Growing Greener Cities

THE CITY IN THE TWENTY-FIRST CENTURY

Eugenie L. Birch and Susan M. Wachter, Series Editors

Published in collaboration with the Penn Institute for Urban Research

Growing Greener Cities

Urban Sustainability in the Twenty-First Century

EDITED BY EUGENIE L. BIRCH
AND SUSAN M. WACHTER

PENN

University of Pennsylvania Press

Philadelphia

Published by
University of Pennsylvania Press
Philadelphia, Pennsylvania 19104-4112

Printed in the United States of America on acid-free paper
10 9 8 7 6 5 4 3 2 1

A Cataloging-in-Publication record is available from the Library of Congress
ISBN 978-0-8122-2037-7

Contents

Preface: Common Ground, Common Good   ix
AMY GUTMANN

Introduction: Urban Greening and the Green City Ideal   1
EUGENIE L. BIRCH AND SUSAN M. WACHTER

Part I. Greening at Every Scale: Nation to Roof Tops

1. Taking the Initiative: Why Cities Are Greening Now   11
TOM DANIELS

2. Growing Greener Regions   28
ROBERT D. YARO AND DAVID M. KOORIS

3. The Inter-Regional Dimension: The Greening of London and the Wider South East   46
ROBIN THOMPSON

4. Greening Cities: A Public Realm Approach   60
ALEXANDER GARVIN

5. Growing Greener, New York Style   84
RACHEL WEINBERGER

6. Greener Homes, Greener Cities: Expanding Affordable Housing and Strengthening Cities Through Sustainable Residential Development   106
STOCKTON WILLIAMS AND DANA L. BOURLAND

Part II: Getting Greening Done

7. Urban Stream Restoration: Recovering Ecological Services in Degraded Watersheds   127
RUTHERFORD H. PLATT, TIMOTHY BEATLEY, SARAH MICHAELS, NANCY GOUCHER, AND BETH FENSTERMACHER

8. The Role of Citizen Activists in Urban Infrastructure
Development   152
PAUL R. BROWN

9. Blue-Green Practices: Why They Work and Why They Have Been So
Difficult to Implement Through Public Policy   170
CHARLIE MILLER

10. The Roots of the Urban Greening Movement   187
VICTOR RUBIN

11. Leveraging Media for Social Change   207
HARRY WILAND AND DALE BELL

12. Transformation Through Greening   227
J. BLAINE BONHAM, JR., AND PATRICIA L. SMITH

13. Community Development Finance and the Green City   244
JEREMY NOWAK

14. Growing Edible Cities   259
DOMENIC VITIELLO

Part III. Measuring Urban Greening

15. Ecosystem Services and the Green City   281
DENNIS D. HIRSCH

16. Metro Nature: Its Functions, Benefits, and Values   294
KATHLEEN L. WOLF

17. Green Investment Strategies: How They Matter for Urban
Neighborhoods   316
SUSAN M. WACHTER, KEVIN C. GILLEN, AND
CAROLYN R. BROWN

18. Measuring the Economic Impacts of Greening: The Center for
Neighborhood Technology Green Values Calculator   326
JULIA KENNEDY, PETER HAAS, AND BILL EYRING

19. What Makes Today's Green City?   346
WARREN KARLENZIG

Afterword   364
NEAL PEIRCE

Notes   369

List of Contributors   381

Acknowledgments   391

Plates follow Chapter 6

Preface: Common Ground, Common Good

AMY GUTMANN

I have loved cities for as long as I can remember. Born in Brooklyn, I grew up in rural New York but made regular pilgrimages back to the enchanting place we called "the City." There was no finer treat for me as a child than seeing a Broadway show after spending the day on the Lower East Side, first with my parents and later with my friends, hunting for bargains and drenching my senses in all the intense sights, smells, and sounds of the city, which linger to this day.

When the urban cacophony overloaded my senses, I discovered sanctuary in Central Park and drank in the refreshing calm of lawns and meadows, tranquil lakes, and miles of tree-lined paths. As a child I must have assumed that these "natural wonders" had always graced the island of Manhattan.

Later, I learned that Central Park was the result of a monumental 15-year greening project during the mid-1800s that demolished neighborhoods, removed more than 10 million cartloads of soil and rock, and planted more than 4 million trees, shrubs, and plants.

I also learned that Central Park was the vision of landscape architect Frederick Law Olmsted, who considered equitable access to green and open spaces as part and parcel of the right to life, liberty, and the pursuit of happiness. Describing the Central Park project as "a democratic development of the highest significance," Olmsted dispensed valuable advice to the growing nation: If you want a healthy democracy, you must cultivate greener cities.

My appreciation of this vital link between healthy democracies and greener cities deepened when I came to Philadelphia to become president of the University of Pennsylvania in 2004. Penn is embarking on a once-in-a-century campus development project that will extend the university eastward across fallow industrial parcels of land toward the center of the city. As we discussed our future with neighboring residents and businesses and with our own students, faculty, and staff, my colleagues and I more fully discerned how our plans for greening surface parking lots would dramatically boost the cultural, recreational, and economic health of Philadelphia while securing Penn's future as a premier urban teaching and research university.

Our plan, which we call Penn Connects, has been embraced enthusiastically by all our constituents while earning several awards for design and planning. Today, as we begin transforming those parking lots into urban parkland, we at Penn look to seize this moment in time to serve our city, country, and world as a leading agent of long-range urban thinking and action, which will help to sustain humankind today, tomorrow, and for generations to come.

Thanks to a confluence of factors—including the popularity of former Vice President Al Gore's documentary on global warming *An Inconvenient Truth,* the tragic devastation caused by a tsunami and Hurricane Katrina, and the alarming escalation of gasoline prices to all-time highs—many Americans now consider securing a healthy future for our planet to be the defining challenge of our time.

What critical roles can today's research universities play in meeting this global challenge? How can we help to maximize the potential for progress unleashed by our growing sense of urgency?

I believe institutions of higher education can make a profound difference in three ways: as generators of ideas, as models of best practices, and as catalysts for collaborative approaches to urban sustainability.

First, we can assure that the best research and scholarship informs global strategies for addressing these complex issues.

Back in the 1950s, while large-scale development projects were, in Jane Jacobs' words, "reducing city and countryside alike to a monotonous, unnourishing gruel," Penn created its path-breaking department of landscape architecture and regional planning. The department's founder, a passionate Scotsman named Ian McHarg, pioneered the concept of designing built projects *with* nature. He created a series of maps that enabled designers to incorporate essential elements such as wildlife habitat, historic landmarks, scenic views, and existing land use into their planning. His maps laid the groundwork for the development of computer-based geographic information systems (GIS), on which urban planners rely today. By 1960, the charismatic McHarg was hosting a nationally televised series called *The House We Live In,* which introduced millions of Americans to the religious, ethical, and philosophical issues surrounding the environment.

While McHarg was integrating nature into analysis, his colleague David Wallace, a professor in the Department of City and Regional Planning, was working with cities to redevelop their degraded industrial sites, especially those along the waterfront. Baltimore's Inner Harbor and Lower Manhattan's Battery Park City resulted from this work.

The work that McHarg and Wallace began at Penn seeded a generation of urban planners, designers, and budding environmentalists.

Penn faculty members today remain at the forefront of enhancing global sustainability. They are advising Central American governments on strategies to preserve vital biodiversity. They are using cutting-edge technology to design more energy-efficient buildings with partners in Europe and Asia. They are exploring more efficient ways to use solar energy. They are addressing the business, legal, and ethical considerations inherent in today's environmental issues. At the same time the university is establishing new environmental research programs and corporate internships and developing a new post-graduate degree program to train future leaders.

Yet urban research universities can and must do more than help to answer questions and solve problems. In his book *The Idea of the University*, the eminent historian Jaroslav Pelikan observes, "The university as institution, employer, wage-payer, and property-owner contributes to its local society and in turn depends on it: if either of these partners is sick, the other suffers as well."

As anchor institutions, universities like Penn have a responsibility to serve as models for creating and implementing best practices in sustainable development. For example, Penn for some time has been one of the largest private purchasers of wind power in the nation, obtaining 30 percent of our energy from wind-generated power. We also are a national campus leader in the adaptive reuse of existing buildings and materials. We are cutting energy usage during peak hours by nearly 20 percent and are testing vehicle fuel made from kitchen waste.

Equally important, we are engaging our students in sustainable activities, including recycling, managing energy use, supporting local farmers, and composting. Earlier this year, we signed a historic higher education pact to develop a comprehensive sustainability plan by 2009. We are committed to finding ways to do more to point the way toward excellent environmental citizenship.

At the same time, the challenge of sustainable development is global in scope. According to the UN Commission on Population, half the world's population live in cities. Many of the world's problems—including housing, rising infant mortality, asthma and obesity, poor nutrition, illiteracy, income inequality, and crime—arise with greater frequency and intensity in cities, gravely threatening a sustainable future.

Yet urban greening projects are generating tides that can lift other boats. For example, North Philadelphia artist Lilly Yeh launched her Village of Arts and Humanities by transforming a blighted site into a sculpture garden. Today as a vibrant community enterprise comprising 260 square blocks of art-filled gardens, green spaces, and a working tree farm, the village has jump-started efforts to improve neighborhood health care and social services, education, and safety.

Urban research universities have the capacity and the resources to build effective partnerships for greening initiatives that simultaneously generate momentum to revitalize our communities. We also have strong ties to the government, business, nonprofit, and civic interests that must work together to make our cities more livable. Why not leverage these relationships to mobilize a new framework of collaboration for the sustainable good of our cities?

Penn's Institute for Urban Research took the first steps toward developing such a framework in Philadelphia when it joined with the Pennsylvania Horticultural Society in organizing the conference Growing Greener Cities at Penn on October 16 and 17, 2006. More than 200 community leaders, policymakers, nonprofit developers, horticulturalists, and researchers discussed issues ranging from the business prospects for "green building" practices to race in environmental education.

The essays compiled in this volume present some of today's most creative strategies for sustainable urban thinking, planning, and practice. They also highlight how much work remains to be done to create cities where all urban residents can see and live green.

Jaroslav Pelikan reminds us that the Italian Renaissance was primarily an urban phenomenon, created in Florence by the interaction of "civic humanism" and "classicism." Today, the dynamic interaction between the powerful teaching and research engines of great universities and the cities in which they are fortuitously anchored can spark what future generations will describe as the "Great Urban Renaissance of the Twenty-First Century." Thus we will greatly improve the prospect that generations of children to come will inherit the riches of great urban parks, a healthy democracy, and a sustainable planet.

Introduction: Urban Greening and the Green City Ideal

Eugenie L. Birch and Susan M. Wachter

The convergence of several phenomena is pushing urban greening to the forefront of American thought and action. A population that is more than 70 percent urban, growing concern about global warming, rising energy prices, the unabated pace of globalization, and terrorist threats emanating from petroleum-producing countries confront today's decision makers with the need to find ways to adapt U.S. life to these modern exigencies (United Nations 2005; Friedman 2007). One important approach is growing greener cities, the subject of this book.

Growing greener cities involves the promotion of activities that employ, recognize, or conserve nature in its many helpful forms to sustain urban life while limiting or reducing its depletion. This ranges from supporting regional ecosystems and improving the functioning of municipal infrastructure to the valuation of greening in real estate and public capital investment decisions. It also includes building energy-efficient and resource-conserving homes and providing multipurpose, varied-sized open space meeting needs for respite, recreation, aquifer protection, storm-water management, flood control, and urban agriculture. Implementing these new ways has become the primary mission of many. They are working through government, advocacy groups, professional organizations and partnerships, and as individuals.

Where Did Urban Greening Come From?

The modern urban greening effort stems from a generation of environmentalism that in itself has deep roots in American culture that can be traced back to Thomas Jefferson, the great parks designer Frederick Law Olmsted, and Theodore and Franklin Roosevelt. It has a broad base of support from the public, private, and nonprofit sectors. There is increasing recognition that action by all levels of government, by the private sector, and by individuals acting on their own and in groups is required to innovate the green behaviors necessary for achieving the green city ideal.

Today, many state and local government agencies are taking a lead in sponsoring urban greening projects. For example, Pennsylvania Governor Edward Rendell's Growing Greener I and II programs have directed more than $600 million to state agencies, primarily the departments of Environmental Protection, Conservation and Natural Resources, and Community and Economic Development for innovative greening efforts that include underwriting renewable energy, innovative wastewater treatment, brownfield remediation, watershed and park restoration, acquisition of conservation easements to protect aquifers and other natural resources, and creation of nature trails and other projects. Other states have similar initiatives.

A huge civic infrastructure, rich in social capital, intelligence, money, and energy, also undergirds urban greening. The Natural Resources Defense Council, Environmental Defense League, and Trust for Public Land are but a few of the national organizations that are active. State and regional advocates include 10,000 Friends of Pennsylvania, myregion.org (Florida), New York Regional Plan Association, TreePeople (Los Angeles), and many others too numerous to list here. Between New York City and Philadelphia alone, groups range in scale, focus, and capacity from the Pennsylvania Horticultural Society's Philadelphia Green and New York's Green Guerillas, which promote community gardens, to Philadelphia's Friends of Fairmount Park and New York's conservancies for Central Park, Prospect Park, and Battery Park, which support citywide facilities. More general local environmental groups like Sustainable Philadelphia are raising citizen consciousness and voting power through citywide reports, forums, and media campaigns. Meriting special mention are environmental justice groups that have focused attention on the degradation of low- and moderate-income communities, calling attention to their severe public health concerns (for example, high rates of asthma due to air pollution) and quality-of-life issues. The Green Worker Cooperatives, whose executive director Omar Freilla is the first winner of the Jane Jacobs Medal for New Ideas and Activism, is an example.

Local and national foundations play a pivotal role in supporting these groups as have print, broadcast, and Internet media. Newspapers spotlight problems and success stories in the area. A typical example is coverage from the *Philadelphia Inquirer*. In just two days in June 2007 the newspaper featured Jennifer Lin's "More Rain, Old Sewers Make for a Nasty Story" (June 14, 2007), a discussion of the storm runoff problems, and Stephanie Salisbury's "Council Backs Appointed Parks Commission" (June 15, 2007), heralding a governance change aimed to improve the care of the city's 9,200-acre open space inventory. In the broadcast arena, *Eden's Lost & Found*, a four-hour PBS special focusing on urban greening in Seattle, Los Angeles, Chicago, and Philadelphia, is exemplary. Finally, the Internet has become an enormous source of information and communication. With daily dispatches from national groups to bulletins about local activities, it fosters and supports important civic dialogue.

Urban greening involves many types of people in a variety of initiatives and processes. It incorporates inclusive citizen planning efforts to help strategize about where and how to green. It demands the expertise of city planners, environmental engineers, landscape architects, and others to help determine the form and structure of greening efforts. It calls for widespread media campaigns to share information, data, and techniques. It has room for new public-private partnerships to deliver key elements and craft creative financing arrangements. It inspires entrepreneurs and social activists to pursue or make improvements to broaden life's green opportunities in their areas of concern.

Defining and Measuring a Green City

What is a green city? First, it is an ideal, yet to be attained by any urban place in the world but certainly achievable in the twenty-first century. In its most perfect form, a green city is carbon neutral and fully sustainable. According to economist Matthew Kahan, a green city is a healthy place that has "clean air and water, pleasant streets and parks." It is "resilient in the face of natural disasters and faces little risk of infectious disease. Its residents have strong, green behavioral habits, like taking public transit, practicing recycling and water conservation, using renewable energy" (Kahan 2006: 4).

Answering the question of what is a green city also requires distinguishing between existing places and ones to be built in the future. Existing places have their basic form and structure while new ones do not. Existing places may have to adapt and mitigate nongreen conditions while new ones can invent their own approaches. Older industrial cities have extensive park systems but also have massive brownfields or combined sanitary and storm sewers. Newer, rapidly growing, spread-out cities have little parkland, rely heavily on automobiles, and accommodate their growth through greenfield conversion under zoning ordinances legislating low-density, large-lot sites and single uses, but increasingly they are implementing strategies to preserve open space through open space initiatives.

Whether old or new, green cities have one central feature in common:

they take full advantage of their natural environments to sustain human life. They use the sun, the earth, and its vegetation to supply, use, and reuse the basic necessities. They reduce or minimize their imprint on the land. They employ common sense and modern technology to meet these ends.

Measuring the "greenness" of a city takes many forms, ranging from rankings designed to attract the media and popular attention to those based on indicators related to such specific disciplines as public health, ecology, city planning, and economics. Among the popular rankings are the *National Geographic* Green Guide and the Earth Day Network and SustainLane surveys that integrate data from a variety of sources to derive lists of top cities.[1] Public health measures tabulate the incidence of disease and mortality related to environmental conditions. In addition, in the past five years the Centers for Disease Control and Prevention (CDC) has begun the National Environmental Health Tracking Program to create a national database on hazard (presence of harmful environmental agents in air, water, soil or other media) and exposure data (presence of a harmful environmental agent in an individual) that will, when completed, be a useful tool for measuring the public health aspects of greening (Levin 2007). City planners map and measure land uses and modes of transportation and their integration with natural landscape features. They balance regional environmental assets and urban growth. Ecologists who look at natural factors estimate a place's "ecological footprint" or the amount of natural resources consumed by individuals, aggregating it to many levels from the city to the state or the nation (see http://www.ecofoot.org/). Economists have focused on understanding the impact of urban greening on market prices—especially real estate—using regression analysis pinpoint-specific features (Kahan 2006). They have also developed techniques to value ecosystem services, including air and water purification and reclamation of rain runoff (Pagiola, Ritter, and Bishop 2004).

By any measure, some places are already more advanced than others in their march toward being green. Some are consciously attempting to undertake the necessary reforms in lifestyle and others are either unwilling or unable to make the required changes. The names of some cities—Portland, Oregon, Denver, Seattle, Oakland, and Minneapolis—appear repeatedly as leaders in urban greening.

Urban Greening: From Industrial Cleanup to Global Warming

A generation ago, the federal government led initiatives to clean up air, water, and polluted lands. Through the Clean Air (1970) and Clean Water (1972) acts, the nation established minimum standards. Subsequent legislation focusing on transportation, sewerage treatment, and brownfields supplemented the original laws, offering substantial funding for specified initiatives. Driven by concerns about environmental quality, not by broader greening issues, this legislation has achieved major milestones in cleaning up industrial pollution and thus has contributed to growing greener cities.

Additionally, in addressing various interest group needs, the federal government has tinkered with the laws over time but has never conceived them as part of an overall policy related to the concerns now driving today's greening efforts. For example, federal transportation legislation, in calling for compliance with federal air quality minima, has successfully forced localities to consider the environmental implications of their mobility investments. However, the monitored pollutants include six emissions (nitrogen dioxide, sulfur dioxide, lead, carbon monoxide, particulates, and ozone) but do not cover carbon dioxide (CO_2), a major contributor to global warming. The twentieth-century clean air vision was one that dealt with the outcomes of the polluting agents, not the producers of CO_2 coming from the petroleum-fed vehicles and coal-stoked power plants so central to the American lifestyle.

Tied up in complex political considerations revolving around the failure of the United States to endorse the Kyoto Accords (1997) and disputes about the cost of compliance to greenhouse gas reduction targets, the federal government has continued a piecemeal approach to greening into the twenty-first century. This approach has had varied effects on cities—their air and water are definitively cleaner—but is offset by other population-dispersing/sprawl-inducing federal policies including highway construction in outlying areas and income tax relief for homeownership. These elements in themselves do not cause sprawl but have had the unintended effect of doing so.

In the absence of comprehensive federal policy on greening, cities and states have begun to take it up with varied success. Recently, concerns with global warming are driving these efforts, making urban greening not the focus but a by-product of emerging local policies. Since 2005, under the leadership of Seattle Mayor Greg Nickels and working through the U.S. Conference of Mayors, 600 mayors have signed the U.S. Mayors' Climate Protection Agreement. This pact sets a 7 percent reduction in 1990 CO_2 by 2012, a higher target than the Kyoto Accords. Pledging to reach that goal, the mayors are focusing on transportation, land use, building codes, and municipal energy consumption. Chicago, the self-declared greenest city in America, has promoted many measures, including green roofs (it has approximately 200, encompassing about 2.5 million square feet, some supported by a specially legislated tax increment financing district in the Loop and others through city grants), tree planting (400,000 in the past decade, with approximately 5,000 in 60 miles of new, vegetated street medians), and bike lanes (about 250 miles). More recently, New York issued PlaNYC 2030, pledging a 30 percent reduction in CO_2 by 2030, but failed to secure congestion-pricing, a key component, from the intransigent state legislature. Nonetheless, it is pursuing a million-tree planting program and continuing regional land purchases aimed to protect its watershed and avoid construction of an industrial-sized water filtration plant.

State level initiatives are also emerging. In the past year, the governors of four states—California, New Jersey, Hawaii, and Florida—have instituted measures aimed to reduce greenhouse gases according to strict targets. Concerned with protecting their extensive coasts and mitigating other climate-warming problems, California and Florida have each set a goal of achieving 80 percent of the 1990 levels by 2050. In addition, 10 northeastern states have signed on to the Regional Greenhouse Gas Initiative (RGGI) whose initial project is to design a cap and trade program covering power plant CO_2 emissions but may, in the future, take on other initiatives that would contribute in other ways to urban greening.

The Emergence of Greening Standards

Among the more notable efforts in urban greening has been the institution of green building standards under the Leadership in Energy and Environmental Design Green Building rating system (LEED), which was initiated by the U.S. Green Building Council, the Congress for New Urbanism, and the Natural Resources Defense Council in 1998. To date, U.S. Green Building lists approximately 6,000 projects worldwide as having registered for the LEED ratings (U.S. Green Building 2007). Recently, the group has added a new program, LEED-ND, to its LEED green building rating system. Piloted in 2007–2008, LEED-ND rewards dense, compact development, awarding points for location (near existing development and infrastructure or infill), walkability (wide sidewalks with shade trees and other interesting features), mixed use (proximate location of housing, stores and workplaces), multimodalism (access to public transit, bike trails), and water and energy conservation (use of landscape features to minimize runoff, rain collection gray water recycling, solar panels, or other renewables). The LEED measures are important tools for achieving greener cities because the anticipated increase in the U.S. population by an additional 100 million people in the next 30 years will stimulate an enormous building boom to accommodate the growth. By 2025, analysts predict that half the built environment will be new and will include the construction or rebuilding of 50 million housing units and 100 billion square feet of nonresidential building (Nelson 2006; Nelson and Lang 2007).

Urban Greening Worldwide

The United States has much to learn about urban greening from around the world. Exemplary European cities are compact, have multimodal transportation systems and extensive open space systems, and practice energy conservation. England, for example, has a tradition dating from the end of World War II of containing its largest cities with greenbelts. Its Docklands brownfield reclamation project transformed a 8.5-square-mile area into a twentieth-century mixed-use green city. More recently, London has mandated global warming preventive measures in the Mayor's Climate Change Action Plan (2007) addendum to the comprehensive plan. Copenhagen and other European cities have encouraged biking and walking by providing an extensive network of routes reaching from downtown to the outskirts and traffic-calming devices to guarantee pedestrian and biker safety. Singapore is a model of greening, with an integrated land use and transportation strategy starting more than a generation ago with a Long Range Concept Plan (1972) that ringed the central business district with new towns linked by mass transit. Successive revisions (1991 and 2001) have concentrated development in four high-density regional centers served by public transit and the city-state is focused on transforming heavy industrial land into mixed use, raising residential densities, doubling and upgrading open space, and addressing the jobs/housing balance.

An Achievable Goal

The authors of *Growing Greener Cities*, drawn from practice and academia, provide insights into the urban greening topics discussed in this introduction. They wrestle with the difficulties of breaking old, anti-greening habits and introducing new practices. They detail successful strategies and practices ranging in scale from regional watershed management to rain barrel placement. They demonstrate that with focus, will, and determination, transforming urban places into green cities is an achievable goal for the twenty-first-century city.

References

Friedman, Thomas. 2007. "The Greening of Geopolitics." *New York Times Magazine*, April 15: 40–51, 67, 71–72.
Kahan, Matthew E. 2006. *Green Cities, Urban Growth, and the Environment*. Washington, D.C.: Brookings Institution Press.

Levin, Aaron. 2007. *Keeping Track . . . Promoting Health: CDC National Environmental Public Health Tracking Program.* Atlanta: Centers for Disease Control and Prevention.

Nelson, Arthur C. 2006. "Leadership in a New Era." *Journal of the American Planning Association* 72, 3 (Autumn).

Nelson, Arthur C., and Robert E. Lang. 2007. "The Next 100 Million." American Planning Association, February. http://www.vt.edu/spotlight/next_100_million.pdf.

Pagiola, Stefano, Konrad Ritter, and Joshua Bishop. 2004. *Assessing the Economic Value of Ecosystem Conservation.* Washington, D.C.: World Bank.

United Nations. 2005. *World Urbanization Prospects: The 2005 Revision.* Nairobi: Department of Economic and Social Affairs/Population Division.

U.S. Green Building Council. 2007. "Certified Project List." April 12. http://www.usgbc.org/DisplayPage.aspx?CMSPageID=1452&.

Part I
Greening at Every Scale:
Nation to Roof Tops

Chapter 1
Taking the Initiative: Why Cities Are Greening Now

Tom Daniels

Nearly 40 years ago, the federal government began to put into place a series of laws designed to improve the nation's environmental quality. At the time, almost two-thirds of America's waterways were not fit for swimming or drinking. Smog from cars and factories clouded cities with a brownish haze. Tens of thousands of former industrial sites sat abandoned, containing unknown levels of hazardous substances. Mass transit systems were falling apart. Cities—especially in the Northeast—were seen as the hostile, rusting, graying remains of a rapidly passing industrial era. The suburbs presented a healthier, greener, and safer place to live.

Why have cities only recently seen an upsurge in "greening"—from green roofs to new parks to tree planting to more energy efficient buses—despite the fact that sweeping federal environmental legislation was enacted more than 30 years ago? Quite simply, city leaders are recognizing that a cleaner environment is needed both to provide residents with a good quality of life and to compete in the global economy. America's manufacturing-based economy of the twentieth century has been transformed into a service-based knowledge economy. For the information age economy, environmental quality is a major economic asset. Skilled workers are increasingly footloose, able to settle just about anywhere there is broadband Internet access, and they are drawn to healthy, aesthetically pleasing environments. Moreover, green cities are demonstrating that the alleged trade-off between jobs and the environment is a false dichotomy. A quality environment produces jobs; a polluted environment costs jobs.

A green city enables a choice of transportation options, areas in which to enjoy recreational activities, and opportunities for social interaction on the street and in public spaces. And there are indications that living in a city is healthier than residing in a suburb. A 2003 study reported that people in cities weighed on average six pounds less than suburbanites and had lower blood pressure, too, because they walked more and drove less (Ewing et al. 2003).

A green city has value in promoting civic pride and serving as an example to other cities. Chattanooga, Tennessee, was America's most polluted city in 1969. Today it is the nation's cleanest city and a thriving tourist destination (Beatley and Manning 1998). In 2007, New York City Mayor Michael Bloomberg put forth an ambitious plan comprised of 127 projects to improve air quality, protect water supplies, promote mass transit, plant a million trees, and expand park space (*Economist* 2007). Mayor Bloomberg hoped that New York's green initiatives would serve as a model for other American cities to become economically, environmentally, and socially sustainable. The New York City example also reflects an effort by local leaders and citizens to do their part in addressing national and global environmental challenges, such as energy conservation and climate change.

Many cities face the likelihood of substantial growth in the coming decades. The U.S. Census Bureau has projected that the population of the United States will reach 419 million in 2050, an increase of more than 130 million from the 2000 census (U.S. Bureau of the Census 2004). New York City is expecting nearly a million more inhabitants by 2030; it and other cities must become greener in order to maintain as well as enhance their livability (*Economist* 2007).

Ironically, another reason for the growing popularity of green cities is the absence of environmental leadership at the federal level and in most states since the administration of President George W. Bush came to office in 2001. In fact, the shortage of federal and state direction goes back to the presidency of Ronald Reagan when the U.S. Environmental Protection Agency (EPA) was seen as blatantly pro-business and anti-regulation (Lash et al. 1984). Then, under the Clinton Administration, the EPA began to turn over the monitoring and enforcement of several federal environmental programs to the states. As a result, the enforcement of federal environmental laws has been inconsistent, if not extremely lax (Coequyt and Wiles 2000).

Federal environmental laws set standards for air and water quality to protect the public health. They have established the environmental impact statement approach to evaluate the environmental effects of proposed development projects, and have provided major funding for sewage treatment plants, multimodal transportation projects, and some brownfield remediation. But the federal laws have largely established a reactive "command and control" system that does not promote the development and maintenance of good places to live and work (Shutkin 2001).

Many city leaders have recognized that they cannot turn to the federal or state government for specific advice or for funding on how to create green cities. New Orleans provides a tragic case in point. The city relied on the federal government to maintain the levees along the Mississippi River and Lake Ponchartrain, only to see the levees fail in 2005 during Hurricane Katrina and leave the city flooded. On the other hand, New Orleans contributed to the devastation by allowing the draining and filling of hundreds of thousands of acres of wetlands, which then lost the ability to absorb floodwaters.

The bottom line is that U.S. cities have become aware that they need to take responsibility for their environmental quality. This means investment in the city by local government, businesses, and property owners and a change in lifestyles. At the same time, an abundance of nonprofit organizations has sprung up to promote urban greening activities, from watershed alliances to park associations to community gardens to farmers markets. As a result, the greening of cities has evolved into a local public-private partnership. The federal government has provided some tools for environmental improvement, especially in the areas of clean air and clean water. Yet, the cities themselves deserve credit for creating the changes that have instilled green urbanism in people's lives.

Laying the Foundation for Green Cities

The federal environmental laws enacted between 1970 and 2005 form the foundation for the current focus on making cities greener (see Table 1). These laws created a set of rules of behavior for individuals, companies, and governments to protect air and water quality and public health. The laws and their regulations have influenced local environmental planning efforts, and have led to improvements in the nation's air and water quality (Daniels and Daniels, 2003). They combine reactive planning in responding to pollution damage and proactive planning in preventing pollution or degradation.

THE NATIONAL ENVIRONMENTAL POLICY ACT

The National Environmental Policy Act of 1970 (NEPA) established a process for federal agencies to review their projects and policies that could affect environmental quality and result in the irreversible use of natural resources. Thus, any federal project in a city must first go through the NEPA review process to determine its potential environ-

TABLE 1. MAJOR FEDERAL ENVIRONMENTAL LAWS THAT AFFECT CITIES, 1970–2005

1970 National Environmental Policy Act (PL Law 90-190)
      Clean Air Act Amendments (PL 91-224)
      Resources Recovery Act (PL 91-512)
1972 Federal Water Pollution Control Act Amendments (Clean Water Act)
      (PL 92-500)
1973 Safe Drinking Water Act (PL 930-523)
1976 Resource Conservation and Recovery Act (PL 94-580)
1980 Comprehensive Environmental Response Compensation and Liability Act
      ("The Superfund Law") (PL 96-510)
1984 Hazardous and Solid Waste Amendments (PL 98-616)
1986 Superfund Amendments and Reauthorization Act (PL 99-499)
1990 Clean Air Act Amendments (PL 101-549)
1991 Intermodal Surface Transportation Efficiency Act (ISTEA) (PL 102-240)
1996 Safe Drinking Water Act Amendments (PL 104-182)
1998 Transportation Equity Act for the 21st Century (TEA-21) (PL 105-206)
2002 Small Business Liability Relief and Brownfields Revitalization Act
      (PL 107-118)
2005 Safe, Accountable, Flexible, Efficient, Transportation Equity Act: A Legacy
      for Users (SAFETEA-LU (PL 109-59)

mental impacts. This "look before you leap" approach to the environment was lacking in the urban renewal projects of the 1950s and 1960s.

NEPA contains several important concepts for green cities: that each generation is a trustee of the environment for succeeding generations and that all Americans should have safe, healthful, productive, and aesthetically and culturally pleasing surroundings. Other key concepts include attaining the widest range of beneficial use of the environment without degradation, or risk to health or safety; preserving important historic, cultural, and natural aspects of our national heritage, and maintaining an environment that supports diversity and a variety of individual choice; achieving a balance between population and resource use that will permit high standards of living and a wide sharing of life's amenities; and enhancing the quality of renewable resources and approaching the maximum attainable recycling of depletable resources (see, 42 U.S.C., Section 4331 et seq.)

NEPA created the Environment Impact Statement (EIS) process for federal agencies to evaluate the potential environmental effects of their proposed projects, funding, permits, policies, and actions. An EIS must describe and evaluate

• the current conditions and the environmental impact of the proposed action;

- any adverse environmental effects that cannot be avoided should the proposal be implemented;
- alternatives to the proposed action, and the likely effects of those alternatives;
- the relationship between local short-term uses of man's environment and the maintenance and enhancement of long-term productivity;
- any irreversible and irretrievable commitments of resources that would be involved in the proposed action, should it be implemented; and
- ways to minimize the negative impacts of the proposed action (42 U.S.C., Sec. 4332(2)(c)).

A federal agency first decides whether NEPA applies to a specific project or action. If NEPA does apply, the agency must determine whether an EIS is required before the project or action can begin. The purpose of the EIS process is to provide full disclosure of the impacts of federal actions that may affect the environment. State and local governments and the public have the opportunity to participate in the EIS process and may challenge the findings of an EIS in court. In the 1970s and 1980s, more than 20 states adopted their own EIS process, which also require cities to use the EIS approach in reviewing the potential environmental impacts of city projects and policies and those of proposed private developments.

A shortcoming of NEPA is that it is reactive planning, designed to react to proposals rather than serve as a proactive planning tool. NEPA involves a case-by-case review of projects, not a cumulative assessment of the impact of development projects on the environment over time. Moreover, an EIS is supposed to be based on "good science." The debate about what is good science appears endless, but knowledge about human effects on the environment does change. Yet, the slowness of the Bush administration to acknowledge the effect of human actions on climate change has led some cities to take action on their own to reduce emissions of greenhouse gases.

In urban areas, NEPA usually involves large federal projects. But more relevant for the environmental quality of cities are air and water quality and brownfield redevelopment programs, which have traditionally been administered by the EPA. Yet, since the early 1990s, the EPA has ceded greater control over these programs to the individual states, and with varying success.

President Richard Nixon created the Environmental Protection Agency in 1970 to administer the environmental legislation that had begun to emerge. The EPA has broad regulatory powers that affect every industry and city in the nation. EPA implements and enforces several environmental laws, such as the Clean Water Act, the Safe Drinking Water Act, the Clean Air Act, the Toxic Substances Control Act, the Resource Conservation and Recovery Act (RCRA), and the Comprehensive Environmental Response, Compensation, and Liability Act (CERCLA) (the Superfund for toxic waste cleanup) (see table 1). Large cities have formed environmental quality departments to carry out and comply with EPA regulations (see chapter 40 of the Code of Federal Regulations).

The EPA has wide-ranging authority that directly affects urban environments. It has the ability to:

- block large development projects that EPA feels cause irreversible environmental damage or violate federal environmental laws;
- bring enforcement actions against state and city government agencies that are not carrying out environmental laws and regulations;
- undertake legal action and levy fines on violators of environmental laws and standards;
- initiate the cleanup of hazardous waste sites;
- withhold federal highway funds from states and metropolitan regions that do not meet federal air quality (Daniels and Daniels 2003).

The EPA is supposed to guard America's public health and the environment. But in attempting to carry out its responsibilities the agency has been subject to the whims of whichever political party is in the White House. Moreover, because EPA has largely turned over the monitoring and enforcement of the Clean Air and Clean Water Acts to the states, EPA today has less impact than it did 15 years ago.

Air Quality

Air quality is a primary public health issue. Polluted air can cause or exacerbate asthma attacks, bronchitis, emphysema, lung cancer, or circulatory problems, as well as lead to premature death. EPA employs two air quality standards. Ambient air-quality standards set the maximum allowed level of certain pollutants in the air. EPA also determines air pollution emissions standards for new stationary sources of pollution (power plants and factories) and for mobile sources (cars and trucks). EPA, states, and metropolitan regions share responsibility for maintaining and improving air quality. Governments, businesses, and individuals bear responsibility for controlling their air pollution emissions.

The Clean Air Act of 1970 gave EPA the authority to set National

Ambient Air Quality Standards for six "criteria" pollutants: nitrogen dioxide, sulfur dioxide, lead, carbon monoxide, particulates, and ozone. Cities, states, and metropolitan regions must meet the air quality standards or draft plans to come into compliance. EPA has a cleanup schedule that allows jurisdictions from 3 to 20 years to achieve compliance. This schedule has not been seriously enforced; only Denver among dozens of "nonattainment" cities has come into compliance with the Clean Air standards (Daniels and Daniels 2003). Furthermore, the Clean Air Act standards create an incentive for new businesses to locate in areas that meet the federal air quality standards as opposed to selecting nonattainment cities that may need the economic development.

The 1990 Clean Air Act amendments required each major city to become part of a Metropolitan Planning Organization (MPO) to link transportation planning with air quality as well as to qualify for federal transportation funding. The Intermodal Surface Transportation Efficiency Act (ISTEA) gave each MPO greater local control of federally funded transportation projects. This was a welcome change from the neighborhood busting that occurred with the construction of interstate highways through cities. ISTEA emphasized multiple modes of transportation that would include alternatives to car travel. Some ISTEA funds were set aside for bike lanes and pedestrian access. Yet, the large majority of the more than $600 billion in ISTEA funds and subsequent transportation funding acts have been spent on highway construction and repair, mainly in the suburbs, rather than on urban mass transit systems (APTA 2007, Daniels and Daniels 2003).

Each MPO must adopt a transportation planning process that will either maintain the region's good air quality or else move a nonattainment region toward meeting the federal air-quality standards in three-year intervals (42 U.S.C.A. Sec. 7511a(g)). The transportation plans must include a 20-year regional transportation plan, which must be consistent with both the state transportation plan and state air-quality improvement plan, and a three-year transportation improvement plan (TIP), which updates the regional plan. The three-year plans must show that any increase in vehicle miles traveled and vehicle trips will not hinder the improvement of air quality. The three-year plans include specific transportation projects recommended for federal funding and projects to be paid for entirely with state, local, or private money. Third, individual transportation projects, such as new roads, bus routes, or rail lines, must be listed on both the regional transportation plan and TIP, and must be consistent with the state transportation plan and the state TIP and the state air-quality improvement plan in order to qualify for federal funding.

Under the 1990 Clean Air Act amendments, EPA can withhold federal funds for new highway construction in cities and regions where air quality is below the federal standards. EPA has used this power only once, in the case of greater Atlanta between 1998 and 2000. But EPA could legally withhold highway funds from dozens of cities that do not comply with the federal air quality standards. Apparently, EPA is reluctant to risk curbing economic growth and incurring the political wrath of congressional representatives and local politicians.

From 1970 to 2000, America's overall air quality improved as emissions of the six criteria pollutants fell by 29 percent (U.S. EPA 2001a). The number of air-quality alert days in major cities also declined by half, to fewer than 300 per year. But ozone caused by smog and motor vehicle emissions and particulates from motor vehicles and coal-fired power plants remain problems in many urban areas.

Greenhouse gases and climate change. The United States has not yet established standards to reduce emissions of carbon dioxide and other greenhouse gases that contribute to climate change, even though a reduction in carbon dioxide emissions would also lower emissions of particulates, ozone, and nitrogen and sulfur oxides (Dunn and Flavin 2002). The Kyoto Protocol of 1997, signed by 163 countries, called for industrialized nations to set limits on the emission of carbon dioxide and other greenhouse gases. But the U.S. Senate failed to ratify the Kyoto Protocol, believing that the cost of compliance would be too high. In 2007, the U.S. Supreme Court ruled that the EPA has the authority to regulate emissions of greenhouse gases, such as carbon dioxide, under the Clean Air Act (U.S. Supreme Court 2007). Meanwhile, several American businesses have set their own targets for reducing greenhouse gasses. More than 20 states and several cities have adopted portfolio standards for the percentage of electricity obtained from renewable sources as a way to reduce reliance on fossil fuels and thus lower carbon dioxide emissions.

SIDEBAR: THE LAND USE, TRANSPORTATION, AND AIR QUALITY CONNECTION

A city can offer multiple modes of transportation to move people and goods within the city and to connect the city to the outside world: cars and trucks, buses, trains, subways, bicycles, foot, boats, and airplanes. Transportation modes greatly determine the physical environment and development patterns of a city, but modes vary considerably in their financial costs, use of energy, and effects on air and water quality. In particular, cities are realizing that they cannot build more highways to solve congestion, especially if they want to maintain or improve air quality. The doubling of oil prices since 2003 has encouraged cities to seek alternative means of transportation, and mass transit ridership is on the rise (American Public Transportation Association 2007).

Federal transportation funding through ISTEA and subsequent acts and the 1990 Clean Air Act amendments have provided money and the regulatory incentive for cities to pursue transit-oriented development (TOD). For instance, in the 1990s, greater Portland, Oregon produced two remarkable studies that tied together land use, transportation, and air quality. Between 1991 and 1997, 11 Land Use Transportation and Air Quality (LUTRAQ) reports were written and concluded that mass transit has less environmental impact and is more energy efficient than the automobile (1000 Friends of Oregon 1991–1997). The reports proposed expanding the light rail system that served Portland's eastern suburbs into the western suburbs. In 1998, the west side light rail line was opened, thanks in large part to federal funding.

The LUTRAQ reports also featured transit-oriented developments designed by New Urbanist architect Peter Calthorpe, who sought to recreate the streetcar suburb of the early twentieth century. A TOD typically has a core area of about a quarter-mile radius, and a secondary area that extends outward for an additional quarter mile. Within this area, development occurs at a full range of densities—houses, apartments, pocket parks, and commercial space within walking or biking distance of a transit line and an easily accessible town center at the transit hub.

The 2040 plan of Metro, greater Portland's regional elected government, identified 35 potential transit-oriented developments (Metro 1995). These centers could occupy about one-fourth of the metropolitan area and contain about half of the region's people. A number of U.S. cities have taken note of the success of Portland's light rail system. Light rail commuter lines now exist in more than 25 metropolitan areas and are being proposed in several others.

WATER QUALITY AND SUPPLY

Clean fresh water and the treatment of wastewater are essential for the sustainable functioning of a modern city. The new mantra for water use is reduce, reuse, and recycle. This is especially true in the Sunbelt, where water is becoming increasingly scarce. On the other hand, many wastewater treatment systems are old and in need of major upgrades to reduce nitrogen loadings and to avoid overflows and the release of raw sewage during rainstorms. Meanwhile, more development means more impervious surfaces in the form of roads, parking lots, and buildings, and an increase in storm water runoff—the leading cause of urban water pollution.

The Safe Drinking Water Act of 1974 (SDWA) gave the EPA the

authority to set national drinking water-quality standards; require water-quality monitoring, water treatment, and reports from water suppliers to the public about contaminants in drinking water (the EPA has set mandatory maximum contaminant levels for about 90 drinking water contaminants); fund source water protection programs to protect watersheds and groundwater from contamination; and regulate public water systems that provide drinking water to the nation's cities.

Since 1989, the EPA has adopted a series of rules that protect surface water supplies, the main source of urban drinking water. Under the Enhanced Surface Water Treatment Rule of the SDWA, all public water systems that use surface water or surface-influenced groundwater must filter and disinfect the water before distributing it to consumers. This new regulation was sparked in part by an outbreak in 1993 of *cryptosporidium*, a microbe that contaminated the drinking water supply of Milwaukee, Wisconsin, killing more than 50 people and making 400,000 people sick (Daniels and Daniels 2003).

The EPA may grant a waiver from the Enhanced Surface Water Treatment Rule if a city water system has good water quality and a water source protection program, and can control potential contamination. New York City, for example, has avoided building a $6 billion filtration plant by protecting water supplies in the Catskill and Delaware watersheds in upstate New York. But New York City will have to spend $1.5 billion on a filtration plant in the nearby Croton watershed where urban runoff has reduced water quality.

The Safe Drinking Water Act requires state and local governments to take a watershed management approach to protect their drinking water supplies. A watershed is the geographic area that drains into the water bodies from which the city draws its water. A city must first identify its watersheds. A major portion of the water supplies of several large cities comes from sources many miles away. New York, Boston, and San Francisco obtain their water supplies from distant reservoirs.

The Clean Water Act of 1972 contains several provisions that affect water quality in urban areas (see Table 2). In the early 1970s, point sources of pollution from factories and municipal sewage treatment plants were identified as the major causes of water pollution. Through Section 201 of the Clean Water Act, EPA has made over $30 billion in grants to states and localities to build sewage treatment plants. As a result, sewage treatment capacity has increased significantly to where nonpoint sources are now seen as the main causes of water pollution (Daniels and Daniels 2003).

Each state must determine the maximum amount of pollution an impaired waterway can assimilate and still meet the drinkable or swimmable standards. The states must also identify and place pollution limits

TABLE 2. CLEAN WATER ACT PROGRAMS THAT INFLUENCE URBAN
WATER QUALITY

Section 201—Grants for construction of public sewage treatment plants

Section 303(d)—Identifying impaired waterways and drafting Total Maximum
Daily load plans to clean up these waterways to drinkable or swimmable
standards

Section 319—State plans and programs and federal loans and grants for control
of nonpoint source pollution and to publish reports

Section 402—NPDES permit system for point and nonpoint sources of water
pollution, including stormwater management permits and the monitoring of
urban stormwater discharges into regulated streams

Section 403—Pretreatment of industrial sewage before discharge into municipal
sewage treatment plants

Section 404—Permits for dredging or filling wetlands in navigable waterways

---

on the individual point sources (such as factories) and nonpoint sources
(such as construction sites) so that maximum pollution levels are not
exceeded. Finally, states must enforce the TMDL pollution budgets for
each waterway. Much more work on TMDLs needs to be carried out in
order to clean up urban waterways.

Section 402 requires any government, business, or individual that discharges from a point source (for example, a factory or sewage treatment
plant) into a navigable waterway to obtain a National Pollutant Discharge Elimination System (NPDES) permit from the state environmental agency or EPA. Since the early 1990s, EPA has turned over most of
the NPDES permitting, monitoring, and enforcement to the states.

Federal legislation separates the NPDES stormwater program into two
phases and generally covers two types of runoff: from storm sewers and
from construction sites. In Phase I, medium and large municipal separate storm sewer systems (MS4s) and construction sites greater than five
acres must obtain NPDES permits from EPA. Phase II requires NPDES
permits for stormwater runoff in municipalities with fewer than 100,000
people and for construction activities that disturb one to five acres of
land.

About 700 cities have combined sewer systems, and combined sewer
overflow continues to be a major source of water pollution. During
heavy rainstorms or snowmelts, dangerous levels of bacteria-laden sewage are released into waterways, threatening drinking water supplies and
often leading to beach closings.

Section 404 regulates dredging and filling wetlands in navigable
waters. Landowners, developers, and governments proposing to dredge
or fill a wetland in navigable waters must first obtain a permit from the
U.S. Army Corps of Engineers. Parts of many older cities were built on

floodplains and still experience periodic flooding. Wetlands and flood-plains play an important role in absorbing floodwaters. This was a lesson that greater New Orleans learned the hard way when Hurricane Katrina hit; hundreds of thousands of acres of wetlands had been dredged and filled, greatly reducing the capacity to absorb floodwaters. Loss of wet-lands and the increase in impervious surfaces make flood events more severe by increasing water velocity and soil erosion.

Urban water supply. The federal government has promoted water supply planning through the source water protection program and the well-head protection program of the Safe Drinking Water Act. Water supply planning is especially important in cities that are experiencing rapid population growth and development, and where water must be brought in from a distance. A particular challenge for cities is implementing careful land use planning to accommodate more people and develop-ment while protecting water supplies. For instance, cities can use the Drinking Water State Revolving Fund under the Safe Drinking Water Act to install green infrastructure such as permeable pavement, green roofs, rooftop gardens, and other measures that help reduce the urban heat island effect, save energy, and control storm water runoff. Cities can also use this funding to purchase land and conservation easements to land to protect water sources.

The Barton Springs watershed in greater Austin, Texas, provides an interesting example of local water protection efforts. The watershed cov-ers over 360 square miles and the aquifer supplies water to 45,000 peo-ple. In 1992, the city of Austin passed an ordinance limiting the amount of new impervious surface to 15 to 25 percent of any tract over the Bar-ton Springs aquifer. In 1998, Austin voters approved a $65 million bond issue to purchase sensitive lands and conservation easements on land in the Barton Springs contributing and recharge zones (Daniels and Dan-iels 2003).

Cities need to be alert for potential mismatches between water sup-plies and population growth, the uncertain replenishing and expansion of water supplies, and threats to water supplies from competing jurisdic-tions and pollution sources. Increasingly, cities must plan regionally and at a watershed level to ensure they have adequate supplies of clean fresh-water over the long run.

BROWNFIELDS

The cleanup and reuse of brownfield sites has become one of the most important efforts that older industrial "rust belt" cities can undertake for revitalization and greening. The EPA defines brownfields as "abandoned, idled, or underused industrial and commercial facilities where expansion or redevelopment is complicated by real and perceived contamination" (USEPA Brownfields Home Page 2001). There are an estimated 500,000 brownfields in the United States, mainly in cities. The U.S. Conference of Mayors cited brownfield cleanup as its top priority in 1994 because of the potential number of jobs, new business investment, tax revenues, new residents, and neighborhood revivals that would result (Daniels and Daniels 2003).

Brownfield sites include gas stations abandoned because of leaking underground storage tanks, former dry cleaners, and empty factories. Brownfields often have the advantage of good access to transportation networks, sewer and water facilities, and nearby residents. Brownfields have been redeveloped into offices, housing, technology parks, new factories, warehouses, museums, restaurants, and parks. Brownfield redevelopment has involved both new construction as well as the adaptive reuse of existing buildings.

Cities and private developers have faced a variety of obstacles in redeveloping brownfield sites. For years the major problem was liability. In 1980, Congress passed the Comprehensive Environmental Response Compensation and Liability Act (CERCLA), better known as the Superfund law. CERCLA addressed the need to clean up large hazardous waste sites and to establish liability to recover cleanup costs from those responsible for dumping the waste. The strict liability provision of CERCLA made all previous and current owners or waste dumpers liable for cleanup costs, even if a person or company purchased a property without knowing that it contained hazardous waste. The "joint and several" clause of CERCLA allowed the EPA to make one company or individual liable if others could not be found or if others had no money to pay for cleanup costs. The risk of liability made businesses and local governments reluctant to purchase and rehabilitate property on which any hazardous waste had been dumped.

Brownfield sites show a moderate amount of contamination from hazardous waste, but not high enough levels to be placed on the EPA's priority list for the Superfund program. Even so, brownfields may pose a threat to public health and may be expensive to clean up. The successful cleanup and redevelopment of brownfield sites depends on limits to future cleanup liability, a reliable assessment of the contamination, risk-based cleanup standards, and financial incentives. In addition, brownfield redevelopment occurs as a partnership between public regulatory and funding agencies on the one hand, and private investors, developers, and neighborhood groups on the other.

In the 1990s, the EPA began to give the states considerable responsibility for the identification, monitoring, and redevelopment of brownfields, and recovery of cleanup costs (Johnson 2002). States can grant relief from liability under the Superfund law to companies and investors that redevelop lightly to moderately polluted properties. A state environmental agency and a developer enter into an agreement that spells out the conditions of cleanup, based on an assessment of the contamination on the brownfield site before any remediation takes place. The Small Business Liability Relief and Brownfields Revitalization Act of 2002 limited liability of buyers of brownfields as a way to encourage remediation and reuse of brownfield sites.

Limits on future landowner liability are essential for brownfield developers because lending institutions require an assessment of the possible existence of hazardous waste, leaking underground storage tanks, or asbestos before they will issue a loan for the purchase of commercial real estate. Also, through site-by-site cleanup agreements, the state can set cleanup standards that match the proposed redeveloped use; for instance, a warehouse project would involve less remediation than a park.

Cleaning up brownfields is expensive. Since 1993, the EPA has funded national and regional brownfield cleanup and redevelopment projects through grants to states and cities. The grants have enabled communities to assess and inventory brownfield sites as a first step toward redeveloping those properties. For instance, Baltimore has used an EPA grant to set up a Geographic Information System (GIS) identifying available vacant and underutilized properties, about half of which are brownfields (Johnson 2002). The 2002 Brownfields Act also provides federal grants for brownfield assessment and cleanup.

Building on the Foundation of Federal Environmental Laws

The federal government has helped urban environments mainly through air and water quality regulations and infrastructure grants. But the federal government has not passed much pathbreaking environmental legislation since the 1990 Clean Air Act amendments. In particular, the federal government has exerted little leadership in energy conservation and the development of alternative energy systems. Further improvements in urban air quality will depend in large part on increased use of mass transit (fewer car trips and miles driven), renewable energy (less fossil fuel), and overall energy conservation. Federal transportation funds have been skewed toward road construction and maintenance. The MPO approach is serving some cities well, such as San Francisco and Washington, D.C. But most of the 341 MPOs are still wedded to road construction and motor vehicle travel. The federal government needs to put much more money into mass transit as the nation approaches 400 million Americans.

Meanwhile, some cities are promoting alternative energy and energy conservation both to improve air quality and to reduce greenhouse gases that contribute to climate change. In 2007, New York City's Mayor Bloomberg proposed imposing America's first congestion pricing schedule on cars and trucks to encourage New Yorkers to use mass transit (congestion pricing places a toll on drivers who enter a part of the city during certain hours as a way to reduce traffic by discouraging driving). Moreover, the proceeds from the congestion tolls would be spent on improving bus and subway service.

Mayor Bloomberg also proposed reducing the city's greenhouse gas emissions by 30 percent by 2030 (*Economist* 2007). There is an element of self-interest here because New York City is a flood-prone coastal city, vulnerable to rising sea levels brought on by climate change from greenhouse gases. Dozens of other U.S. coastal cities are equally vulnerable.

To reduce greenhouse gas emissions, 23 states and a few cities, such as Columbia, Missouri and Jacksonville, Florida, have adopted renewable portfolio standards requiring local electricity providers to obtain a percentage of their electricity from renewable energy sources. The federal government has imposed no such renewable portfolio standards on electric utilities.

The nonprofit sector has played an increasingly important role in promoting energy conservation. The U.S. Green Building Council's Leadership in Energy and Environmental Design (LEED) certification of buildings has attracted the attention of developers, investors, and end-users. Cities including San Francisco, Boston, and Austin have adopted ordinances that all new municipal buildings and major renovations to existing municipal buildings must meet LEED standards.

Green space is essential for urban revitalization. Mayor Bloomberg set out a goal that every New Yorker should live no more than 10 minutes from a park (New York City has already produced a greenprint map of the green spaces in the city). Some federal funding for parks has come through the Land and Water Conservation Fund and the Urban Park and Recreation Recovery program for economically distressed urban communities. But Land and Water Conservation Fund monies are spread throughout the United States and tend to favor rural projects, whereas the Urban Park and Recreation Recovery program has not been funded since 2002. Thus, cities have had to look for other ways to pay for new parks, greenways, and trails. Indianapolis has a 35-mile greenways trail system; Chattanooga is building a 75-mile trail system. Again, the nonprofit sector is helping to create and maintain urban green spaces. For instance, the Pennsylvania Horticultural Society, profiled in the book and video *Edens Lost & Found*, has worked with neighborhoods to create community gardens, restore parks, and generally upgrade appearances. The Trust for Public Land, founded in 1972, works with cities nationwide to protect and create public spaces for recreation and social gathering.

The federal government has established no standards for the recycling of household waste. In cities, solid waste disposal is typically the third-largest government expense after education and transportation. Recycling has several benefits, such as avoiding waste incineration and the resulting air pollution, and reducing carbon dioxide emissions by requiring fewer trees to be harvested. The national recycling rate is currently about 30 percent, far lower than in Japan or Germany, where rates are 70 percent or higher (Daniels and Daniels 2003). California requires cities to recycle half of their waste, a standard Los Angeles has met.

An important emerging practice in cities is setting benchmarks for environmental improvement. For instance, in 2001 Columbus, Ohio published a report on environmental progress against benchmarks (Columbus Health Department 2001). This allows elected officials to better identify successes and shortcomings in their greening efforts; and the voters of Columbus can hold their elected officials accountable.

The Urban Future

The slogan "Think Globally, Act Locally" holds considerable relevance for cities involved in greening efforts. America is the world's leading producer of greenhouses gases and the world's leading consumer of energy and natural resources. Meanwhile, our trade deficit and dependence on foreign oil supplies continue to grow. This is not a sustainable situation.

In 1990, the U.S. census indicated that America had become a suburban nation: more people were living in the suburbs than in central cities. The suburban lifestyle relies heavily on cheap and plentiful oil supplies and the ubiquitous automobile. Moreover, if another 100 million Americans are to be accommodated with a minimum of impact on the environment, then cities will have to provide attractive places to live and work. The suburban model is simply not sustainable.

Greening the cities is not just an attempt to improve the quality of life of current residents. It is also a matter of national security. It is an effort to live with a smaller ecological footprint in greater harmony with nature, and to create places that provide a quality future for generations to come.

References

American Public Transportation Association. 2007. *Ridership Report: Fourth Quarter, 2006*. Washington, D.C.: APTA.

Beatley, Timothy, and Katherine Manning. 1998. *The Ecology of Place: Planning for Environment, Economy, and Community*. Washington, D.C.: Island Press.

Coequyt, John, and Richard Wiles. 2000. *Prime Suspects: The Law Breaking Polluters America Fails to Inspect*. Washington, D.C.: Environmental Working Group.

Columbus Health Department. 2001. *Environmental Snapshot, 2001*. Columbus, Ohio: Columbus Health Department.

Daniels, Tom, and Katherine Daniels. 2003. *The Environmental Planning Handbook: For Sustainable Communities and Regions*. Chicago: American Planning Association.

Dunn, Seth, and Christopher Flavin. 2002. "Moving the Climate Change Agenda Forward." In *State of the World 2002: A Worldwatch Institute Report on Progress Toward a Sustainable Society*, ed. Linda Starke. New York: Norton.

The Economist. 2007. "Greening the Big Apple." April 28: 34.

Ewing, Reid, Tom Schmid, Richard Killingsworth, Amy Zlot, and Stephen Raudenbush. 2003. "Relationship Between Urban Sprawl and Physical Activity, Obesity and Morbidity," *American Journal of Health Promotion* 111, 12.

Johnson, Mark. 2002. "Brownfields Are Looking Greener." *Planning* 68, 6: 14–19.

Lash, Jonathan, Katherine Gillman, and David Sheridan. 1984. *A Season of Spoils: The Reagan Administration's Attack on the Environment*. New York: Pantheon.

Metro. 1995. Metro Growth Concept. www.metro-region.org/article.cfm?article ID=231.

1000 Friends of Oregon. 1991–1997. *Land Use Transportation and Air Quality (LUTRAQ) Reports*. Portland: 1000 Friends of Oregon.

Shutkin, William A. 2001. *The Land That Could Be: Environmentalism and Democracy in the Twenty-First Century*. Cambridge, Mass.: MIT Press.

U.S. Bureau of the Census. 2004. *Census Bureau Projects Tripling of Hispanic and Asian Populations in 50 Years: Non-Hispanic Whites May Drop to Half of Total Population*. Washington, D.C.: Bureau of the Census.

U.S. Environmental Protection Agency. 2001a. *Latest Findings on National Air Quality: 2000 Status and Trends*. Washington, D.C.: EPA.

———. 2001b. http://www.epa.gov/swerosps/bf/index.html.

U.S. Supreme Court. 2007. *Massachusetts et al. v. Environmental Protection Agency et al.* 549 U.S. Supreme Court No. 05–1120 (2007).

Wiland, Harry, and Dale Bell. 2006. *Edens Lost & Found: How Ordinary Citizens Are Restoring Our Great American Cities*. White River Junction, Vt.: Chelsea Green.

Chapter 2
Growing Greener Regions

Robert D. Yaro and David M. Kooris

In 2007, the population of the United States reached 300 million; that of the globe recently hit 6 billion. Climate change and ecological damage unparalleled in recent history echoed these milestones. Storms have become more erratic and extreme. The first plot of habitable land recently gave way to rising sea levels in coastal India. Deforestation, desertification, and sprawling development are drastically reducing the world's biological diversity and available arable land. Global warming is no longer under dispute. The most recent report from the Intergovernmental Panel on Climate Change links human behavior with higher land and ocean temperatures and rising sea levels over the past century and into the future (IPCC 2007). The greatest impetus for growing greener is thus the impending crises stemming from climate change.

Human activities are responsible for many of these ecological problems. For example, in America's Appalachian region and other mining districts around the world, miners eliminated mountains, filled river valleys, and left gaping holes carved into the earth's crust to reach the underlying natural resources. The use of fossil fuels for transport and manufacturing concentrates pollution in the air, oceans, animals, and, most worrisome, in those who use them and their children. Just as humans have created these problems, they can also relieve them by promoting greener patterns of growth. Most important, they can reduce the demand for energy through promoting green regional design to achieve a greater balance between the built and natural environments, curbing greenhouse gas emissions.

Intervention at the regional scale is not only feasible but also necessary to counteract the dangers of climate change. In this essay we define the key aspects of green regional design. We then use the New York-New Jersey-Connecticut metropolitan area as a case study of the application of regional design, detailing its use in the creation of open space, transportation (and related land uses) and energy networks that frame an area's growth and development. We show how it makes the area more livable and competitive while addressing global warming.

Global Challenges Require Regional and Local Solutions

The largest source of greenhouse gas emissions (primarily carbon dioxide) comes from vehicles and power plants. Cars and trucks consume nearly a third and buildings almost half of U.S. energy. A heavy dependence on fossil fuels to feed these uses means that the United States is the largest emitter of carbon dioxide in the world. While the per capita emissions in the Northeast are lower than most other regions in the country, the volumes are still high (U.S. EPA 2006).

While climate change is a global challenge, the current U.S. political system indicates that few solutions will be put into place even at the national level. Though virtually every other industrialized country has instituted national policies to cap carbon emissions and achieve a development future that is more in balance with the environment, the United States has not. Thus, for the near future, the lower levels of government will have to take the lead outlining and implementing green strategies. The way in which they decide to allocate and arrange growth will be the foundation of this process because the form of the built environment fuels the demand for energy and drives the extent of greenhouse gas production,

In the past 60 years a common vernacular—low-density suburban sprawl—has dominated American development. Characteristic of this pattern are spread out metropolitan areas tied together by highways and streets, a pattern that relies on the automobile with its high consumption of carbon-based fossil fuels. It is a reflection of how modern industrial society has dominated nature and managed ways of achieving a common ideal, regardless of the particular opportunities or constraints of a specific place. This one-size-fits-all approach to city and regional design is becoming an unsustainable ethos in the age of expensive energy and climate change.

Today, 80 percent of Americans live in metropolitan regions, a pattern that will continue in the future. With the nation's population projected to grow by 40 percent, reaching 420 million by 2050, accommodating this growth will require the construction of nearly as many places to live, work, and shop between now and midcentury as have been built over the past two centuries. By just 2025, more than half the built environment will not have existed in the year 2000 (Nelson 2006). In addition, as students and faculty at the University of Pennsylvania and staff at the Regional Plan Association (RPA) have recently documented, 10 connected "mega-regions"—integrated networks of several metropolitan regions in every corner of the United States—will capture more than 70 percent of this projected growth. These mega-regions have shared demographics, economies, mobility networks, and environmental support systems linking their present situations as well as their futures. Because they command such a dominant share of the nation's growth, the ways in which metropolitan regions and mega-regions decide to plan for this expected development will have profound implications for the environment. Regions choose the way they grow. They can develop in ways that either aggravate or mitigate climate change. If they adopt green regional design, they can balance a desire to be truly green with competitiveness and prosperity.

Defining Green Regional Design

Although no standard definition of green regional design exists, at the most basic level it includes creating places in which inhabitants recycle materials and consume locally grown organic produce. In highly urbanized regions, it incorporates high rates of transit ridership and building codes that require LEED—Leadership in Energy and Design—certification. A green region is one that is in balance with its environment.

A green region also is one that embodies design strategies that respond to its particular environmental conditions, made up of both natural and built components. Green regional design must, therefore, embark on a path that responds to both the natural and climatological conditions of a geography, but also to the manmade infrastructure and built environment spread across the landscape. A green region can take many forms, as will be seen in the following case study.

A Case Study of the New York-New Jersey-Connecticut Metropolitan Area

This case study will detail green regional design approaches that deal with open space, mobility (and associated land use), and energy systems in place, being planned, or in concept stages in the tri-state (New York-New Jersey-Connecticut) metropolitan region. The area's open space systems support its "green infrastructure" of water supplies, ecological reserves, and farms and forests. They are also the region's aesthetic and recreational backbone. Its mobility systems shape how individuals make travel choices based on a combination of the availability and convenience of different modes and the distribution and concentration of land uses and activities. Each mode of transport is more or less suited for particular environments and each has profoundly different implications for climate change, air quality, and public health. Finally, its energy generation and distribution systems power the region's buildings and transit systems.

OPEN SPACE SYSTEMS IN THE NORTHEAST TRI-STATE REGION

In green regional design, determining where to grow and where not to grow is the first step in achieving a balance between the built and natural worlds. In the tri-state region, one of the America's most highly urbanized areas, a network of regional landscapes (foremost among them the Appalachian Highlands and their vast surface water supplies) provides natural resources as well as psychological sustenance. These landscapes, a form of "Greensward," are the yin to the area's urban yang. They ensure the availability of clean drinking water for the region's population—it would cost a fortune to replicate the services that the forested hills, lakes, and river valleys provide naturally. These large systems, with their pristine aesthetic quality and diverse, well-located recreational opportunities, also form the foundation of the region's quality of life. Workers in the knowledge and information economy are increasingly making choices about where to live and work based on quality of life factors, giving rise to the success of locations such as Portland, Oregon, Austin, Texas, and San Francisco (Florida 2002).

The "Greensward" frames the tri-state region, incorporating more than a dozen large natural systems, ranging in size from the 3-million-acre Appalachian Highlands to the 100,000-acre Long Island Pine Barrens. Preservation efforts have successfully targeted their most ecologically sensitive cores. Planning efforts have also paid attention to their fringes where sprawling development patterns are jeopardizing their integrity. As described later, a multistep preservation strategy has been successful in protecting the region's most valuable ecological resources.

In true McHargian tradition, RPA first prioritized the region's rural and natural landscapes based on a series of ecological and green infrastructure factors (for example, the quality and extent of public water supplies within each system) and determined the most important areas for preservation in Region at Risk, RPA's third regional plan. They identified the five large systems that provide the majority of the regional water supply, constitute a commanding share of the region's undeveloped land, and make up the foundation for the region's networks of parkland and trails. The large water supply landscapes follow the spine of the Appalachian Mountains through the tri-state region. They include the Appalachian Highlands, the Kittatinny and Shawangunk Mountains (which stretch northeast from Delaware Water Gap just west of the highlands), and the Catskill Mountains in central New York state. Two other large groundwater systems—the Long Island Pine Barrens and New Jersey Pinelands—provide additional potable water supplies (see Plate 1).

The Greensward also contains all or portions of three major rivers: the Delaware, the Hudson, and the Connecticut. These waterways drain into a network of estuaries, including New York Harbor, Long Island Sound, Peconic Bay, and the coastal bays on Long Island and the New Jersey shore, whose integrity relies largely on what happens in upstream developed lands. These natural systems and water bodies are the essential elements of the landscape that make the tri-state region unique; destruction of any part of them would have negative implications for the quality of life and economic vitality of the entire region.

As early as the 1920s, pioneering regional planner Benton MacKaye identified the important role of the Appalachian Highlands. He proposed the preservation of the whole Appalachian region as a permanent greenbelt for the Northeast. As a result of his advocacy, the national and several state governments established parks and forests from Maine to Georgia, linked by the landmark Appalachian Trail. But preservation efforts in the New Jersey-New York-Connecticut portion of the highlands lagged until recently.

RPA was an early supporter of highland preservation measures. In its first (1929) and second (1968) regional plans, RPA proposed ambitious efforts to protect the area. Because of RPA's sustained advocacy, state legislatures established or expanded several key state parks, including New Jersey's Ringwood State Park (1964, 1966, and 1995) and New York's Minnewaska State Park (1993 and 2006). In the late 1980s RPA began a new initiative to protect the highlands, culminating in the preservation of the 25,000-acre Sterling Forest along the border between New York and New Jersey.

In the 1990s, increased pressures from suburban development near the highlands led the RPA and other groups to advocate broader preservation strategies for the whole ecosystem. By 2004 Congress had enacted the Highlands Stewardship Act, allocating federal funds for planning and land and resource conservation efforts in a four-state region stretching from Pennsylvania to Connecticut. In the same year, the New Jersey state legislature adopted the Highlands Water Protection and Planning Act, authorizing the creation of a 400,000-acre highlands planning and preservation area administered by the Highlands Council. RPA is now pressing for similar measures in New York and Connecticut.

Key to preserving these ecological treasures is protecting the landscapes located along their edges. What happens along the fuzzy boundaries between natural and urban areas is important because it is here that biodiversity can be greatest, and it is at this line where society decides the level of integration that it will allow to occur between the natural world and the built. Virtually all the Northeast is subdivided into municipal governments with responsibility for administering land use along with planning and zoning and providing subdivision regulations. This political fragmentation requires coordination and cooperation among adjacent towns and with other agencies to protect large resource systems, such as the highlands. Today a number of experiments are under way to coordinate planning and zoning among the municipalities near the highlands.

One example is in southeastern Orange County in New York. The area sits on the northern edge of the New York Highlands, an area threatened by suburbanization leapfrogging over the preserved mountain range from the more heavily developed towns and villages closer to the metropolitan core. Some equally ecologically sensitive but presently unprotected lands near Harriman State Park, Palisades Interstate Park System, West Point Military Academy, and Sterling Forest Reserve are threatened by the rising demand for residential subdivisions and retail malls. While the threat to the natural environment was apparent to many residents of the region and acknowledged as threatening their quality of life, traffic and roadway congestion was the most apparent externality of unmanaged growth. In 1998, seven municipalities (three towns and four villages), concerned primarily about traffic and transportation issues, formed a joint planning task force under the auspices of the Orange County Planning Commission. After participating in a transportation study that resulted in several concrete transportation improvement projects presently undergoing implementation, the partners concluded that these measures only slightly mitigated growing traffic congestion. They saw that the only way to address the problem would be through a coordinated, intermunicipal approach to land use planning.

Working with these municipalities and several other stakeholders, RPA was commissioned by the county of Orange and the Orange County Planning Department to link today's land use decisions with tomorrow's transportation and quality of life implications. A main objective of the project was to demonstrate in easily accessible graphic language the future development paths available to the region. As a first step, RPA undertook a build-out analysis under the existing zoning and associated regulations. The resulting "business as usual" scenario laid out anticipated development, parcel by parcel, showing building footprints and road networks that echoed the development style embodied by recent subdivisions. With limited arterials spanning the region and much of the landscape unprotected, the result was automobile-dependent sprawl that dumped traffic onto the few primary roads. Under these conditions, the conversion of thousands of acres into areas dominated by single-family homes on cul-de-sacs and large commercial establishments ringed by seas of parking would lead to continued congestion, loss of open space, and an overall reduction in the area's quality of life. Recent trends in southeast Orange County have demonstrated that the preponderance of a uniform development type—a single-family house on a large lot—has lead to a marked decline in affordability throughout the region.

To develop an alternative to the status quo, RPA convened a professional workshop, consisting of nationally recognized urban designers, landscape architects, land use law professionals, and local stakeholders. They began by mapping the area's most ecologically sensitive landscapes and then identified priority growth areas, recommending development strategies that targeted infill and placemaking in the area's centers. The ecologically sensitive landscapes formed a green network that not only integrated the seven municipalities but also connected their cores to the surrounding parkland. The resulting green infrastructure permeated each village and hamlet center. It originated in a wilderness park, moved through active recreation areas, traveled from rail to trail to a green street, and terminated in a village green.

This planned green network consists of the area's river corridors, floodplains, wetlands, agricultural lands, and ridges as well as other lands necessary to bridge the elements. Preserving these lands provides other regional benefits, including storm-water management, groundwater replenishment, flood hazard prevention, recreational opportunities, and other quality of life enhancements. In sum, the green infrastructure signals where not to grow and provides the framework within which all future development will occur.

Mobility Systems: Transportation and Associated Land Uses

In green regional design, once the landscapes for preservation are protected, the next step is to determine supportive transportation investments and associated land uses. Ideally, these two streams of planning occur iteratively so that the transportation infrastructure is best suited to accommodate the spatial distribution of land uses and the development patterns reinforce the transportation investment.[1] The primary assumption of green regional design is that a hierarchy exists in a regional mobility system that ranges from pedestrian ways to highways to rails. Green regional design rejects transportation plans that take a "one-size-fits-all" approach relying only on wide traffic lanes, on-street parking, and minimum sidewalks. In green regional design, nonautomobile transportation receives priority from the mega-region to the neighborhood. At the largest scale, green regional design aims to strengthen and improve existing regional rail networks, connecting centers, suburbs, and hinterlands. At the smaller scale, it seeks to create nodes of pedestrian activity for short distances, combined with bike lanes and transit for longer distances. It views the automobile as useful for occasional trips to outlying locales, inconvenient locations, and for recreational use. Its goal is to gear mobility spending to enhance the pedestrian realm, bicycle infrastructure, and mass transit.

The tri-state region and the larger Northeast mega-region are examples of places that can capitalize on green regional design because they have well-developed mass transit systems, strong regional centers, and historic downtowns and village centers originally developed at the scale of the pedestrian. Urban and suburban municipalities across the nation have been trending in recent years toward higher-density and pedestrian-oriented developments in order to replicate the quality of life and vitality found throughout the historic centers of the New York metropolitan region. As concerns over both energy security and climate change become more pronounced, communities will continue to look to the precedents of New York City and its regional centers since they have the country's lowest per capita energy consumption and carbon emissions.

Historically, transportation shaped the tri-state region. First, it grew around its streetcar, subway, and commuter rail networks and, later, it spread out along its highways. Today, the growth of the population and employment base of New York City—it added more than a million residents in the 1990s—and a regional network of suburban centers has created congested highways and pushed ridership to crushloads on many of the region's subway and commuter rail lines. New York City is expected to add a million more people by 2030. The whole region expects to add 4 million residents and 3 million jobs over that period. Accommodating this growth will require expansion of the regional rail network.

The New York metropolitan area currently boasts the world's most robust regional rail, subway, and light rail network; it has more than 900 stations distributed over several thousand square miles. The region's transit agencies have invested over $60 billion in capital improvements over the past 25 years. New Jersey, in particular, has instituted system-expanding projects consisting of three new light-rail lines, new transfer points, and line upgrades, and is examining the reactivation of several lines decommissioned in the latter half of the last century. The recent construction of the Secaucus transfer station cut travel times by allowing a direct connection into New York's Pennsylvania Station for lines that previously terminated in Hoboken, New Jersey, which provided connections to ferries and the PATH rail line for the trip to New York. Midtown Direct, the electrification of several formerly diesel rail lines, has had a profound impact on both travel times as well as property values within walking distance of the rail stations.

The system in New Jersey serves the more than 5 million passengers daily who travel to New York City and these investments have allowed mass transit to become an option for many trips, particularly as the area's highway system has become more congested and less reliable in recent years. Currently, New Jersey Transit is planning another $6 billion investment, the "Access to the Region's Core" (ARC) project, a two-track commuter rail tunnel under the Hudson River serving a new New Jersey Transit terminal north of Penn Station in Manhattan's West Midtown district. This will permit continued growth around New Jersey Transit's extensive commuter rail network (see Plate 2).

The region is also moving forward with two additional "mega-projects" designed to meet increased mobility needs: the construction of the Second Avenue subway and Long Island Railroad's East Side Access (ESA). Representing the first major expansion of the region's transit network in more than 60 years, these projects will be funded by New York's Metropolitan Transportation Authority (MTA), the Port Authority of New York and New Jersey, and the federal government. Located at the heart of the region, the Second Avenue subway, beginning construction in the spring of 2007, will run the length of Manhattan's East Side and may eventually extend north to the Bronx and south into Brooklyn and Queens, linking JFK airport to the job centers in midtown and lower Manhattan via a one-seat ride. It will relieve the overstressed Lexington Avenue subway line and provide modern transit service to an economically diverse population that currently has poor transit access. The ESA project will create a spur of the Long Island Railroad (LIRR), branching off in Sunnyside, Queens before entering the tunnel to Pennsylvania Station and leading to a new terminal under Grand Central Terminal in Manhattan's East Midtown district. This investment will reduce travel times by up to 20 minutes for more than 100,000 daily commuters whose ultimate destination is Midtown's east side. This will concurrently free up platform space at the LIRR existing Penn Station hub and track space under the East River, while expanding the transit commuter shed 20 miles farther into Long Island. The ESA and what has been termed the Access to the Region's Core projects will have a significant impact on the regional rail system, enabling one-seat through service between Connecticut, New Jersey, and New York. A great number of population and employment centers throughout the region will then be linked with reliable and efficient transit connections.

In addition to these major fixed right-of-way transit investments, the region is also moving forward with less expensive and more flexible "bus rapid transit" (BRT) lines. These projects, in sync with green regional design, decrease dependence on autos and, when they incorporate new propulsion technologies such as hybrid or even hydrogen-powered buses, reduce greenhouse gas emissions. New York has a long tradition of employing BRT. For example, the Port Authority's Lincoln Tunnel has had exclusive BRT lanes for decades. Building on this success, the New York City Department of Transportation and the MTA are jointly looking to establish five additional BRT lines in the city's outer boroughs. Outside of New York City, two promising BRT projects are on the horizon. In Hartford County, Connecticut, the Connecticut state Department of Transportation has planned a BRT route between Hartford, the state capital, and New Britain, the county's second largest city. It will use an abandoned rail line parallel to I-84 to link the communities. New Jersey Transit is planning a second BRT in Essex County, New Jersey. Its two lines will radiate from Newark's Penn Station, the area's major transit hub, to suburban Irvington and Bloomfield. These BRT lines absorb a small fraction of the cost and time needed for construction of new light-rail systems. They will also have the potential to become catalysts for creation of new transit-oriented development nodes around each stop.

Just as these improvements will lead to a regional transit system that limits carbon emissions and environmental impact by reducing the amount of trips made by automobile within the metropolitan region, transportation advocates are eyeing similar strategies that would provide a green and efficient transit alternative for intercity trips. The Northeast mega-region, stretching from Boston to Washington, first identified by geographer Jean Gottman in his book, *Megalopolis* (1961), represents the most appropriate scale for addressing the challenges of intercity rail. The density along this corridor offers a rare opportunity in this nation to support high-speed rail linkages and should serve as a model for future transportation policy within the other emerging mega-regions across the United States. The Northeast has two-thirds of the nation's transit ridership, and more than 80 percent of its commuter rail passengers. While the mega-region's Northeast Corridor rail system carries more than half of Amtrak's national ridership, it has remained uncompetitive with automobiles and air shuttle services because of its relatively slow and expensive service. Amtrak's Acela express trains were designed for 140-mph service, but travel most of the distance between Boston and Washington at less than half that speed. Nonetheless, Acela ridership is high, proving significant demand for an efficient and reliable alternative to the congested motorways and airports for trips between 100 and 500 miles.

While the United State struggles to maintain even the Northeast Corridor with limited funding for rail travel, other industrialized nations have identified rail's environmental and efficiency benefits at the scale of the mega-region. Since 1964, Asia and Europe have built extensive high-speed rail (HSR) networks, clearly demonstrating the potential for

HSR to compete effectively with cars and planes in similar mega-regions. Kip Bergstrom, the director of the Rhode Island Economic Policy Council, has predicted that HSR will become the preferred mobility system for travel between metropolitan centers in twenty-first-century mega-regions, such as the Northeast, stretching over 500 miles. In this sense, they will enable the growth and integration of mega-regions, in much the same way that limited-access highway networks enabled the growth of late twentieth-century metropolitan areas. Achieving a viable rail alternative for intercity travel within the Northeast and other mega-regions will require substantial financial investment coupled with substantive institutional change.

To realize the full potential of mobility investments, local governments and planning agencies must organize land uses to take advantage of new and improved transit systems through transit-oriented development (TOD). Walkable and pedestrian scaled, mixed-use nodes at key stations serve as built-in ridership for the transit system while providing a variety of destinations at stops along each line. While no one-size-fits-all TOD solutions exist, each community, in taking the greatest advantage of its rail or bus station, should plan for densities related to the level of service at its stations. The density at a suburban rail station served by a single line would be of an order of magnitude several scales lower than the density at an urban station served by regional rail and multiple subway lines.

At the most urban edge of the density spectrum are recent plans for new TOD opportunities on the West Side of midtown Manhattan, directly adjoining Penn Station. Identified as early as 1964 by RPA as having the potential to become Manhattan's third mixed-use employment center, the concept was resurrected in the Third Regional Plan in 1996; beginning in 2004 a massive rezoning allowing for up to 50 million square feet of mixed use development is making this idea a reality. With Penn Station (presently served by 14 regional rail lines and new connections discussed earlier, six subway lines, and PATH service to New Jersey) as a transit hub, the area is appropriate for intense development. Current plans calling for major improvements to Penn Station—including transforming the nearby landmark Farley Post Office into a new "Moynihan Station" and modernizing the existing Penn Station site into a twenty-first-century transportation center—would make the Penn Station area the hub of the largest TOD district in the country.

A second example from Manhattan, albeit with less transit accessibility than the region's core but a greater framework for pedestrian- and bicycle-oriented development, is in the West Village in a district known historically as the Meatpacking District. While the wide cobblestone streets speak to the district's industrial past, meat packing has largely left the area, and so has the truck traffic on which the area was so dependent. In their place has grown one of the most hip neighborhoods in the entire region. Restaurants, boutiques, galleries, luxury hotels, condominiums, and nightclubs have transformed the neighborhood's gritty economic heritage. Other anticipated investments—including the Whitney Museum, which will open an annex, and the southern terminus of the High Line, the city's newest park along the linear viaduct formerly used for freight rail—will attract many more people to the area. Initial efforts to make the area more pedestrian friendly include activation of formerly blank street walls with new boutiques, installation of limited streetscape amenities including new lighting and trash cans in portions of the district, and greening through planting and landscaping of a median at the intersection of Fourteenth Street and Tenth Avenue.

RPA has worked with local community leaders to convene a series of design charrettes looking at more comprehensive strategies to better balance the automobile and pedestrian realms throughout the district. The New York City Department of Transportation has agreed to remove two northbound travel lanes from Ninth Avenue between Fourteenth and Sixteenth Streets, allowing for new public spaces and the transformation of a wide thoroughfare into a green boulevard. Additional opportunities for new public spaces and a unified streetscape program consisting of greening strategies as well as pedestrian amenities is being developed with the community and will be implemented in the coming years. Every street and block in a city is unique and demands a unique design based on the fine balance at that location between the various modes of mobility. St. Mark's Street in the East Village, Fulton Street in Lower Manhattan, and many other high-pedestrian-volume locations throughout the city require an approach that responds much more appropriately to the overwhelming demand for a quality pedestrian environment in these areas.

Improvements to a variety of transit options and the pedestrian realm will make these necessary alternatives to the automobile more attractive for certain trips. The tri-state region could additionally institute other reforms that would enhance another aspect of green regional design by limiting the attractiveness of the automobile for those trips most appropriately managed by other modes, namely congestion pricing and other incentive and regulatory measures. It could learn from London, where congestion pricing reduced traffic volumes in the city's core by one-third, allowing for the reclamation of a significant area of roadway for reuse by bikes and pedestrians. The tri-state region contains dozens of pedestrian-scale cities, town centers, villages, and hamlets that could consider this technique.

Opportunities exist throughout the tri-state region to capitalize on more sustainable transportation options than the automobile. Robust TOD opportunities exist in the area's 10 regional centers outside Manhattan, identified by RPA as it has worked for more than 40 years to transition the tri-state area into a multinucleated metropolis. Recent RPA activities in two centers, Newark, New Jersey, and Bridgeport, Connecticut, demonstrate how their revitalization can become models of green regional design. Crucial to the reestablishment of these cities to their former glory is to rebrand them from gray to green. Each city has robust remnants of its industrial past, underutilized and decaying waterfronts, a solid stock of housing and aging, underserviced transportation infrastructure that can be capitalized on to transition them to sustainable centers—models within the metropolitan region.

In Newark, in partnership with a newly elected progressive mayor, RPA launched a community-based planning process. Participants aimed to consolidate the best suggestions of past planning efforts, fill in the gaps with new and innovative ideas, and move the city out of its current blighted position. A positive element of Newark's recent urban history has been an extensive investment in the city's transit infrastructure. Based on its successes with the Hudson-Bergen Light Rail and the River LINE along the southern Delaware River, New Jersey Transit upgraded the Newark subway stations and rolling stock in 2001 and opened a new line connecting the Pennsylvania and Broad Street regional rail stations in 2006. In addition, it has undertaken important large-scale downtown redevelopment projects, including an arena (under construction), a performing arts center, a medical school, office buildings, and several residential conversions, achieving a full range of land uses into a true 24-hour community.

Severely lacking, however, is the city's connection to its Passaic River waterfront and its natural surroundings. None of the recent office buildings constructed along the city's waterfront made any effort to respond to this amenity, turning their backs to the river and most often placing parking garages and surface lots along that façade. A proposed new riverfront park would connect the northern end of downtown around the Riverfront Stadium and Washington Park to central downtown around the New Jersey Performing Arts Center and Military Park and on finally to Riverbank Park and the Ironbound neighborhood. This first phase of waterfront parkland would link the disparate elements of the city via a green amenity that would redefine the city by reestablishing its gateway, seen from the train, car, and plane entering the city, as a green ribbon linking the city to its principal natural resource, the river. This network would then be expanded throughout the city grid in a series of green streets and pedestrian and bike-priority corridors linking the downtown and its waterfront with Branch Brook Park, Weequahic Park, and the many diverse and vibrant neighborhoods throughout the city (see Plate 3).

Downtown Bridgeport is also working on revitalization, initiating programs that incorporate greening to make it a more desirable place for TOD development. Bound on three sides by interstate highways and on the fourth by the Metro-North railroad viaduct, it is isolated from its major waterfront assets, the Pequonnock River, and the Long Island Sound. Bridgeport is the only city on the northeast corridor Amtrak line from Washington to Boston that has a world-class beach within walking distance from the train station. This beach is set within the idyllic setting of a Frederick Law Olmsted-designed park, Seaside Park. In addition, the Pequonnock River links this park to another Olmsted-designed facility, Beardsley Park, located in one of the city's northern neighborhoods. Greening the various underpasses that link the downtown with its surroundings and connecting the two parks with a greenway and promenade along the Pequonnock River will create the aesthetically pleasing pedestrian experience essential to breaking the downtown out of its transportation-ringed bounds. The revitalization and greening of this waterfront will link the population of Connecticut's largest city with two of its greatest parks and form the first link in a trail and park network that may connect the population centers of the state's gold coast with both its beaches and rolling hills further north.

Both Newark and Bridgeport represent additional opportunities to institute green building design, most notably green roofs. Both have tens of acres of vacant land within the heart of their downtowns and can capitalize on this asset in an increasingly tight real estate market in the New York metropolitan area. The magnitude of potential development on the horizon for these two cities represents a nearly unparalleled opportunity in the metropolitan area to combine best practices in sustainable neighborhood and building design.

ENERGY SYSTEMS: POWERING REGIONS

The landscape preservation and strong links between transportation and land use planning encompassed in green regional design will go a long way toward reducing a region's ecological footprint and its impact on climate change. But green regional design also includes an energy component because the built environment, even in its most efficient of forms, has high demands for power. In general, the energy demand of buildings is composed of three broad categories: lighting, appliances, and heating and cooling. Energy conservation focuses on two areas: reducing the demand of individual structures through modern green building technologies, and finding new green energy supplies to diversify the mix in a region's power generation portfolio.

Encouraging the transition to more energy efficient lighting and appliances by private homeowners and by businesses requires both price incentives as well as stocking incentives so that the correct products are available to the consumer. While the prices of low-energy light bulbs and Energy Star appliances have come down, providing incentives to accelerate their use by both businesses and consumers may still require policies at the state and local level to reach the optimal price and availability. One example is New York's Energy Research and Development Agency (NYSERDA), which has pioneered an incentive program for stocking and purchasing of Energy Star air conditioners. It has been very successful in getting nearly 250,000 inefficient air conditioners removed from homes and apartments throughout the state and replaced with more efficient air conditioning units.[2]

With regard to supply, the tri-state region has many opportunities to diversify its sources that are as yet largely unrealized. In addition to energy saving and demand reduction measures in building design, several of the most ambitious green building projects incorporate power generation within the structure to meet much of the remaining supply needs. For example, the Condé Nast building at Four Times Square and the Bank of America building at One Bryant Park contain a variety of photovoltaic panels, hydrogen fuel cells, and, in the Bank of America building, a combined heat and power generator to meet the building's base load energy needs. Combined heat and power plants as well as district heating and cogeneration (in which electric generating plants use waste heat to provide heat and hot water in nearby buildings) are also in evidence. Most of Midtown and Lower Manhattan functions as the nation's largest district-heating service area. Steam ducts running from the area's power plants under most city streets serve large offices, stores, and apartment buildings. District cooling has also been successfully demonstrated in Toronto, Ontario, which draws water from Lake Ontario to cool an energy transfer station on the lake's shore in the summer.

In the speculative realm are other solutions, including solar radiation, wind power, lunar tide energy generation, excess heat capture, and geothermal cooling. Thousands of buildings in the tri-state region receive solar radiation. Presently, this energy is a liability, breaking down roof materials and causing costly replacement every decade or so. Harnessing this energy to generate electricity, a broadly accepted practice throughout the world, has not occurred in the tri-state region. However, recent work by New York City's Department of Long-Term Planning and Sustainability determined that the city could theoretically generate 18 percent of its electricity from solar panels installed on existing buildings.

Wind power generation is not as prevalent in the tri-state region as in the northern Great Plains or Denmark's North Sea, despite the many opportunities for both land-based and offshore turbines close to the population and job centers of the three states. However, upstate New York farmers struggling to keep up with rising property taxes and energy costs have constructed several small-scale wind farms. The resulting source of income is allowing them to harvest wind, making their land more profitable. Even greater than the wind potential upstate, however, are the strong winds of the Atlantic Ocean off the shorelines of the East Coast. An offshore wind farm south of Jones Beach, Long Island, consisting of up to 40 windmills that could generate between 100 and 140 MW of electricity—enough to power 30,000 to 40,000 homes—has been proposed by the Long Island Power Authority, but local property owners oppose it. The primary opposition stems from the visual disruptions to the horizon for the wealthy homeowners along the south shore. Concurrently, however, plans are moving ahead to construct a new natural gas generation facility adjacent to one of the more economically challenged communities on the island. Meeting the region's future energy needs will require the use of many distributed generation possibilities located in and around the demand and population centers (Figure 1).

An almost completely untapped energy source is the lunar energy derived from daily tidal fluctuations. Few places exist in North America where tidal power is strong enough to be harnessed for this purpose, but New York Harbor and the East River have some of the most promising potential. In one experiment dating from 2006, Verdant Power, the pioneer in kinetic hydropower systems, has tested this method by anchoring turbines in the East River adjacent to Roosevelt Island. This demonstration consists of several turbines that will power a grocery store on the island. If successful, Verdant is poised to install 400 turbines, generating 10 MW of electricity in the coming years. NYSERDA and New York University have identified the potential for between 600 and 1000 MW of kinetic hydropower generation in New York state, and Verdant Power is aiming to harness at least half that potential. This generation method is extremely reliable and as predictable as the tides, completely renewable and sustainable, and out of sight completely from all but the most hardy divers and sea creatures. For these reasons, growth in this green generation technology has enormous potential to serve New York City and other areas of the region with strong tidal flows, including areas of Connecticut and Long Island adjoining Long Island Sound and nearby bays and inlets.

Conservation and innovation will only partially meet the region's

Figure 1. Small-scale wind farms allow farmers to "harvest" the wind and increase the value of their land. David M. Kooris.

energy demand, leaving coal and nuclear power as other options. While poor mining practices, combined with air pollution and greenhouse gas production, make the prospect of reliance on coal far from appealing, the United States has the world's largest coal reserves, making selection of this option likely. For this reason, the United States needs to invest in new clean coal technologies, including gasification and carbon sequestration. Of equal concern are the attempts at mitigating the negative externalities of nuclear power. Even under the strictest safety regimen, disaster remains a possibility, and storing the waste for tens of thousands of years is a locally undesirable land use few if any communities are willing to accommodate. These solutions are not easy. There will be some methods of electricity generation in the future that clearly fall on the green side of things, such as solar panels and wind turbines, and others, such as nuclear, that blur the boundary between green and brown.

Green Regional Design and the Future

Global warming with its climate change effects will be a constant challenge in the twenty-first century. America is a major source of the greenhouse gas emissions that contribute to these problems. The form of the built environment and the structure of our nation's and region's mobility systems drive our demand for energy and result in our emissions of greenhouse gases. Green regional design offers an ameliorative approach. As outlined in this chapter, green regional design factors open space, mobility, and energy systems into determining the distribution and intensity of uses and the means to travel among them. It begins with preserving the most sensitive ecological landscapes and infiltrates green systems into urban areas. It organizes development around pedestrian, transit, and other sustainable forms of mobility. It recognizes that even in the most compact, transit-oriented regional development patterns, the demand for energy remains high. Thus it calls for the use of innovative, green alternatives for power generation. This nation anticipates growth rates greater than any of the other industrialized nations; how our society chooses to accommodate this growth will determine the quality of our environment and our competitiveness for several generations to come.

References

Adams, Thomas et al. 1929. *Regional Plan of New York and Its Environs.* New York: Committee on Regional Plan of New York and Its Environs.

Florida, Richard L. 2002. *The Rise of the Creative Class: And How It's Transforming Work, Leisure, Community, and Everyday Life.* New York: Basic Books.

Gottman, Jean. 1961. *Megalopolis: The Urbanized Northeastern Seaboard of the United States.* Cambridge, Mass.: MIT Press.

Intergovernmental Panel on Climate Change (IPCC). 2007. *Climate Change 2007.* IPCC Fourth Assessment Report.

Nelson, Arthur C. 2006. "Leadership in a New Era." *Journal of the American Planning Association* 72, 4: 393–407.

Regional Plan Association. 1964. *The Second Regional Plan.* New York: RPA.

———. 2006. *America 2050: A Prospectus.* New York: RPA.

U.S. Environmental Protection Agency. 2006. *EGRID 2006.* Version 1. Washington, D.C.: EPA.

Chapter 3
The Inter-Regional Dimension: The Greening of London and the Wider South East

ROBIN THOMPSON

The greening of our cities can only be fully effective if the regional dimension is taken into account. Some of the most pressing green issues demand policy and action at the strategic level associated with regional forms of governance: the challenges of climate change are an obvious example. Cities have powerful interactions with their hinterlands in the form, for example, of flows of water and energy into the city and wastes into the hinterland. Urban plans often feature green belts, green grids, green wedges, and other devices that extend into the surrounding areas. Major metropolitan areas have especially strong interdependence with the regions in which they are set; many have ecological footprints that extend far beyond the city limits.

This can be seen in London's efforts to promote green issues and its attempts to integrate these efforts with the approach being taken in the Wider South East region, which surrounds London. This chapter describes the metropolitan region and the current strategies to greening, including policies to contain rapid urban growth, promote sustainable development, and develop an inter-regional comprehensive approach. It concludes that preoccupation with containing growth and weak mechanisms for inter-regional collaboration are inhibiting an otherwise vigorous effort to promote greening at the strategic level.

The Regional Context

The Wider South East region of the United Kingdom is a megacity region (similar to the northeastern seaboard cities in the United States) (Hall and Pain 2006). It has a population of about 19 million, of whom almost 8 million live within the London boundary. As seen in Plate 4, it stretches north to Oxford and Cambridge and south to the coast of England. Diverse in character, it is essentially monocentric, dominated by London and with a galaxy of small and medium-sized towns.

Over the past century there has been an enduring tension between London and its hinterland, driven by the tendency of population and industry to move outward into the Wider South East. Considerable thought and strategic planning effort have gone into managing this spread of development. This has included Ebenezer Howard's Garden Cities concept, the postwar new towns movement, several central government attempts at producing an overall regional strategy and, most recently, the government designation of growth areas as part of its sustainable communities initiative.

Despite these and other initiatives, coordinating the planning of the wider region has been a problem (Wannup 1995). Residents in the areas beyond the London boundary have been reluctant to accept new housing developments designed in part to accommodate the overspill from the capital. Local government in London has, until recently, been lethargic about the city's relationship with its hinterland. Central government has been consistently unwilling to devolve strategic planning powers to a region that contains a third of the UK population and its economic engine room.

Regional Institutions

For much of the last century, there was reluctance by all parties to accept that the wider region needed its own planning institution. In 1962 the government created a body called South East Regional Planning (SERPLAN) to serve as a significant vehicle for coordinated planning. Its membership included representatives of local authorities from London and across the wider region. It had the duty of preparing formal regional planning guidance for the Wider South East, although the central government made the final decision on the content of the published guidance. Nonetheless, SERPLAN had an honorable track record of conflict resolution across the wider region and of introducing new initiatives. For example, it was an early and vigorous proponent of sustainable development. However, the perennial divisions over the amount and location of housing development to be supported in the wider region proved to be its ultimate undoing and it was disbanded in 2000.

In the same year, as part of its devolution program, the government established new regional boundaries and institutions for England, ostensibly to delegate more planning responsibilities to the regional level. In the Wider South East, a bizarre set of boundaries was used. As seen in Plate 4, the London boundary was unchanged: broadly following the limits of built development up to the Green Belt that surrounds the core city. However, the surrounding areas were distributed between two regions: the South East occupies an L-shaped section and the East of England partly includes the remainder of London's surrounds. These boundaries have no relationship to historic boundaries, to the wider region's traditional concentric pattern of development, or to any feelings of community identity or allegiance. Their configuration smacks of a divide and rule approach by central government. The boundaries have contributed to difficulties in coordination among the three regions.

The regional institutions are also complex. The South East and East regions have regional assemblies composed of representatives from local authorities, business, and voluntary agencies and supported by small permanent officer teams. These assemblies produce the initial draft Regional Spatial Strategies (RSS), which set out long-term plans for a whole region (these are the successors to regional planning guidance and take a much wider and more strategic approach). These, however, have to be forwarded in draft form to the central government for finalization and publication. Indeed, regional government offices, acting as watchdogs for central government, "guide" each assembly. In addition, the government appoints regional development agencies that exercise substantial powers of economic development with significant budgets of their own. These arrangements heavily circumscribe the action space for the indirectly elected assemblies.

These regional arrangements fit within the statutory planning policies in the United Kingdom, dating essentially from 1947. The Town and Country Planning Act of that year established a framework of statutory plans implemented through a comprehensive system of development control. The development plans, which now include the RSS, are considerably more powerful than those in the United States. A plan has the force of law: this applies to the RSS. Development control is a more complex and rigorous regime than zoning. All developments (with small and minor exceptions) require planning permission, a relatively tough and open procedure in which a developer must demonstrate that his or her proposal is compatible with the local, regional, and national planning policies.

Partly to reflect Prime Minister Tony Blair's admiration for the American city mayor system, the government also established a new office of the mayor in London. This office has the power to produce and finalize an RSS. Still, many key actions lie beyond the spatial planning powers of the mayor. For example, although London's mayor has significant economic development and transport planning powers, Whitehall has its own government office watchdog in London and retains many decisions about major transport and other infrastructure investment. Furthermore, as much of the responsibility for local planning and regulation lies with the London boroughs, the mayor's implementation powers are limited, though law requires boroughs to conform to the policies of what is called the London Plan.

In 2000, Londoners elected Ken Livingstone as their first mayor. He is now serving a second 4-year term. In 2004, Livingstone produced the "London Plan" as his first RSS. The London Plan anticipates continuing rapid population and economic growth in the city and seeks to contain that growth within its own boundaries. Although this will increase the intensity of growth, especially in central areas, Livingstone believes that self-sufficiency and maximization of resources such as land, energy, and transport infrastructure are essential if sustainable development is to be achieved. As a corollary of higher-density development, the mayor includes a powerful policy forbidding any loss of open space. In addition, the London Plan places emphasis upon the need to link green spaces: it recognizes that, in a highly developed urban area with very high land prices, the creation of major new parks will be extraordinarily difficult and that well-linked sequences of green space can provide a satisfactory alternative. Indeed, the Lea Valley regional park already provides a good example of such a linear set of spaces.

To implement the plan, Livingstone is taking vigorous action as the leader of London's community to work with agencies that can contribute to sustainable development. He has, for example, established his own London Climate Change Agency to provide practical advice and take radical measures such as substituting fuels that emit less or no carbon in the London Transport vehicle fleet and support for more decentralized forms of energy supply.

Overall, in the devolution program initiated by the Blair government, the powers of regional authorities remain substantially less than those of the states and major cities under the U.S. system. Central government is more interventionist, retains far more controls over expenditures, and is deeply reluctant to empower authorities at the regional level. Nor has the new regional system improved coordination among the three regions. SERPLAN was a statutory body with its own officer support; it commanded respect within and beyond government. The three new regional bodies meet on a voluntary basis in an Inter-regional Forum, which has no executive powers, no resources and no officer support. The coordination of greening policies and proposals across the three regions takes place in an unpromising institutional context.

Greening the Cities in the Wider South East

The greening cities movement can claim a long ancestry in the UK. From the seventeenth century onward, British writers extolled the virtues of parks and open spaces. The tradition of rus in urbe is deeply rooted in British culture. Adam Smith promoted the model of the successful man of business who makes his fortune and then retires to the country estate. Philanthropists built parks both inside and outside the cities. Landscape and garden design have a distinguished tradition in the UK. As early as 1877, the Metropolitan Open Spaces Act provided a legal basis for the extension of open space in London.

The effects of the Industrial Revolution in terms of poor health and loss of open land led to some of the earliest town planning legislation, notably in the early part of the twentieth century. At that time, the Garden Cities movement arose as an early advocate for the containment of urban growth around the central city through development of satellite towns characterized by extensive green spaces, low densities, gardens, and high levels of self-sufficiency. Some early garden cities, such as Letchworth, retain many of these characteristics. However, despite this powerful effort by largely voluntary agencies, the government did not produce an effective overarching regional plan for the Wider South East; its efforts foundered on the institutional tensions discussed above.

The most effective greening initiative in London came in the 1945 Greater London Plan, drawn up by Sir Patrick Abercrombie. Anticipating many of the objectives and policies of the contemporary green movement, Abercrombie called for a system of parks, linked to form green wedges and connecting to a Green Belt surrounding the city. These green areas would have a multitude of functions, including amenity and recreation. Abercrombie also set open space standards (four acres per thousand population) that have proved to be durable and are used as targets to this day. His plans had an immense impact on London and many other cities. A 1947 act of Parliament created the Green Belt around London. It survives to this day as a major instrument of spatial planning (see Plate 4).

The Greater London Development Plan of 1976 introduced the concept of Metropolitan Open Land to designate green space for protection. It applied not only to parks but to golf courses, nursery gardens, woodlands, cemeteries, and other spaces.

In 1996, the government's Regional Planning Guidance set out a hierarchy of open spaces that local authorities should seek to achieve, ranging from regional parks to local spaces.[1] This hierarchy has been updated and refined, most recently in 2004 (Table 1). Planning Policy Guidance 17 (ODPM 2002) sets out national policy on open space, sport, and recreation. It emphasizes some of the wider benefits of greening, including community health and well-being, support for social inclusion, and promotion of biodiversity and nature conservation. It represents a holistic vision of the green city and a powerful instrument in

Table 1. London's Public Open Space Hierarchy

Open space category	Size guideline	Distance from homes to open space	Distance (taking into account access barriers)
Regional parks	Over 400 hectares	3.2–8 kilometers	
Metropolitan park	60–400 hectares	3.3 kilometers or more	
District park	20–60 hectares	1.2 kilometers	
Local park	2–20 hectares	400 meters	280 meters
Small local parks	0.4–2 hectares	400 meters	280 meters
Pocket parks	< 0.4 hectares	400 meters	280 meters
Linear open spaces	Variable	Where feasible	

Source: Mayor of London (2004b).

the prevention of loss of green space, extension of the green and public realm, and recognition of the importance of providing better access for people regardless of their income and mobility.

Despite this impressive history of open space planning in London—and to a lesser extent in the cities around it—it lost some of the impetus in the latter years of the twentieth century. For example, by 2003 the loss of school playing fields (ascribed to pressures for housing land and financial benefits to the education authorities) contributed to the motivation behind the Blair government's Sustainable Communities Plan (ODPM 2003). The plan introduced a renewed and powerful emphasis on the benefit of green and sustainable development in cities. It called for more, better, and readily accessible open spaces, deeming them essential for urban regeneration, sustainable development, protection of the countryside from urban sprawl, and enhancement of the landscape.

Green Policies in London

The policies of the three regional authorities are consistent in their emphasis on retention and expansion of green space. In London in particular, Mayor Livingstone envisages continuing population and economic growth in a sustainable form, viewing increased densities, redevelopment of previously used land, and the retention of green spaces as essential. As a result, the 2004 London Plan (Mayor of London 2004a) contains highly protective policies for open space and requires each of the 32 local planning authorities—the boroughs—to produce its own open space strategy. These policies have proved to be highly effective: monitoring reports show that about 97 percent of all developments in London are on previously used brownfield sites. Livingstone has published guidance on how these open space strategies should be produced and what they should include (Mayor of London 2004b).

Alongside the recognition over the past decade of the value of green spaces has come the development of a more coherent approach to sustainable development and, increasingly, to the need to mitigate climate change and adapt to the effects that are already present. In London the mayor, who has responsibility for the production of a set of environmental strategies, has published policy documents on air quality, biodiversity, ambient noise, climate adaptation, energy, and municipal waste. Under a recent extension of his powers, he will have responsibility for a strategy on climate change. The spatial policies of each of these mayoral environmental strategies are contained in the London Plan and thereby given the force of law. There is a comparable emphasis on sustainable development in both the draft Regional Spatial Strategies for the South East and the East of England regions.

Increasingly concerned about climate change, Livingstone is altering the London Plan after only three years, largely to strengthen its policies in this area.[2] The draft alterations to the plan contain radical policies to address climate change (Mayor of London 2006a). They recognize that London's environmental vulnerabilities to flooding, subsidence, overheating, and shortfalls of water supply could be exacerbated by climate changes that cause rising sea levels, heavier winter rainfall, higher tidal surges, and hotter, drier summers. The central thrust of the revised London Plan is that all development should minimize carbon dioxide emissions, use sustainable design and construction measures, and support decentralized forms of energy generation, including renewables. Its long-term carbon reduction target is 60 percent by 2050 (the same as that adopted by California and a number of other agencies), with an interim target of 20 percent by 2015.

The plan requires all major planning applications to demonstrate the ways in which the development would use sustainable forms of design and construction and to provide an assessment of its energy demand and levels of carbon emission. All developments should achieve a reduction in carbon dioxide emissions of 20 percent from onsite renewable energy sources. Although acknowledged as a longer-term aim, the plan promotes the use of hydrogen as an alternative to fossil fuels. The plan also contains measures to improve adaptation to the unavoidable effects of climate change. These include policies to minimize overheating and the heat island effect, to maximize solar gain, and to contribute to the reduction of flood risk, improve water use efficiency and quality, and promote sustainable drainage systems.

The London Plan alterations were tested by a formal process of

"Examination in Public" in front of a government-appointed panel appointed in summer 2007. The development industry has opposed some of the policies on the grounds that they were prohibitively costly and would make London an uncompetitive location for future development. The outcome of the examination will not be known before the end of 2007, but the impetus of scientific and indeed public concerns about climate change makes it probable that Livingstone's approach will be largely endorsed.

Containing Growth in the Wider South East

The Wider South East has experienced sustained population and economic growth over many decades and will continue to do so. The principal focus for the green movement across the area has therefore tended to be on the protection of green space from the insatiable demands for development. Sir Peter Hall has characterized UK planning policy as essentially about "the containment of the city" and this has certainly been true in the Wider South East (Hall 1974).

For decades, the emphasis has been on finding a strategy that could accommodate growth in the most sustainable and least controversial way. For example, the postwar New Towns initiative sought to concentrate growth in a set of planned towns that ringed London beyond the Green Belt. The initiative served as a model for many countries and had a measure of success. However, the new towns were unable to absorb the sheer scale of population growth and never achieved the levels of self-sufficiency for which they were designed. Other mechanisms have included town expansion programs in which London's "overspill" population was housed in towns across the wider region. Again, these programs were insufficient to meet the scale of need and often experienced difficulties in integrating the incomers with the existing population.

SERPLAN, for all its qualities as a consortium, was unable to fashion a strategy for growth that had sufficient conviction and realism to satisfy the government. Ultimately, local and protectionist interests proved too powerful to permit an incisive and convincing plan to emerge. Government also found itself compromising. There is a clear strategic case for promoting development in the eastern half of the Wider South East, where there is relative underinvestment, and for constraining growth in the western half, where high demands have created congestion, land price increases, and labor shortages. While the government was willing to support growth in the east, it was unwilling to dampen growth significantly in the west because of the potential effects on national economic performance.

The government set out its strategy for growth and sustainable development in its 2003 Sustainable Communities Plan, as described earlier. This encouraged the formation of more self-sufficient, green, balanced communities across the country. It designated four major growth points within the Wider South East (see Plate 5). By far the most substantial of these in terms of new development and regeneration is the Thames Gateway area, stretching on both sides of the Thames from central London to the coast. The government has committed heavy public investment in transport, regeneration, and subsidies to support the gateway as the flagship for urban renaissance in the east. It also designated the London-Cambridge-Stansted-Peterborough growth area along the M11 motorway to the northeast of London and another at Ashford, where a station has been built on the Channel Tunnel rail link. The fourth growth point is around Milton Keynes and the South Midlands to the northwest of London.

This strategy for the Wider South East provides a strong direction for accommodation of growth and backs this with substantial public spending. However, it offers only a partial solution to planning growth because the majority of new development will still have to be identified in areas of the South East outside the growth areas shown in Plate 5. Many of these areas have high landscape or historic value, and development will often be vigorously challenged by local societies and conservation groups. Moreover, the Sustainable Communities Plan was essentially imposed on the regional and local authorities by the central government. The three regions were left to complete the process of long-term planning through their RSSs. Mayor Livingstone published his London Plan in 2004 and is now at an advanced stage in the updating and revision of the plan. The two other regions have produced draft RSSs, both of which are going through the process of government appraisal.

While Mayor Livingstone has been able to identify most of the growth areas within London, mainly by encouraging higher densities, the South East and East of England have struggled to allocate sufficient capacity in their strategies. The unpopularity of additional housing, often in areas of relatively high landscape value, and the vigor and resourcefulness of green and community interest groups has made locally nominated politicians fearful of supporting extensive housing growth when they step into the Regional Assembly chamber. The government has shown increasing impatience with the slowness and lack of ambition of the process of identifying locations for growth. Indeed, the chancellor of the exchequer targeted the mismatch between housing demand and supply as a key cause of spiraling house prices and lack of affordable housing for key workers. In 2005 the government launched its own review of the planning process in the hope of finding a solution (Barker 2006).

The resulting report (Barker 2006) has considered a number of ways to expedite plans and planning decisions in order to meet demand, including a reduction in the number of minor proposals that need formal planning approval through the development control process. It has also identified the Green Belt as potentially ripe for change. The Green Belt has remained essentially sacrosanct for governments at all levels since its inception immediately after World War II. It has clearly prevented the kind of unfettered urban sprawl that has disfigured a number of American and other cities. However, some argue that the Green Belt is unsustainable. For more than half a century, London-driven growth has skipped over the Green Belt to the areas immediately beyond. As a result, enormous amounts of energy and emissions are expended in commuter and other journeys that cross the Green Belt every day. One strategic option is to allocate growth along the major transport corridors traversing the Green Belt, making more effective use of the major green wedges that would remain protected between them. This would be akin to the Scandinavian "green finger" form of development. All three regional bodies would fiercely resist such a change, united by a common hostility to the notion of incursion into the Green Belt, fearing that the process, once initiated, would be very difficult to stop.

Agencies Promoting Greening at the Regional Level

While the attention of the government and regional authorities has been focused on the need to contain growth and protect green space, there have been a number of initiatives that seek to create a common approach to positive greening across the three regions. Both within London and beyond, local authorities have undertaken a number of "Green Grid" initiatives. They aim to create networks of interlinked, high-quality open spaces that connect town centers with public transport nodes, the Green Belt, the water systems and the main housing and employment areas. For example, Mayor Livingstone has published the East London Green Grid Framework (Mayor of London 2006b). Livingstone seeks to coordinate the further development of an already well-established grid of open spaces with the wider regeneration programs for the area in order to offer a green lung for East London, promote biodiversity, and encourage a variety of landscapes and opportunities for recreation. The grid covers an extensive area, which includes the Thames Gateway, and engages a formidable number of partners at national, subregional, and local levels. It contains six subareas and sets out opportunities for expansion of open space and biodiversity in each, identifying the main ecological and landscape zones and open space deficiency areas at all levels.

The East London Green Grid stops at the London boundary, where the mayor's power ends. However, an equivalent Green Grid is being developed in the part of the Thames Gateway beyond the London area, so that, in practice, an integrated system is evolving.

A number of "Green Arc" partnerships have been formed in areas that tend to cover sectors of the outer areas of London and the contiguous parts of the areas on the other side of its border. These informal partnerships characteristically include representatives from the regional and local authorities working with bodies such as the Woodland Trust, Trees for All, the Forestry Commission, Natural England Groundwork, and a variety of community and voluntary agencies often supported by partial government funding. For example, the East Green Arc covers 400 square miles to the north and east of London (see woodland-trust .org.uk). Its recent activities have included the purchase of more than 50 hectares of arable land in the Green Belt for conversion to woodland to help safeguard more than 1,000 plant and animal species and the natural regeneration of existing forest. More than 65,000 trees will be planted by school children, and the area will be accessible to all. One objective of this Green Arc is to help mitigate the effects of the growth designated in and around it. The government has committed £24 million to "green space projects" as part of the Sustainable Communities Plan, and this has helped to support all the arc partnerships.

One of the features of these partnerships is the very extensive participation of communities within them, not least as volunteers undertaking planting, clearing, and other tasks. One of the difficulties of formal planning at the regional scale is that it tends to operate at too high a spatial level to engage the interest of many people, who relate more immediately to their local environments. The Green Arcs operate at a subregional level, so that their greening strategies are more accessible and can be exemplified through action projects in which local groups enthusiastically participate.

Within London, the London Parks and Green Spaces Forum acts as a bridge between the city's overall greening strategy and the multitude of local groups within the city. The forum promotes the sustainable use of London's parks, acts as a network for the exchange of expertise, experience, and information, collects data, identifies best practices, and acts as an influential lobby at city and national levels. It engages with community and user groups on issues such as improving access, especially for those with the greatest needs and difficulties. It was a key contributor to the development of a strategy for major open spaces in London (EDAW/Greater London Authority 2006).

London has also been able to benefit from the experience of other European cities in greening their areas. It is participating in the European Union-supported SAUL (Sustainable and Accessible Urban Landscapes) initiative under the EU Interreg program. Undertaken by a consortium of urban areas that includes, in addition to London, Amsterdam, Frankfurt, Luxembourg, Rhein-Ruhr and Saarland in Germany, SAUL, with a budget of 22 million euros, explored greening in these urban areas. It found that nurturing high-quality urban landscapes formed a key part of the most competitive city regions. Its examples of good practice draw particular attention to greening programs that have involved local communities at all stages as advocates, advisers, volunteers, and maintainers (SAUL 2006).

Perhaps the most significant new initiative is the collaboration between the climate change partnerships in the three regions of the Wider South East. In 2005, they established the Three Regions Climate Change Group to coordinate action. It has produced a checklist of ways in which development should take account of climate change (Three Regions 2005). The London Climate Change Partnership has itself published an authoritative guide, *Adapting to Climate Change*, which reviews best practices in a number of cities across the world and draws conclusions for London from this review (London Climate 2006). Although these efforts have no legal status, they contribute significantly to the growing shift in UK opinion in favor of stronger action on climate change.

These efforts reflect the attempts at a strategic approach to greening. There are of course many other greening initiatives across the Wider South East, although most energy inevitably goes into more local programs, which are too detailed to consider in this strategic overview.

Conclusions

In theory, consensus exists in the United Kingdom and the Wider South East about the need to defend green spaces and to improve and extend them wherever possible. There is a general recognition that this requires the full involvement of local people in a country that has always placed high value on open space and landscape. There is widespread acceptance of a partnership approach engaging agencies and communities at all levels and across all sectors.

Under law, statutory planning policy in the UK flows from central to regional to local level, aiming for consistency of approach within and between regions. It is indeed true that all planning documents aspire to retention of open space and to sustainable development. It is also true that both plans and planning decisions on individual developments have become far more sensitive in recent years to matters such as biodiversity, quality of access, landscape design, and impacts of natural resources.

There is also a growing impetus toward the integration of climate change mitigation and adaptation into plans and decisions.

However, in practice there is tension around the achievement of a coherent inter-regional approach to greening. This is largely because the debate is dominated by the questions posed by high and continuing levels of growth. Regional governance seeks to reconcile the national and local policy dimension, but this can leave it vulnerable to frustration by either or both of the national and regional tiers. The lack of an effective mechanism for reconciliation of planning policies among the three regions means that disputes continue on the most appropriate overall strategy for accommodation of growth. The vacuum created by this lack of a pan-regional strategy is regularly filled by the central government, despite its professions about delegation.

The lack of a common strategy among the three regions for planning of growth tends to obscure the richness of some of the initiatives that are taking place in response to the greening, sustainable development, and climate change agendas. The arbitrary nature of the regional boundaries inhibits more effective inter-regional working on these issues. However, more informal mechanisms, less tied to administrative boundaries, are proving a valuable means of achieving cross-border collaboration as the Green Arc initiatives demonstrate.

The prospects are for a more coordinated inter-regional approach. Each of the three regions has been preoccupied with the establishment of new institutions and with developing its own regional strategy. With this process largely completed, there should be more opportunity for the regions to look more fully across their own boundaries. Indeed, collaboration is noticeably on the increase. More than this, the ever-growing recognition of the threat of climate change will inevitably draw strategic decision makers closer together.

References

Barker, Kate. 2006. *Review of Land Use Planning.* London: HMSO.

EDAW/Greater London Authority. 2006. *London Strategic Parks Project Report.* London: Greater London Authority.

Hall, Peter Geoffrey. 1974. *The Containment of Urban England.* London: Allen and Unwin.

Hall, Peter Geoffrey, and Kathy Pain, eds. 2006. *The Polycentric Metropolis: Learning from Mega-City Regions in Europe.* London: Earthscan.

London Climate Change Partnership. 2006. *Adapting to Climate Change: Lessons for London.* London: Greater London Authority.

Mayor of London. 2004a. *London Plan.* London: Greater London Authority.

———. 2004b. *Best Practice Guidance: Guide to Preparing Open Space Strategies.* London: Greater London Authority.

———. 2006a. *Further Alterations to the London Plan.* London: Greater London Authority.

———. 2006b. *East London Green Grid Framework.* London: Greater London Authority.

ODPM (Office of the Deputy Prime Minister). 2003. *Sustainable Communities Plan.* London: HMSO.

———. *Planning Policy Guidance 17.* 2002. London: HMSO.

SAUL. 2006. *Vital Urban Landscapes.* London: Greater London Authority.

Three Regions Climate Change Group. 2005. *Adapting to Climate Change: A Checklist for Development.* London: Greater London Authority.

Wannup, Urlan A. 1995. *The Regional Imperative: Regional Planning and Governance in Britain, Europe, and the United States.* London: Jessica Kingsley.

Chapter 4
Greening Cities: A Public Realm Approach

ALEXANDER GARVIN

During my senior year in college, my roommate gave me a book that changed my life: *The Death and Life of Great American Cities* by Jane Jacobs, published in 1961. The following year, a second book appeared that changed the lives of many others: *Silent Spring* by Rachel Carson. Without that book, we would not be talking about greening cities, for it opened a whole new way of thinking. *Silent Spring* and works that followed Carson's led to the passage of the National Environmental Policy Act of 1969 (NEPA), with its public disclosure requirements and environmental impact assessments that help us evaluate the effects of large federal projects on their surroundings. This environmentally conscious approach is continued today with the Leadership in Energy and Environmental Design (LEED) standards, which analyze how well a building conserves resources. With widespread discussion of climate change, we also have attempts to create sustainable cities that try to achieve energy self-sufficiency.

And yet, I believe that all these efforts have resulted in an overly narrow, even miserly, view of greening of our environment. The current approach to greening is largely reactive and conservative, not the routinely progressive part of the development process it should be. We should not foster greening through litigation in reaction to development, nor should we attempt to restore the "natural" conditions of some distant past, real or imaginary. We must recognize that sometimes doing nothing is *not* the best thing for the environment, and that development can improve as well as harm it. Moreover, we need to place people at the center of our thinking, making human activity and public participation important elements of the planning process.

Fortunately, there is someone whose work can guide us through this territory. Nobody has better understood the complex interaction between nature and America's cities than Frederick Law Olmsted, America's first landscape architect, and, in my opinion, its greatest planner.

Olmsted was a great lover of nature from his boyhood on, but nature, as he understood it, was not something separate from mankind. On the contrary, he recognized that humankind inevitably has an effect on nature—and, just as important, that nature can have a profound influence on us.

No project better illustrates this complex interrelationship than his work on Boston's Emerald Necklace. In the late nineteenth century, the city of Boston held a competition to design a park for an area called the Fens. Originally a salt marsh at the mouth of the Charles River, the construction of several railroads trestles had cut off tidal flow to the upland portion of this waterway, making it a polluted swamp and a fetid dump for malodorous garbage and vermin-infested trash. When city officials asked Olmsted his opinion of the competition submissions, he remarked that half were drainage plans and half were recreation plans, but none were both. They then hired Olmsted to design an entire park system that included the Fens. The resulting Emerald Necklace is nothing short of a masterpiece.

Although the Emerald Necklace was a new park system, it was anything but untrammeled nature. For example, Olmsted rechanneled the Muddy River, which flowed into the Fens, regrading and relandscaping its banks. Where a railroad line—now the MBTA Green Line—ran along one edge of the river, he created a berm to shield the park from the train. As a result, to this day strollers in the park are unaware of the train, while commuters enjoy the benefits of a sylvan setting (Figure 1). The result was a drainage system, a recreation facility, a transit line, and a framework for real estate development on both sides of a new linear park.

But it was also more than that. The Emerald Necklace restored nature to the city of Boston; in the Fens, Olmsted artfully created a salt marsh not dissimilar to what once been there. But of course this salt marsh was also a product of human artifice, with carefully framed views and a complex drainage system. Olmsted "improved" on nature. At the same time, he expected that nature would improve the citizens of Boston, providing them with a place to relax, meditate, and contemplate nature's wonders.

So the first lesson Olmsted teaches us is that the present landscape is the product of human alteration and the future landscape will be no less so. Consequently, contemporary planning should reflect the best ecological practices, rather than attempt to freeze existing conditions or recreate a previous situation. By their very nature, best ecological practices preclude single-function planning. They aim to produce a mixed-use public realm that accommodates and sustains every form of flora and fauna, including people.

Figure 1. A snippet of Olmsted's masterpiece: a portion of the Muddy River flowing through the Emerald Necklace. Alexander Garvin.

Good Development—and Bad

Contrast what today is deemed the environmentally correct way of building in an area with Olmsted's approach. Current practice looks at drainage, vegetation, topographical contours, soil, energy usage, local flora and fauna, and other aspects of the natural environment—all good things to consider. But because these elements are typically considered separately from one another, and separately from the human activities that surround them, the resulting landscape is often undesirable. For example, such a landscape often includes water retention ponds, which

Figure 2. The Westside Highway in 1981. New York City Parks Department.

may take care of the drainage but are often eyesores, not assets to the environment. Such landscapes may retain habitats for endangered species of flora and fauna, but they do nothing to improve daily life for people.

Although planning for basic environmental conditions is a necessary first step in greening urban areas, it is insufficient because it treats nature in isolation without consideration of human beings or, when it deals with human activity, it acts as if it were separate from nature. I propose that we stop thinking only about how to prevent or mitigate the degradation of the natural environment and start thinking about how the human species and the natural environment can interact with one another to their mutual benefit.

Let me illustrate with an unfortunate story about New York City's West Side Highway, a 4.2-mile elevated artery in Manhattan that ran along the Hudson River (Figure 2). Known as the Miller Highway, this 1920s project was begun more than a decade before Robert Moses took charge of the city's arterial construction program. By the early 1970s it was falling apart. In fact, in 1973 one section collapsed, leading to its closure and creating a hardship for drivers because it was an important commercial artery. In response, New York City and the state of New York proposed to rebuild it as part of the Interstate Highway System, putting forward a plan, "Westway," bold for its time, that called for routing the highway

Figure 3. Westway envisioned. New York City Parks Department.

under 178 acres of new landfill that would have created independent sites of 82 acres for parkland, 35 acres for housing, and 53 acres for manufacturing (Figure 3). To satisfy NEPA requirements, Westway's proponents dutifully conducted the mandated environmental review, producing a study of the highway and various rebuilding alternatives. Conforming to the law, the review had a narrow scope, focusing on transportation and its impact on traffic flows and environmental elements in its path. It did not question whether several billion dollars should be spent on transportation rather than on public schools, police protection, or anything else New York City might need. Nor did it study whether money for transportation ought to be spent for mass transit or highways, or for freight or passenger movement. It only studied different alternatives for building a highway.

Immediately, the study came under legal attack from environmental protection groups. The Hudson River Fisherman's Association asserted that it failed to consider properly Westway's effect on the spawning habits of the striped bass (a major element of New York's fishing industry). A court agreed and ordered another study. Government officials under litigation pressure canceled Westway, not through a broad examination that would have evaluated it as the best or most cost-effective way to use federal money in New York City or even because it was the correct action to take in response to large environmental concerns.

In fact, this outcome resulted from a flawed decision-making process that is now widely ingrained. We have an environmental review process

Figure 4. Hudson River Park: an example of the public realm approach to planning. Alexander Garvin.

that focuses on environmental factors, not human factors. Perhaps one of its most important deficiencies is that it casts the whole discussion in terms of single functions—in this case, the single function of transportation. Even the Interstate Highway System, begun in 1956, was conceived as a way of moving goods and people, not as a government action that affected the communities on either side of it. Now this may be acceptable in rural Nebraska, where the highways are generally flanked by cornfields. But it does not make sense where the highways run through a complex city like New York.

However, this story has a happy ending. With the defeat of Westway, the state went back to the drawing board. It replaced the West Side Highway with West Street, an at-grade eight-lane boulevard, bounded on the west by Hudson River Park, a five-mile, 550-acre ribbon extending from Battery Park to Fifty-Ninth Street. It conceived of this park and boulevard combination as a place with multiple users—bicycle riders, people sitting in the sun, joggers, automobiles, trucks, and buses (Figure 4). The process began with a fight among various players who only considered the highway, but what resulted is a facility that also takes into account the residents of the surrounding community, users from neighborhoods throughout New York, and traffic. If we are to have greener cities, we need planning that provides this more balanced view, which includes human beings, not just "endangered wildlife," and a complex mix of uses, not just transportation. This is what I call a *public realm* approach to planning.

The potential opportunities for environmentally and financially sustainable public realm improvements should be the priority of any major planning or development project. The public realm presents the single largest opportunity to create greener cities. As a framework for development, it can set the standard so that future growth can embrace all the benefits of a healthy environment and make our cities more vibrant places to live and work for generations to come.

A project I am currently working on provides an example of how to apply the public realm approach. At the request of the Department of Parks and Recreation of Prince George's County, Maryland, GB Development (a local real estate development company) hired me to redesign a proposed 150-acre park surrounded by what was slated to become a conventional suburban development. The initial thinking about the park was seriously flawed. The site is complicated. A roadway, whose standards are determined by the state of Maryland's Department of Transportation, will bisect it. In addition, several already polluted streams cross it but were excluded from the program for "environmental reasons" by Maryland's Departments of the Environment and of Natural Resources. They had the misguided belief that "protecting" streams (part of the Chesapeake Bay watershed) from people would somehow prevent further pollution from people. They set all land within 50 feet of the streams off-limits to park users, even though the streams would be the first places that dogs, children, and just about anybody else would want to go. This prohibition struck me as particularly strange, because Maryland and Prince George's County have been creating parks out of streambeds since the 1920s. As I forged the plan, I decided on three guiding principles: (1) unify the site into a single park; (2) apply sound hydrological principles to establish a self-sustaining ecological environment; and (3) allow men, women, and children of all ages to enjoy the park without causing environmental degradation.

Once again, it was Olmsted's work, especially his plans for two major parks, Yosemite National Park and Niagara Falls, that inspired this strategy. Olmsted always conceived of parks and people together. Appointed in 1864 by the governor of California to lead a commission to decide what to do with a new property ceded to the state by the Congress of the United States called Yosemite, Olmsted wrote:

It is but sixteen years since the Yosemite was first seen by the white man, several visitors have since made a journey of several thousand miles at large cost to see it, and notwithstanding the difficulties which now interpose, hundreds report to it annually. Before many years if proper facilities are offered, these hundreds will become thousands, and in a century the whole number of visitors will be counted by millions. (Olmsted 1993: Introduction)

Figure 5. Visitors at Yosemite. Alexander Garvin.

Olmsted designed a park that preserved for public enjoyment one of the world's most extraordinary natural landscapes. More than a hundred years after he completed his work, his prophecy had come true. In 1999, 3.6 million people visited Yosemite (Figure 5). That is what a true public realm approach to environmental planning is about: accommodating 3.6 million people in one of the wonders of the world, without doing harm to it.

Twenty years later, while working on a design for the preservation of Niagara Falls, Olmsted posed the question more explicitly: "How can the natural scenery suitable to Niagara Falls be restored and maintained against the riotous action of a mob unconscious of wrong purposes and indignant at obvious constraints upon what it regards as harmless conduct?" (quoted in Beveridge 1985). Olmsted knew what Maryland environmental officials did not: that people occupy and use the natural landscape. So he designed the 200-acre Niagara Frontier State Park accordingly. He designed trails that allowed visitors to enjoy this spectacular setting without degrading it as a habitat for indigenous plants and animals.

Following Olmsted's lead I decided to make the streams in my Maryland project part of the park in a way that assumed the presence, not the absence, of people. I also decided to clean the polluted water entering the park by restoring the type of wetlands that would have been there before the area was cleared for farming. I called for eliminating the 50-foot buffers around the streams. At the same time, I decided to transform the streams into a water feature that would achieve other aims as well. By widening the section of the stream that passed underneath the roadway, I created a lake. This unified the site into a single park. The lake became its central feature and the road that bisected the park was transformed into a small bridge crossing the lake (Figure 6). In sum, I followed Olmsted's recommendations: I thought about environment planning as an approach to the public realm that included nature with people.

Integrating People with Nature

Olmsted was a master at integrating nature with people, in a fashion that has been a constant inspiration to me. His design for Boston's Emerald Necklace has been particularly influential. From the day I first visited the Emerald Necklace, I have been inspired by Olmsted's ability to combine hydrological engineering, transportation corridors, animal habitats, recreation facilities, and urban development. Equally important, I have come to think of well-designed parks as part of a mixed-use public realm, carefully laid out to permit a multitude of uses occurring independently and simultaneously without intruding on one another.

I tried to take this Olmstedian approach in my work as managing director of planning for New York's Olympics 2012 bid. One example is my proposal for the required 2,000-meter flat-water rowing facility (Figures 7 and 8). In contrast to the design at the 2000 Sydney Olympics, which placed the rowing facility 20 or 30 miles outside town, I was determined to find a place for rowing within New York City so that my fellow

Figure 6. Integrating nature and people in Prince George's County, Maryland. Alexander Garvin.

Figure 7. The lakes at Flushing Meadows Corona Park. Alexander Garvin.

Figure 8. The proposed rowing facility for New York City's 2012 Olympic bid. Alexander Garvin.

New Yorkers could use the facility after the Olympics were over. After an extensive search I selected Flushing Meadows Corona Park, which had two leftover lakes from the World's Fairs of 1939 and 1964.[1]

Long ago the area had been marshland, washed by the tides of Flushing Bay. But a garbage dump blocked the old marshland. Robert Moses, who created the park, turned the marshland into the two lakes, channeling the flow of water through an underground conduit to the bay. Two heavily traveled arteries, the Van Wyck Expressway and the Grand Central Parkway, which pass alongside the park, polluted the lakes with their runoff. Consequently, the lakes did not support much in the way of fish or other wildlife. I proposed dredging and connecting these water bodies and restoring their surrounding wetlands by planting appropriate vegetation that would clean the runoff, making the lakes swimmable and fishable for humans, and the whole area habitable for dozens of native birds, fish, and plant species. Unfortunately, London, not New York, won the 2012 Olympic bid, so this plan will not be implemented.

Can we expand this approach to create a greener way of planning? I believe we can. Above all, we have to stop thinking in single functions and start thinking about simultaneous, multiple uses of land. Although earlier I used New York's West Street/Hudson River Park to illustrate

Figure 9. Cars only: a remnant of the failed Westway project in Lower Manhattan. Alexander Garvin.

mixed use, it is not a perfect example. Between Battery Park and Canal Street, West Street is a 240-foot-wide remnant of the failed Westway project that had been conceived of as a traffic artery for motor vehicles. It is so difficult to cross that in some places the city has erected elevated pedestrian bridges (Figure 9). There is another street about the same width that is a far better example of what I am talking about: Paris's Champs-Élysées (Figure 10). This boulevard is 230 feet across and moves a great deal of traffic (perhaps even more than West Street), but it serves as more than a traffic artery. The Champs-Élysées is a place to sit in a café and have a cup of coffee, or go for a stroll, or shop, or ride a bicycle, or do any of a number of things. It shows how we can stop thinking about the public realm in single function terms and start thinking about how it works on multiple levels simultaneously.

When we think in terms of this sort of mixed-use public realm, we become true environmental planners. One example of this type of thinking in the United States is New York City's Greenstreets program overseen by the Department of Parks and Recreation. This program reclaims and greens unused traffic islands and other odd spaces left by the city's road systems. A good instance is the small patch of land at West 116th Street and Claremont Avenue. This form of greening provides visual and physical respite to people (Figures 11 and 12). It provides cli-

Figure 10. People and autos share the Champs-Elysées in Paris. Alexander Garvin.

Figure 11. Before Greenstreets. New York City Parks Department.

Figure 12. After Greenstreets. Alexander Garvin.

mate amelioration. (It is estimated that if a city's tree canopy is increased by 5 percent, temperatures will drop between 2 and 4 degrees Fahrenheit, because tree foliage reduces the ambient air temperature. Cooling occurs as the trees transpire.) It also mitigates air pollution. If the ambient temperature is lower, then demand for electricity for air conditioning is also lower. In addition, trees filter the air and remove some of the dust. Finally, the trees add to the city's ecosystem as the green patches become connective tissue for corridors that shelter and support birds, butterflies, bees, squirrels, and other urban wildlife. In short, the Greenstreets program reclaims abandoned portions of the public realm and creates substantial environmental benefits.

We need to reconsider how we use the public realm to increase mobility as a healthy alternative to single-function motorways. We have U.S. examples, but they are flawed. One is the much-admired Embarcadero in San Francisco. Although the Embarcadero has carefully marked bike lanes (Figure 13), they are narrow, exposed to traffic, and often blocked by motor vehicles that encroach on them. The bicyclists, quite sensibly, mostly stick to the sidewalks, where they are safer but where they, in turn, become hazards for the pedestrians. New York's Hudson River Park is much better because its bike lanes are physically separated from motor vehicles and pedestrians (Figure 14). It is better, but it still is not good enough. The problem with these examples is that the bike lanes are isolated and not part of a comprehensive network.

Figure 13. Bicyclists have turned to sidewalks because of the narrow bike lanes along San Francisco's Embarcadero. Alexander Garvin.

Figure 14. The bike lanes in New York's Hudson River Park provide a buffer from traffic and pedestrians. Alexander Garvin.

Figure 15. Copenhagen has long experience integrating bicycle riders and drivers. Alexander Garvin.

Copenhagen offers the best example. Here planners have incorporated cycling into the city's transportation system, providing dedicated lanes and regulating behavior. (Bicycle riders use hand signals to indicate they are stopping, they dismount at red lights, and motorized drivers respect their space; see Figure 15.) Copenhagen began creating bike lanes in the 1930s, and, by 2005 it had built 343 kilometers of protected bike lanes throughout the city. The system allows cyclists to ride to any destination within the city. In addition, the city maintains 900 free bicycle stands and places to rent inexpensively one of more than 2,000 bicycles for an unlimited period. As a result, every morning and afternoon, 36 percent of the working population of Copenhagen are on bicycles, 32 percent use mass transit, and only 27 percent commute by automobile. The city has reduced the number of parking spaces for motor vehicles from 3,100 in 1995 to 2,700 in 2005. Notably, Copenhagen is not as polluted as cities that are totally dependent on automobiles, trucks, and buses, and its population is healthier. With regard to transportation, Copenhagen has created a remarkably successful mixed-use public realm. Consequently, its citizens do not think of streets only as a corridor for moving people in cars.

Not only do we need to rethink how we deal with the functions in a city, we need to redefine sustainable planning to make it inclusive. As vice president for planning, design, and development for the Lower Manhattan Development Corporation (LMDC)—the entity charged with rebuilding the World Trade Center site after the 9/11 terrorist attacks—I reinforced my belief in the importance of public participation. If you were following the news at the time, you may recall that "experts" put together six reconstruction proposals and that the LMDC, working with a number of other organizations, solicited public opinion through a one-day event called "Listening to the City." Unparalleled in the history of planning, it assembled 4,500 people to discuss those six plans. By the end of the session, the attendees offered a loud and clear verdict: the plans were not good enough. They told the experts to start all over again.

Some of us were very pleased. We took the opportunity to organize what became an international competition to create a master plan for Ground Zero. Nine of the world's most famous designers proposed quite different schemes. Some were feasible, some were not. The LMDC displayed the schemes on its website, where they generated millions of hits. The LMDC also sponsored a public exhibit with models and large images of the designs. Tens of thousands of people saw them and contributed written comments. In the end, the LMDC, the governor of New York, and the mayor of New York City selected Daniel Libeskind's plan. An astonishing thing happened: in a city as contentious as New York, almost nobody criticized the selection. People accepted the choice because they had been actively involved in the planning process.

I used a similar approach to arrive at an acceptable plan for the Olympic Village for New York's 2012 Olympic bid. One of my biggest problems in planning this bid was mobility: moving 500,000 spectators, 1,500 athletes and coaches, 25,000 journalists, and 75,000 workers each day to all the Olympic venues. Subways could easily move half a million spectators around New York City. I solved the rest of the problem by devising an "X" that used two types of transit for athletes, coaches, journalists, and VIPs (Figure 16). The north/south axis of the X was a ferry system and the east/west axis the Long Island Railroad and Amtrak. I sited the Olympic Village where the two systems crossed, on land that the city was trying to develop for new housing. Then I used a participatory process to help inform the design of the Olympic Village.

I formed a series of advisory panels. One consisted of Olympians who had competed in prior games and knew what it was like to live in an Olympic Village. Another included environmentalists who wanted a green Olympics. The third consisted of developers and public officials who were involved in projects throughout the city and knew what it

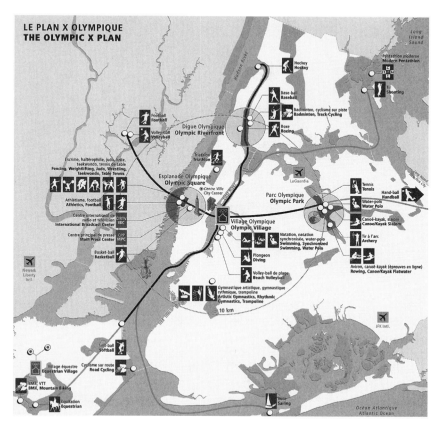

Figure 16. New York City's bid for the 2012 Olympics included a plan to move hundreds of thousands of spectators and thousands of Olympic Village inhabitants across the metropolitan region. Alexander Garvin.

would take to make the village a reality. A fourth was made up of residents and organizations from the surrounding neighborhoods.

I then developed a request for qualifications based on their input. A jury that included architects, environmentalists, Olympians, developers, property managers, and public managers selected five finalists. Over a three-month period, the finalists developed more refined plans that we then exhibited in Grand Central Terminal and on the NYC2012 website. Once again, there were a lot of opinions. We selected the winning proposal, by a team of designers led by mOrphosis, an architecture firm from Santa Monica (Figure 17), because it included items from the community wish list, recommendations from Olympians, and green ele-

Figure 17. The winning proposal for the Olympic Village that New York submitted as part of its bid for the 2012 Olympics. Alexander Garvin.

ments. Once again, the contentious New Yorkers readily accepted the winner as having created a suitable and very desirable design.

Bringing Boston's Nineteenth-Century Emerald Necklace to Twenty-First-Century Atlanta

Can a public realm framework shape private market reactions? Once again, Olmsted's Emerald Necklace provides the answer. As discussed earlier, the Emerald Necklace begins as a marshland at the mouth of the Fens and continues up the Muddy River as a trail for strolling, jogging, bicycling, and sitting in the sun on one side of the tracks of the MBTA Green Line at the Longwood Station area, making the neighboring land attractive for residential use. From there, the Necklace threads its way through the city of Boston to Jamaica Pond, where it becomes a location for seasonal recreation (fishing, boating, and ice skating). Next it passes down a tree-lined parkway—the Arborway—to the Arnold Arboretum, a park setting for a display of trees from around the world. The necklace then follows another Arborway to end at Franklin Park, a 527-acre terri-tory whose thin, rocky soil was too expensive to transform into a fancy park. Here Olmsted reshaped the earth and rocks to create wooded areas, open meadows (which later became a golf course), and even a lovely pond. It is important to underscore once again that the Emerald Necklace is not a natural landscape. It is a man-made system of trails, waterways, playing fields, woods, and meadows. In the years following its

Figure 18. Boston's Emerald Necklace has shaped the development of the property surrounding it. Alexander Garvin.

construction, the Necklace shaped the entire future of development of the property surrounding it (Figure 18).

How does one devise a public realm that, like Boston's Emerald Necklace, will reshape a city? In the summer of 2004, the Trust for Public Land asked me to tackle a problem in Atlanta, Georgia. That city had only 3.5 percent of the land surface devoted to parkland, a shockingly low figure compared to 12 percent of Philadelphia's land area and 19 percent of New York's. Atlanta did not even rank in the first 50 large cities in the percentage of territory devoted to public parkland.

Atlanta did have a belt of freight lines that ringed its downtown. Some years earlier, Ryan Gravel, a graduate student at Georgia Tech, had proposed reusing the freight lines for a transit line, an idea that had begun to gain support. When I began working on the project, I remembered Olmsted's Emerald Necklace and specifically the spot on the Emerald Necklace at Longwood Station, where parks and transit joined. It inspired me to propose a Beltline Emerald Necklace for Atlanta—a 20-mile transit line loop combined with a 23-mile trail (Figure 19). I proposed 13 parks as jewels on that necklace. Four were new parks consisting of 204 acres, four were expanded parks of another 185 acres, and five were mixed-use, park-centered development areas of about 2,000 acres. Together they created a 2,500-acre park system, only 500 acres of

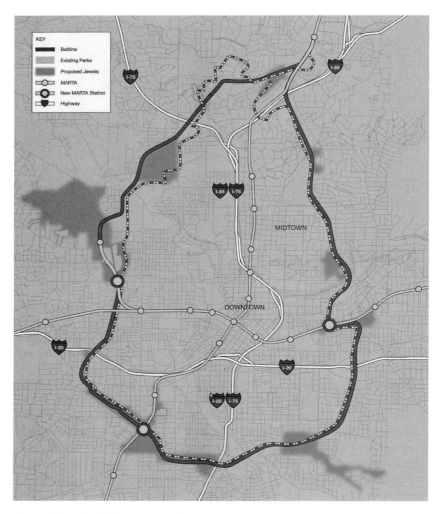

Figure 19. The Beltline Emerald Necklace that will loop around Atlanta.
Alexander Garvin.

which was already in place. One of the existing and probably best-known
jewels was 185-acre Piedmont Park, which I proposed to expand. Potential new park-centered developments included a reservoir fenced off
from the public, a freight yard about a mile from Peachtree Street,
Atlanta's main downtown artery, and a quarry only three miles from the
center of town.

I completed the Beltline Emerald Necklace proposal in December

2004. It immediately captured public support. One year later, the Atlanta City Council approved the Belt Line Emerald Necklace as a tax allocation district. In April 2006, Mayor Shirley Franklin announced that the city was buying the quarry, which will become the city's largest park.

When I envisioned the parks I never thought of the jewels only as nature preserves—although in many places they will provide space for plants and animals as well as people. I conceived them as settings around which there would be substantial new residential development enhanced by the 23-mile park system. The Beltline Emerald Necklace thus became more than simply a transit line or a park—it became a mixed-use public realm that would provide the framework for Atlanta's twenty-first-century future.

A Philadelphia Story

Is a mixed-use public realm worth the money? A half-century ago, Philadelphia demonstrated that a clever investment in such a mixed-use public realm is definitely worth the money. In 1950, the Dock Street Market was in active use as Philadelphia's produce distribution center. Traffic at four and five o'clock in the morning was noisy. The vermin generated by the spilled produce made living there unpleasant. Edmund Bacon, the planning director of the city, believed that the market did not belong at that location, just as in Atlanta I believed that a quarry was not the highest and best use of property three miles from Peachtree Street. He convinced the city to move the produce market to South Philadelphia and to spend $17 million for land acquisition and infrastructure investment. In addition, the businesses that used the market invested another $100 million.

At that time, the area the produce market had occupied, known as Society Hill, was not in great demand as a residential neighborhood. The neighborhood of choice was Rittenhouse Square, where in 1950 houses sold for $15,000. (At that time Society Hill residences went for $5,000, and the average price of a house in the city of Philadelphia was $3,700.) Bacon proposed to reuse the market site for apartment buildings that would create a beacon announcing the revival of downtown. The city held a competition that was won by developer William Zeckendorf and architect I. M. Pei. Today it is the site of Society Hill Towers.

The neighborhood surrounding the old market included vacant and abandoned properties that Bacon decided to reuse for new and renovated housing and new and restored public open space. He also transformed existing streets into places that recalled their charming eighteenth- and early nineteenth-century character. Bacon created a new public realm framework of greenways connecting small parks, land-

Figure 20. The Greenways of Philadelphia's Society Hill give the
neighborhood a distinctive character. Alexander Garvin.

marks, churches, and other destinations within the area. Federal urban
renewal funding paid for two-thirds of the cost of the project, including
the cobblestone streets, granite curbs, brick paving, gas lamps, and
street trees. It also provided mortgage insurance for housing rehabilitation and construction.

The area has changed substantially since the 1950s. Today, Society
Hill's greenways connect neighborhood destinations and give the area a
distinctive character (Figure 20). Since 1950, the value of an apartment
or a house in Society Hill has increased 78 times compared to only 18
times in Rittenhouse Square and 16 times in Philadelphia as a whole.
Society Hill has become the neighborhood of choice in Philadelphia. It
represents what I describe as successful planning in my book, *The American City*: "public action that generates a widespread and sustained private market reaction." This widespread private market reaction was

possible because Bacon created a public realm framework that was not restricted to a single function. It was a park, it was a transportation system, it was a setting for people's houses, and much more. It changed Society Hill into a better, greener place to live. And it was certainly worth the money.

These experiences convinced me that the first way in which we should redefine "environmental" planning is to include people. The second is that we must think of the public realm as the framework around which private property owners develop. A sustainable public realm framework does make a city a better place to live and work. We have learned the benefits of planning with public participation. However slowly, we are beginning to build greener cities. But, in order to further cultivate the environmentally sustainable mixed-use public realm, we must take the next step—we must bring public realm opportunities to the forefront of any planning effort. Public realm improvements present the single greatest opportunity to make our cities greener. It is time not only to plan for the symbiotic relationships of humans to the earth, but also to make this vital issue the driving force of any planning or development project. Only such a cultural change of priorities will galvanize a widespread and sustained reaction to create greener, more sustainable, more livable cities.

References

Beveridge, Charles E. 1985. *The Distinctive Charms of Niagara Scenery: Frederick Law Olmsted and the Niagara Reservation.* Niagara Falls, N.Y.: Niagara University.

Carson, Rachel. 1962. *Silent Spring.* Boston: Houghton Mifflin.

Garvin, Alexander. 1996. *The American City: What Works, What Doesn't.* New York: McGraw-Hill.

Jacobs, Jane. 1961. *The Death and Life of Great American Cities.* New York: Random House, 1961.

Olmsted, Frederick Law. 1993. *Yosemite and the Mariposa Grove: A Preliminary Report, 1865.* Yosemite National Park: Yosemite Association.

Chapter 5
Growing Greener, New York Style

RACHEL WEINBERGER

Cities around the world are striving to meet the challenges of greening their transportation systems. London implemented a congestion charge in 2004, reducing auto usage and increasing its commitment to public transportation. Paris has reallocated a highway along the Seine as Paris Plage, converting the road to a pedestrian space and manmade beach for several weeks each year. Paris has also installed thousands of bicycles throughout the city that can be rented for short journeys around town. These bikes may be picked up at any bike stand location and returned at any other location. In the United States, major cities such as Salt Lake City, Chicago, San Francisco, and Denver are contributing through their transit and bicycle initiatives to a budding revolution in sustainable/green transport.

New York City is making an especially noteworthy effort to put in place a green transportation plan. PlaNYC 2030, issued by Mayor Michael Bloomberg in April 2007, will contribute to the city meeting its pledge to reduce carbon emissions 30 percent by 2030 and setting New York on course for further reductions in the future. This chapter discusses this initiative and the question of transportation in New York City generally by first discussing the negative externalities of transportation and showing how these led to the guiding principles the city adopted. New York City has a transit advantage relative to other U.S. cities: residents rely heavily on this transit infrastructure and the city will leverage this strength in the plan. Next it outlines New York's current mobility needs, providing a window on future patterns. How the city has defined its transportation problem is a critical step in proposing a solution. The chapter ends with a description of the PlaNYC initiatives proposed to reach the city's sustainability goals.

New York is unique in its low levels of auto ownership and high transit usage, two positives it must preserve and build on to achieve greater levels of sustainability. Despite its uniqueness, the city can, and should, serve as a model for other cities. Even while it has improvements to make, it is a living example of the possibility of sustainability in the transportation arena.

The Negative Externalities of Transportation

The transportation system is the lynchpin of the New York City's success. Failure to manage it well will put a serious strain on the city's ability to grow. With an expected 10 percent increase in city population by 2030, New York can expect a commensurate increase in the demand for transportation.[1] In addition, the city expects a surge in suburban commuters and visitors, further increasing pressure on the transportation system. The challenge is to provide for additional movements in a system that is, in many places and at many times of the day, already stretched beyond capacity, and to do so while decreasing carbon emissions. To accommodate these new demands will require approaching transportation resources with a new strategy.

As New York develops solutions to ensure future mobility, it must bear in mind the environmental implications and land requirements of its transportation system. A desirable solution minimizes environmental damage and preserves as much land as possible for other uses. There are at least three negative externalities of transport that New York City sought to address in planning the transportation system:

1. Pollution. Motorized transportation degrades air quality causing adverse health effects. In 1994, the U.S. Environmental Protection Agency (EPA) identified driving a car as the single most polluting activity of most Americans (USEPA 1994). This is an enduring phenomenon, according to the National Safety Council (NSC 2002).
2. Congestion. When a transportation system reaches capacity, its users impose unreasonable delays on themselves and each other. For example, when a train is full, passengers hold the doors to squeeze on, preventing the next train from entering the station, making the ride longer for those already on the train and delaying the next train as well. Likewise, when too many vehicles attempt to use a bridge, tunnel, or road simultaneously, the facility's capacity is diminished. Beyond lost time, these delays impose additional costs on a city's economy, as deliveries are slowed and thus made more expensive.
3. Land. Space requirements associated with transportation compete with other needs for a city's land. The space required to surface park 50 cars is equal to that needed for a small playground or to house 30 people in medium density dwellings.

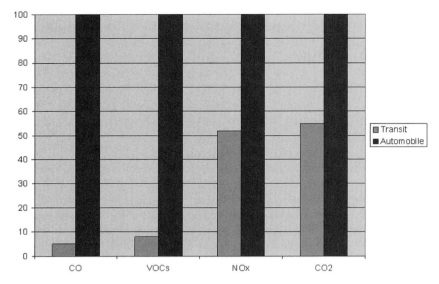

Figure 1. Emissions level per passenger mile: public transit compared with private automobile. Shapiro, Hassett, and Arnold (2002).

Understanding these externalities guided the transportation element of PlaNYC. Each is described in more depth below.

POLLUTION

Emissions contribute to both air and water problems. Burning fossil fuels to power cars, buses, and trucks adds to air pollution, air toxins, and greenhouse gases. In accordance with the Clean Air Act Amendments of 1990, the EPA monitors six air pollutants included in the National Ambient Air Quality Standard: ozone, volatile organic compounds, carbon monoxide, nitrogen oxides, particulate matter 2.5 and 10, and lead. However, the National Ambient Air Quality standard does not cover air toxins, which include other airborne substances that can also cause cancer, respiratory diseases, and leukemia and other blood disorders. Some examples of these toxins are benzene, formaldehyde, acrolein, toluene, acetaldehyde. In addition, heat-trapping or greenhouse gases, such as carbon dioxide, nitrous oxides, and methane, are by-products of burning fossil fuels.

Nationally, public transportation uses about half the amount of fuel per passenger mile as automobiles (Figure 1). In New York the savings are higher. Buses use 60 percent less fuel and the subway system is even more fuel efficient. Emissions per passenger mile are considerably lower for transit than for cars. Nationally, the rate of carbon monoxide emissions per passenger mile on transit is 5 percent that of private auto emissions, volatile organic compounds 8 percent, nitrogen oxides 52 percent, and harmful greenhouse gas carbon dioxide 55 percent.

In New York City, cars and light trucks are responsible for 78 percent of transportation carbon dioxide equivalent (CO_2e) emissions, yet they carry only 60 percent of motorized trips. In contrast, 40 percent of people traveling by motorized transportation in the city use public transit, yet are responsible for only 12 percent of transportation CO_2e emissions. Public transit is more than four times more carbon efficient at current usage rates. If New York is successful in its new policy direction, transit will become even more carbon efficient. Furthermore, as will be shown, the better an environment is for transit, the better it will be for walking and bicycling, which will further contribute to emissions reductions. Today, comparing cars with other modes combined shows that private motorized transport is 10 times more polluting than public transit or walking and bicycling in New York City.

Despite its per passenger efficiency, New York City produced a high level of air pollutants. Burning 1 gallon of gasoline in a passenger car emits nearly 1 pound of carbon monoxide, .07 pounds of nitrogen oxides, and 20.7 pounds of carbon dioxide. Drivers in New York City currently register about 51 million miles per day, thus creating 837 metric tons of carbon monoxide, 103 metric tons of nitrogen oxides, 2.8 metric tons of coarse particulate matter, and 34,000 metric tons of CO_2e each day from on-road vehicles alone. Taxis and for-hire vehicles contribute significantly to air pollution and greenhouse emissions because of the high mileage driven by each vehicle. Together, these vehicles emit approximately 1.6 million metric tons of CO_2e each year—almost 3 percent of the city's total. Forty percent of the roughly 100,000 miles driven by a medallion taxi each year are driven cruising for fares, resulting in the annual emission of more than 230,000 metric tons of CO_2e. While strategies to reduce cruising should be pursued, the city's robust livery industry also contributes to New Yorkers' low auto ownership rates, a very important factor in the city's relatively low per capita auto emissions. The livery system as a complement to the transit system means New Yorkers use cars less frequently than other Americans. The option of not owning a car contributes significantly to the high walking and transit use rates among New York City residents.

CONGESTION

Roads have different capacities at different speeds. For example, a highway designed to be safe at 50 mph has a per lane capacity of about 600 cars per hour at its maximum design speed. Capacity increases as the speeds slow. The 50-mph facility reaches a maximum per lane capacity of about 1,500 vehicles per hour when vehicles operate at speeds around 35 or 40 mph (*HCM* 2000). Thus the mobility of individuals is said to decrease but the overall system performance and aggregate mobility are improved. Beyond the maximum capacity, speeds slow even further and both system performance and individual mobility suffer. All the access routes to New York City's main business districts, in particular bottle-neck facilities like tunnels and bridges, are operating beyond their maxi-mum capacity for substantial parts of the day. If fewer people tried to use these facilities at once, more people would be able to flow through during a given day. To meet this challenge, New York has adopted a demand management strategy to reduce peak-time usage of these facili-ties.

In transit, when a passenger holding subway doors delays subsequent trains, the individual may succeed in saving a few minutes on his own journey, but delays to the system likely delay him as well, and surely cause the entire system to operate below capacity, serving fewer passen-gers than it otherwise could. For example, on New York's most crowded subway line, the Lexington Avenue line, in-station delays prevent the Metropolitan Transportation Authority (MTA) from dispatching all the available trains, leaving the line operating at only about 90 percent of its capability during the busiest parts of the day.

The city's approach is to encourage the more efficient—both from a space and carbon perspective—transit and walking trips by providing additional transit facilities and to manage the auto system to redistribute some of those trips to different times of day or on to the transit and nonmotorized parts of the transportation network.

LAND

Transportation requires a large amount of land to move and store vehi-cles. New York City's 19,000 lane miles of streets translate to approxi-mately 23,000 acres (almost the same size as the Bronx). Furthermore, the cars New Yorkers own would occupy about 5,500 acres, about seven times the size of Central Park. This does not account for trucks, taxis, and other for-hire vehicles and the thousands of cars that commuters and residents of adjacent counties drive into the city on a regular basis. The cars New Yorkers do not own (that is, if they owned vehicles at the same rate as average Americans) would require 11,000 acres or almost all of Manhattan just to park them side by side and end to end. Other modes of transportation are far more space efficient. Automobiles not only consume land, they also contribute other environmental problems.

Impervious surfaces such as asphalt and concrete roadbeds prevent rainwater from percolating into the ground. As the runoff from streets enters the storm sewer system, it carries tire dust, oil, and antifreeze spills and other pollutants into the waterways. Figure 2 shows how much of Manhattan would be devoted to parking additional cars. Figure 3 shows how many people can travel one mile, two miles, and five miles in one standard lane by walking driving, and cycling in the first two and by driving, cycling, and bus in the third.

The New York Advantage

Cities across the country scramble to build new urbanist communities and encourage transit-oriented development in a style that New York takes for granted. Steeped in the growing consensus that cars have an important place in transportation systems, but that auto dependence is not healthy for the environment, economies, or communities, these cities are trying to create transit systems, transit nodes, and pedestrian-oriented plazas. In all but the largest cities these communities are just beginning to build the basic elements of rail transit systems. Houston is expanding its light rail, and Denver has an ambitious program to build 120 miles of new commuter rail, light rail, and bus rapid transit (BRT). Salt Lake City has recently built light rail also. The country is moving in this direction to take advantage of what transit can offer, ease auto dependence, increase transport choices, and satisfy mobility needs in less space and with fewer pollutant and greenhouse gas emissions.

As shown in Figure 4, New York City's transit network carries more passengers than the five next largest transit systems in the United States.[2] The city's transit system—and walkability—provides far more efficient mobility than would be possible with exclusive auto dependence. According to the New York MTC 1998 household travel survey (the most recent available), New York's street system served 6 million daily trips on its 19,000 miles, while the subway served 3.5 million trips on 660 miles of track, making the subway 17 times more space efficient than the street system. At maximum capacity the subway system is potentially 25 times more space efficient and buses could be 10 times more space efficient (Figure 5). In fact, the city would need to increase street capacity by at least 50 percent to accommodate the same level of usage that the transit system provides. Curiously, unlike most cities, New York is in the peculiar position of having no direct jurisdictional control over its public transportation systems. Instead, it must work to align the interests of its regional partners with its own interests to achieve this high level of ridership.

Even with these tremendous efficiencies, tailpipe emissions from

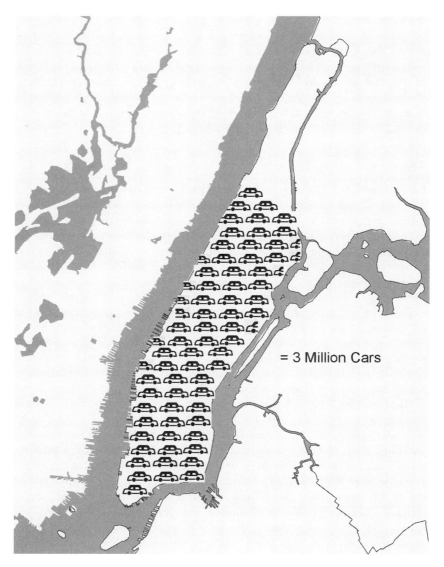

= 3 Million Cars

Figure 2. Nearly all Manhattan would be required as parking space if New Yorkers owned cars at the same level as the rest of the nation. New York City Mayor's Office of Long-Term Planning and Sustainability.

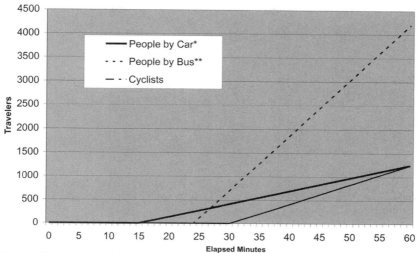

* assumes 1.5 passengers per vehicle
** assumes 35 buses per hour (aprox. 1/2 the capacity of bus rapid transit)

Figure 3. Hourly productivity of a 10-foot-wide New York avenue lane, 5-mile movement. * assumes 1.5 passengers/vehicle. ** assumes 35 buses/hour (approximately half the capacity of bus rapid transit).

transportation still account for 61 percent of the city's carbon monoxide emissions, 7 percent of the more dangerous particulate matter (PM2.5), 32 percent of nitrogen oxides, and 26 percent of volatile organic compounds emissions (EPA 1994). The latter two form ozone, which is the main component of urban smog. New York City does not meet federal air quality standards, and a large percentage of New Yorkers face an elevated risk of developing respiratory diseases such as asthma.

Relative to residents of other United States cities, New Yorkers rely heavily on transit, but compared with global competitors the city could do much better. In London, a city that is generally lower density and harder to serve by transit, people use transit more than twice as intensively as New Yorkers (Figure 6).

New York is a multimodal city. New Yorkers, more than other Americans, can match their trip needs to the most appropriate travel mode relative to their personal circumstances and destinations. For example, New Yorkers do not have to drive to the theater because the transit system does not stop running late at night, leaving them no way to get home. And if they are tired, or if it is raining, they can hail a cab or call a car service with relative ease. They can satisfy many trips by walking. New Yorkers make more than one-third of their trips on foot because

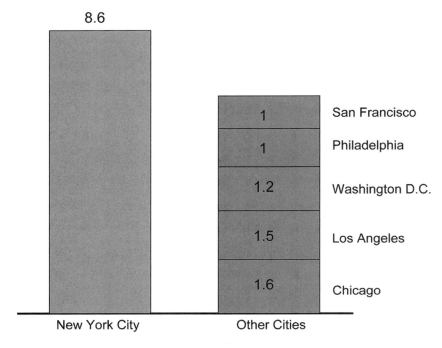

Figure 4. Daily transit riders (millions of passengers). American Public Transit Association (2006).

the city's unique land use and extensive transit system allow its residents to use and own automobiles by choice rather than by necessity.

Nationally, 90 percent of households own one or more vehicles and 88 percent of the population commute to work by car, truck, or van. More than 75 percent drive alone. Most have little choice but to own a car. Indeed, across the country all but the poorest citizens and those unable to drive—due to age or physical disabilities—own cars. In most of New York City the story is different. In Staten Island, the borough with the highest auto ownership per household, and arguably the most similar to the rest of the nation with respect to land use, 82 percent of households own private vehicles. But overall, only 44 percent of New York City households own cars, with as few as 22 percent of Manhattan households owing an auto. Only 26 percent of the population drives to work (less than 5 percent to Manhattan); indeed, only 33 percent of all trips are made by private automobile. The remaining trips are made by ferry, rail, subway, bus, bicycle, and foot.

While nationally auto ownership is highly correlated with income, in

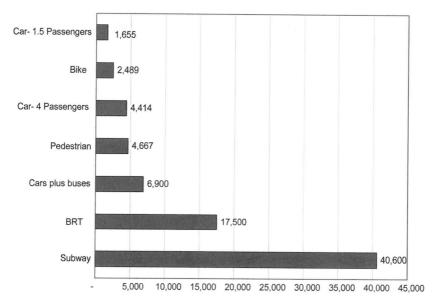

Figure 5. Trips per lane per hour. *Highway Capacity Manual* (2000).

New York City it depends on income and other factors. Density and transit access are stronger predictors of auto ownership. For example, people in the lowest income brackets in Staten Island are more likely to own cars than people in every income bracket in Manhattan. Brooklyn households with earnings over $150,000 are less likely to own private vehicles than those in the $100,000 to $150,000 bracket, and they are less likely to own vehicles than Staten Island households in the $25,000 to $50,000 and any higher bracket. These differences are due to the nature of the urban fabric and transit access where the non-auto-owning households locate.

New York City's Mobility Patterns

Understanding the different trip purposes and their essential characteristics—such as their distance and what time of day they occur—guides planning and helps determine the best mode and transportation system configurations.

As is the case in every city, transportation is an integral part of New Yorkers' lives. To get to work or school, to go shopping, visit friends, or enjoy the parks, people travel. Every day, New Yorkers have access to a wide range of options for these personal trips: they can walk, ride bikes,

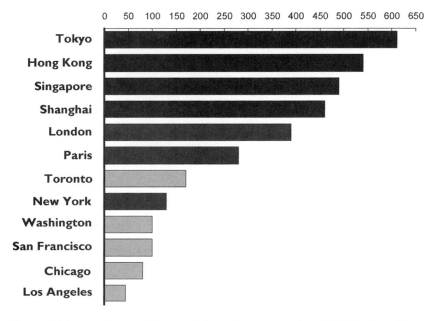

Figure 6. Metropolitan region transit boardings per capita, 1995. Institute for Sustainability and Technology Policy, Murdoch University.

hail cabs, take personal cars, ride buses, or take trains. Forty-five percent of work trips are made to Manhattan's central business district and the newer centers in Long Island City, Downtown Brooklyn, Flushing, Jamaica, and the Bronx hub. Residents also depend on the timely delivery of goods to supply local stores, carry packages, deliver construction materials, and haul trash. Trucks carry nearly all this freight. This section describes in some detail the trips New Yorkers make.

Streets and sidewalks are the most basic element of New York's transportation infrastructure. Subway and commuter rail trips generally begin with a walk to a station; most auto trips in the city also include a walk to a parking spot or garage. As mentioned earlier, walking is the means of travel for more than a third of all trips and is part of nearly all trips. Walkers and cyclists transporting themselves, automobiles and taxis serving individuals, buses providing mass transit, and trucks moving freight share the city's streets. Street space must be allocated efficiently to accommodate all the required trips.

New Yorkers daily take millions of trips around the city and throughout the region. The average New Yorker makes 3.4 trips and travels a total of 21 miles a day. Family and personal business, including shopping and trips to the doctor, account for 44 percent of all trips. Social and recreational trips, including exercise and sports, going out to eat or for entertainment, and visiting friends, constitute 25 percent of trips; commuting to work 16 percent; and trips to school and religious activities another 11 percent. Just over half of all trips are less than 20 minutes, regardless of mode, and one third are less than one mile in distance.

MOBILITY NEEDS

Currently, the citywide modal distribution of trips is 34 percent by walking, 33 percent by private automobile, 19 percent by rail or ferry, 11 percent by bus, and 3 percent by taxi or shared ride. In 2006, all vehicles combined logged 20 billion miles on New York City's streets and highways. Automobiles and light trucks, typically associated with personal transport, accounted for 95 percent of city vehicle mileage, with heavy trucks accounting for 3 percent and buses 1 percent. Analysts expect auto traffic to increase 10 percent and truck traffic, growing much faster, to increase 64 percent by 2030.[3]

Data from several sources form the basis of the analysis in the following sections that describe the characteristics of trips and trip makers for different trip purposes.[4] They detail mode split, travel times, trip lengths, and volume at different times of the day and week that allow for better service planning and transportation interventions to ease congestion, improve air quality, and reduce vehicle emissions.

FAMILY AND PERSONAL BUSINESS TRIPS

For New Yorkers, family and personal business is the largest category, accounting for 44 percent of all trips. This category includes shopping, doctor and dentist visits, traveling to day care, and other family and personal obligations. On weekdays, family and personal business trips are spread between 9 a.m. and 7 p.m.; on weekends, the greatest amount of travel of this type occurs between 9 a.m. and 1 p.m., gradually decreasing through the rest of the day. Family and personal business trips are shorter during the week, averaging about 3.1 miles compared to 5.2 miles on the weekend. Two-thirds of family and personal business trips are less than 20 minutes long, and nearly half of those are less than 10 minutes. Trips for family and personal business are fairly evenly split between walking and driving, with only 14 percent on public transit.

Among the family and personal-business trip types, shopping is the shortest, averaging 16 minutes. Only 6 percent of these trips are to Manhattan from the other boroughs. Most shopping is on foot or by auto, with the relative share of these modes varying significantly across the five boroughs. In Manhattan, 70 percent of shopping trips from home are on foot; in the Bronx, Brooklyn, and Queens, walking shares are 55 percent, 47 percent, and 42 percent respectively. On Staten Island, where auto ownership and car dependency are highest, only 9 percent of shopping trips are on foot. Citywide, 36 percent of shopping trips are by auto. However, only 6 percent of shopping trips in Manhattan use an auto compared to 85 percent in Staten Island. Other types of personal business rely more heavily on transit—40 percent in Manhattan and 28 percent citywide.

SOCIAL AND RECREATIONAL TRIPS

Social and recreational trips, accounting for one quarter of all trips, include vacations, visiting friends, eating out, exercising or playing sports, and other entertainment. Weekdays, the largest share (36 percent) is evening trips between 7 p.m. and 10 p.m. On weekends, New Yorkers make twice as many social and recreational trips as on weekdays, and travel more than three times farther than during the week. On the weekend, the longest trips of any type are for social and recreational purposes, with an average distance of 10.6 miles.

Social and recreational trips are somewhat longer than family and personal business trips, averaging 27 minutes. Weekday social and recreational trips having their origins and destinations within the city vary greatly by borough with regard to modal split. For example, on Staten Island, more than three-fourths of these trips are by auto but the proportion is much lower in Queens (50 percent), Brooklyn (37 percent), the Bronx (18 percent), and Manhattan (9 percent).

JOURNEY TO SCHOOL

For younger New Yorkers, the "commute" to school is their most important daily trip. With 1.5 million New Yorkers attending preschool, elementary school, or high school, and another half million in college or graduate school, citywide, 35 percent walk to school, 30 percent take a bus, 20 percent ride the train or ferry, and 15 percent come by car.

As with the other trip purposes, significant cross-borough variations exist. On Staten Island, 41 percent of students commute to school by car, 42 percent take a bus, and 13 percent walk. In Queens 40 percent take the bus while in the Bronx and Manhattan less than 20 percent use this mode. The subway accounts for 20 percent or less in the outer boroughs. Walking has a lower share in Manhattan than in the Bronx, possibly due to the concentration of magnet schools and universities in

Manhattan to which students commute longer distances, typically by transit.

Journey to Work

The journey to work is the most studied area of trip making, possibly because it is the most stable and predictable. Consequently, planners tend to have the most data about this type of trip. Despite the amount of attention journey to work receives, it accounts for only 16 percent of trips by New Yorkers. About 43 percent of New Yorkers are in the labor force. Commuting trips tend to be the longest trips New Yorkers make, averaging 8 to 12 miles and taking about 34 minutes. Ironically, while New Yorkers' long commute times are due to their use of transit—an inherently slower way to travel—if New Yorkers commuted predominantly by car the times would be much longer because the street system simply does not and cannot have the capacity to serve their number efficiently.

Most New Yorkers work within the borough in which they live, but a significant portion (47 percent or 1,372,000 trips) of commuting trips are to Manhattan below 96th Street. The volume of commuters varies by borough: 530,200, Manhattan; 329,000, Queens; 325,600, Brooklyn; 135,400, the Bronx; and 51,700, Staten Island. While mass transit accommodates the majority of trips to the Manhattan hub, many drive. Queens is the borough with the highest number of drivers—60,000, including carpoolers. Staten Island, with only 16,000 car commuters, has the lowest absolute number of drivers, but the highest share of its Manhattan-bound commuters coming in by car (32 percent) (see Plate 6 for the origins of commuters to below 96th Street by census tract and Plate 7 for the highest concentrations of drivers).

Freight

As New York City has increasingly supported a service-oriented economy, it imports nearly all its material goods—from food to office supplies to construction materials—from other states or overseas. It exports its waste because it has no active landfills or waste-to-energy plants. Nearly 99 percent of this freight travels on trucks.

Over the last 20 years, the city's rising population and booming economy have been accompanied by a 35 percent increase in truck traffic. As was mentioned earlier, truck traffic is expected to grow another 64 percent by 2030. New York's congested roads slow trucks and delay deliveries, imposing significant costs on businesses and the freight industry. Truck traffic also imposes heavy costs on the city. Trucks are a small fraction of the total vehicles on the road, but have disproportionate impacts on pollution and safety. In terms of greenhouse gases, for example, heavy trucks emit three times as much CO_2 per mile as do automobiles and light trucks. Moreover, because they are used commercially they log more miles, using the street system more heavily than cars. Not only do trucks contribute to regional air pollution, in neighborhoods with high concentrations of truck traffic their emissions exacerbate public health problems such as asthma and other respiratory diseases. Truck traffic in those neighborhoods is also a significant safety hazard for pedestrians.

In recent years, New York has taken a number of steps to reduce trucking's negative impacts. For example, the Department of Sanitation's Solid Waste Management Plan (approved in 2006) uses barges and trains to export 90 percent of the city's residential trash. The program is expected to cut truck traffic in the city by nearly 3 million miles per year. The Department of Transportation Truck Route Management and Community Impact Reduction Study (released in March 2007) calls for improved signage and enforcement of truck routes and establishment of an Office for Freight Mobility. Such steps could improve safety in neighborhoods with high concentrations of truck traffic.

Defining the Problem

PlaNYC defines New York City's transportation problems in terms of accessibility and sustainability. Historically, transportation performance measures have revolved around mobility—how much distance can be covered by people and vehicles. Recently, the notion of accessibility has taken center stage. Accessibility, defined in terms of how many people can reach a certain place in a certain amount of time, is a function of the surrounding land uses and their densities. Thus, mobility combined with land use defines accessibility.

The transportation/land use connection is mediated by how much land must be devoted to the transportation infrastructure and the capacity of the transportation system. An area served only by automobile-designed streets (an auto/highway network) cannot accommodate high-density development because it is physically impossible to bring high volumes of people to a particular place by automobile—an inherently low-capacity mode. Furthermore, the amount of space that must be devoted to the carriageway for autos and to parking cars diminishes the amount of space that can be developed for other uses. Similarly, an area zoned for low-density development cannot have robust transit options because it lacks sufficient population to support frequent and comprehensive transit. Thus, areas zoned and built for auto use (low-density places with parking requirements) are virtually guaranteed to have auto-use dominance. To address this problem, the 2030 plan calls for development of more mass transit infrastructure and rationalization of land devoted to transportation in order to facilitate movement of more efficient modes—rail, bus, bicycle, and walking. Fortunately, these more space-efficient modes tend to be more fuel efficient as well.

With regard to sustainability, New York City considered the impact of transportation on air quality and its contributions to global warming stemming from the burning of fossil fuels. It identified three areas where intervention could reduce negative impacts of the transport sector while preserving the city's special accessibility characteristics:

1. Burn less fuel while satisfying the same travel needs. This would include shifting trips to more energy efficient modes, for example, auto to bus trips, bus to train trips, bus, train, and auto to walking or biking trips. It would also include vehicle replacement to more fuel-efficient vehicles. In addition to the city's own vehicle fleet this could include the taxi fleet and incentives for private citizens to adopt more fuel-efficient vehicles. It also includes reducing idling by reducing double parking, reducing traffic tie-ups, and enforcing anti-idling laws.
2. Burn cleaner fuels (biofuels and removal of toxins such as benzene from gasoline).
3. Burn fuel more cleanly (ensure better vehicle maintenance through more regular and rigorous inspection, regular engine tune-ups, and particulate filters, especially on diesel fuel trucks and buses).

The latter two interventions would not only address issues in the transportation sector but are also would have an impact on energy production and consumption, the construction industry, and other sectors. The 2030 plan treated these areas under its air quality initiatives. The plan emphasized the first impact area, burning less fuel, under its transportation initiatives, calling specifically for the reduction of private automobile use and developing policies to ensure more trips by nonmotorized and more fuel-efficient per capita modes. Thus the transportation element of the 2030 plan focuses on strategies to burn less fuel while meeting travel needs.

In sum, New York City adopted a strategy to match every trip need to the mode with the smallest pollutant and carbon footprint possible. In so doing, it seeks to allocate transportation resources to favor the most space-efficient and productive modes, taking into consideration the different characteristics of trips and the surrounding conditions: distance, whether items need to be carried, and the availability of options at the trip's origin and destination. For example, typically, a person can make an intra-neighborhood trip for grocery shopping on foot, car, bus, or bicycle. In promoting accessibility and sustainability, the 2030 plan sets a policy direction and contains initial provisions to position walking as the most pleasant, convenient, and desirable way to make that trip. For longer trips, people choose bicycle, bus, subway, or automobile. Again, the 2030 plan supports efforts to facilitate biking and transit as the most convenient, pleasant, and reliable ways to travel. Routine journey-to-work trips that are too long to walk or bicycle are usually best served by transit. And for unique trips like a family visit between parts of the city that are not now well connected to each other—for example, a trip between Brooklyn and the Bronx—the city seeks to develop greater connectivity. Meanwhile, the automobile may be the best choice, either in a private auto or in a livery car. To the extent that New Yorkers can rely on livery for car trips, their needs for individual auto ownership will be reduced, in turn lowering their propensity to default to the auto for other trips where more sustainable options exist. Over time, this would result in a reduction of the land resources required to accommodate automobiles.

Accompanying its decision to make trips by transit and nonmotorized modes the most pleasant and convenient, the city developed basic planning principles for transit access and pedestrian space to guide decision making:

- Provide safe, secure pedestrian connections with transit stations.
- Design transit stations to facilitate transfers to other transit services.
- Guarantee a pedestrian environment that is comfortable, safe and supportive of mixed uses where appropriate.

Station access is a critical piece of transit planning because potential riders may be discouraged if arriving at and departing from the stations makes the trip by mass transit more costly, time intensive, unreliable, or otherwise more difficult than using another mode, such as private automobile. The goal is to create a mass transit system that provides seamless, intermodal connections, offering riders a high level of comfort, ease, and satisfaction. Designing pedestrian access to a station involves creating safe, secure, and direct routes. Pedestrians tend to seek the shortest paths, often choosing routes that compete with cars, buses, or bicyclists. Planning direct and safe paths must meet pedestrian needs while providing protection from other traffic. Another concern is ensuring adequate sidewalks at bus stops and subway entrances to increase safety and comfort.

Stations should also be designed to facilitate transfers to other transit services, such as bus, subway, or rail. Way-finding systems, appropriate signage, comfortable waiting areas, and real-time information about wait times for connecting services can all help to make the trip more predictable and provide a consistent high level of service throughout the journey. Bicyclists should also be accommodated in station access planning. Bicyclists must have safe, convenient, and available parking near a station attendant or in a high-volume area, protected from inclement weather when possible.

While walking is the earliest and most basic form of mobility, it was not frequently considered a serious mode of transportation until 1991, when federal legislation mandated planning for bicycle and pedestrian facilities in federally supported projects. Walking holds numerous benefits. It is the most environmentally sustainable form of transportation. It produces no emissions, no noise impacts, and requires less space per person than other forms of transport. It also promotes economic activity and is good for local businesses. Walking has well-documented physical and mental health benefits. In New York, an extraordinary number of residents walk for transportation, rather than for just recreational purposes; as previously noted, 34 percent of trips are made on foot.[5]

In designing sidewalks and other pedestrian ways, safety, accessibility, comfort, and the visual variety that comes from mixed land uses or well-landscaped streets are key ingredients. These elements are not always compatible, and the challenge for planners and designers is to strike the right balance among them, prioritizing where necessary. To the extent that investing in pedestrians can encourage a shift away from automobiles, pedestrian planning is a critical strategy in reducing New York's traffic congestion and emissions. In addition, making walking a more attractive alternative for short trips has the added advantage of also making bus and car trips more productive. The road space freed by shifting trips to walking brings demand for the road space more in line with capacity, serving the long trips that cannot reasonably be made by walking.

New York's Transportation Initiatives for 2030

In developing the 2030 plan, New York City assessed its past and future potential. The mayor, Michael Bloomberg, concluded that both realizing the potential and being a good global citizen would require auto-reducing and transit-enhancing strategies. Thus, with a commitment to reducing greenhouse gas emissions and a recognition of the physical impracticality of accommodating the city's expected growth by replicating and expanding the existing transportation configuration, the plan outlined four focal areas for sustainable transportation improvements:

(1) building and expanding transit infrastructure; (2) improving existing transit; (3) promoting other sustainable modes; and (4) improving traffic flow by reducing auto use and its attendant congestion. The plan includes an additional critical element: the introduction of congestion pricing. Congestion pricing, part of the fourth focus, addresses the traffic problem and creates a revenue stream that can be leveraged to implement other parts of the plan.

The first focal area aims to clear the backlog of major transit improvements that have already been identified as important to the city and region. These projects include construction of the Second Avenue subway; completion of the East-Side Access project, which will allow Long Island Rail Road trains that currently serve only Penn Station to travel into Grand Central Station; building Access to the Region's Core, a project to add a rail passenger tunnel under the Hudson River, which will increase transit capacity between New York City and New Jersey. Of these projects, some date from the 1920s (Second Avenue subway) and others were conceived more recently. All are long-term infrastructure improvements that will take several years to complete and require a commitment of substantial resources. In reality, many are the primary responsibility of the city's regional partners, not the municipal government. PlaNYC's contribution is to articulate their need strongly, clear city-related obstacles to their implementation, and contribute funds to fill chronic financing gaps.

In the second focal area, improving existing transit, the 2030 plan identifies a series of short-term transit improvements that the city can make, in cooperation with the Metropolitan Transportation Authority, to attract and accommodate additional riders in the next few years. One project that the city and the MTA will bring on-line shortly is a bus-rapid transit pilot project that supplements the subway system. An associated effort is the creation of additional exclusive bus lanes on city streets and bridges to enhance the efficiency and reliability of the existing bus system. Other bus and subway service initiatives include improving station access, changes in routing, and adding or supplementing transit service to underserved areas. In addition, the city will address congested bottlenecks on the auto-highway system by developing multi-modal corridor plans and will develop pedestrian plazas throughout the city to reinforce its commitment to promoting a lower carbon lifestyle.

The 2030 plan calls for supporting other sustainable transportation modes including bicycles and ferries. By completing the 1,800-mile bike master plan and installing more than 1,000 on-street bicycle racks, New York hopes to increase the cycling mode share beyond its current 1 percent of journey-to-work trips. The city has already replaced a couple of on-street car parking spots with bicycle storage racks near a subway station in Williamsburg, Brooklyn. Additional reallocations will follow. In addition, it is taking measures to partner with private ferry operators to provide service along the East River. This service will help meet the transportation needs of prospective residents of the new waterfront developments in Brooklyn and Queens that were stimulated by the 2006 rezoning of this former industrial area. Ideally, the ferry operators will provide seamless connections to the city's mass transit network through bus service and fare integration.

The most publicized element of the plan 2030's transportation strategy is its congestion pricing recommendation. The plan envisions using this mechanism to reduce automobile traffic in the main business district, Manhattan south of Eighty-Sixth Street while raising money to fund the major infrastructure improvements discussed earlier. By charging drivers a fee to enter Manhattan at the busiest time of day, the city expects to see a 6.3 percent reduction in vehicle miles traveled within the priced zone. It also anticipates significant revenues—an estimated $400 million per year. Other cities such as London, Stockholm, and Singapore have found congestion pricing to be an effective tool in reducing gridlock, not only within the pricing zone, but also in peripheral neighborhoods that had experienced traffic bound for the priced zone. To implement this element requires approval by the state legislature.

Loathe to endorse the plan without a careful examination, the legislature delayed an up or down vote in the last legislative session. Instead, it voted to form a commission to develop a workable congestion pricing plan or to propose an alternative plan that would accomplish the same objectives. The head of the commission, Marc Shaw, sees his role as ensuring a workable plan. The key to its success, he asserts, is to show how the revenues will be used to improve mass transit (Neuman 2007). A U.S. Department of Transportation grant of $354 million is conditioned on this commission's positive recommendation of a program that includes road pricing. The city is working assiduously with the legislature and the commission to pass an effective resolution allowing the city to pilot the plan.

Looking Beyond PlaNYC

The strategy outlined in PlaNYC—expanding transit capacity, improving existing service, encouraging other sustainable modes, and managing traffic and raising revenues through congestion pricing—has set a strong precedent for New York City to use transportation policy as a means of attaining broader goals, especially reducing its carbon footprint. One important benefit of this large-scale planning effort is that it raises consciousness about a host of issues, initiating widespread dialogue about the city's future. The congestion pricing strategy, for example, would make people think twice before taking their cars, especially if they have a comparable mass transit option.

PlaNYC is a dynamic document stimulating change in many areas. To implement it, the New York City Department of Transportation (NYC-DOT) has retooled, creating a new Department for Planning and Sustainability led by a deputy commissioner. New York City and the New York State MTA,[6] frequently pursuing competing agenda, are now enjoying an unprecedented level of cooperation, evidenced by their successful submission of a joint application to the U.S. Department of Transportation for $354 million to be used for transit improvements in anticipation of implementing congestion pricing. Other tangible results include the mandatory replacement of the 13,000-vehicle taxi fleet with all hybrid vehicles by 2012, announced by Mayor Bloomberg in May 2007. The conversion of the iconic symbol of New York City, the yellow taxi, from a 14-mile-per-gallon gas guzzler to a 30-mile-per-gallon energy conserver, saves almost 50 million gallons of gasoline every year and makes a strong statement about the city's commitment to its sustainability goals.

New York City's plan is both ambitious and cautious, striving to make important changes palatable to the body politic while setting the stage for dramatic changes in the future. As the city continues with its implementation, sustained outreach is essential to communicate the plan's underlying values and to put the various initiatives in context. Understanding the broader benefits to a congestion charge, which include less traffic, improved air quality, faster bus service, and funding to support mass transit, makes paying a modest fee to drive into the zone more palatable. Moreover, critical to the plan's success is the city's ability to garner broad-based support that will last beyond the Bloomberg administration, which ends in 2009. Stakeholders can help hold future administrations accountable and keep sustainability issues at the forefront of political agenda. In particular, the city must work to maintain good relationships with its regional partners—including the MTA, Port Authority, and New Jersey Transit—which all have a role in bringing the planned projects to fruition.

References

American Public Transit Association. 2006. http://www.apta.com/research/status/ridership/riderep/ documents/06q2rep.pdf, accessed July 1, 2007.
Highway Capacity Manual (*HCM*). 2000. U.S. Customary Version. Washington, D.C.: Transportation Research Board.
National Household Travel Survey (NHTS). 2001. http://nhts.ornl.gov/.

National Safety Council. 2002. *Outreach and Education on Air Quality, Climate Change, and Transportation: Youth Initiatives.* http://www.nsc.org/ehc/mobile/ozone.htm.

Neuman, William. 2007. "Members Named for Panel Studying Traffic Cutting Plan." *New York Times,* August 22.

New York Metropolitan Transportation Council (NYMTC). 1998. Regional Travel Survey. 1998.

Shapiro, Robert J., Kevin A. Hassett, and Frank S. Arnold. 2002. "Conserving Energy and Preserving the Environment: The Role of Public Transportation." Report prepared for the American Public Transportation Association. July. http://www.apta.com/research/info/online/shapiro.cfm.

U.S. Census Bureau. 2000. *Census Transportation Planning Package. Journey to Work.* Washington, D.C.: U.S. Census.

U.S. EPA Office of Mobile Sources. 1994. *Automobile Emissions, an Overview.* http://www.epa.gov/otaq/consumer/05-autos.pdf.

Weinberger, Rachel. 2007. *New York City Mobility Needs Assessment 2007–2030.* New York: City of New York.

Chapter 6

Greener Homes, Greener Cities: Expanding Affordable Housing and Strengthening Cities Through Sustainable Residential Development

STOCKTON WILLIAMS AND DANA L. BOURLAND

Sustainable design and development practices are becoming more common in the construction and rehabilitation of affordable housing in many cities. "Greening" affordable housing can create healthier living environments for low-income and minority families, who suffer disproportionately from asthma and other health problems exacerbated by poor indoor air quality. More sustainable affordable homes also can reduce utility and operating expenses in affordable multifamily buildings, cutting costs for residents and boosting building reserves. And green affordable housing development at scale can contribute to broader strategies for cities to enhance environmental quality, improve public health, and encourage interagency collaboration to solve local issues.

While there are encouraging signs that green building is catching on among affordable housing developers, with a demonstrable surge in just the last few years, sustainability remains a new concept for many affordable housing professionals. More work remains to be done to educate affordable housing providers about the benefits of sustainable development and to build their capacity to incorporate green features into projects on a cost-effective basis. Additional research is required on the costs and benefits of green affordable housing. Public policies must also evolve to support smarter and healthier affordable homes. Progress in these areas may encourage financial institutions, appraisers, and other market actors to consider new ways of underwriting and assigning value to green affordable housing developments, which could create a "tipping point" at which sustainable practices become the mainstream in affordable housing. Cities and their low-income residents would stand to gain greatly from such a market transformation.

A word about a few key terms. For the purposes of this essay, "affordable" is defined as for-sale homes reasonably affordable to owners whose incomes do not exceed 80 percent of area median income, and rental apartments reasonably affordable to residents whose incomes do not exceed 50 percent of median income; the latter are considered "very low-income" for the purposes of federal housing programs.

Housing problems are especially acute for very low-income renters. According to the U.S. Department of Housing and Urban Development (HUD), nearly 6 million very low-income U.S. households have "worst case needs." They do not receive federal rental housing assistance and either pay more than half their income for rent or live in severely substandard housing. Worst case needs have increased 16 percent since 2003, according to HUD (HUD 2007: 1). In addition, HUD reports that only 77 units are affordable, available, and physically adequate for every 100 very low-income renters, down from 81 in 2003 (HUD 2007: 4).

For the purposes of this essay, "green" or "sustainable" are conceptual terms, used interchangeably, that refer to a broad-based set of design, building, and maintenance features of an apartment building or single family home intended to improve the efficiency, performance, and durability of the property, enhance the health of its residents, and mitigate the building's environmental impacts in construction and operation. Most important, the concept is holistic, encompassing more than a single green component, and includes both site and location features (such as density, walkability, and transit access) as well as building elements (including energy efficient systems, healthy and recycled materials and features to improve indoor air quality).

Green Homes Yesterday and Today

Although the Greeks incorporated green features in their homes in the fifth century B.C., visionaries, pioneers, and iconoclasts have, until recently, been the chief advocates of sustainable dwellings. Ancient Greek house plans maximized the warming benefits from the sun and mitigated the cold winds during the winter, as noted by the playwright Aeschylus, who wrote that only primitives and barbarians "lacked knowledge of houses turned to face the winter sun, dwelling beneath the ground like swarming ants in sunless caves." Starting in the 1930s, Buckminster Fuller's three prototype Dymaxion houses adopted many techniques to reduce resource use, such as a "fogger" shower head, a packaging toilet, and a vacuum turbine for electric power. The 1970s saw the solar home fad as well as "bioshelters" like the Ark community for Prince Edward Island, which used wind-based water pumping and electricity and a closed loop sewage reclamation system that recycled human waste into sanitized fertilizer for fish tanks. "Earthships" built of tires filled with earth and relying entirely on the sun for heat and rain for water also emerged in the 1970s and can still be found today in some states.

Green homes became more mainstream during the 1990s through local initiatives that promoted practical ways to save energy and conserve resources in home building. Austin, Texas was first, followed closely by Boulder and Denver, Colorado; Santa Barbara County in California; Kitsap County in Washington; and Scottsdale, Arizona ("Green Building Comes Home" 2004: 34–35). Usually sponsored by state or local governments, local homebuilder associations, utility companies or nonprofits, the local programs typically provided "a checklist of factors related to energy usage, waste management, site work, water conservation and indoor environmental quality. Builders [who attained] a sufficient number of credits [could] label their homes 'green,' thus benefiting from market differentiation, positive public image and improved relations with local government officials who [controlled] zoning, construction permits and building codes" ("Green Building Comes Home" 2004: 34–35). According to the U.S. Green Building Council, more than 70 local green residential programs exist today ("Frequently Asked Questions" n.d.).

Precise data on the number of green homes do not exist. A 2003 survey found that "more than 30" local green residential programs had certified more than 30,000 homes ("Green Building Comes Home" 2004: 34). Two years later, an analysis by the National Association of Homebuilders reported that more than 61,000 homes had been certified under local programs, including 14,000 in the prior year alone.

Most green homes certified under local programs have been single-family, market-rate homes and interest in green homes among market-rate builders is growing. A 2006 survey of National Association of Homebuilders members projected that green homebuilding will grow to 10 percent of all new housing starts by 2010 from 2 percent in 2006. The survey estimated that the market for green homebuilding will rise to between $19 billion and $38 billion by 2010 from $2 billion in 2006. "Green home building is at a tipping point among the builder population. . . . Within 10 years, every builder will be incorporating green practices into what they do," according to one of the study's authors.[1] Many speculate that to the extent the conventional residential real estate industry adopts sustainable practices, the ripple effects among architects, contractors, and suppliers should increase awareness among affordable housing developers.

Figure 1. Oleson Woods, a Green Communities development in Tigard, Oregon, outside Portland, conserved a mature tree canopy, expanded a wetland, and created a rainwater filtration system around 32 healthy, efficient homes on a site that encourages walking and biking. Carleton Hart Architecture.

Several local programs are already focusing on encouraging affordable housing. Among them are Southface's EarthCraft House Mutlifamily program, Advanced Energy's SystemVision program, the city of Seattle SeaGreen initiative, Portland, Oregon's Office of Sustainability Design and Construction Guidelines for Affordable Housing, and the New Jersey Department of Community Affairs Green Homes Office. And green development has already become more widespread among affordable housing developers in the last several years. In 2006 the *Chronicle of Philanthropy*, noting that "more charities are incorporating environmentally friendly building practices into their work," reported that several national housing organizations were offering training and technical assistance. The Home Depot Foundation had begun to focus grantmaking on green affordable housing and the "biggest push thus far" had come from the $555 million commitment from Enterprise (formerly the Enterprise Foundation) for its Green Communities initiative (Wallace 2006: 60) (Figure 1).

The Green Communities Initiative

Enterprise launched Green Communities in 2004 to take to scale the emergent green affordable housing movement with the ultimate goal of making all affordable homes in the United States environmentally sustainable. Through Green Communities, Enterprise provides financial support and technical expertise to enable developers to build and rehabilitate homes so that they are healthier, more energy efficient, and better for the environment—and without forcing developers to incur infeasible extra costs. Green Communities also assists state and local governments to ensure their housing and economic development policies are smart and sustainable. By mid-2007, Enterprise had invested $425 million to support nearly 9,000 homes in almost 200 Green Communities developments in 23 states. In addition, Enterprise had trained more than 3,000 affordable housing professionals in sustainable affordable development and worked with state and local agencies to craft policies to create greener projects in more than 20 cities and states.

Green Communities homes are built according to the Green Communities Criteria, the first national framework for sustainable development developed specifically for affordable housing. The criteria were developed in 2004 by a working group assembled by Enterprise that included the American Institute of Architects, the American Planning Association, the Natural Resources Defense Council, Southface, Global Green USA, the Center for Maximum Potential Building Systems, and the National Center for Healthy Housing. They were designed to create healthier, better performing homes through proven, cost-effective building strategies, without burdening developers with undue complexity or infeasible costs. The working group based the Green Communities Criteria on leading local green building programs specifically designed for affordable housing, especially Seattle's SeaGreen program (see below) and the U.S. Green Building Council Leadership in Energy and Environmental Design (LEED) rating system for large multiunit buildings. The council began to pilot test a national residential rating system called "LEED for Homes" in 2006, with plans for a formal release in 2007.[2]

Affordable Green Housing Efforts at the State and Local Levels

Another indicator that green affordable housing is poised to become more common is in the adoption of policies at the state and local level to encourage it. State housing agencies that administer the federal Low Income Housing Tax Credit, which accounts for almost all newly rehabilitated and constructed rental apartments for low-income people, are increasingly encouraging and, in some cases, requiring developers to use sustainable practices in order to receive tax credits through competitive scoring processes. Virtually every state now encourages some level of sustainable principles and in many states, proposed developments must include green features to be in the strongest competitive position to receive credits. Significantly, 28 state agencies added new green policies to their Low Income Housing Tax Credit programs from 2006 to 2007 and 36 agencies have done so since 2005.[3]

State action on sustainable affordable housing has not been limited to Low Income Housing Tax Credit programs. The Maine State Housing Authority requires comprehensive green building criteria for virtually all its programs. The Minnesota Housing Finance Agency has integrated green criteria into its rental and single-family initiatives as well. The state of Washington has adopted holistic green criteria for its affordable housing trust fund, which supports 4,500 new homes every two years.

Cities are providing examples of exciting leadership as well. For many, the threat of climate change has galvanized a new way of thinking about urban redevelopment. Former President Bill Clinton, whose Clinton Climate Initiative is helping large cities worldwide reduce their greenhouse gas emissions, framed the issued in a speech announcing the work of the initiative:

> Every country has got this challenge. How are we going to meet it? By a serious commitment to a clean energy future, that's how. We can create jobs out of wind energy, out of solar energy, out of bio-fuels, out of hybrid engines, out of a systematic determination to change the lighting patterns, the insulation patterns, the efficiency standards of all buildings and all appliances. We could make, in America, there is no telling how many jobs we could create if we'd just made a decision that in the rebuilding of New Orleans, it could become America's first "green" city. We would restore all the wetlands, and every building would have solar cells. (Clinton 2005)

Leading mayors understand that green affordable housing is integral to a truly sustainable city.[4] For example, since 2002 Seattle, under Mayor Greg Nickels—who has made greening affordable housing part of his agenda—has encouraged developers to incorporate environmental principles through its SeaGreen initiative. This groundbreaking program provides detailed information on incorporating green features into affordable housing developments in Seattle (Office of Housing 2002: ii). In 2005, San Francisco Mayor Gavin Newsom committed to ensure that all city-supported affordable housing developments would include holistic environmental standards based on Enterprise's Green Communities Criteria (Office of the Mayor 2005).

Other cities are integrating sustainable affordable housing strategies into broader efforts to reshape the urban fabric in environmentally sustainable and economically competitive ways. In January 2007 Washington, D.C., became the first city to require private developers to meet U.S. Green Building Council LEED standards for commercial projects and

Green Communities Criteria for housing.[5] The legislation applies to new construction and significant renovations of older buildings. Boston has shown how a commitment to sustainable affordable homes can enhance interagency cooperation and secure resources for affordable housing from new funding sources—both often elusive goals for local governments. Mayor Thomas M. Menino formed the city of Boston Green Affordable Housing Partnership, consisting of the Department of Neighborhood Development, Boston Housing Authority, Boston Redevelopment Authority, Boston Public Health Commission, the Mayor's Office, and the Environmental and Energy Services Cabinet. The partnership received a $2 million grant from the Massachusetts Technology Collaborative, Renewable Energy Trust, plus an additional $100,000 from an anonymous local donor, to provide outreach, training, and project management assistance to green affordable housing developers and photovoltaic installations to serve 200 affordable apartments.

Federal Support for Affordable Green Housing

The federal government's primary support for green housing has been through the Energy Star program, a joint initiative of the U.S. Department of Energy and the U.S. Environmental Protection Agency (EPA). Launched in 1992, Energy Star certifies products, equipment, and buildings—including homes—that meet verified levels of energy efficiency (www.energystar.gov). Energy Star homes are at least 15 percent more energy efficient than homes built to the 2004 International Residential Code and can include a variety of energy-efficient features, such as effective insulation, high performance windows, tight construction and ducts, efficient heating and cooling equipment, and Energy Star-qualified lighting and appliances. EPA reports that there are nearly 750,000 Energy Star homes, 200,000 of which earned the designation in 2006 alone. These homes will generate $180 million in annual savings for homeowners, according to EPA (EPA 2007). Homes of three stories or less can participate in the program; almost all to date have been market-rate homes. An Energy Star program for larger multifamily buildings that holds significant promise for affordable housing developments is being pilot tested.

Even though Energy Star is generally limited to energy efficiency, it has been an important contributor to green residential programs that have a broader focus. Many green residential programs reference Energy Star as part of their criteria. In addition, the home energy rating system for the Energy Star homes program has expanded the national infrastructure of professionals who are equipped to measure the energy performance of homes through duct leakage and blower door tests. That infrastructure has made it possible for programs such as Green

Communities and LEED for Homes to link national rating systems to quantifiable performance measurements.

The federal government has other areas where it could support affordable green housing policy and could, in addition, realize substantial cost savings. For example, HUD spends an estimated $4 billion a year on energy, more than 10 percent of its annual budget, for utility allowances in connection with rental assistance payments to low-income renters and indirect operating subsidies to public housing authorities. By instituting green energy requirements that could yield savings it would have more resources to contribute to affordable housing—a savings of just 5 percent a year over five years could generate $1 billion. In 2006 HUD provided a report to Congress outlining administrative and regulatory steps to reduce energy costs in public and assisted housing (HUD 2006).

In 2007, HUD announced a nationwide pilot program to encourage owners of multifamily properties to rehabilitate and operate their buildings using green principles. Through the initiative, HUD will cover almost all the costs apartment owners are otherwise required to pay for building improvements under certain HUD regulations when they refinance their properties if those improvements are environmentally sustainable.

The start of the 110th Congress in 2007 saw a surge of legislation to encourage green affordable housing. Leading members of the House of Representatives introduced proposals to require green criteria in large-scale public housing redevelopments; to create incentives for Fannie Mae and Freddie Mac to purchase mortgages on homes with environmental features; to ensure cities and states consider the extent to which affordable housing developments meet the Green Communities Criteria in awarding resources from a proposed national affordable housing trust fund; and to provide cities and states with new bond authority to finance green affordable housing and economic development projects. Each of these proposals advanced in the House of Representatives in 2007; stakeholders were optimistic about Senate consideration of them in 2008.

The Benefits of Green Affordable Housing

The most compelling reason for greening affordable housing lies in the potential benefits, ranging from healthier environments to lower costs for utilities and transportation, for low-income people. A growing body of research has shown that the built environment can have "profound, directly measurable" physical and mental health outcomes, "particularly adding to the burden of illness among ethnic minority populations and low-income communities. . . . Studies have shown that negative aspects of the built environment tend to interact with and magnify health disparities, compounding already distressing conditions" (Hood 2005). Green development can be seen as a public health strategy. "By using green building techniques to increase energy efficiency and environmental sustainability of new and renovated housing, the community at large may benefit from reduced exposure to emissions associated with burning fossil fuels and negative health impacts linked to smog, acid rain and air pollution" (Cohen 2006: 6).

Housing conditions in particular have long been seen as important factors influencing health. According to David E. Jacobs, research director of the National Center for Healthy Housing and former director of the U.S. Department of Housing and Urban Development, Office of Healthy Homes and Lead Hazard Control: "The physical structure of housing, together with the social and psychological aspects of home and the surrounding neighborhood are related to many key determinants of health. . . . Specific housing hazards include exposure to allergens that may cause or worsen asthma, lead-based paint hazards, mold and excess moisture, unintentional injury, pesticides, indoor air quality and others" (Jacobs 2005: 25).

Green building practices can address such housing problems, although researchers and public health professionals are only beginning to fully understand the interaction of specific building practices and health outcomes. Jacobs argues that "there is new evidence that housing interventions are indeed effective in reducing the onset and severity of asthma [and] there is similar evidence for other health outcomes . . . [but] considerably more research is needed to understand which interventions hold the greatest promise" (Jacobs 2005: 41). Similarly, Howell, Harris and Popkin (2005: 283) noted "suggestive evidence for a relationship between poor quality housing and the onset of asthma" and concluded that that "one major benefit of improving housing quality may well be the improved health status of children, because housing quality may have a pronounced effect on the onset and severity of asthma for the youngest children," but cautioned that "direct inferences about the relationship between housing quality and health are difficult to make."

While researchers remain cautious, many public health professionals and a growing number of affordable housing developers believe sufficient evidence exists to justify adoption of basic "healthy homes" practices to keep homes dry, clean, well ventilated, and free of pests, combustible products, and toxic materials (see Tohn 2006). Such practices are embedded to various degrees in leading green affordable housing programs.

The potential to provide financial benefits to low-income people through green affordable housing in the form of energy and water efficiency features is also important. Utility bills often impose a substantial financial hardship on low-income households, forcing many to make tradeoffs between heat or electricity and other basic necessities. In 2005 the National Energy Assistance Directors' Association issued the results of a nationwide study of more than 1,100 households that received assistance under the Low Income Home Energy Assistance Program (LIHEAP). The study documented the choices that LIHEAP recipients make when faced with unaffordable home energy bills. During the prior five years, 57 percent of nonelderly owners and 36 percent of nonelderly renters went without medical or dental care; 25 percent made a partial payment or missed a whole rent or mortgage payment; and 20 percent went without food for at least one day (National Energy Assistance Directors Association 2005: i-iv).

A recent study by New Ecology and the Tellus Institute found strong evidence of the financial benefits of green affordable housing for low-income residents over time. "For residents of affordable housing units, the lifecycle financial outcome is almost always positive, ranging from a [net present value] of −$140 to $59,861 per unit. In 14 of the 16 cases, owners/residents receive a net benefit from greening; in one case, there is no impact on the financial condition of residents, since they are not responsible for any of the utility costs; and in one case residents experience higher net costs from greening, though the project developer attributes this to anomalies in project design and resident demographics" (Bradshaw et al. 2005: 10).

Finally, green affordable housing programs that enhance mobility can provide substantial savings. Transportation costs consume a large share of low-income family incomes—according to the Surface Transportation Policy Project (STPP), families at the poverty level pay more than 40 percent of their income for transportation. Furthermore, STPP's study of 28 metropolitan areas found that families with incomes between $20,000 and $50,000 spend an average of 29 percent of their income on transportation and an average of 28 percent on housing. In the past, poorly planned development isolated low-income people in distressed areas distant from jobs (see McCann and Ewing 2003) (Figure 2).

The benefits of green affordable housing are not necessarily limited to low-income residents. Green rental apartments can generate operating cost savings and perform better over time for their owners and operators, suggesting that they could be more valuable real estate assets for their owners as well. While these benefits are to some extent speculative, initial research, discussed later in the essay, has yielded encouraging results.[6]

Figure 2. Trolley Square, a Green Communities development in Cambridge, Massachusetts, has walkable access to mass transit and a community park as well as energy and water conservation features in the building and on the surrounding site. ©2007 Lloyd Wolf.

Issues in Green Affordable Housing

One of the primary barriers to broader adoption of green building among affordable housing developers and policymakers has been concern about increased cost. Generally, there is a direct correlation in affordable housing between higher costs and either fewer affordable units or lesser affordability—a tradeoff most affordable housing developers and policymakers are unwilling to make (in fact, it is common for affordable housing subsidy programs to place limits on overall construction costs, as well as subsidy allocations, for this reason). There is, however, increasing evidence that affordable housing can achieve significant levels of environmental performance on a cost-effective basis.

The aforementioned analysis looked at 16 green affordable developments around the country. The average "green premium" was only 2.4 percent. These incremental costs were largely due to increased construction, as opposed to design, costs (Bradshaw et al. 2005: 10). Early evaluation results by Enterprise of Green Communities developments generally show a similarly small average development cost increase.

A central tenet of sustainable development generally is that costs on a longer-term or "life-cycle" basis are lower as a result of green design and construction practices and more than offset any higher up-front costs. There is substantial evidence for this proposition for larger nonresidential buildings. The definitive study on costs and financial benefits of green building, which analyzed 33 LEED-registered office and educational buildings, found the average development cost premium to be slightly less than 2 percent of total development cost. The report found that the financial benefits associated with lower energy, waste, water, environmental, operations and maintenance costs, plus increased productivity and health, were 10 times the additional cost (Kats 2003: v).

The same is likely true with respect to holistically green affordable housing developments and homes. The cost/benefit analysis by New Ecology and the Tellus Institute found that

From a life-cycle net present value perspective, the case studies show that the benefits of green affordable housing are real and, in some cases, substantial. In virtually all the cases, energy and water utility costs are lower than their conventional counterparts. In many cases, decreased operating expenditures alone more than pay for the incremental initial investment in greening the project in present value terms. The use of more durable materials and equipment in several of the case study projects result in reduced replacement costs and provide additional life-cycle financial benefits. Moreover, the value of improved comfort and health for residents, as well as reduced environmental impacts, is substantial, although not captured quantitatively in our analyses. (Bradshaw et al. 2005: 10)

The cost issue is particularly complex for affordable housing because much of the stock is in multifamily rental properties whose developer (which generally would bear any additional costs for greening the building) is often not the owner/operator of the property (and so would not realize the financial benefits of the green features). The problem may persist even when the owner makes green improvements, since most of the benefits will accrue to tenants, who typically have little involvement in the green upgrades. The New Ecology/Tellus Institute study found that in 5 of the 16 cases, developers received net benefits from greening; in 2 cases greening the project had no net financial effect on the developers, while in 9 cases the developers experienced net losses relative to investing in comparable conventional projects.

In market-rate housing, developers can pass on additional development costs to tenants and buyers. Affordable housing almost always has restricted rents, required by public funding programs, so higher developments costs generally must be absorbed by the developer's profit or building reserves.

Part of the solution in affordable housing is found in the policy of low-income rental assistance programs that typically provide for a "utility allowance" as part of the total rent owners can charge low-income tenants, generally no more than 30 percent of monthly income. When a public housing authority or private owner pays for utilities directly, the assisted household pays the 30 percent amount. When a household pays a utility company directly, the household receives a reduction in rent (the utility allowance) to cover the expected costs of consuming a reasonable amount of utilities. Thus to the extent utility bills are reduced, and the utility allowance lowered through green features, owners have the opportunity to capture additional cash flow and reinvest it in the property, pass it through to tenants, or both.[7]

An important part of the solution is also educating developers that certain green improvements may actually have lower first costs than conventional construction practices and could help compensate for any incrementally higher costs associated with other green features in the project. Properly sized HVAC systems may be smaller and less expensive, advanced framing may use less lumber, and recycling construction waste may reduce tipping fees, just to cite three examples. (More broadly, denser development may save localities in infrastructure costs.)

Another issue in sustainable affordable housing is an uneven capacity among developers to successfully incorporate holistic green elements into a project on a cost-effective basis, especially in areas where the community-based affordable housing infrastructure itself is comparatively weak. Sustainability remains an unfamiliar—although often appealing—concept for many affordable housing developers.

Encouragingly, a number of grassroots affordable housing developers have gained the experience to build highly sustainable developments at little or no higher cost; their developments show what is possible. And programs such as Green Communities (see Figure 3) that combine technical assistance with modest financial incentives have shown promise to enhance green building capacity among affordable housing developers. More resources are needed to provide education, training, and technical assistance to these organizations, as well as the contractors, engineers, and architects that are on their development teams.

In addition, certain kinds of affordable housing developments can pose special challenges for integrating sustainable practices. Rehabilitation of existing buildings, an inherently sustainable activity itself and the bedrock of community development in many neighborhoods, requires a careful cost-benefit analysis and energy modeling to determine the most cost-effective green improvements. Ensuring that affordable housing rehabilitation developments, both single-family houses and multi-unit apartments, are as sustainable as practical, given budgetary, building, and siting constraints, is an emerging area of focus for green affordable housing stakeholders.

Figure 3. Spring Terrace, a Green Communities development in Austin, Texas, consists of 140 homes in a renovated motel for extremely low-income and formerly homeless families. The development integrates solar energy, rainwater harvesting, and healthy building materials. Foundation Communities.

Achieving smart and sustainable sites that facilitate walking and transit access and ensure environmentally responsible (while contextually appropriate) densities is also a challenge in smaller towns and rural communities, where lack of existing infrastructure or restrictive zoning policies may be beyond developers' abilities to change.

Another issue is research. More data are needed on the development costs, financial benefits, long-term performance, and health impacts of green affordable housing. As more green affordable developments come on line, there will be rich opportunities to carry out these kinds of evaluations and they must be a high priority for green building stakeholders. Data from such research would have a number of worthwhile applications, such as enabling organizations supporting green affordable housing to develop more effective resources for developers and ensuring that mayors and other policymakers committed to supporting sustainable affordable homes can justify their decisions and expand their leadership.

Performance data, as well as information on developer experience, are also critical to changing the policies and products of mainstream financial institutions, which ultimately may have the greatest potential to accelerate a market transformation to make sustainability the mainstream in affordable housing. If banks were willing, based on property appraisals and other data, to provide lower-cost loans or more flexible underwriting to green residential developments based on their greater durability and superior performance compared to conventional properties, it would likely have powerful effects throughout the affordable housing industry.

There are signs that some banks are thinking along these lines. A number of large banks have made broad-based environmental commitments. As of July 2007, more than 50 banks had adopted the Equator Principles for managing environmental and social issues in project finance, and it is estimated that the principles now cover approximately 80 percent of global project lending.[8] Among the banks that have adopted the principles are Bank of America, Citigroup, HSBC, and Wells Fargo.

A few banks have begun to pilot efforts to incorporate environmental priorities into their domestic community reinvestment activities. In March 2007 Bank of America announced a $20 billion commitment to environmentally focused lending and investing that broadly referenced several housing initiatives, including a "green mortgage program" and a commitment to support green affordable housing through the Bank of American Foundation. Wells Fargo has a "Green Equity Equivalent Investments" product that provides capital to nonprofit organizations that engage in environmentally responsible practices in low-to-moderate income communities, such as sustainable affordable housing development, including affordable housing on transportation corridors or with access to public transportation. Los Alamos National Bank has set aside $50 million for "EcoSmart" land and home loans. These loans will offer significantly lower costs to builders and developers that embrace LEED concepts and standards. The bank also set aside another $10 million in consumer loan funds with lower borrowing costs for the purchase and installation of energy saving cars, appliances, fixtures, and equipment. The bank plans to fulfill this $60 million dollar commitment in Eco-Smart lending in the next two years.

Another potentially powerful factor that could convince banks to provide more favorable terms and conditions to green affordable developments is evidence that the properties are worth more than conventional residences over time; this could be especially important for multifamily properties, whose owners often choose to sell their interests at a certain point in the future. There is not yet enough experience to test the premise that green affordable homes and developments are more valuable real estate assets. There are however indications that sustainable commercial and office buildings—of which more have been in operation for longer periods—may be more valuable than nongreen buildings. For example, a recent survey by Turner Construction found that 84 percent of executives involved with green building believe that green construction yields higher property values. Furthermore, 75 percent of those executives said their green properties earned a higher return on investment than non-green buildings (Turner Construction 2004: 1).

The UK-based Royal Institution of Chartered Surveyors (RICS), which represents and promotes the work of 110,000 property professionals in 120 countries, released a study of greener buildings that reveals what the study characterized as a "a clear link between the market value of real estate and its environmental friendliness." The RICS study found that green buildings can earn higher rents and prices, attract tenants and buyers more quickly, cut tenant turnover, cost less to operate and maintain, and benefit occupants. The study also found that green buildings can attract subsidies that increase energy efficiency, improve business productivity for occupants and retain tenants, and generate cost savings that are "more than the underlying asset cost or value" (RICS 2005: 3).

Finally, public polices must evolve to support more sustainable affordable housing. Notwithstanding the encouraging progress noted earlier in many states and some cities, it is too often the case that housing programs, zoning policies, and building codes impede the development of healthier, more energy efficient affordable homes for low-income people. The aforementioned cost caps imposed by many affordable housing programs, for example, should be reconsidered in cases where construction expenditures make a development longer lasting and less expensive to operate, reducing the likelihood that it will need future infusions of public funds. Cities and towns should use zoning as a tool to generate mixed-income development at appropriate densities near transit, parks, and services. Local building codes, often initially established to promote public health, should be revised when it is clear they are impeding healthier building practices.

A Vision for Greener Homes in Greener Cities

Cities around the country are developing broad-based plans for reducing their carbon emissions, creating healthier environments, and improving the quality of life for their citizens. A commitment to sustainable affordable homes should be a central component of any sustainable city effort.

Affordable housing at the local level often struggles to receive sufficient funding and encounters neighborhood opposition by residents who fear it will decrease their quality of life. Ensuring that affordable housing is sustainably developed and maintained could help change those realities. Imagine green affordable homes and developments that capture and filter stormwater; actively or passively use solar energy; reuse construction waste or use materials in the construction process that could be deconstructed and reused in the future; employ affordable technologies to reduce water and energy consumption in the home while retaining resident comfort; and encourage native plants that require little or no irrigation and do not invade other species, contributing to a sense of place and historical context. The small but rapidly growing number of green affordable housing developments shows that affordable housing can incorporate these features on a cost effective basis.

Truly sustainable cities should be able to reduce their capital budget needs over time and reallocate the savings to meeting pressing needs, including the construction or rehabilitation of affordable housing. (One small, tangible example: Denver saves an estimated $800,000 a year from using more energy efficient traffic lights and dedicates part of the savings homeless assistance.) By ensuring that the city's affordable housing is green, further savings and other health and environmental benefits become part of the feedback loop of sustainability.

In the end, the strongest reason for cities to adopt green affordable housing and sustainability as an overarching priority more broadly is to improve life for their residents. Affordable housing should be green as part of a healthy city infrastructure that includes both the human and the physical capital side. James Rouse, the visionary planner, developer, and founder of Enterprise, believed that cities should be gardens to grow people. Cities have the opportunity to lead in the effort to make green building and affordable housing one and the same as part of broader strategies to become such gardens. Now is the time for cities to seize that opportunity.

References

Bradshaw, William et al. 2005. *The Costs and Benefits of Green Affordable Housing.* Boston: New Ecology.

Clinton, Bill. 2005. Remarks by President William J. Clinton at the United Nations Climate Change Conference, Palais des Congrès, Montréal, Québec, Canada, December 8.

Cohen, Rebecca. 2007. *The Positive Impacts of Affordable Housing on Health: A Research Summary.* Washington, D.C.: Center for Housing Policy and Enterprise.

"Frequently Asked Questions: LEED for Homes." U.S. Green Building Council. www.usgbc.org.

"Green Building Comes Home." 2004. *Building Design and Construction*. Supplement: Progress Report on Sustainability. November.

Hood, Ernie. 2005. "Dwelling Disparities: How Poor Housing Leads to Poor Health." *Environmental Health Perspectives* (May).

Howell, Embry M., Laura E. Harris, and Susan J. Popkin. 2005. "The Health Status of HOPE VI Public Housing Residents." *Journal of Health Care for the Poor and Underserved* 16.

Jacobs, David E. 2005. "Housing and Health: Challenges and Opportunities." Keynote Address, Proceedings of the 2nd WHO International Housing and Health Symposium, WHO European Centre for Environment and Health (Bonn Office), Noise and Housing Unit, Bonn Germany, September 29–October 1, 2004.

Kats, Greg. 2003. *The Costs and Financial Benefits of Green Buildings: A Report to California's Sustainable Building Task Force*. Washington, D.C.: Capital E.

McCann, Barbara, and Reid Ewing. 2003. *Measuring the Health Effects of Sprawl: A National Analysis of Physical Activity, Obesity, and Chronic Disease*. Washington, D.C.: Smart Growth American and Surface Transportation Policy Project.

National Energy Assistance Directors Association. 2005. *2005 National Energy Assistance Survey*. Washington, D.C.: National Energy Assistance Directors Association.

Office of Housing, City of Seattle. 2002. *SeaGreen: Greening Seattle's Affordable Housing*. Seattle: Office of Housing.

Office of the Mayor, City and County of San Francisco. 2005. "San Francisco Becomes First City in the Country to Adopt Green Building Standards." Press release, August 2.

Royal Institution of Chartered Surveyors. 2005. *Green Value: Green Buildings, Growing Assets*. London: Royal Institution of Chartered Surveyors.

Tassos, James. 2006. *An Even Greener Plan for Affordable Housing*. Columbia, Md.: Enterprise Community Partners.

Tohn, Ellen. 2006. *Building Guidance for Healthy Homes*. Rev. ed. Dorchester, Mass.: Asthma Regional Council of New England.

Turner Construction. 2004. "Turner Green Building Market Barometer." Sacramento, Calif.: Turner Construction.

U.S. Department of Housing and Urban Development (HUD). 2006. *Promoting Energy Efficiency at HUD in a Time of Change: Report to Congress*. Washington, D.C.: U.S. Department of Housing and Urban Development.

———. 2007. *Affordable Housing Needs 2005: Report to Congress*. Washington, D.C.: U.S. Department of Housing and Urban Development).

U.S. Environmental Protection Agency (EPA). 2007. Press release, July 12.

Wallace, Nicole. 2006. "Building Green." *Chronicle of Philanthropy* (October 26).

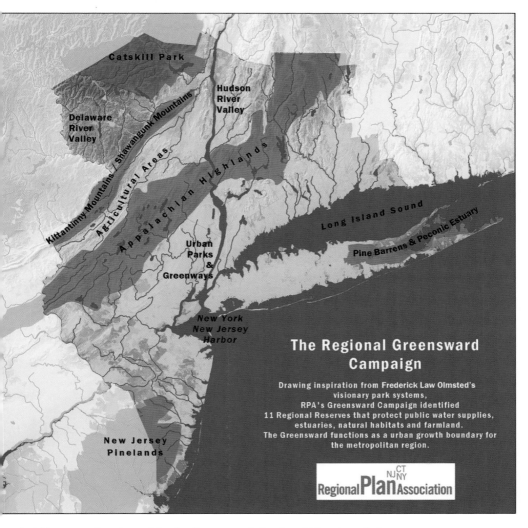

Plate 1. Tri-state region framed by the Greensward. Regional Plan Association.

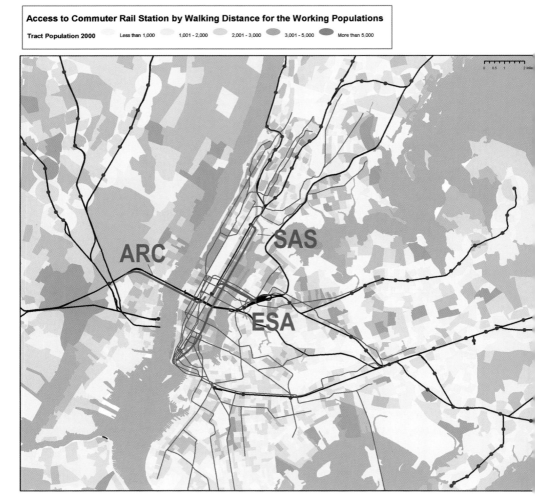

Plate 2. Proposed major transit programs in the New York Metropolitan Area. Regional Plan Association.

Plate 3. Artist's conception of the "Green Ribbon" linking the diverse neighborhoods of Newark, New Jersey, with each other and the Passaic River. Regional Plan Association and Porto Folio, Inc.

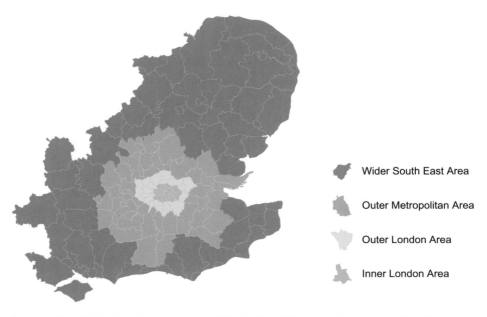

Plate 4. The Wider South East region of the United Kingdom. Greater London Authority.

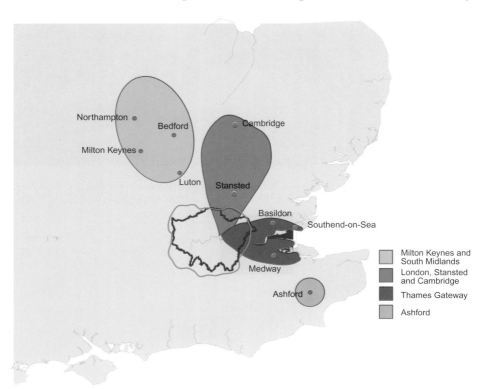

Plate 5. The four areas designated as major growth points in the Wider South East. Greater London Authority.

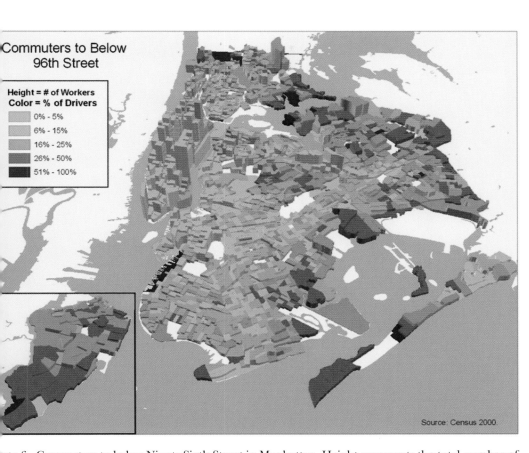

ate 6. Commuters to below Ninety-Sixth Street in Manhattan. Height represents the total number of
ıb-bound commuters. Color represents the percentage of workers who drove alone; darker means a
gher percentage of drivers, lighter means more people using transit. U.S. Census CTPP and New
ırk City Office of Long-Term Planning and Sustainability.

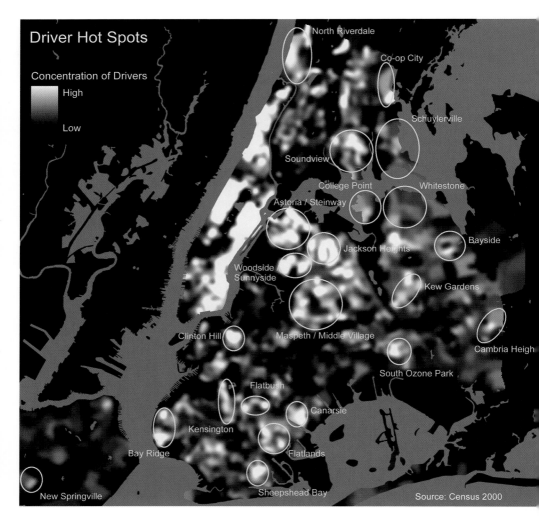

Plate 7. Concentrations of Manhattan-bound drivers. U.S. Census CTPP and New York City Office of Long-term Planning and Sustainability.

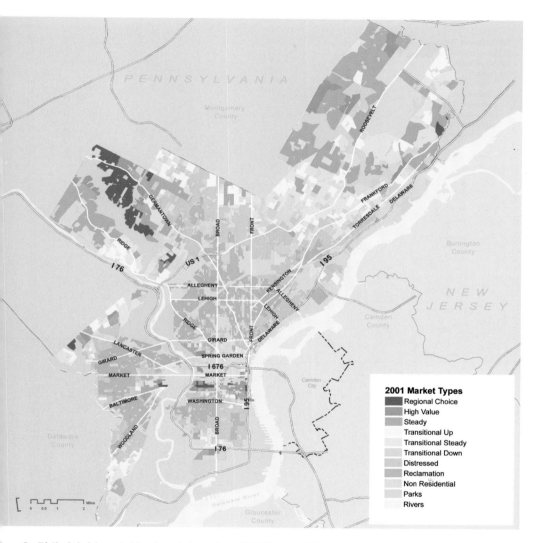

2001 Market Types
- Regional Choice
- High Value
- Steady
- Transitional Up
- Transitional Steady
- Transitional Down
- Distressed
- Reclamation
- Non Residential
- Parks
- Rivers

Plate 8. Philadelphia neighborhoods based on NTI Market Value Analysis. The Reinvestment Fund.

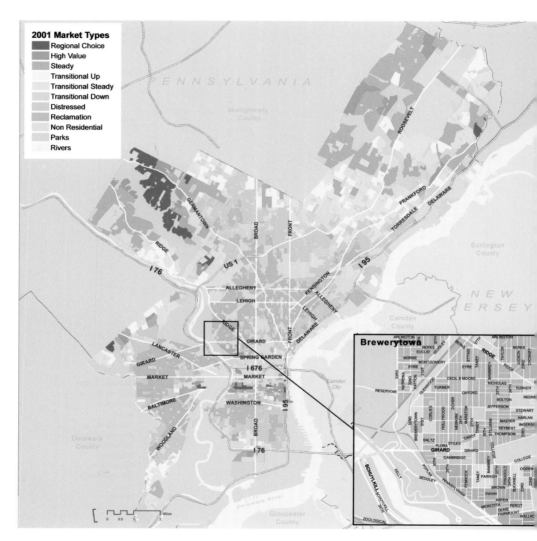

Plate 9. Philadelphia cluster analysis with Brewerytown highlighted. The Reinvestment Fund.

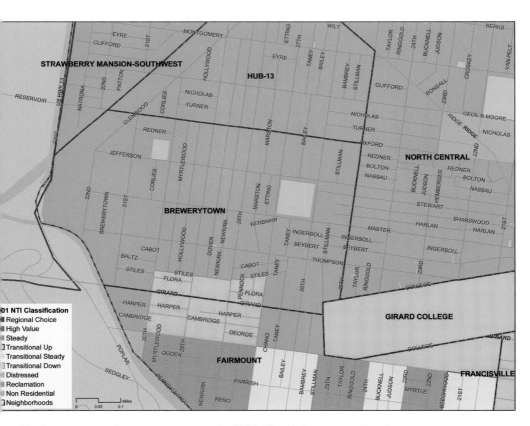

Plate 10. Brewerytown cluster arrangement in 2001. The Reinvestment Fund.

Plate 11. Brewerytown cluster arrangement in 2003. The Reinvestment Fund.

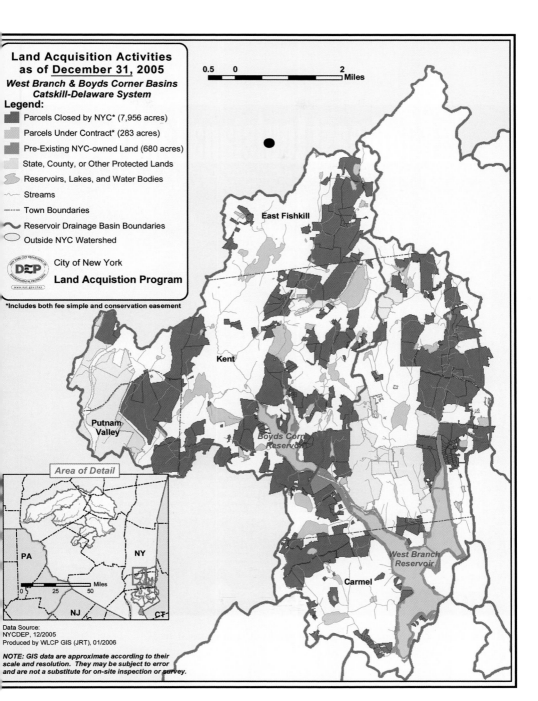

Plate 12. New York City watershed, 2005. New York City Department of Environmental Protection.

Southeast Louisiana Land Loss

*Historical and Projected Land Loss in the Deltaic Plain

Lake Pontchartrain

New Orleans

Lake Borgne

Lake Salvador

Breton Sound

Houma

Atchafalaya Bay

Barataria Bay

Terrebonne Bay

Port Fourchon

Gulf of Mexico

Land Loss 1932- 2050

* The Land Loss between 1932-2000 is historical. The Land Loss between 2000-2050 is projected based on historical trending if no further action is taken as documented in the "Historical and Projected Coastal Louisiana Land Changes: 1978-2050" (www.Lacoast.gov/LandLoss/NewHistoricalland.pdf)

0   7.5   15   22.5   30
Kilometers

7   0   7   14   21   28
Miles

Coastal Louisiana has lost an average of 34 square miles of land, primarily marsh, per year for the last 50 years. From 1932 to 2000, coastal Louisiana lost 1,900 square miles of land, roughly an area the size of the state of Delaware. If nothing more is done to stop this land loss, Louisiana could potentially lose approximately 700 additional square miles of land, or an area about equal to the size of the greater Washington D.C.- Baltimore area, in the next 50 years.

N

For more information about the land loss analysis or to see an animated time series of wetland change, visit www.LaCoast.gov/LandLoss

Data Sources:
1932-1956 Land Change Analysis
U.S. Army Corps of Engineers, New Orleans

1956-1990 Land Change Analysis
1978-2050 Land Change Analysis
U.S. Department of the Interior
U.S. Geological Survey
National Wetlands Research Center
Lafayette, LA

Prepared by:
U.S. Department of the Interior
U.S. Geological Survey
National Wetlands Research Center
Lafayette, LA

Map ID: USGS-NWRC 2005-16-0001
Map Date: December 6, 2004

BTNEP   USGS
science for a changing world

Plate 13. Historical and projected land loss in Louisiana's coastal areas.

Largest 50 US Cities Ranked According to Sustainability Factors

#	City	Score
1.	Portland, OR	85.08
2.	San Francisco	81.82
3.	Seattle	79.64
4.	Chicago	70.64
5.	Oakland	69.18
6.	New York City	68.20
7.	Boston	68.18
8.	Philadelphia	67.28
9.	Denver	66.72
10.	Minneapolis	66.60
11.	Baltimore	64.78
12.	Washington, DC	63.14
13.	Sacramento	62.64
14.	Austin	62.00
15.	Honolulu	61.42
16.	Milwaukee	60.42
17.	San Diego	57.18
18.	Kansas City, MO	56.64
19.	Albuquerque, NM	56.10
20.	Tucson, AZ	55.86
21.	San Antonio	54.60
22.	Phoenix	54.50
23.	San Jose	54.28
24.	Dallas	54.58
25.	Los Angeles	52.28
26.	Colorado Springs	51.36
27.	Las Vegas	50.24
28.	Cleveland	50.10
29.	Miami	50.00
30.	Long Beach	49.46
31.	El Paso	49.10
32.	New Orleans**	49.04
33.	Fresno, CA	48.96
34.	Charlotte, NC	47.58
35.	Louisville, KY	47.14
36.	Jacksonville, FL	46.80
37.	Omaha	46.56
38.	Atlanta	45.20
39.	Houston	44.68
40.	Tulsa, OK	43.74
41.	Arlington, TX	41.80
42.	Nashville, TN	40.70
43.	Detroit*	40.30
43.	Memphis*	40.30
45.	Indianapolis	38.40
46.	Fort Worth	37.50
47.	Mesa, AZ	36.70
48.	Virginia Beach, VA	34.00
49.	Oklahoma City	32.92
50.	Columbus, OH	32.50

1-10: Sustainability Leader
11-19: Sustainability Advances
20-29: Mixed Results
30-39: Sustainability Challenged
40-50: Sustainability in Danger
* denotes tie
** reflects pre-Katrina data

Plate 14. City rankings according to SustainLane's sustainability index. SustainLane.

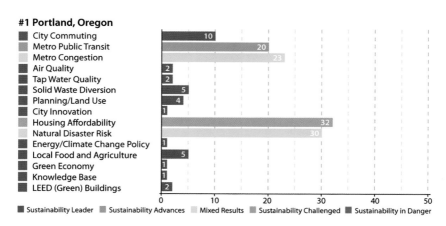

#1 Portland, Oregon

City Commuting	10
Metro Public Transit	20
Metro Congestion	23
Air Quality	2
Tap Water Quality	2
Solid Waste Diversion	5
Planning/Land Use	4
City Innovation	1
Housing Affordability	32
Natural Disaster Risk	30
Energy/Climate Change Policy	1
Local Food and Agriculture	5
Green Economy	1
Knowledge Base	1
LEED (Green) Buildings	2

■ Sustainability Leader   ■ Sustainability Advances   ■ Mixed Results   ■ Sustainability Challenged   ■ Sustainability in Danger

Plate 15. Portland, Oregon, was the top-ranked sustainable city according to SustainLane's 2006 sustainability index. SustainLane.

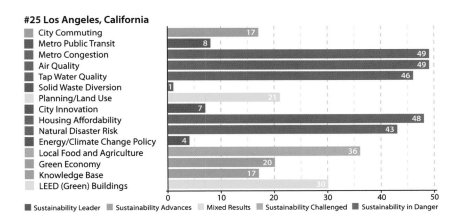

#25 Los Angeles, California

	Value
City Commuting	17
Metro Public Transit	8
Metro Congestion	49
Air Quality	49
Tap Water Quality	46
Solid Waste Diversion	1
Planning/Land Use	21
City Innovation	7
Housing Affordability	48
Natural Disaster Risk	43
Energy/Climate Change Policy	4
Local Food and Agriculture	36
Green Economy	20
Knowledge Base	17
LEED (Green) Buildings	30

■ Sustainability Leader ■ Sustainability Advances Mixed Results ■ Sustainability Challenged ■ Sustainability in Danger

Plate 16. Although it scored high in public transit and energy/climate change policy, Los Angeles had significant air and tap water quality challenges in 2006, which helped lower its sustainability ranking. SustainLane.

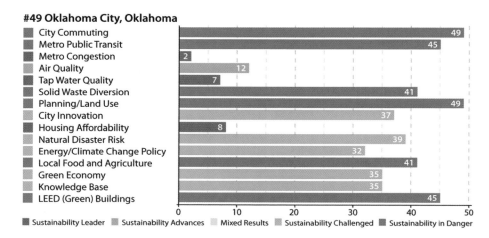

#49 Oklahoma City, Oklahoma

	Value
City Commuting	49
Metro Public Transit	45
Metro Congestion	2
Air Quality	12
Tap Water Quality	7
Solid Waste Diversion	41
Planning/Land Use	49
City Innovation	37
Housing Affordability	8
Natural Disaster Risk	39
Energy/Climate Change Policy	32
Local Food and Agriculture	41
Green Economy	35
Knowledge Base	35
LEED (Green) Buildings	45

0   10   20   30   40   50

■ Sustainability Leader   ■ Sustainability Advances   ■ Mixed Results   ■ Sustainability Challenged   ■ Sustainability in Danger

Plate 17. Oklahoma City ranked near the bottom in the 2006 sustainable city rankings. Transportation issues—especially lack of mass transit usage—lowered the ratings. SustainLane.

Part II
Getting Greening Done

Urban Stream Restoration: Recovering Ecological Services in Degraded Watersheds

RUTHERFORD H. PLATT, TIMOTHY BEATLEY, SARAH MICHAELS, NANCY GOUCHER, AND BETH FENSTERMACHER

The Ecological Cities Project, based at the University of Massachusetts, Amherst, recently completed a three-year reconnaissance study entitled "Urban Watershed Revitalization in the U.S.: Comparative Regional Experience in Multi-Objective Management."[1] The study hypothesized that urban communities (neighborhoods, cities, regions) are beginning to recognize and restore "ecological services" rather than ignore or seek to replace them through technology. The researchers conducted case studies of regional experiences in pursuing multiple environmental, social, and economic goals at the urban watershed scale. Five overarching questions guided their research: (1) How are urban watersheds organized? (2) How are policy issues and management goals identified? (3) What is the role of science and scientists in watershed restoration? (4) What watershed management strategies are used? (5) How do federal/state laws influence management of urban watersheds? The discussion that follows summarizes the findings of three case studies that together represent different scales and government approaches to urban watershed revitalization: the Anacostia River in the Washington, D.C., area, Nine Mile Run in Pittsburgh, and Laurel Creek in Waterloo, Ontario.

The Anacostia: Beltway River Politics[2]

In the past, the Anacostia, often called Washington, D.C.'s "other river," was largely ignored by local residents and government leaders, even though it flows only 2,000 feet from the U.S. Capitol building. Like most urban river systems, the Anacostia watershed has suffered from development pressures. Expanding population, increased pollution, and unsustainable land management practices have all taken their toll on this once productive ecosystem. Recently the river has begun to show signs of a comeback as policymakers at the city, county, and state levels have begun to address the environmental problems of the river and its watershed. While still nascent, these restoration activities collectively offer new hope that the Anacostia will emerge as an inviting and multifunctional regional resource.

The Anacostia River Watershed drains 176 square miles, of which 87 percent is shared by Montgomery and Prince George's Counties in Maryland, with the remainder downstream in the District of Columbia. Lying entirely in metropolitan Washington, it is densely developed and populated with over 800,000 residents. Crisscrossed by many highways, including Interstate 95 and the Capital Beltway, and by commuter and mainline railways, about 70 percent of its land surface was developed by 2000 (Figure 1).

The Anacostia watershed contains the most economically distressed areas in the entire metropolitan region. According to the Brookings Institution (1999), the district and its suburbs are starkly divided along lines of income and race. Additional data from the 2000 census indicate that Washington, D.C., and Prince George's County account for 56 percent of the region's population living below the poverty line. In addition, these two jurisdictions are home to nearly 80 percent of the region's welfare caseloads. They are also home to a majority of the region's African American population, of whom approximately 70 percent live either in the district or in Prince George's County (Brookings Institution 1999). While poor neighborhoods line both banks of the river in Washington, upstream in Maryland there is a relatively low incidence of poverty.

Washington is a profoundly divided city where opportunities and life circumstances vary dramatically depending on one's neighborhood and socioeconomic status. The Anacostia River is a rough approximation of the social and economic dividing line between the affluence of the Northwest and the poverty and despair of the Southeast. Revitalizing the Anacostia may help to overcome some of the social and economic fractures that exist in this city.

Years of extensive urbanization throughout the watershed left it highly degraded. Unmanaged development resulted in habitat loss, erosion, sedimentation, destruction of wetlands, channelization, and toxic pollution. These impairments eliminated such recreational opportunities as swimming, fishing, and boating and severed most ties between the river and its increasingly dilapidated communities and waterfront areas.

The watershed consists of three main subdrainage areas: the Northeast Branch, the Northwest Branch, and the tidal river basin. The two

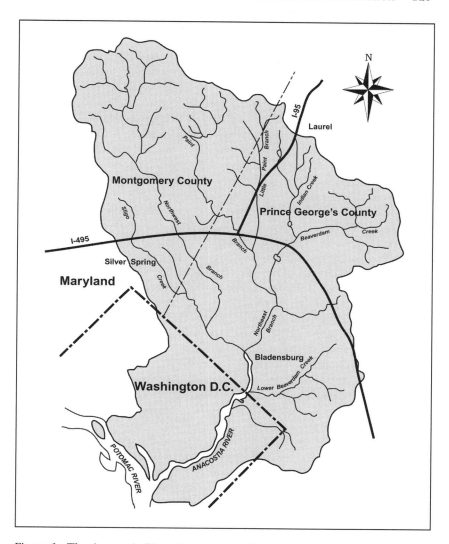

Figure 1. The Anacostia River Watershed in Maryland and the District of
Columbia. Adapted from http://anacostiaws.org.

branches converge at Bladensburg near the District border to form the
main stem of the Anacostia River. The latter flows 8.4 miles through the
Northeast part of Washington to its mouth at Hains Point on the Potomac River. With a very shallow gradient and tidal action from the Poto-

mac, the lower Anacostia flows very gradually. The river's sluggishness retards flushing of pollutants. In essence, it acts as a shallow lake, collecting and trapping sediment that contains extensive pollutants and toxins.

The look, feel, and condition of the Anacostia vary greatly depending on which reach is considered. The shorelines within the District of Columbia are highly engineered with many floodwalls and storm outfalls. In Southwest Washington the riverfront is inaccessible due to the presence of the Washington Navy Yard, the Anacostia Freeway, the National Arboretum (except for visitors), and a new baseball stadium now under construction for the Washington Nationals. Upstream in Prince George's and Montgomery Counties, the river and its tributaries retain a somewhat more natural appearance.

Concrete and other impervious land surfaces cover about half the watershed. Urban development has heavily altered the river's ecology and natural conditions. Dredging or filling fringing wetlands and marshes and cutting forests and natural habitats have diminished the watershed dramatically. Only 25 percent of the watershed's land area is still forested. Most of the cover that remains is highly fragmented except for several thousand acres of forest in the Beaverdam Creek subwatershed in eastern Prince George's County. Wetlands comprise only 3 percent (3,200 acres) of the watershed's land area. According to the Anacostia Watershed Network, in the past 300 years agricultural and urban development have destroyed an estimated 4,000 acres of nontidal wetlands and 2,500 acres of tidal wetlands. Currently, only 180 acres of tidal wetlands remain, a 90 percent loss of the total original acreage.

The Anacostia is one of the ten most polluted rivers in the country (www.nrdc.org/water/pollution/fanacost.asp). Every year it conveys an estimated 20,000 tons of trash downstream. Annually, it receives more than 2 billion gallons of stormwater and sewage discharged from Washington's antiquated combined sewer overflows (CSOs), yielding fecal coliform counts up to 21 times the federal limit (Fahrenthold 2007). Industrial activities, institutions, the Washington Navy Yard (designated as a Superfund site by the U.S. Environmental Protection Agency), Washington Gas and Electric, St. Elizabeth's Hospital, and the Barney Circle landfill are other sources of pollution. (Ironically, as this heavily polluted river flows in the shadow of the Capitol, federal properties contribute 18 percent of the river's runoff; NRDC n.d.) Upstream pollution sources in Maryland come from broken pipes, illegal sewer connections, and nonpoint runoff from street drains and parking lots. Fecal coliform counts by the Anacostia Watershed Society often show higher amounts at Bladensburg, Maryland, than anywhere downstream in the District (Forgey 2004: C4).

Sediments in the Anacostia have played a role in trapping a number of different toxic contaminants in the river. Polychlorinated biphenyls (PCBs), pesticides, herbicides, and heavy metals typically cling to particulate matter suspended in the water and can be ingested by fish and other aquatic organisms. Several studies of the tidal river have detected harmful levels of PCBs, DDT, chlordane, and trace metals. In 1995, these findings prompted the Metropolitan Washington Council of Governments Chesapeake Bay Program to name the Anacostia River one of three sites in the Chesapeake Bay watershed that poses "significant risks to aquatic life" (MWCOG 1998).

STAKEHOLDERS IN THE WATERSHED CLEANUP

For much of the twentieth century, few recognized the Anacostia River's economic, recreational, and ecological values. Those who lived within its watershed had neither the political nor the economic influence to effect any changes. Residents of more affluent regions on the western side of the city had little incentive to take any action since they rarely ventured into Southeast Washington or Prince George's County. While the Potomac River experienced a major rebirth as a recreational and an economic engine for the region, the Anacostia languished on the impoverished eastern side of the city.

In the early 1980s, area environmental groups and local governments began to recognize the connection between the quality of the Anacostia watershed and the health of local and downstream communities. Grassroots support for a large-scale restoration effort gradually began to spread among local government representatives. Today, several intergovernmental and public-private arrangements address various aspects of upgrading the Anacostia River and its watershed.

The leading intergovernmental institution, the Anacostia Watershed Restoration Committee (AWRC), established in 1987 by the Anacostia Watershed Restoration Agreement, is a joint effort of the state of Maryland, the Maryland counties of Montgomery and Prince George, and the District of Columbia, which are equal partners in efforts to reinvigorate the watershed. The federal government also has representatives on the AWRC, including the Army Corps of Engineers, the Environmental Protection Agency, and the National Park Service (as the largest single landholder in the watershed). The Metropolitan Washington Council of Governments (MWCOG) coordinates the activities of the ARWC.

AWRC plans and coordinates watershed restoration projects to be implemented by its member agencies and units of government. By 1990, the AWRC had identified 207 stormwater retrofit, stream restoration, wetland creation, and riparian reforestation projects within the watershed (MWCOG 1998). In 1991, the committee adopted a "Six-Point

Action Plan for Restoring the Anacostia River" as a blueprint for action over the next two decades (Table 1).

Also active in restoration efforts is the Anacostia Watershed Toxics Alliance (AWTA), a public-private partnership created in 1999 to focus and coordinate cleanup efforts along the river. Its 25 member organizations encompass key federal and state agencies, including the members of the AWRC. "By pooling available fiscal and technical resources, AWTA has been successful in developing a watershed based approach to address the problem of contaminated sediments" (EPA 2003). AWTA's program focuses on developing a "comprehensive contaminated sediment management strategy" to guide future cleanup and restoration work. As of early 2007, the Anacostia still did not have a comprehensive basin-wide cleanup plan.

The Anacostia Watershed Society (AWS) is a key nongovernmental advocate for a cleaner, healthier Anacostia. Formed by Robert Boone in 1989, its efforts involve wetlands restoration projects, tree planting, water quality monitoring and flagging, debris removal, community outreach, and watershed education. AWS provides some of the glue and a good bit of the vision for managing the larger watershed, working with many different groups and serving as an umbrella for smaller organiza-

TABLE 1. SIX-POINT ACTION PLAN AND INDICATORS AND TARGETS FOR ANACOSTIA RIVER

Goal 1: Dramatically reduce pollutant loads such as sediments, toxics, CSOs, other nonpoint inputs, and trash delivered to the tidal river and its tributaries in order to meet water quality standards and goals.

Goal 2: Protect and restore the ecological integrity of the Anacostia River and its streams to embrace aquatic diversity, increase recreational use, and provide for a quality urban fishery.

Goal 3: Restore the natural range of resident and anadromous fish to historical limits.

Goal 4: Increase the natural filtering capacity and habitat diversity of the watershed by sharply increasing the acreage and quality of tidal and non-tidal wetlands.

Goal 5: Protect and expand forest cover throughout the watershed and create a continuous riparian forest buffer adjacent to its streams, wetlands, and rivers.

Goal 6: Increase citizen and private business awareness of their vital role in both the cleanup and economic revitalization of the watershed, and increase volunteer and public-private partnership participation in watershed restoration activities.

Source: AWRC (2001).

tions. The society, moreover, sees its mission, in part, as promoting a new code or creed for the watershed.

AWS has energized an extensive network of volunteers, estimated to number over 41,000 people, since the organization's founding in 1989. The volunteers participate in activities ranging from cleanups to river tours. A special focus is on involving young people in AWS projects and programs. Engaging children, Boone argues, not only changes their outlook on the river but also fundamentally redirects young lives

Through its volunteers, AWS has planted more than 11,000 trees, stenciled more than 1,100 storm drains, and removed 500 tons of trash and 11,000 tires from the river. Its annual paddleboat regatta and weekly canoe tours have introduced thousands of people to the river and its varied environmental conditions and problems. Some 5,500 school children have participated in the Watershed Explorer River Habitat education programs (www.anacostiaws.org).

AWS has also engaged in environmental litigation, using pro bono legal services from local law firms. It sued the D.C. Water and Sewer Authority (WASA) to expedite the construction of a stormwater detention and treatment project known as the Long-Term Control Plan. Its other lawsuits have addressed specific projects affecting the river. It has also sued EPA to hasten implementation of its Total Maximum Daily Load (TMDL) program for controlling nonsource pollutants in the Anacostia.

AWS president Robert Boone describes current efforts as "a body without a head." He identifies a lack of coordination and even communication among the many stakeholders. He views the Metro Council of Governments as supplying the appearance of coordination but lacking the resources and leadership to genuinely provide it. He is impatient with the pace of programs and real restoration work, which he characterizes as "slow as molasses."

The Earth Conservation Corps (ECC), formed in the 1990s by television producer/director Robert Nixon, is another key NGO working on site restoration in the Anacostia watershed. Its headquarters, the Matthew Henson Earth Conservation Center, is a demonstration of model restoration strategies, notably low-impact development (LID). A former pump house, it sat idle for many years with four large tanks containing lead and asbestos actively leaking pollutants into the river. Restored for reuse with the help of Navy SeaBees, it now has administrative and educational spaces. It also has an extensive and beautiful green rooftop and several rain gardens.

Like AWS, the ECC emphasizes the need to build community support for and commitment to the river. For the ECC, involving kids from the surrounding communities is essential. Many young people living geographically near the river have never seen it, or even know it is there. For others it is about "demysticizing" the river and debunking the myths and prejudices that these kids grew up with, such as that the river is dead and the river is dangerous or harmful (which it was in the past). ECC has now taken some 4,000 kids on the river. Among other activities, the ECC takes youths out on its "buy boat," where they draw water samples and trawl for fish. However, as recounted by Robert Nixon (2003), the ECC has lost several of its young participants, victims of street violence in the vicinity of the Anacostia waterfront in the district.

One of ECC's major projects is creating an Anacostia riverwalk and trail similar to the Mount Vernon trail along the Potomac. The idea of a riverwalk has been under consideration for some 30 years. It is now becoming a reality; most segments of the right-of-way along the river have been secured. The Navy Yard has agreed to open its promenade as part of the trail. With funding from the D.C. Department of Transportation, the ECC is building three demonstration sections of the riverwalk, including one next to its headquarters building on First Street. The ECC has designed the trail to serve as a rainwater retention and rainwater garden. It will also have other LID elements.

Several other groups are working on the Anacostia cleanup. They include the Chesapeake Bay Foundation (CBF), which has an "Anacostia River Initiative," and the Anacostia River Business Coalition, which galvanizes the businesses community to improve the river. Among its annual activities are its Anacostia Watershed-Stewardship Award, recognizing exemplary businesses. Award winners have included the Super Salvage Company and Maryland Park for their stormwater containment, and recycling and spill prevention programs. Several companies, including Pepco and the Results Gym, have been recognized for their use of LID techniques, such as rain barrels and installation of rain gardens. The Shaw ecovillage has also been noted for both its use of LID techniques and for its youth education program (www.potomacriver.org/arbc/arbc.html).

THE DISTRICT OF COLUMBIA INITIATIVES

In 2004, the District of Columbia unveiled its Anacostia Waterfront Initiative (AWI) as the guiding framework for the redevelopment of areas bordering the river within the district. Featured in a major exhibit at the National Building Museum in early 2004, the AWI has received extensive press coverage because it is the first comprehensive waterfront process undertaken for the Anacostia addressing both sides of the river. Many compare AWI's bold vision to the 1902 MacMillan Commission Plan for

Washington, D.C., that led to the rehabilitation of the Mall and the expansion of the park system. The AWI reorients the city:

With Washington's downtown nearly built out, the city's pattern of growth is moving eastward toward and across the Anacostia River. The destiny of the city as the nation's capital and a premier world city is inextricably linked to re-centering its growth along the Anacostia River and making its long-neglected parks, environment and infrastructure a national priority. The recovery of the Anacostia waterfront will help to reunite the capital economically, physically and socially. (www.planning.dc.gov/planning/cwp/view,a,1285,q,582130,planning Nav_GID,1708. asp)

The AWI Framework Plan identifies five main themes or clusters of goals:

1. a clean and active river;
2. eliminating barriers and gaining access;
3. a great urban river park system;
4. cultural destinations of distinct character;
5. building strong waterfront neighborhoods.

The first detailed element of the AWI is the development plan for the Southwest waterfront that aims to create a "true urban waterfront where commercial, cultural, residential and neighborhood life can come together" (AWI 2003: 1–3). The plan covers a one-mile strip from the tidal basin to Fort McNair. It envisions new public spaces—a market square and a civic park, as well as other smaller plazas and parks linked by an expanded and improved waterfront promenade. It calls for a "grand public pier" extending from the civic park. These public investments would stimulate new residential development—6- to 12-story, mixed-use buildings, supplying 800 units of housing. A new light rail line along Maine Avenue, supplemented by water taxis and ferries, would connect the Southwest waterfront to the rest of the city.

The District of Columbia has forged consensus around AWI implementation through execution of a Memorandum of Understanding (2000) signed by 18 federal and local agencies, including the District, National Park Service, Office of Management and Budget, Army Corps of Engineers, D.C. Housing Authority, Sports and Entertainment Commission, and Water and Sewer Authority. Described as a "new partnership" that "envisions an energized waterfront for the next millennium," the agreement calls on the parties to work together to "cause the dream of a new waterfront . . . to become a reality" (District of Columbia 2000).

The planning and management of this waterfront represents a tremendous political challenge in terms of reconciling the interests of

AWI's 18 member organizations and agencies, numerous other stake-holder associations, governmental agencies and community groups. While the D.C. Office of Planning has spearheaded this initiative, implementation of much of its development falls to the National Capital Revitalization Corporation (NCRC), specially created in July 2004.

A major concern among lower-income residents of the Anacostia neighborhoods is the fear of gentrification—replacement of low-rent housing with high-end condos and apartments (Wilgoren 2004). To address that concern, the AWI has planned several major projects, including a new HOPE VI project to replace 700 existing units of public housing with 1,000 affordable housing units. It will incorporate some low-impact development requirements and will facilitate connections to the river for residents of the project.

Despite the extensive public participation in developing AWI plans, there is still concern that the interests of developers and builders will win out over citizens and the surrounding communities. ECC's James Willie, a member of the Anacostia Citizen Advisory Committee, believes residents along the river remain skeptical and suspect that the nice images of the vision of the AWI will not be realized, and that many pieces will be subtracted or negotiated away in the mechanics and realities of real estate transactions.

In addition to the AWI activities, the District of Columbia is dealing with water pollution control issues generated by its combined sewer overflow system. About 60 percent of the Anacostia watershed is drained through this antiquated system, including some 17 main combined sewer outflows. According to the Metro Council of Governments (1998), overflow events occur between 40 and 50 times per year and result in the discharge of some 1.3 billion gallons of sewage into the river. NRDC puts the "outflow" each year at 2 to 3 billion gallons (NRDC n.d.).

The Water and Sewer Authority (WASA) has the primary responsibility for addressing the combined sewer overflow problem within its service area. Based on evaluation of regulatory compliance, cost effectiveness, and an extensive public outreach and comment period, in July 2002 it released its final Long-Term Control Plan (LTCP) (WASA 2002). The plan recommended retrofitting of WASA's own facilities to reduce combined sewer overflows through improved conveyance, storage, treatment, and consolidation of discharges to the Anacostia, the Potomac, and Rock Creek. Specifically, WASA proposes the construction of two underground storage tunnels at an estimated cost of $770 million, about four-fifths of the $940 million total cost of Anacostia improvements. It predicts that for an average year these improvements will contain 97.5 percent of overflow, and reduce the annual number of overflows per year from 75 to only 2 (WASA 2002: ES-12). WASA dismisses the option of separating the storm and sanitary sewage system as "not economically feasible" and too disruptive.

A major limitation of WASA's ability to relieve the bacterial pollution of the lower Anacostia is the prevalence of upstream stormwater and nonpoint sources in Maryland: "As WASA and the District develop provisions to implement the LTCP, consideration should be given to formation of a watershed based forum to reduce the other pollution sources" (WASA 2002: ES-19). At this writing no such forum or watershed-wide water quality program has been established. The district is thus at the mercy of the determination of the state of Maryland and the U.S. Environmental Protection Agency to enforce federal and state water pollution laws, especially "total maximum daily loads" (TMDLs) for nonpoint sources.

An important question is whether low-impact development represents a viable alternative to the $1 billion approach proposed by WASA. LID would involve a variety of small-scale buildings and site-oriented techniques for containing and treating stormwater. Among them are green rooftops, bioswales, raingardens, and rain barrels, among many others. The National Resources Defense Council has been the most vocal group advocating this alternative strategy—one they believe will be less costly and more environmentally preferable. There remains considerable disagreement about whether LID, even extensively applied, could sufficiently resolve the Washington combined sewer overflow problem. NRDC argues that there are many regulatory barriers that discourage or prohibit LID. The D.C. building code, for example, requires roof gutters to be connected with the city's storm sewers, precluding use of rainbarrels and other creative diversions of storm water (NRDC 2002).

The Anacostia watershed cleanup involves various governmental and NGO stakeholders that share responsibility for the river and watershed. They include several regional agencies—WASA, MWCOG, and the Capital Regional Planning Council—that facilitate actions at a regional or watershed level and some smaller subwatershed citizens or community groups (for example, Eyes of Paint Branch, Friends of Sligo Creek, and Citizens Concerned for Indian Creek) that work locally. These diverse stakeholders may or may not share a common vision and a comprehensive strategy for the Anacostia does not exist.

One clear tension among them revolves around the approach to restoration: promoting many small projects in the watershed versus a single grand solution. AWS's Robert Boone believes there is a bias against the small-scale LID approach, which he colorfully describes as "pennies." Many believe in the big dollars and discount the pennies, he says. For Boone, much centers around issues of fundamental fairness. He argues that we should no longer tolerate the great spatial inequalities in the

District of Columbia and work simultaneously to elevate awareness and enjoyment of this historically undervalued watershed. For example, the district's Anacostia Waterfront Initiative explicitly envisions a "recentering" of energy and activity to the east and—through new parks, development, infrastructure, amenities (a waterfront trail, for example), and greater efforts to connect and make the river accessible—the potential exists to improve conditions and opportunities and quality of life in the (now) most marginalized areas of the city. Balancing revitalization of poor neighborhoods near the Anacostia with mitigation of the effects of gentrification is a major ongoing challenge.

Watershed Challenges

The Anacostia River Watershed faces a daunting series of challenges to those who envision it as a cleaner, more accessible, and more ecological resource for metropolitan Washington, D.C. One challenge, common to most urban watersheds, is its political fragmentation, namely among two Maryland counties and the District of Columbia, as well as among the many federal agencies which play various roles in the watershed. A second challenge is the multiplicity of problems, including poor water quality, loss of wetlands and other habitat, inaccessibility to local communities, and the socioeconomic contrasts between suburban communities upstream and the District downstream. A third challenge is to reconcile low-impact development with the proposed LTCP as competing strategies for controlling combined sewer overflows. And finally, there is the challenge of gentrification: if the Anacostia Waterfront Initiative is substantially realized, how will it affect the present residents of the lower-income neighborhoods that now border the river? The jury is still out on these and related issues that complicate all attempts to revitalize the Anacostia.

Nine Mile Run: "Small Is Beautiful"[3]

Nine Mile Run is a local tributary to the Monongahela River (the "Mon") in the Pittsburgh metropolitan area (Figure 2). It drains a tiny 6.5-square-mile watershed that overlies parts of the city of Pittsburgh and three adjoining communities: Wilkinsburg, Swissvale, and Edgewood. The watershed was the focus of one of the largest urban renewal land acquisition projects in the city's history, and it is now the scene of a significant aquatic ecosystem restoration under the management of the Army Corps of Engineers. The NMR watershed is home to close to 48,000 people, as well as 250 plant species, 22 different mammals, and 189 types of birds (Ferguson et al. 1999). The restoration of this water-

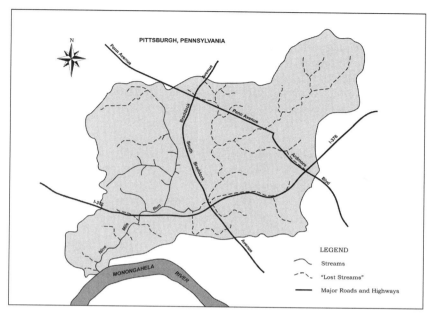

Figure 2. The Nine Mile Run Watershed. Adapted from Nine Mile Run
Watershed Association, www.ninemilerun.org.

shed provides a model of how to pursue multiple goals—stream restoration, brownfield remediation, housing, environmental education—
within the geographic framework of a small urban watershed. It also
demonstrates the potential for community level action stimulated by
charismatic leaders and a strong watershed organization.

In the early twentieth century, approximately two-thirds of Nine Mile
Run was relegated to an underground culvert to alleviate flooding in the
area. The stream first emerges from the culvert in Pittsburgh's Frick
Park and flows 2.2 miles through the park and local neighborhoods to
the Mon River. At high flow, NMR gushes out of its culvert with such
velocity that it erodes away the stream banks of the free-flowing sections
of stream. This leads to tons of eroded sediment being carried downstream to the Monongahela along with tons of debris. Also, at the mouth
of the concrete culvert, four municipal combined sewer overflow pipes
discharge directly into the creek. Some of these pipes have reportedly
been connectors for both waterlines and sewer lines, and during storm
events it is not uncommon for raw sewage to drain directly into Nine
Mile Run (www.nmwra.org).

In addition to the stream erosion and combined sewer overflow problems, the watershed contains the site of the former Homestead Steel Company. Its former presence is marked permanently by a 238-acre, 21-story pile of slag, a byproduct of steel manufacturing close to the Mon River. The site represented the largest stretch of open riverfront land in the city of Pittsburgh. Although in the early twentieth century, efforts were made to clean up the site; instead, it was gradually buried under as much as 120 feet of additional industrial by-products and wastes (Ferguson et al. 1999).

In 1995, the EPA, through the newly inaugurated Brownfields Economic Redevelopment Initiative, provided $200,000 to the Pittsburgh Urban Redevelopment Authority (URA) for two brownfield evaluation projects, one of which was the Nile Mile Run site. The grant—among more than 120 national and regional brownfield assessment pilot projects funded by the EPA—helped the city evaluate the 238-acre slag pile site, which the URA later purchased for future redevelopment.

Once it owned the Homestead site, the URA commissioned a master plan for its redevelopment. The plan initially proposed the construction of 1,200 housing units (later reduced to about 700 units) and the development of 100 acres of public space. It called for paving over additional stretches of Nine Mile Run, a proposal that met strong opposition from environmentalists.

In response, a group of researchers at the Carnegie Mellon University Studio for Creative Inquiry began a public process and study to develop an alternative plan that would save the stream, fearing that the URA master plan would "destroy the stream once and for all" (Ferguson et al. 1999). In October 1998, they held a three-day design charrette with participation from a panel of 60 local and national designers, engineers, artists, planners, policy analysts, and local citizens The group addressed the entire 6.5-square-mile watershed, not just the 238-acre slag pile site. They called for a "restorative redevelopment" approach to the sewers, ecosystem, and communities, arguing that "retrofit and redevelopment projects that are technically and economically feasible can improve the value and livability of the city while effectively restoring the watershed's natural functions" (Ferguson et al. 1999). Their long- and short-term proposals responded not only to the ailing stream and watershed but also to community revitalization.

This alternative plan attracted the attention of the URA and the city of Pittsburgh. The URA decided to integrate stream restoration—including wetland enhancement and streambed erosion reduction—into its housing development plan. The revised plan called for a pedestrian-friendly community with an open space network and "transit-oriented design" features. The ensuing residential development proposals were so popular that the units were sold lottery-style.

The Army Corps of Engineers undertook the Nine Mile Run stream restoration projects in the new development plan. The major goal was to restore aquatic habitat for invertebrates and amphibians that were dependent upon the stream. The corps reestablished the stream banks, rechanneled parts of the stream into historic wetland areas, and created additional wetland areas.

It divided the project into three phases:

- Phase 1A. Stream rechanneling and infrastructure improvements (reducing impervious surface in the lower Frick Park parking lot) (completed 2002)
- Phase 1B. Stream channel modifications and improvements to the Fern Hollow/Falls Ravine tributary (completed fall 2005).
- Phase 2. Stream channel modifications and improvements beginning at Commercial Avenue to just before the railroad crossing in Duck Hollow (completed June 2006).

The total cost of the restoration was $7.7 million. The $5 million federal contribution to the project was paid for through Army Corps of Engineers Section 206 funding. The nonfederal match of $2.7 million came from the city of Pittsburgh and the Three Rivers Wet Weather Demonstration Program.

The ecosystem restoration was only one step in restoring the NMR watershed to full health. Polluted runoff from residential areas in the upper watershed also degrades water quality. To continue with improvement efforts in this area, the CMU studio project also stimulated the creation of the Nine Mile Run Watershed Association (NMWRA) in 2001. Since its project's inception, NMRWA has undertaken an educational mission. In addition to its bimonthly tours of the restoration site, NMRWA leaders "support residents' efforts to implement lot-level solutions to stormwater problems, provide citizen training for urban ecological stewardship, and act as an information clearinghouse about key watershed issues" (quoted on www.nmrwa.org website). Under the leadership of current executive director Marijke Hecht, NMRWA has sponsored several programs, including:

- The Rain Barrel Initiative, which was begun in 2004, to mitigate the effects of storm water on the Nine Mile Run. Stormwater runoff is a direct cause of sewage overflows and stream bank erosion in the Nine Mile Run stream. By holding rainwater in a barrel, water is released gradually, giving the water the chance to soak through the ground and enter the water table instead of rushing into the stream all at once. The NMWRA aims to have 4,000 rain barrels in place at homes throughout the watershed. In addition to improving the health of Nine Mile Run, a rain barrel also provides homeowners with free, untreated water for plants and gardens.

- The Regent Street Gateway Park, which is now in the design stages. This open space will serve as a new entrance to Frick Park, where the stream first flows aboveground. It incorporates sustainable stormwater management and landscaping to clean and store excess rain and snowmelt. The CMU studio first proposed this park.

- Urban EcoStewards is a citizen group of 24 volunteers to work along Nine Mile Run, monitoring and removing invasive plant species, picking up litter, and cataloguing native plants. The Pennsylvania Department of Conservation and Natural Resources provides training for the Urban EcoStewards.

- Green Links is a program to increase the amount of tree coverage in the watershed. In 2005 it enlisted more than 125 residents to plant trees throughout the community of Wilkinsburg. In 2006, the NMWRA began to inventory the health and number of existing trees and the need for future tree plantings in the watershed. Street trees absorb excess stormwater runoff, reduce air pollution, increase property values, and reduce heating and cooling costs for residents and businesses.

A SUCCESS STORY

The Nine Mile Run experience to date is a success story of brownfield redevelopment, stream restoration, and building a sense of "watershed community." The project has moved ahead despite straddling parts of four political jurisdictions and several neighborhoods of broad social and economic diversity. In comparison with the Anacostia, Nine Mile Run has benefited from the unity of perspective and initiative represented by the Nine Mile Run Watershed Association and its leadership. Its limited geographic size has also helped foster local involvement and "buy-in." As E. F. Schumacher put it: "Small is Beautiful."

Laurel Creek: A Canadian Perspective[4]

Laurel Creek is the principal stream flowing through the city of Waterloo, Ontario, and its vicinity. It is a small but important tributary of the Grand River, one of the largest river systems in southern Ontario, which in turn flows to Lake Erie (Figure 3). Most of the 28.7-square-mile Laurel Creek Watershed (LCW) is located at the northwestern end of the regional municipality of Waterloo. About 78,000 people live in the

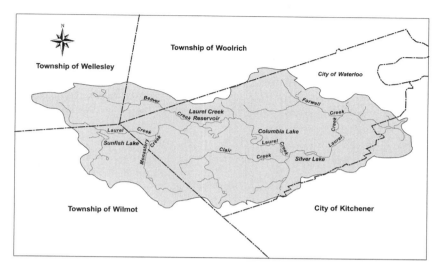

Figure 3. Grand River Watershed. Adapted from Grand River Conservation Authority map.

watershed, mostly in the urban area of the city of Waterloo (LCWS 1993).

Laurel Creek's headwaters lie in the rural landscapes of the townships of Woolwich and Wellesley and drain into the Grand River in the city of Kitchener. Laurel Creek's main tributaries include Clair Creek, Forwell Creek, Beaver Creek, and Monastery Creek, each of which drains portions of Waterloo. Well-drained soils and moraines that enable groundwater recharge and the sustainability of relatively large aquifer systems characterize the watershed. In its original state, the groundwater would contribute to the base flow of Laurel Creek and its tributaries to provide for productive coldwater fisheries. The moraine system also supports a wide range of plant, animal and bird species.

The LCW physical landscape is dominated by glacial kame deposits, known locally as the Waterloo Moraine or Sandhills. Major aquifers lying beneath this landscape serve as a source of drinking water for at least 300,000 people in the Waterloo region (City of Waterloo 2003a). Furthermore, numerous spring-fed wetlands and small ponds are found in the area. Soils in the LCW are generally sandy loams and the topography consists of the varied gradients typical of glaciated terrain. In pre-European times, dense deciduous and coniferous forest and extensive marsh wetland dominated the watershed. Common native trees include Aspen, Beech, Manitoba Maple, Oak and White Pine (Nelson et al. 2003).

The creek has influenced the development of Waterloo, including the location of its downtown, the layout of its street plan, and the nature of its industries, past and present. As the city developed, the quality of the creek and its watershed was degraded through the clearing of land and draining of wetlands. In the first half of the twentieth century, Laurel Creek underwent a number of structural-related changes for the purpose of flood and erosion control to protect life and property.

Waterloo originated as a center of lumbering and agriculture that evolved in the nineteenth century into a commercial and educational city with the growth of local insurance companies and two institutions of higher learning: the University of Waterloo and Wilfred Laurier University. Historically, the creek served as a source of drinking water and waterpower, and as a site for breweries and a distillery. Today, while there is not much left of the historic mills, two of the breweries are still functioning and the buildings from Seagram's Distillery have been restored as residential lofts.

In the early 1900s, widespread clearance of forests and filling of wetlands made Laurel Creek especially prone to flooding in the spring during snow melts and heavy rainfall. It was a virtual sewer in the dry summer months (LCWS 1993). Flood control planning began in the 1930s for the Grand River Watershed, including Laurel Creek. After World War II, the Grand River Conservation Authority (GRCA), a regional unit of government established under the 1946 Conservation Authorities Act, oversaw planning for Laurel Creek. Conservation authorities in Ontario, which have few if any counterparts in the United States, follow these principles:

1. Local Initiative: Local political and citizen support is required prior to consent to create a conservation authority.
2. Cost Sharing: Costs of projects are shared by the province and municipalities.
3. Watershed Jurisdiction: Conservation authorities are given power to set regulations within the watershed jurisdiction to allow them to adequately manage issues like flood control (Conservation Ontario 2003).

Pursuant to this institutional arrangement, the GRCA constructed several projects to control flooding and erosion—dikes, channel improvements, and bank stabilization—in the Grand River Watershed during the 1960s and 1970s (GRCA 1983; Boyd et al. 1999). One of these projects, the Laurel Creek Reservoir, completed in 1966, would become the centerpiece of GRCA's Laurel Creek Conservation Area. The authority originally acquired lands for the conservation area for flood control but soon were valued as open space in the midst of rapid urban development. Around this time, the GRCA also built Columbia and Laurel Lakes, largely to serve aesthetic and recreational functions rather than flood control (LCWS 1993).

Today, upstream Laurel Creek traverses a still-rural landscape of farmland and a few remnants of woodlands and wetlands. Fecal coliform from livestock grazing in and near the stream, as well as soil erosion, pesticides, fertilizers, and other agricultural chemicals degrade the water quality. The creek then enters the Laurel Creek flood control reservoir. As streamflow slows, the creek deposits silt and contaminants and its temperature increases because of lack of shade and the shallowness of the lake. At times waterweeds and the excrement of resident flocks of ducks and geese add to the pollution. Below the reservoir, landscape nutrient runoff and warming in downstream lakes and ponds further degrade the creek. Beyond the University of Waterloo campus, the creek disappears into a 500-meter (1,640-foot) culvert, from which it emerges at the Waterloo city center. Its final reach is subject to bank erosion from riparian development and is used as a dumping ground for yard waste and hazardous household products.

The Laurel Creek Watershed Study

In 1993 the GRCA initiated the Laurel Creek Watershed Study (LWCS), marking the advent of comprehensive planning and management in contrast to single-purpose structural interventions of the past. The LCWS addressed six concerns relevant to rapidly urbanizing watersheds: flooding, water quality, streambank erosion, sedimentation, groundwater, and natural resources (Table 2). It used a systems approach to develop indicators to measure the overall health of the ecosystem and the impact of ecological stresses (LCWS 1993).

One of the key land-use elements of the LCWS has been the identification of "constraints areas" that define the level of development permitted in particular areas or zones. The LCWS designates all of the Laurel Creek Watershed as one of three constraint categories: (1) lands that protect and enhance natural environmental functions and processes; (2) lands that could provide valuable ecological functions but are degraded and would require management and rehabilitation to improve functioning; and (3) lands not serving specialized ecological functions.

The area known as Waterloo's Moraine on the west side of the city exemplifies the special attention accorded to areas classified in category 1. Although the LCWS identified these moraine lands as significant to both groundwater and biodiversity, the city intended to allow the area

TABLE 2. Issues, Goals, and Conclusions in the Laurel Creek Watershed Study

Issue	Questions to be addressed	Goals	Conclusions
Flooding	• Will further development result in further flooding?	• Minimize risk to life, property and natural resources • Preserve natural floodplains and hydraulic functions	• Identified 10 areas in watershed as being "high risk" • Reservoirs play a role in controlling floods • Natural storage areas (i.e., bogs) help reduce floods • Natural floodplains control floods and should be maintained • Major cause of flooding in uptown results from urban runoff • New development in Waterloo will increase flows unless volumes, timing, and flows are controlled
Streambank erosion	• Will further development lead to further erosion?	• Preserve and protect aquatic resources and water supply	• Rehabilitate streambanks and channels
Surface erosion and sedimentation	• Are existing agricultural and urban practices causing erosion of open areas leading to sediment deposits?	• Preserve and protect land, water, forest, and wildlife	• Some areas have high sediment loads and suspended solids from erosion

Water quality	• Can urban growth continue without more degradation? • What is the impact of reservoirs on water quality?	• Restore, protect, and enhance water quality and associated aquatic resources and water supplies	• Bacteria in reservoir and Columbia Lake prevent recreational use • Reservoirs warm water, add nutrients, and degrade aesthetics • Hard for fish to survive because of low dissolved oxygen, high water temperatures, and high stream vegetation • Phosphorus causes algae blooms and degraded aesthetics
Groundwater	• How will groundwater use affect wells in the area and groundwater fed streams?	• Protect and restore both quality and quantity of groundwater	• Maintain in and outside Laurel Creek watershed: infiltration with greatest potential in upper watershed • Deeper aquifers to provide water supply • Shallow aquifers sustain river flows
Natural resources	• Can urban growth continue and not degrade natural areas further? How can we protect these resources?	• Restore, protect, develop and enhance ecological, historical, cultural, recreational, visual amenities of both rural and urban origin particularly around streams	• Terrestrial resources are extensive and relatively well connected but are experiencing intense pressure • Remaining areas have important natural resource functions • They should be divided into three constraint areas with different management strategies

Source: LCWS (1993).

to be residentially developed. Resulting negotiations led to city-imposed strict guidelines on development to promote water infiltration and to a vigorous program of environmental education. The latter included interpretive signage along neighborhood trails and brochures distributed to all area residents explaining the sensitivity of the lands. Furthermore, the city of Waterloo website includes descriptions of the history, geology, and rare species found in the area and the importance of the moraine for groundwater. Under its new zoning category for the moraine called "Flexible Residential," the city requires 49- to 98-foot vegetative buffers around woodlots, waterways, and wetlands. It also mandates that at least 50 percent of each lot allow water to infiltrate, thereby limiting expansion of driveways, building footprints, and decks (City of Waterloo 2002).

The Laurel Creek Citizens Committee (LCCC), initiated in 1990 to protect, rehabilitate, and enhance the creek, has played a strong role in the formulation and implementation of the LCWS and its offshoots. LCCC and other nongovernmental organizations such as the Waterloo Citizens Environmental Committee participate in city steering committees for studies relating to Laurel Creek Watershed and the rest of the city. With a small cadre of members and volunteers, LCCC each year works on various projects of which the following are representative:

- planting native species along Laurel Creek and its tributaries;
- pollandering (debris and obstruction removal) along Laurel Creek and its tributaries;
- stream rehabilitation and activities at Silver Lake;
- stream rehabilitation, erosion control along Laurel Creek and its tributaries; and
- stream assessment.

THE LAUREL CREEK EXPERIENCE

The Laurel Creek Watershed experience to date is noteworthy for the dominating influence of a single agency (Grand River Conservation Authority) and its plan, the 1993 Laurel Creek Watershed Study, in prescribing environmental stewardship in the watershed. The study provided baseline watershed health indicators for monitoring environmental progress and thereby influence the regulation of further development in the watershed.

The Watershed Approach: An Evaluation

The three case studies discussed in this chapter offer different approaches and outcomes to recent urban watershed management experiences. Attempts to draw comparisons among them must recognize that each involves a different physical and political geography, program goals and timeframes (river improvement takes time, and the oldest of the three programs, Laurel Creek, dates back only to 1993). With these caveats in mind, the "effectiveness" of these watershed programs (in terms of realizing stated objectives) *seems to be inversely proportional to watershed size.*

Nine Mile Run, the smallest of the three (6.5 square miles), is already enhanced by a wetlands restoration project completed by the Corps of Engineers in 2006, based on designs initiated by the Carnegie Mellon University Studio for Creative Inquiry in the late 1990s. The Nine Mile Run Watershed Association, formed in 2001, has a broad and ambitious agenda of other projects in progress—for example, the Rain Barrel Initiative, Eco-Stewards, Green Links, and Regent Street Gateway Park. However, at this stage there is no comprehensive plan for the entire Nine Mile Run watershed and political oversight is fragmented among several units and levels of government.

The medium-sized (28.7 square miles) Laurel Creek Watershed in Ontario, unlike the U.S. study sites, has both a regional watershed management agency (Grand River Conservation Authority) and a comprehensive plan: the 1993 Laurel Creek Watershed Study. Under these instruments, management of the watershed has used a broad array of both structural and nonstructural interventions. Land-use planning and development restrictions, such as those applied by the city of Waterloo pursuant to the LCWS, appear to be more proactive than is politically feasible in the United States. Unlike Nine Mile Run, the Laurel Creek example has no "signature" restoration project, but it has achieved many small-scale projects to reduce flooding and bank erosion under the GRCA. Citizen groups are engaged in on-going local clean-up, replanting, and stream-monitoring activities.

Finally, the much larger (176 square miles) Anacostia River Watershed abounds with public and private sector programs but lacks either an umbrella agency for overall management or a comprehensive watershed plan. The most ambitious project proposed for the Anacostia is the District of Columbia's Anacostia Waterfront Initiative, an urban renewal project with a strong river improvement component. Its goal to upgrade the blighted and forbidding Anacostia waterfront in the nation's capital is commendable, and the plan does envision improved public access to and along the river. But without buy-in by upstream jurisdictions (Montgomery and Prince George's Counties in Maryland), the AWI cannot hope to improve the river's abysmal water quality. The other massive response to the water quality problem, the proposed billion-dollar WASA project to limit combined sewer overflow discharges from district sewers, likewise addresses only the downstream portion of the water-shed. The January 9, 2007, *Washington Post* offered a gloomy assessment of prospects for cleaning up the Anacostia: "Polluted Waters Stain D.C.'s Shining Vision; Rejuvenation Near the Anacostia may Leave One Component Behind: The River."

Apart from their many contrasts, all three cases reflect growing recognition that a host of urban and environmental problems may be productively and synergistically addressed at the scale of local drainage systems. As discussed above, watershed approaches potentially embrace such public objectives as water-quality improvement, flood hazard mitigation, restoration of aquatic and riparian habitats, encouragement of outdoor exercise, and enhanced awareness of the natural settings of urban communities. The lack of geographic correspondence between watersheds and political jurisdictions may be turned to an advantage as a condition demanding interjurisdictional communication and cooperation. Ideally, pursuit of watershed improvement efforts may help to overcome the trend toward social and economic stratification and privatism that afflict metropolitan areas everywhere.

References

Anacostia Waterfront Initiative (AWI). 2003. The Southwest Waterfront Development Plan and AWI Vision. February 6.

Anacostia Watershed Restoration Committee. 2001. "Working Together to Restore the Anacostia Watershed." AWRC Annual Report.

Boyd, Dwight, Toni Smith, and Barbara Veale. 1999. "Flood Management on the Grand River, Ontario, Canada: A Watershed Conservation Perspective." *Environments* 27, 1: 23–47.

Brookings Institution. Center on Urban and Metropolitan Policy. 1999. "A Region Divided: the State of Growth in Washington, D.C."

City of Waterloo. 2002a. Environmental Strategic Plan. Waterloo, Ontario.

City of Waterloo. 2002. Height and Density Policy Study. Discussion Paper. Waterloo, Ontario.

Conservation Ontario. 2003. Corporate Profile http://www.conservation-ontario.on.ca/profile/profile.htm.

District of Columbia. 2000. "Memorandum of Understanding: Anacostia Watershed Initiative." March 22.

District of Columbia Water and Sewer Authority (WASA). 2002. "WASA's Recommended Combined Sewer System Long Term Control Plan." Executive Summary. July.

Fahrenthold, D. A. 2007. "Polluted Waters Stain D.C.'s Shining Vision." *Washington Post,* January 9.

Ferguson, Bruce, Richard Pinkham, and Timothy Collins. 1999. *Re-Evaluating Stormwater: The Nine Mile Run Model for Restorative Redevelopment.* Snowmass, Colo.: Rocky Mountain Institute, September.

Forgey, Benjamin. 2004. "Coming Clean About the Future: With Recreation

Central to Plans, Pollution Curbs Can't Be Swept Aside." *Washington Post,* July 13.

Grand River Conservation Authority (GRCA). 1993. Laurel Creek Watershed Study. Waterloo, Ontario.

Ivey, Janet. 2002. "Grand River Watershed Characterization Report." Guelph Water Management Group, University of Guelph. http://www.uoguelph.ca/gwmg/wcp_home/Pages/G_home.htm.

Laurel Creek Watershed Society. 1993. *Laurel Creek Watershed Study.* Waterloo, Ontario: The Society.

Metropolitan Washington Council of Governments (MWCOG), Department of Environmental Programs. 1998. "Anacostia Watershed Restoration Progress and Conditions Report." May.

Natural Resources Defense Council. 2002. *Out of the Gutter: Reducing Polluted Run-Off in the District of Columbia.* Washington, D.C.: NRDC.

———. n.d. "Cleaning Up the Anacostia River." http://www.nrdc.org/water/pollution/fanacost.asp.

Nelson, James Gordon, Jim Porter, C. Farassoglou, S. Gardiner, C. Guthrie, C. Beck, and Christopher J. Lemieux. 2003. *The Grand River Watershed: A Heritage Landscape Guide.* Heritage Landscape Guide Series 2. Waterloo, Ontario: Heritage Resources Centre, University of Waterloo.

Nixon, Robert H. 2003. "Endangered in Anacostia." *Washington Post,* October 26.

Platt, Rutherford H. 2006. "Urban Watershed Management: Sustainability One Stream at a Time." *Environment* 48, 4 (May): 26–42.

Sievert, Laurin N. 2006. "Urban Watershed Management: The Milwaukee River Experience." In *The Humane Metropolis: People and Nature in the 21st Century City,* ed. Rutherford H. Platt. Amherst: University of Massachusetts Press and Lincoln Institute of Land Policy. 141–53.

U.S. Environmental Protection Agency (EPA) Mid-Atlantic Superfund. 2003. Anacostia River Initiative Current Site Information.

Wilgoren, Debbi. 2004. "Hope, Fret Along the Anacostia." *Washington Post,* July 18.

Chapter 8

The Role of Citizen Activists in Urban Infrastructure Development

PAUL R. BROWN

Integrated programs for water management and environmental services that combine large-scale infrastructure with demand-side management are gaining wide acceptance throughout the United States. These programs, whether in the areas of water supply, wastewater, stormwater, or solid waste, alter relationships between utilities and their customers. Because they rely on changes in community practices and behavior, integrated programs benefit from citizen activists and community interest groups who are partners in the achievement of program goals. These partnerships can benefit from improved communications and collaboration between established utilities and the independent world of community interest groups and their inspirational leaders.

From Landmark Infrastructure to Integrated Resources Plans

Since the nineteenth century, the United States has been on a long, often reactive path toward large-scale environmental infrastructure. President Theodore Roosevelt realized this in his often-quoted speech at the Sorbonne in 1910. He lauded the individual citizen as the foundation of a successful republic, but specifically singled out urban water-supply and drainage as examples of societal problems best solved by government:

Individual initiative, so far from being discouraged, should be stimulated; and yet we should remember that, as society develops and grows more complex, we continually find that things which once it was desirable to leave to individual initiative can, under changed conditions, be performed with better results by common effort. . . . For instance, when people live on isolated farms or in little hamlets, each house can be left to attend to its own drainage and water-supply; but the mere multiplication of families in a given area produces new problems which, because they differ in size, are found to differ not only in degree but in kind from the old; and the questions of drainage and water-supply have to be considered from the common standpoint. (Roosevelt 2004: 790)

Addressing issues like drainage (which in 1910 could refer to both stormwater and sewage—often combined), water supply, and solid waste from "the common standpoint" remained the primary approach taken by growing municipal utilities, both large and small, for decades to come.

The many early examples of municipal civil engineering projects, conceived and executed through "common effort," were essential to the growth and prosperity of the cities they served. For example, responding to years of poor quality water epidemics, New York City completed the Croton Aqueduct in 1842, bringing fresh water 40 miles from Westchester County (Koeppel 2000). Chicago built the Sanitary and Ship Canal, reversing the flow of the Chicago River in 1900 to prevent contamination of the city's water supply (Hall 2000), and Southern Californians constructed the 226-mile Los Angeles Aqueduct (1913) and 242-mile Colorado River Aqueduct (1941), both developed and engineered by the larger-than-life William Mulholland to ensure the area's growth and economic prosperity (Hundley 1992). These examples are representative of hundreds of large-scale infrastructure projects that have provided the foundation for the country's public health and safety, quality of life, and economic success.[1]

In addition to its accomplishments in building large-scale infrastructure systems, the United States has also increased government regulation to preserve community health, causing, at times, a "clash between individual liberty and the public welfare" (Duffy 1992: 3). Through both large-scale infrastructure and increasing public health, safety, and environmental regulation, the United States has created urban infrastructure that functions as a command-and-control system with protective "barriers" between individuals and the physical environment. This approach has not asked much of citizens other than the timely payment of their taxes and utility bills.

Though not without eloquent opponents from the outset,[2] during the last decades of the twentieth century confidence in large-scale infrastructure projects—as the sole solution to future growth and urbanization—waned. Marked for many by the publication of Rachael Carson's *Silent Spring* (1962), the ongoing environmental movement began to take shape as a national force. With the federal clout of the 1970 National Environmental Policy Act (NEPA) passed in 1970 and subsequent federal and state legislation, opponents to major civil engineering projects succeeded in delaying, significantly modifying, and occasionally stopping proposed projects. Significant concerns regarding the direct and indirect impacts of major structural investments altered public policy in the direction of approaches that minimized investments in large-scale facilities by optimizing the performance of existing assets and reducing user demands on the system (through conservation, improved efficiency, and recycling).

After a struggle initially played out in courtrooms,[3] a more balanced approach to the development of urban infrastructure emerged within many agencies and utilities. For example, in 1996 the Metropolitan Water District of Southern California, the agency Mulholland had established to finance the Colorado River Aqueduct, completed an Integrated Water Resources Plan (IRP) for Southern California that announced a new role for the engineer and builder of some of the world's largest infrastructure projects. The IRP replaces "exclusive dependence on Metropolitan for supplemental water with coordinated approaches developed in conjunction with local resources" (MWD 1996). Under this plan, the Metropolitan Water District (MWD), serving approximately 18 million people in a 5,200-square-mile area is fulfilling its water supply responsibilities through a combination of imported water, local facilities, and demand management (including conservation and recycling).

Although MWD is only one agency among many thousands responsible for urban infrastructure, the change at MWD reflects a transition occurring throughout the country. Integrated resources planning and demand management, concepts that originated in the energy industry, rapidly spread throughout the water industry as well. Today, many municipal utilities support and work cooperatively with customers to reduce their demands on large-scale infrastructure systems, opening the door to many smaller-scale technologies that serve as substitutes for reliance on centralized systems.

The purpose of this brief history is to highlight the significance that demand management and its associated small-scale technologies have acquired as large-scale "landmark" projects become increasingly rare. It also highlights the inevitable tension that results from changing views regarding the appropriate scale of energy and environmental technology in a rapidly urbanizing world. Large-scale systems reach farther away for their resources and often have equally long distances to travel in disposing of their wastes. The impact on the environment at both the source of supply and ultimate disposal site has, in many cases, become a constraint on system expansion, whether dealing with water supply, wastewater effluent disposal, biosolids disposal from wastewater treatment plants, or solid wastes to landfills.

As the impacts and costs of expanding large-scale systems increase, the desirability of efficient, small-scale substitutes increases as well. And with the rise of small-scale technologies comes an inevitable reliance on the individual user to take personal responsibility for the operation, care, and maintenance of the tools and systems providing services. This is essential if the small-scale solutions are to prove more efficient, less damaging to the environment, and less dependent on external resources and disposal sites. Real people ensure that small-scale solutions work and are maintained.

The shift reflected in utilities' commitment to demand management practices that reduce resource dependence and the need for infrastructure redefines their relationships with their communities. In the past, the function of municipal utilities was to remain largely invisible to customers and ratepayers. They would "go public" periodically, seeking support for capital improvement programs and other projects that "disappear" into the fabric of cities and suburbs, only reemerging in the public consciousness when they were malfunctioning, or making noise, or emitting odors. However, as much as they know about the process of planning, permitting, designing, constructing, and operating large-scale environmental facilities, many agencies and utilities are just learning about the process of mobilizing, energizing, deploying, and supporting community groups and citizen activists needed to deliver the anticipated benefits of increasing levels of demand-side management.

All these emerging approaches to providing reliable services, while managing resources, and protecting the environment, rely on an engaged citizenry with an engrained stewardship ethic. These imply deep cultural changes, not simply superficial behavior modification and technology improvements. Deep cultural change always originates in passionate, committed individuals and small groups with a vision of hope.

Institutional Success Involving Citizens and Managing Demands

This is not to say that there has not been progress integrating large-scale system improvements and demand-side management programs—or, looked at from an organizational standpoint, integrating large-scale municipal bureaucracies and individual citizens and community groups. Utilities have successfully incorporated citizen activists and interest groups into the policy and planning decision-making process for some time. They have also been successful in implementing demand management programs in water, solid waste, energy, transportation, and stormwater management. The initial success of these initiatives is reason to be hopeful that future demand management, waste reduction, and efficiency improvements can have ever increasing impacts.

Public Participation in Decision Making

While the transition to integrated structural and nonstructural programs was taking place, a related and equally important trend was occurring simultaneously. Municipal leaders invited public stakeholders to participate in the decision-making process, taking traditional public hearings and public information toward full citizen involvement and public participation. Fueled by the same environmental movement and federal legislation that buttressed successful assaults on large-scale projects, citizen activists were able to move from after-the-fact courtroom confrontations into front-end planning and decision making for proposed infrastructure projects and programs.

On occasion, some utilities have feared heavy involvement of citizen stakeholders in their decision-making processes. They expect the worst: chaos, delays, opposition to action, public controversy, "hijacked" projects, and bad publicity. They base their expectations on the litigation during the early years of the environmental movement mentioned above. When done correctly, however, fully integrated stakeholder involvement is the best means of preventing all of these outcomes from occurring. Heavy reliance on nonstructural and small-scale solutions to complement large-scale infrastructure must include the community. This entails listening to what is important to them; and engaging them for the long haul of implementation, maintenance, and care for the small-scale features that provide a reliable level of service. Examples of successful consensus-based decision making built on full public participation in California and Colorado are well documented (Rodrigo and Brown 2005).

Water Conservation

Widespread water conservation programs and initiatives have produced significant reductions in water use. In its annual progress report to the California state legislature on its achievements in conservation, water recycling, and groundwater recharge, MWD estimates that it conserved 112,300 acre-feet of water during 2005 through "active conservation," including "device retrofits, process improvement, landscape efficiency improvements, updating plumbing codes, and other efficiency measures used in the commercial, industrial and residential sectors" (MWD 2006: 5–15).

An acre-foot of water is roughly the amount needed to meet the annual water demands of two typical families in California (325,851 gallons). For 2005, MWD conservation savings represented the equivalent of taking almost 650,000 people "off the grid"—a population roughly the size of Ventura County. While the amount of water saved is impressive—nearly 6 percent of the total amount of water delivered by MWD to its member agencies in 2005 (approximately 1.98 million acre-feet)— equally impressive is the number of programs and initiatives that MWD actively supports in its ongoing efforts to increase water savings and meet its long-term IRP goals. In addition to its residential programs to replace toilets and appliances, MWD supports landscape programs; commercial, industrial and institutional programs; builder and retail partnerships; consumer research; and public education. MWD reports its cumulative investment in active conservation at $234 million.

Looking at the national perspective, the director of the California Urban Water Conservation Council reports that

the United States has made significant progress in water efficiency during the past decade. Although the amount of conservation varies from region to region, water efficiency has become the first choice for many water utilities in lieu of expanding facilities or purchasing more expensive sources of water. (Dickenson 2006: 11)

Solid Waste Recycling

Solid waste is another area where progress has been impressive. The growth in curbside recycling programs requiring homeowner separation of waste prior to pickup is one of the most successful examples of a structured programmatic response to the need for behavioral change in the community. Solid waste recycling programs, both voluntary and mandatory, have proliferated across the nation.

Recycling programs increased in 2005, recovering slightly over 32 percent (79 million tons) of the municipal solid waste stream, which is up from less than 10 percent (14.5 million tons) in 1980. There were about 8,550 curbside recycling programs in the United States in 2005. About 3,470 yard trimmings composting programs were reported in 2005 as well (EPA 2006).

Stormwater Management

In the area of stormwater management and flood control, low-impact development (LID) approaches have also gained rapid acceptance and support. LID reduces runoff and its impacts on drainage, flooding, and resulting water quality. It is "innovative technology to control stormwater quantity/quality impacts at the source using microscale management practices distributed and integrated throughout the landscape" (France 2002: 297).

The Philadelphia Water Department is demonstrating the benefits of

LID as an effective alternative to investments in large-scale underground storage facilities for meeting its regulatory commitment to reduce combined sewer overflows (CSOs). Their integrated watershed management program includes controlling stormwater at the source through LID and redevelopment retrofits, as well as new stormwater regulations and practices such as street tree-planting and riparian buffer restoration. Together these measures improve water quality, protect beneficial uses, restore stream habitat, and provide residents with cleaner and safer streams. At the same time, they make demands on existing and future infrastructure. The Philadelphia case illustrates that the significant capital costs associated with buried infrastructure can be partially offset through implementation of integrated watershed management plans that include community greening initiatives. The combination of lower costs and increased community benefits explains the burgeoning enthusiasm for LID practices (Maimone et al. 2006).

WASTEWATER TREATMENT

With overall support for distributed small-scale approaches growing, the interest in decentralized wastewater treatment has grown as well. For example, urban "gray water" systems and composting toilets (for "black water") are finding acceptance in many communities. Recognized for decades as a means of both reducing the amount of wastewater delivered to the sewer system (or septic tank) and the demand for potable water supply (for both residential irrigation and urban farming), gray water systems separate and capture nontoilet wastewater from sinks, showers, and laundry produced in a residence and reuse it on-site. A household can virtually eliminate all wastewater discharge by combining gray water systems with composting toilets. Only a few states like California and Arizona permit these systems.

In fact, the area of decentralized wastewater management may be one of the most contentious topics in the world of demand-side management. What is the difference between potable water conservation and decentralized wastewater management? Both ask consumers to take more active roles in thinking about their environment, modifying behaviors, and relying less on large-scale, centralized infrastructure. The difference involves the fact that water conservation requires altered patterns of use that can be achieved without taking customers off the grid, through a combination of low-cost technology improvements like low-flow toilets and shower heads augmented by voluntary changes in behavior such as shifting the time of use to off-peak hours. Every positive action creates a benefit, while failure to participate is handled by the large-scale system: customers use less but remain connected to the centralized system.

When customers take themselves off the grid with microscale technologies, they are responsible for the management of a technology and local ecosystem that will function properly only with knowledgeable, active maintenance. This raises an important question: Does turning to microscale technologies that depend on a higher level of user engagement than is generally associated with flushing a toilet jeopardize the earlier public heath benefits so painfully achieved? The limited data available on the performance of small-scale systems make that question difficult to answer.

The Centers for Disease Control *Healthy Housing Reference Manual* highlights the fears of individual customers and small communities managing their own urban ecosystem and the issues associated with public health and safety. The chapter on "On-site Wastewater Treatment" begins by establishing the relative importance of proper handling of wastewater and essential principles for its safe management:

Safe, sanitary, nuisance-free disposal of wastewater is a public health priority in all population groups, small and large, rural or urban. Wastewater should be disposed of in a manner that ensures that

- community or private drinking water supplies are not threatened;
- direct human exposure is not possible;
- waste is inaccessible to vectors, insects, rodents, or other possible carriers;
- all environmental laws and regulations are complied with; and
- odor or aesthetic nuisances are not created. (CDC 2006: 10-1)

The requirement to separate all human or nonhuman contact with wastewater is itself a "barrier" to customer or community engagement with wastewater treatment and stormwater runoff at any scale. In fact, with little explanation except as evidence of the threat posed by poorly implemented on-site disposal systems, the manual presents photos of a direct discharge into a creek with the following description:

In (the) Figure . . . a straight pipe from a nearby home discharges untreated sewage that flows from a shallow drainage ditch to a roadside mountain creek in which many children and some adults wade and fish. The clear water . . . is quite deceptive in terms of the health hazard presented. A 4-mile walk along the creek revealed 12 additional pipes that were also releasing untreated sewage. Some people in the area reportedly regard this creek as a source of drinking water. (CDC 2006: 10-2)

To ensure that greater levels of direct citizen involvement in the management of the urban ecosystem do not compromise public health and safety, education, monitoring, and feedback regarding performance and results are essential.

These examples represent efforts on the part of large government agencies and municipal utilities to create and support initiatives that reduce the demands placed on the urban infrastructure they manage, thereby extending the life of existing facilities and reducing the costs of expansion. Like similar gains achieved in energy and transportation, many have succeeded in convincing individual customers within their service areas to change their behavior.

Individual and Community Group Success

While anecdotal evidence of tens of thousands of successful high-impact citizen activists and community groups contributing to positive change and environmental restoration in their neighborhoods and cities exists,[4] data regarding who they are; where they are; and, perhaps most important, what they have achieved (expressed in quantifiable measures of performance) are rare and often nonexistent.[5] This lack of information makes it difficult to predict the potential benefits possible from incubating, nurturing, and providing ongoing support for these efforts. Furthermore, the lack of data discourages utility managers from relying too heavily on these small- and microscale initiatives. For utility managers, "reliability" in supply, facility capacity, facility availability, and response time to outages is a top priority. "Guessing" at the long-term contributions that could result from small-scale initiatives does not meet the standard of care or performance expected of the utility industry.

Nevertheless, the growing case evidence regarding performance is both encouraging and inspirational. The PBS-series *Edens Lost & Found* (produced by Harry Wiland and Dale Bell) is one example of an attempt to document and communicate to others the accomplishments of committed individuals and community groups.[6] They have included the stories of habitat restoration accomplished by Steve Packard's Chicago Wilderness coalition, Michael Howard's Eden Place Nature Center in Fuller Park, the Pennsylvania Horticultural Society's Philadelphia Green program, the amazing Lily Yeh's Village of the Arts and Humanities in North Philadelphia, and TreePeople's transformational tree planting efforts in Los Angeles (Wiland and Bell 2006).

Wiland and Bell—who are dedicated to the transforming power of media in our society—believe that the ability to reach individuals in the privacy of their homes offers far-reaching public enrichment and education for social change. Their mission is to create new urban pioneers by highlighting the work of community activists who are breaking new ground.

Apparently, many more people are interested in volunteering to reduce demands on large-scale infrastructure in their communities than have been effectively mobilized. And while media professionals like Wiland and Bell use their talents to recruit new volunteers to the cause, the skills of infrastructure managers do not always translate well into the motivational and inspirational leadership that changes culture and produces long-term societal progress. So what can be done?

A Truce Between Large and Small Systems Proponents

One change would be to establish a standing truce among advocates for specific technologies. It is not unusual for both institutional and individual stakeholders to begin the planning process with definitive ideas regarding the best solution to their problems. "If we would just build more desalination facilities, all our water problems would be solved." Or, "We don't need to build anything if we just conserve more." These opening positions focus on the "means," not the "ends" of achieving sustainable urban environments that all are trying to achieve. No silver bullet technology can "fix" the urban environment; it takes an entire range of infrastructure, institutional, and cultural innovations to achieve the desired economic, environmental, quality of life, and social justice "ends." Efficiently integrating the full spectrum of available solutions should replace the frequent battles over which specific innovation or technology is good, better, and best.

In fairness, it should be noted that many promising small-scale and distributed technologies have had a hard time gaining acceptance among established municipal agencies, utilities, regulators, and professionals. Often the reasons relate to a general lack of information regarding how they perform, health and safety concerns, uncertainty regarding ongoing operations and maintenance, lack of approved standards, and in many cases obsolete local ordinances limiting their application. At the same time, already neglected large-scale infrastructure needs attention as indicated by the state of disrepair, frequently reported in the press. The ASCE 2005 *Report Card for America's Infrastructure* assigned an overall grade of D, and estimated total investment needs at an astounding $1.6 trillion (ASCE 2007b). Responsibly maintaining and replacing large-scale infrastructure assets (airports, bridges, dams, roads, schools, transit systems, in addition to all the environmental infrastructure discussed above) is just as important to urban sustainability as the behavioral and cultural changes needed at the individual, family, and community levels. The concept of stewardship should apply to both the built environment and the natural world.

This "portfolio" approach does not abandon large-scale infrastructure solutions but combines them with small-scale initiatives that reduce the future need. And yet, for many of the most avid proponents of the small-scale solutions, structures such as dams, aqueducts, regional treatment facilities, and concrete drainage channels are intrinsically undesirable. To begin, all interests should start a real dialogue, a dedicated effort on everyone's part to listen, understand, and empathize with the views of large municipal utilities, businesses, environmental activists, homeowners, renters, and the many, many others who have a stake in the urban environment. All of these groups hold common values but often dispute the "means" of achieving the desired results.

A Safe Haven for Innovation and Occasional Mistakes

Integrated planning and development approaches often highlight the conflicts that exist between institutional authority, with its desire to deliver uniform benefits to the broader community (traditionally in a command-and-control context), and the infinite variability and eccentricity of individuals and small groups, however effective they may be in their homes and neighborhoods. The dilemma is old and pits the individual against established norms and authority. The activist's side of the debate could be summed up in the aphorism, "I would rather be cured by a quack, than poisoned to death by a properly qualified doctor."

In many cases, the most effective individual agents of change are not properly qualified doctors, but they have found effective and often unconventional cures for what is ailing their communities. Their cures sometimes venture to the limits of the properly constituted boundaries of their local communities—at least as those boundaries are defined by local building codes, public health and safety ordinances, and established environmental regulations.

In working to incorporate demand management principles into the institutional framework of cities and counties, public officials need to leave room for the innovative, eccentric, and sometimes unsuccessful attempts of individuals and small groups to make positive change. Every new prototype project will not prove to be a best practice. For the professional community of planners, architects, and engineers, taking that kind of risk usually is not acceptable because of the associated liability issues and the need for wide acceptance and public support in their work.

For example, consulting firms providing both traditional civil engineering as well as nonstructural institutional approaches to meeting urban utility needs must meet client expectations that designed solutions (whether structural or institutional) will meet their objectives.

There is little or no tolerance for engineered solutions that "almost" do the job or fail after initial success.

Increased Use of Systems Modeling Tools

Professional planners have the ability to evaluate formally the relationships between large-scale infrastructure and small-scale, decentralized solutions using system simulation modeling tools and techniques. Using systems modeling they can build elaborate conceptual models that can be run dynamically as a means of evaluating the future contributions and impacts offered by alternative investment approaches—including various levels of decentralized, small-scale improvements, and increased adoption of best management practices (BMPs) by communities. For example, for the city of Los Angeles's Integrated Plan for the Wastewater Program, the consulting team of CDM and CH2M Hill developed a comprehensive integrated systems model that depicted the relationships of elements within the wastewater service function, as well as relationships among wastewater, water, recycled water, and stormwater systems. Most important, the model incorporated decentralized capture and beneficial use of wet weather urban runoff resulting from rainfall, together with water conservation measures affecting water supply and consequent wastewater flows.

The model showed and roughly quantified the benefits of implementing higher levels of conservation and decentralized management practices in reducing beach impacts and pollutant loadings, enabling equal consideration of these alternatives with investments in large-scale pipes and treatment facilities (Lopez-Calva, Magallanes, and Cannon 2001).

Comprehensive integrated systems models representing urban infrastructure are not so common as would be expected, given the availability of the technology and the growing interest in "holistic" approaches. In the absence of these modeling tools, the benefits of small-scale investments and conservation is often left to crude estimates of "mass balance" changes, "boundary condition" assumptions, or unquantified "feel good" assertions regarding the importance of reducing runoff and minimizing waste. The routine use of systems models in public policy and infrastructure decision-making is essential to understanding and properly valuing the contributions offered by action at the individual and neighborhood level.

Improved Monitoring, Data Collection, and Mapping of Results

One of the primary shortcomings of a heavy reliance on the small-scale investments in the infrastructure portfolio is the difficulty encountered attempting to quantify the actual contributions and benefits produced by many microscale solutions. The conclusions of a paper on effectiveness of LID state the case clearly:

LID holds much promise as an environmentally sensitive approach to site development and stormwater management. However, data is lacking to fully support this claim . . . Hopefully, as more data from LID projects become available, and conclusions are reached as to its effectiveness, the regulatory framework of states and municipalities will be more aligned to allow and even encourage . . . LID implementation. (Lombardo and Line 2004)

In this regard, one of the most significant limitations on the use of comprehensive systems models recommended earlier is a lack of data on the actual performance and geographic distribution of small-scale improvements, as well as physical linkages between actions and investments that occur at widely different scales in traditionally isolated service functions like water, wastewater, and stormwater. Much like the overall lack of information on the benefits of volunteerism discussed earlier, more effort has gone into counting the number of parts distributed (for example, number low-flow toilets installed or number of trees planted) than monitoring and tracking the actual service benefits that accrue at the location of the installation. Consequently, calibrating models designed to show quantified reductions in flows or demands on large-scale systems necessarily rely upon gross assumptions and oversimplification.

No doubt, analysts could be more creative in using available information technology and the Internet as a tool for collecting and mapping data, relying on both low-cost sensing and data acquisition, as well as individuals to report on performance at the neighborhood level.

Feedback to Citizens and Neighborhoods

Better data on what was being conserved, reused, and prevented from running off individual properties or neighborhoods could be fed back to individuals and neighborhoods as a virtual report card on performance. The aphorism "what gets measured gets done" is relevant to the behavioral changes, increased awareness, improved understanding, and overall sense of responsibility for the physical environment that immediately surrounds each of us as individuals.

Several years ago, Andy Lipkis, president of TreePeople in Los Angeles, imagined the impact of a large-screen video display on which real-time data regarding conservation, tree planting, installed cisterns, and other household and neighborhood activities (as reported by individual citizens through the Internet) could be plotted on a map of Los Angeles. Such an installation could help all visualize the extent and penetration of household-scale changes on the overall environment of Los Angeles. It would show the breadth and scope of individual initiative and provide a place to monitor the rise and fall of the residents' steward-ship of the urban environment.

Innovative electric utilities are exploring the use of Internet sites and e-mail alerts that help customers schedule their power use into non-peak periods. These shifts in the time of use reduce peak demands and fore-stall the need for additional generating and transmission capacity. A recent *New York Times* article reported on a successful pilot program in Chicago:

Just as cellphone customers delay personal calls until they become free at night and on weekends, and just as millions of people fly at less popular times because air fares are lower, people who know the price of electricity at any given moment can cut back when prices are high and use more when prices are low. Partici-pants in the Community Energy Cooperative program, for example, can check a Web site that tells them, hour by hour, how much their electricity costs; they get e-mail alerts when the price is set to rise above 20 cents a kilowatt-hour. (Johnston 2007)

The possibilities of using the Internet to display citizen feedback are dra-matically illustrated in a project called D-Tower developed by Lars Spuy-broek of NOX Architecture (Spuybroek 2002). D-Tower is a roughly 40-foot sculptural structure that changes color based on the emotional state of a Rotterdam community of approximately 45,000 people, as evi-denced by their responses to a monthly questionnaire administered over the Internet. No doubt, devoting more attention to the relationships between urban infrastructure (at all scales) and media could yield many benefits. For the record, a lighted pylon on the top of the old John Han-cock Building in Boston (now called the Berkeley Building) has pro-vided a colored beacon forecasting the weather (and signaling rainouts at Fenway Park) since 1950. If a neighborhood beacon reported environ-mental data like conservation and waste, how many citizens might be motivated to take action to turn it from red to green? While this is an extreme proposal, clearly the Internet and its associated communica-tions technologies offer many new avenues for citizen participation, feedback, and behavior modification—as yet unexplored.

Institutional Mechanisms for Empowering Individuals

Where ongoing care and intensive maintenance is needed to realize the benefits of a micro-scale solution, communities are relying primarily on (1) individuals and families, (2) volunteer community groups, and (3) the occasional overcommitted, underfunded public utility or municipal agency. Is there a business opportunity to create new "green-collar" industries based on the need to maintain small-scale and micro-scale systems?

Creating a "habitat" or market space for individual empowerment and entrepreneurialism may be an option. Such a solution implies forging a partnership among municipal agencies and community interests that can deal with procurement laws and appropriate business ethics between the public and private sectors, but should not be abandoned because of those necessary complications.

Many are applying a great deal of thought and effort to the best practices for driving the innovation and entrepreneurship of citizen activists across society as a whole. For example, Bill Drayton, who serves as the chair and CEO of Ashoka, a philanthropic organization dedicated to addressing social problems through individual entrepreneurialism, argues that the process of creating "change-makers" is more critical than the individual act of changing personal behavior. He describes empowerment this way:

> The most important contribution any of us can make now is not to solve any particular problem, no matter how urgent energy or environment or financial regulation is. What we must do now is increase the proportion of humans who know that they can cause change. And who, like smart white blood cells coursing through society, will stop with pleasure whenever they see that something is stuck or that an opportunity is ripe to be seized. Multiplying society's capacity to adapt and change intelligently and constructively and building the necessary underlying collaborative architecture, is the world's most critical opportunity now. Pattern-changing leading social entrepreneurs are the most critical single factor in catalyzing and engineering this transformation. (Drayton 2006: 5)

What Drayton and others are promoting is an approach to societal problem-solving that relies on the innovation and entrepreneurship of individuals functioning at a microscale, informed by global databases, and spreading change virally through their highly networked urban ecosystems. This model is as different from the traditional command-and-control utility paradigm as the IBM of 1966 is different from Google in 2007.

It may be less relevant to ask whether the social entrepreneur is an appropriate vehicle for addressing our infrastructure needs than to think about how this new force can be applied to reducing those needs on a wide-scale basis. What are the changes that utilities could make in order to provide for the incubation of innovative ideas, technology solutions, and behavioral modifications that have the potential of "spreading" organically through a community?

For many in the world of small-scale solutions, the technologies and behavioral responses represent more than a means to an end. In many cases, they are an end in themselves, representing a redefined relationship between humans and the environment. The modest scale mimicry of "natural" processes combined with restrained consumption of resources and energy is reflective of fundamental values and attitudes. In this context, how people do things is as important as their results.

One of the important differences is that the activities of traditional utilities rarely speak to or enrich the souls of their customers. Community leaders and volunteers are motivated by a sense of responsibility—as are others in the industry. But the spiritual rewards of their work and the enlightenment it can create in others is an invaluable contribution to the overall health and well-being of cities and their populations. Those intangible benefits on top of functional performance can occasionally redeem the microscale from charges of impracticality, unreliability, and added costs.

But this discussion is not about the pros and cons of decentralized technologies versus large-scale regional alternatives. It focuses on agents of change and improvement, both institutional and individual. While the published arguments for and against decentralized systems tend to focus on their technical performance and relative cost-effectiveness, the underlying tension between the two models is grounded in the more fundamental debate between the respective roles of the individual and government in protecting communal interests.

This current tension again recalls Theodore Roosevelt's Sorbonne speech, where he spoke to the importance of the individual while recognizing the practical benefits of government's role in meeting widespread community needs. Should the individual's right to assert an immediate and personal claim on the future of the environment be accommodated, even encouraged, despite the risks of poor performance and neglected maintenance? The monitoring and reporting networks needed to hold those individuals accountable for fulfilling their promise of lower impacts on the environment exists allowing the incorporation of these ecological pioneers and entrepreneurs into the fabric of established infrastructure systems.

Roosevelt also honored "the man in the arena":

It is not the critic who counts: not the man who points out how the strong man stumbles or where the doer of deeds could have done better. The credit belongs to the man who is actually in the arena, whose face is marred by dust and sweat and blood, who strives valiantly, who errs and comes up short again and again, because there is no effort without error or shortcoming, but who knows the great enthusiasms, the great devotions, who spends himself for a worthy cause; who, at the best, knows, in the end, the triumph of high achievement, and who, at the worst, if he fails, at least he fails while daring greatly, so that his place shall never be with those cold and timid souls who knew neither victory nor defeat. (Roosevelt 2004: 781–82)

The hoped for changes in reducing the impacts of urbanization on the environment will more likely come from those "in the arena" than the consultants and critics. Finding a way to encourage "the doer of deeds" and promote innovation in small and microscale technologies—without neglecting or abandoning the massive national investment in large-scale infrastructure, jeopardizing the health and safety of citizens, or destroying the pioneers whose efforts may fail—is a challenge unlike any yet confronted in the realm of public works.

We are at a point where the analyses of the problem, technological capabilities, and the urgency of the need all point towards empowering thoughtful and committed citizens as part of the solution to today's environmental challenges. It will take ingenuity and innovation on the part of large municipal infrastructure agencies and utilities to harness that energy and make its impact felt on a global scale. Roosevelt's reminder to his 1910 audience still holds true today:

Success or failure will be conditioned upon the way in which the average man, the average women, does his or her duty, first in the ordinary, every-day affairs of life, and next in those great occasional cries which call for heroic virtues. The average citizen must be a good citizen if our republics are to succeed. (Roosevelt 2004: 780)

References

Alm, Alvin L. 2007. "NEPA: Past, Present, and Future." U.S. Environmental Protection Agency (EPA). http://www.epa.gov/history/topics/nepa/01.htm.

American Society of Civil Engineers (ASCE). 2007a. History & Heritage of Civil Engineering. http://live.asce.org/hh/index.mxml.

———. 2007b. Report Card for America's Infrastructure. http://www.asce.org/reportcard/2005/page.cfm?id=103.

Brechin, Gray. 1999. *Imperial San Francisco: Urban Power, Earthly Ruin.* Berkeley: University of California Press.

Browman-Krulm, Mary. 2003. *Margaret Mead: A Biography.* Westport, Conn.: Greenwood Press.

Centers for Disease Control and Prevention (CDC) and U.S. Department of Housing and Urban Development (HUD). 2006. *Healthy Housing Reference Manual.* Atlanta: U.S. Department of Health and Human Services.

Dickinson, Mary Ann. 2006. *A Decade of Progress.* Sacramento: California Urban Water Conservation Council. http://www.cuwcc.com/uploads/tech_docs/Article_Decade_01–10–09.pdf .

Duffy, John. 1992. *The Sanitarians: A History of American Public Health.* Urbana: University of Illinois Press.

Drayton, Bill. 2006. "Everyone a Changemaker: Social Entrepreneurship's Ultimate Goal." *Innovations* (Winter).

France, Robert Lawrence. 2002. *Handbook of Water Sensitive Planning and Design.* Baton Rouge: Lewis Publishers.

Hall, Libby. 2000. *The Chicago River: A Natural and Unnatural History.* Chicago: Lake Claremont Press.

Hundley, Norris, Jr. 1992. *The Great Thirst: Californians and Water, 1770s-1990s*. Berkeley: University of California Press.

Independent Sector. 2001. *Measuring Volunteering: A Practical Tool Kit*. Washington: Independent Sector.

———. 2007. *Giving and Volunteering in the United States 2001*. http://www .independentsector.org/members/ismembers.html.

Johnston, David Cay. 2007. "Taking Control of Electric Bill, Hour by Hour." *New York Times*, January 8.

Koeppel, Gerard T. 2000. *Water for Gotham: A History*. Princeton, N.J.: Princeton University Press.

Lombardo, Laura, and Daniel Line. 2004. "Evaluating the Effectiveness of Low Impact Development." Paper presented at the First National Conference on Low Impact Development, September 21–23, College Park, Maryland. http:// www.mwcog.org/environment/lidconference/.

Lopez-Calva, Enrique, A. Magallanes, and D. Cannon. 2001. "Systems Modeling for Integrated Planning in the City of Los Angeles: Using Simulation as a Tool for Decision Making." WEFTEC 2001, Water Environment Federation National Conference Proceedings.

Maimone, Mark, James T. Smullen, Brian Marengo, and C. Crosket. 2006. "The Role of Low Impact Redevelopment/Development in Integrated Watershed Management Planning: Turning Theory into Practice." Paper presented at symposium, Cities of the Future: Getting Blue Water to Green Cities, July 12–14, Racine, Wisconsin.

Metropolitan Water District of Southern California (MWD). 1996. *Southern California's Integrated Water Resources Plan*. Vol. 1, *The Long-Term Resources Plan*. Report 1107, March.

———. 2006. *Relationships Work: Annual Progress Report to the California State Legislature, Achievements in Conservation, Recycling and Groundwater Recovery*. February.

Rodrigo, Dan, and Paul R. Brown. 2005. "Developing Stakeholder Consensus in Water Resources Planning." Proceedings of the 2005 Georgia Water Resources Conference, April 25–27, University of Georgia.

Roosevelt, Theodore. 2004. *Letters and Speeches*. New York: Library of America.

Spuybroek, Lars. 2002. "The Structure of Vagueness." In *TransUrbanism*, ed. Arjen Mulder, Joke Brouwer, and Laura Martz. Rotterdam: V2Publishing/ NAI.

U.S. Bureau of Labor Statistics (BLS). 2005. "Volunteering in America, 2005." News release dated December 9, 2005. http://www.bls.gov/news.release/ volun.nr0.htm.

U.S. Environmental Protection Agency (EPA), Office of Solid Waste. 2006. *Municipal Solid Waste in the United States: 2005 Facts and Figures*. EPA530-R-06–011. Washington, D.C., October.

Wiland, Harry, and Dale Bell. 2006. *Edens Lost & Found: How Ordinary Citizens are Restoring Our Great American Cities*. White River Junction, Vt.: Chelsea Green.

Chapter 9

Blue-Green Practices: Why They Work and Why They Have Been So Difficult to Implement Through Public Policy

CHARLIE MILLER

Blue-green features reduce the demand for potable water, limit a building's impact on overburdened sewers, improve runoff water quality, protect natural downstream habitats, and conserve energy. They also make use of a free resource—rainfall—to create vital new urban landscapes. While common in Germany, these features are just beginning to be incorporated into buildings in the United States.

Joachim Tourbier coined the term "blue-green" technologies more than 35 years ago.[1] He used it to describe a class of sustainable approaches related to the marriage of landscape design and rainfall runoff management. Blue-green features have the advantage of contributing to the aesthetic content of the built environment while drastically reducing the environmental footprint of development.

Although these might also be described as low-impact development measures, the term blue-green captures the essential interplay of plants and rainfall in achieving the benefit. Some designers, notably, Herbert Dreiseitl, Kevin Robert Perry, Faye Harwell, and Steven Koch, have made the movement of water through their urban landscapes a dominant visual and functional element in courtyards, parking facilities, building terraces, and other public and private spaces. By making the flow of runoff visually exciting, these projects help build broader understanding and support for blue-green design.

The traditional approach in urban design has been to conceal runoff when possible and to rapidly convey it away from new construction. This approach was intended to minimize nuisance flooding. It assumed that runoff could be conveyed harmlessly downstream without consequences. More important, it assumed that sources of potable public water were inexhaustible and inexpensive and it did not recognize harvested rainfall as an asset. Future design must respond to the realities of a more densely populated and resource-constrained world.

I have selected four blue-green features to consider in some detail:

- green roofs;
- courtyard landscapes incorporating biofiltration and rainfall harvesting with water reuse;
- living walls;
- green façades or vine walls.

Each of these features is intrinsically linked to building performance and may be best thought of as a building system. These features are at home in the built environment, where a direct connection to the earth is tenuous or abstract, at best. Unlike many suburban or rural settings, in the city deep percolation may be impractical or inadvisable due to contaminated or compacted soils. Consequently, urban landscapes designed around blue-green features create alternative pathways for rainfall. The movement of water is predominantly horizontal as opposed to vertical. The new urban "watershed" consists of a series of shallow planes related to one another by the movement of water. Veneer landscapes may range in thickness from 4 inches to 4 feet and may incorporate shallow pools, sculpted rivulets, wetlands, meadow-like expanses, and formal gardens. Runoff is often captured in shallow underground cisterns and recirculated into the aboveground landscape (Figure 1).

Water moves circuitously through these miniature landscapes. As it travels it is cleansed, used to nourish plants, and cool occupied spaces, and may be put to use replacing potable water sources. Excess water, filtered and cooled at the end of the cycle, can be discharged at a slow rate to sustain local streams and other natural receiving waters. The inventive use of blue-green approaches can restore both hydrologic function and human delight to the most densely developed urban projects.

By integrating blue-green features, ultra-urban environments can begin to emulate the performance of natural, undeveloped landscapes. In nature, most rainfall does not travel far from where it falls. Through the integration of blue-green features, buildings can become as efficient as forests in how they use the precious water resource. Unlike naturally evolved habitats, however, urban development that incorporates blue-green features represents a conscious act of creation. The success of these projects will depend on how well the designer understands the science surrounding the interchange between soil, water, plants, and the atmosphere.

A piecemeal approach often applied to the implementation of sus-

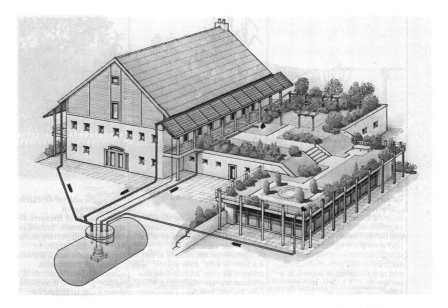

Figure 1. Integrated blue-green measures. Optigrün International AG.

tainable practices conceals the fact that most of these practices work best when combined into networks. One of the most exciting international examples of a highly integrated project is the new high-rise district at Potsdammer Platz in Berlin (Dreiseitl et al. 2001). This project development employs green roofs on all flat roof surfaces, including the tallest of its buildings. In addition, the site design includes numerous terrace and podium-level roof landscapes that serve as preschool play areas, cafes, and meeting areas. On-structure courtyard landscapes at ground level complement the green roofs. Some of the water descending through these features is also routed through shallow reflecting pools populated with rushes and wetland plants. Water released from the features is collected in cisterns. Cistern water is subsequently used for fire protection, toilet flushing, irrigating intensively landscaped areas, and to support a dynamic water feature that is the focus for the central plaza. Excess runoff is directed to a large artificial wetland for additional filtration, and eventually discharges to a tributary of the River Spree.

Potsdammer Platz illustrates another factor in blue-green design. Significant benefits are most likely to be achieved when entire neighborhoods are built (or rebuilt) using these features and when performance objectives for development are clearly articulated. In the case of Potsdammer Platz, a unique opportunity presented itself in which an entire city district was being leveled and rebuilt from scratch. However, the process is typically more gradual, as new ordinances and building codes transform urban neighborhoods over time. In Germany, it has taken decades for city policies promoting or requiring green roofs to transform commercial districts in Stuttgart, Munich, Hamburg, and elsewhere.

Despite the advantages of these features, they are used only infrequently in American designs. There may be several reasons for this, for example,

- Reliable engineering information is incomplete and methods that can stimulate performance are poorly calibrated and not standardized.
- American building owners and managers are skeptical about incorporating living ecosystems into their buildings.
- Most regulations for site development are antiquated and do not provide incentives for managing resources efficiently.
- Fuel remains too inexpensive for alternative methods of cooling buildings to become financially attractive.

Some major metropolitan centers in the United States are, however, beginning to make an investment in blue-green design. Since 2000, when the Chicago City Building was greened, the city of Chicago has been very active in promoting green roofs for new commercial construction in the city. Incentives include expedited planning review and floor area ratio (FAR) bonuses for participating developers. This effort was undertaken as a means of combating the severe effects of the urban heat island phenomenon in Chicago. Millions of square feet of roof surface have been greened as a result of this program. The city also recognizes green roofs as rainfall runoff control measures in its new stormwater ordinance, primarily as a method to reduce runoff volume. However, since preexisting requirements for runoff rate control remain, green roofs can make only a modest contribution in complying with the ordinance.

The cities of Portland and Philadelphia have recently enacted new stormwater ordinances that provide stronger inducements to install blue-green features as rainfall runoff controls. In particular, these cities now treat green roofs and courtyard landscapes as undeveloped open space for the purposes of estimating site runoff. Philadelphia also requires that all new or redevelopment proposals increase pervious area by 20 percent from the existing conditions. Green roofs, as well as landscapes at grade level, are counted as open-space equivalents, and can be used to satisfy the pervious surface requirement.

The Features

Green roofs provide a thin veneer of soil and vegetation at the roof level. For moderate rainfall events, these surfaces will react much like ground landscapes; soaking up rainfall to support plants, filtering runoff, and delaying and reducing the rate at which runoff is released from the site. Consequently, green roofs have been widely adopted in Germany for urban rainfall runoff management. Most of the rainfall intercepted by green roofs will remain on the roof, where it will be taken up by plants. Plants are a critical ingredient that cause green roofs to perform very differently from common ballasted (gravel covered) roofing systems. These features all include components that satisfy four functions: (1) waterproofing to keep water out of the building, (2) a basal drainage layer that collects rainfall or snow-melt that percolates through the cover, (3) permeable soil-like substrate that promotes plant growth, and (4) ground-covering layer of vegetation. Water discharged from a green roof is not, strictly speaking, runoff. The process is more like a shallow groundwater system. The green roof substrate provides a reservoir of moisture that sustains the plants. However, in many climates irrigation is recommended or required. In these cases, consideration should be given to using harvested rainfall or gray water (Figure 2).

Among blue-green features, green roofs are probably among the easiest to retrofit to existing buildings, followed by vine walls. This is especially true in northern cities, where several favorable factors converge. Here buildings are already designed to accommodate significant snow loads. Most buildings were also initially constructed with a heavy felt and asphalt built-up roofing system that was frequently covered with gravel. Moreover, buildings constructed prior to 1940 frequently have massive wood or steel rafters, and many of the old commercial and institutional buildings are of historical value and will be retained. Last, many of these buildings are now reaching a critical point where re-roofing will be required to preserve the buildings or refit them for new uses.

Consequently, old commercial and institutional buildings offer excellent opportunities to install thin, lightweight green roofs. The maximum weight of these assemblies can be as little as 20 pounds per square foot. In many instances, most of this weight requirement can be met by simply removing the existing roofing materials and replacing them with modern lightweight roofing systems. Examples where old buildings have been greened include Chicago's City Hall, Ohio EPA headquarters (the old Lazarus department store), the Kansas City Central Library (the old

Figure 2. Example of a green roof. Charlie Miller.

First National Bank), and Chicago's Cultural Center (the old Chicago Library).

Courtyard landscapes are also veneer features, albeit thicker and more robust than green roofs. They are typically built over underground structures or parking. In addition to benefits associated with green roofs, courtyard landscapes also condition the air column of the courtyard and moderate harsh sunlight. Courtyards are the most practical

Figure 3. Modular cistern installation. Rainwater Harvesting, Inc.

locations to include pools or cisterns to harvest runoff for reuse. Common uses of harvested water include irrigating interior plants, including "living walls"; irrigating exterior landscapes; and providing water for utilities such as flushing toilets and fire protection.

Cisterns for storing harvested rainwater can take many forms. In addition to prefabricated tanks, cisterns can be constructed economically by enclosing plastic modules in a membrane envelope. Using this technique, cisterns can conform to difficult geometric constraints. This technique was used to install cisterns under the walkways of a one-acre elevated courtyard at the Ram's Head complex at the University of North Carolina. These cisterns intercept roof runoff and provide supplemental water to support the trees, shrubs, and grass on the immediately adjacent landscape. The combined cistern and courtyard installation, which is built over a parking facility, is designed to satisfy rigorous stormwater control requirements established by the city of Chapel Hill. Excess runoff is discharged through scuppers in the side courtyard wall into a wooded bioswale. Figure 3 shows installation of a modular cistern for rainwater harvesting.

Interior plantings can be used strategically to condition the air inside buildings. Living walls, plant communities installed into porous wall units, are often mounted inside buildings. Typical plants might include moss and ferns, as well as a range of herbaceous plants including wild ginger, columbine, and linnaea (Sharp 2005). Ideally, these will be irrigated using harvested rainfall. Irrigation systems can include misting systems and capillary methods. The advantage of living walls is that they can be employed to cool the air in the building and promote circulation. As such they offer a functional alternative to more conventional indoor plantings. Examples of indoor living walls are still few. In North America they include the headquarters of Biohabitats, Inc., in Baltimore and demonstrations at Fleming College and Waterloo University, both in Ontario. A massive and well-known, example of an outdoor living wall can be found at the Musée du Quai Branly in Paris.

Like living walls, green façades that use climbing vines can be optimized to become predictable components of building climatization systems. The vines behave like miniature sun-powered pumping networks, lifting water up the face of the building and distributing it uniformly to the leaf surfaces where evaporation occurs. Vines are very effective in providing evaporative cooling measures because of the immense surface area of the foliage and its natural tendency to proliferate in the areas that receive the highest solar radiation. A large working demonstration of this approach has been in operation since 2002 at the Institute of Physics, Humboldt University, Berlin (Schmidt 2000). This project is a unique mixture of high-tech and blue-green technologies. The building uses green façades to reduce the load on its centralized counter-current adiabatic cooling system and its absorption chiller (used at peak load times). The adiabatic system relies entirely on harvested rainwater. In the adiabatic system, incoming air is cooled in a heat exchanger using outgoing (inside) air that has been chilled by evaporating water. Direct contact between the two air streams does not occur (Figure 4).

The vine wall at Humboldt University facilitates the incorporation of operable windows that allow fresh outside air to circulate while not sacrificing cooling efficiency. The benefit is enhanced by the building geometry, in which the vines have been used to cover the walls of four four-story courtyards. Irrigation water is supplied to the plants at the optimum rate to achieve efficient cooling. Unlike green roofs, water supply for irrigation must be provided externally. The Humboldt University project uses harvested rainwater. Another option for similar projects would be using gray water.

Blue-Green Science

In nature, plants and the fungi and bacteria that live symbiotically with them have a valuable role in filtering water, moderating pH, cooling

Figure 4. Vine wall. Charlie Miller.

water, and removing or immobilizing pollutants. The same is true of plant communities incorporated in the built environment. The mineral substrates that support plant growth in green roofs and living walls have high surface areas and pore space capacity. Volcanic rocks, such as pumice and scoria, are frequently used. Also, heat-expanded clay, shale, and slate are common. These materials provide a hospitable environment for beneficial microbial life, and can absorb large quantities of moisture while preserving aerated, well-drained conditions.

The capability of green roofs and managed landscapes to filter suspended solids and neutralize acidic rainfall has been well documented. When managed with water quality as an objective, significant reductions in chemical pollutants and nutrients, including total nitrogen, can also be achieved (Köhler and Schmidt 2003). The largest project being managed in this way is Potsdammer Platz in Berlin. This development integrates green roofs and landscapes and wetlands to polish runoff before it is discharged to the River Spree. Green roofs on the tall buildings (roofs that would not normally be accessible or visible) may not be fertilized according to the local ordinance. Unless they are heavily fertilized, green roofs will become more efficient in sequestering nutrients as they mature. This phenomenon is probably correlated to the increasing biodiversity of the substrate and the gradual accommodation of soil microbes to windborne pollutants. However, by far the most important contribution made by green roofs to improving water quality is the reduction in the frequency of runoff rates that can trigger combined sewer overflows (CSOs) or stream erosion events.

The substrate in green roofs does not act like a simple sponge. Rather, green roofs should be compared to leaky buckets. Water drains by gravity at a rate proportional to the quantity of moisture contained (Zimmer and Geiger 1997). This property is responsible for reducing the peak flow rate and delaying it in time. The effect is indistinguishable from that of a conventional detention device like a runoff basin. In addition, the absorptive capacity of the substrate ensures that the total volume or runoff is also reduced. Detention is a dynamic process in which the pattern of rainfall distribution (the shape of the storm) will affect the outcome. Storms in which the heaviest rainfall occurs early during the event will be affected more strongly than storms in which the peak rainfall rate is preceded by protracted soaking drizzle. As with all rainfall control features, seasonal variables will also affect performance.

In general, the response of green roofs to rainfall can closely emulate that of ground landscapes. However, since these are veneer systems, every green roof has a "threshold" rainfall event. For storms larger than the threshold event, the performance of the green roof will begin to diverge from that of an idealized ground landscape. Thicker green roof profiles, or profiles with higher detention capacities, will be associated with larger threshold events. Choosing appropriate threshold storms is the responsibility of regulators. In many localities, it would make good sense to relate the threshold storm to trigger events that will result in CSOs, a major source of environmental damage to urban steams and watersheds. Designing green roofs that can satisfy the performance requirements for the threshold storm is the job of the green roof designer and engineer. A useful dialogue between these regulators and designers is only now beginning.

The substrate in green roofs and courtyard landscapes will retain water long enough for the plant roots to absorb most of it. Absorbed water will be released primarily by evaporation from the foliage surface (called evapotranspiration). For every gallon of water evapotranspired by plants, approximately 8,150 BTUs (2.38 kWh) of thermal cooling is realized. Experiments conducted on green roofs in Germany (Köhler and Schmidt 2002) determined that evapotranspiration alone could reduce thermal gain on green roof surfaces by over 80 percent. Similar efficiencies are being measured for green façades (Marco Schmidt 2006; personal communication). This represents an enormous energy savings if it can be applied strategically.

Stuart Gaffin has measured a similar effect using data collected at the Pennsylvania State University Green Roof Research Center. He compared the cooling effect of living foliage to solar reflectance of white artificial surfaces (Gaffin et al. 2005). The effective reflectance of the green roofs he evaluated ranged from 0.70 to 0.85, comparable with that of white roof membranes. Furthermore, unless scrupulously cleaned and maintained, the solar reflectance of white roofs will decrease over time. The effective solar reflectance of green roofs and green façades, on the other hand, is permanent and will improve as the foliage cover matures.

In the winter, free water in green roofs will release latent thermal energy as it freezes, maintaining the temperature at 32°F when outside temperatures plummet. This "sheltering" effect can be exploited in cold climates to improve the efficiency of energy conservation measures. However, this benefit can be realized only as long as some liquid water remains in the green roof profile. Therefore, to realize this benefit, thicker and therefore heavier and more expensive green roof assemblies must be considered.

Water is also a good material for absorbing heat. It requires about 8.4 BTUs (2.4 watt hours) to raise the temperature of one gallon of water by one degree F. The heat capacity of wet substrates allows green roofs and living walls to act like massive thermal capacitors, absorbing heat energy during the day and releasing it slowly at night. This effect of moderating the daily temperature fluctuation on roof and wall surfaces will further reduce the flow of heat energy into, or out of, the building. Dry substrates, on the other hand, have comparatively low heat capacities but will make fair insulators. The thermal conductivity of soil ranges from about 0.20 W/m° K to 0.60 W/m° K, depending on moisture content (Çengel 2003). As thermal capacitance increases in response to rising moisture content, insulation value decreases, and vice versa. The physics of energy absorption and conduction through vegetated roofs is currently under investigation by David Sailor at Portland State University. His work focuses on the relationship between energy processes and moisture content of substrates.

The interdependence of energy benefits, water quality improvement, and rainfall runoff management associated with blue-green features is apparent. For instance, decisions concerning the integration of rainfall harvesting or irrigation will also have profound effects on building climatization and energy usage. However, while work by a variety of researchers is currently under way, peer-reviewed computer simulation tools that will allow designers to confidently predict these benefits are not available at this time. When these do become generally available, designers will be able to engineer dynamic urban watersheds that support sustainable living environments.

Clever new ideas for blue-green features are also coming to the fore. For instance, deciduous green façades can be combined with transparent insulation (Schmidt 2006; personal communication). In this strategy a layer of transparent insulation separates the building's masonry wall from the foliage layer. The foliage layer cools the wall surface during the summer months. In winter when the foliage is gone, the sun's radiation is able to penetrate to the masonry wall, producing sensible heat. The transparent insulation prevents the heat from seeping back out of the building. Air circulating freely behind the wall panel is warmed and heats the interior space. A large-scale prototype of this system is currently being monitored. Innovative ideas like this represent a true merging of different technologies that may spur greater interest in blue-green design.

Impediments to Adoption

There are have been two principal impediments to the widespread application of blue-green techniques. One is that most benefits associated with these practices will be realized over long periods of time. This makes direct field measurements of benefits impractical in most instances. Designers must resort to computer simulations to predict potential benefits. In point of fact, most commonly available simulation programs are poorly calibrated, do not include functions to address specific practices of interest, or are based on paradigms that are no longer relevant to sustainable design. Confidence of regulators and developers in blue-green practices is correspondingly low.

The other impediment to the adoption of blue-green features is found in the conservative nature of environmental regulation. Regulatory paradigms once embedded are difficult to dislodge. The tendency is for the revision of existing regulation to take an accretionary approach—new criteria or constraints are added while leaving the old constraints in place. This frequently results in the real benefits of blue-green features being discounted. Nowhere is this more apparent than in the area of stormwater control, where new volume controls (for example, capture of 1/2 or 1 inch of rainfall) are frequently added to existing requirements for large-storm rate control, such as the attenuation of a Natural Resources Conservation Service (NRCS) Type II 100-year, 24-hour storm event. Regulations are rarely focused on environmentally destructive annual CSO events that are smaller and easily controlled using blue-green features. By and large, existing construction codes and regulations do not do a good job of creating incentives for adopting blue-green practices.

Based on our investigation of green roof runoff characteristics using the R-WIN program, we have reached the conclusion that single-storm analyses may not be good indicators of actual performance.[2] The R-WIN program can simulate networks of blue-green features. Components may include a host of features, including over one dozen green roof types. It is typical to run this program using local weather station data, covering periods of 10 years or more. Output from this model includes useful statistical summaries, including

- peak flow rates associated with specified recurrence frequencies (for example, 1-, 2-, 5-, 10-year);
- exceedance frequency for critical flow rates at specified locations in the network (e.g., CSOs).

This approach provides results that will be relevant to the patterns of rainfall in the specific locality of interest, and integrate a broad range of antecedent climatic conditions. Using the same model, it is also possible to simulate isolated prescribed rainfall events (that is, design storms). When the results of long-term simulations using local weather data are compared to the results using single-design-storm inputs, the single-storm simulations are found to be overly conservative.

We conclude that the use of the design-storm approach to simulating complex blue-green networks may significantly underestimate the value of these features. Furthermore, the standard NRCS rainfall distributions, used almost universally in the United States to construct design storms, may not well represent local conditions. Impediments to adopting long-term computer simulations as an alternative to design-storm models in United States include entrenched use of the design-storm approach and emphasis on 25- to 100-year frequency events. Existing weather station databases that incorporate a 15-minute recording interval are rarely long enough to support analysis of a 25-year climate cycle.

Stormwater runoff computer programs that can provide long-term simulations using local weather data, and that are also in common use in the United States, include HSPF (Hydrological Simulation Program-Fortran) and SWMM (Storm Water Management Model). A positive step would be the development of subroutines for these models that can simulate green roofs and other blue-green features.

It is instructive to look at regulations in Germany, where the implementation of blue-green features is much more widespread. The design rainfall event for site development throughout Germany is an intense but short event; approximately one inch of rainfall falling in 15 minutes. An event of this magnitude has been found to be responsible for most of the economic cost associated with flood damage, lost work productivity, infrastructure damage, and stream erosion. Blue-green features are very effective in managing this type of event.

In most German municipalities, building owners are charged for the public water they use, the stormwater they discharge, and the wastewater they discharge. The fees are reasonable reflections of the actual cost to the public of providing these utilities. As a result, there is a strong incentive to reduce potable water usage (by employing rainfall harvesting), runoff (through green roofs and landscaping), and wastewater production (by using efficient appliances and utilities). In some districts new development is not permitted if it will result in the discharge of stormwater in a typical year. These kinds of incentives do not exist in the United States. Even communities that have initiated stormwater utilities and assess a stormwater utility fee to connected properties seldom pass on the full cost of the utility service in their fee.

Of course, a potential impediment to adoption of blue-green features is cost. Financial incentives to install blue-green features may include

- Avoided costs associated with more expensive conventional rainfall runoff control measures. This benefit is highly dependent on the content of local ordinances and permit requirements.
- Longer service lifetimes for completed projects, particularly for green roofs when compared to conventional roofing options.
- Lower fuel requirements.

- Higher rental or sales values associated with desirability linked to aesthetics or environmental consciousness.
- Municipal subsidies, such as FAR bonuses provided in Portland and Chicago.

However, even when potential benefits are taken into account, it is common to find that a positive return on investment will not be associated with a particular project. In large part, this is due to the absence of an experienced and efficient industry to support blue-green projects. For construction prices to decline, the volume of work must be large enough for businesses to train dedicated skilled workforces, negotiate for materials in volume, and invest in specialty material handling equipment. We have seen this transformation occur in Germany, where sustainable construction has been strongly supported by the government.

At present, positive returns on investment are more likely to be associated with commercial or institutional projects in ultra-urban settings. Even in these cases, initial capital costs for buildings that incorporate blue-green measures are likely to be significantly higher than buildings with more familiar designs. However, long-term savings associated with lower fuel consumption and less frequent repair and replacement costs will make these projects good investments in the long run. To make informed decisions, it is a good idea for consumers to ask for engineering analyses to quantify these potential benefits.

All blue-green features are living things and will require some care in order to continue to provide a benefit. The level of maintenance required, and therefore the cost, can vary widely. This annual cost should be included in an assessment of the return on investment. Thin green roofs can, for example, be intentionally designed to require little maintenance. Methods of reducing maintenance include elimination of irrigation; tough, rapid covering groundcover plants; permanent countermeasures against wind damage; supplemental measures to protect the waterproof membrane; durable mineral "soil" material or substrate. Still, owners should plan on some maintenance, including weeding and fertilizing, at least twice annually. A conservative estimate of the maintenance requirement for most projects is 2 man-hours per 1,000 square feet of green roof. Green façades will require a similar level of maintenance. In this case, expect some pruning, fertilization, and periodic attention to irrigation equipment.

Intensively landscaped green roofs (intensive green roofs), courtyard landscapes, and living walls will require the regular attention of a professional landscape maintenance company or gardener. With regard to their maintenance requirements, they will be similar in every way to irrigated gardens incorporated elsewhere in a development plan. As with all landscapes, failure to provide regular and timely maintenance can result in large costs to remediate problems.

It's a Big Country

The application of blue-green features in the United States poses special challenges, due to the tremendous range in climatic variables across the country. As a result national guidelines for the implementation of blue-green features must, of necessity, be generic. Useful indicators of the potential value of blue-green features include seasonal differences between rainfall and potential evapotranspiration (PET):

- rainfall volume associated with the 10-year, 20-minute rainfall event;
- seasonal average daily low and high temperatures.

In many areas of the country rainfall exceeds or keeps pace with PET. These are ideal regions for a wide range of blue-green features. In climates where annual rainfall exceeds PET but summers are dry, it is logical to include rainfall harvesting as part of an overall development plan.

As rainfall runoff management systems, green roofs will be more effective in climates with rainfall patterns dominated by frequent small to moderate-sized events. They are not likely to be as effective in areas of the country with monsoon rains or tropical storms.

Climates with large diurnal swings in temperature will benefit from green roofs since their thermal mass properties will mute the daily highs and lows. All blue-green features are better at cooling than at sheltering buildings from cold. Therefore, greater energy benefits are likely to be realized in warm states. On the other hand, hot and arid areas may be problematic due to a scarcity of water. Also, very high temperatures in some region place absolute limits on the effectiveness of evaporative cooling.

All this diversity further complicates the problem of developing a national public policy toward the implementation of blue-green features. To overcome this problem, trustworthy computer simulation tools must be developed. These tools must be supported by regional efforts to develop calibration data sets. First adopters of blue-green technologies should be identified by state environmental organizations and enlisted in monitoring and reporting programs. This will involve some modest investment by these public entities. Its benefits would far outweigh the costs.

In summary, two conditions are required in order for the potential benefits of blue-green practices to be realized: investment in reliable engineering tools to evaluate and measure benefits, and more flexible codes and regulations that focus on solving the chronic problems associated with development.

References

Çengel, Yunus, 2003. *Heat Transfer: A Practical Approach.* 2nd ed. Boston: McGraw-Hill.

Dreiseitl, Herbert. Dieter Grau, and Karl H. C. Ludwig, eds. 2001. *Waterscapes: Planning, Building and Designing with Water.* Basel: Birkhäuser.

Gaffin, Stuart et al. 2005. "Energy Balance Modeling Applied to Comparison of White and Green Roof Cooling Efficiency." In *Greening Rooftops for Sustainable Communities: Proceedings of the Third Annual Greening Rooftops for Sustainable Cities Conference.* Washington, D.C., May 4–6.

Köhler, Manfred, and Marco Schmidt. 2002. *Roofgreening Annual Report.* Jahrbuch Dachbegrünung. Braunschweig: Verlag Thalacker.

———. 2003. *Study of Extensive Green Roofs in Berlin.* Part III, *Retention of Contaminants.* International Report, Technical University of Berlin.

Schmidt, Marco. 2000. *Energy and Water: A Decentralized Approach to Integrated Sustainable Development.* Internal Report, Technical University of Berlin.

Sharp, Randy. 2005. "Living Walls for the Vancouver Aquarium." In *Greening Rooftops for Sustainable Communities: Proceedings of the Third Annual Greening Rooftops for Sustainable Cities Conference.* Washington, D.C., May 4–6.

Zimmer, U., and Wolfgang F. Geiger. 1997. "Model for the Design of Multi-Layered Infiltration Systems." *Water Science and Technology* 36: 8–9.

Chapter 10

The Roots of the Urban Greening Movement

Victor Rubin

The urban greening movement—the constellation of collective efforts by residents to improve the natural and built environment of their neighborhoods—has evolved into a diverse set of strategies based in at least four distinct but overlapping domains of community organizing and policy change. These domains provide the motivation and conceptual underpinning for a wide variety of local campaigns, programs, and organizations.

The creation and revival of parks, gardens, street trees, creeks, and waterfronts are appealing, tangible, and direct, especially when compared to many of the long-term economic strategies that must also be undertaken to revitalize lower-income urban neighborhoods. Support for the celebration of local cultures through public art, street festivals, and food is innately colorful, life-affirming, and often more enjoyable than many of the complex social and educational programs that must also be part of a community-building strategy. Effective urban greening projects are, in short, not only valuable in the long term to the health of the community but intrinsically rewarding to the participants.

Most urban greening endeavors grow out of the passionate pursuit of specialists and single-issue advocates: those who promote community gardens, self-proclaimed "tree people," creek restoration aficionados, visual artists and their allies with the managerial talent to execute murals and other public art, and entrepreneurs who find environmentally friendly economic niches in the community. Without that kind of deep issue-specific experience and single-minded focus over several years, most of the greening initiatives and projects would never be realized.

At the same time, these specific projects fit within some broader categories of community action. These broader categories of framing and acting on urban issues show that the greening movement is beginning to generate a wider base of political and economic support and that it is becoming allied with powerful forces for social and institutional change.

This essay provides a conceptual framework through which these four domains can be understood, illustrated by a variety of local efforts and recent research. The four domains of organizing and policy reform considered are

1. Advocacy for environmental justice
2. Promotion of community economic development
3. Addressing health disparities through a focus on community factors
4. Advancing equity in urban infrastructure.

Advocacy for Environmental Justice. Low-income communities of color have been the predominant location of many kinds of unhealthy and unsafe facilities and dumping grounds, and this disparity has given rise to the environmental justice movement. Some of the dumping has been the result of lawlessness and official neglect, as when vacant lots are not adequately maintained or policed, but other problems, such as proliferation of refuse transfer stations, incinerators, or power plants, are the result of local policy and planning decisions. Many of the country's most energetic neighborhood redevelopment efforts have started with opposition to these kinds of environmental land use hazards and grown into more proactive efforts to develop new housing, businesses, and open spaces.

Promotion of Community Economic Development. The proliferation of vacant lots and properties in lower-income neighborhoods, including residential, industrial, and commercial sites, has created great need and incentive for community-based developers to turn these sites into productive, safe, inviting environments. Parks, open space, outdoor art, and other aspects of the public realm are critical to this kind of redevelopment of sites of all sizes. Community developers have created environmentally focused businesses as well as parks and open spaces for recreation and cultural gatherings.

Addressing Health Disparities Through Community Factors. The recent heightened concern with fitness and weight control as a public policy issue has generated new support for the creation and improvement of urban parks, trails, community gardens, and other open spaces. The increase in obesity, especially in children, is to some extent a society-wide problem, but it has its most severe incidence and health effects in low-income communities of color, leading to extremely high rates of diabetes and heart disease. Attention to obesity has coincided with a much higher level of awareness that such problems need to be addressed not just as medical issues but as community factors. As a result, foundations and government agencies centrally concerned with addressing health disparities have lent new funding and technical support to scores of community-based campaigns to create or improve local parks, recreation facilities, walking and bicycling trails, and other places for exercise. The movement to provide nutritious produce through community gardens has also benefited from this infusion of support from the effort to address health disparities.

Advancement of Equity in Urban Infrastructure. Parks and open space are a critical element of urban infrastructure. They are essential to the revitalization of cities, and to the health of communities and individuals. Activists from a variety of backgrounds are working to see that parks and related facilities and programs are provided in a way that embodies principles of social and economic equity. The principles apply not only to parks and open space but also to other forms of infrastructure, including school facilities, transportation, water and sewer systems, and even telecommunications technology. The issues covered through the focus on equity include guidance of growth and development patterns, fair allocation of capital and operating funds across neighborhoods in a city and cities in a region, open access to economic opportunities generated by new construction, and promotion of inclusive decision-making processes.

The relevance of all these domains can be illustrated by taking stock of the motivations and sources of support to build a new urban park in a lower-income area where parks have been scarce, poorly maintained, and unsafe. The local community development corporation sees the new park as a cornerstone of its vision for revitalization of a commercial area, an expression of local culture, and the focal point of a neighborhood safety campaign. The local health clinic and county public health agency seek the park as a means to encourage exercise and recreation, especially among the alarming number of overweight children and youth. Local environmental justice groups see the transformation of a former waterfront industrial site into a park as the appropriate remedy for the history of neglect exemplified by such brownfields. And, a national nonprofit park development organization uses the opportunity to generate a larger share of state infrastructure bond funds for this kind of urban project, in contrast to its main prior application for wilderness conservation.

This composite picture is representative of an initiative in Oakland, California,[1] but in its general form it is probably recognizable in many U.S. cities, where efforts to build or revive urban parks have taken on these varied partners and sources of motivation and support. As we examine the four dimensions of the urban greening movement, they will often seem to intertwine closely in support of the same kinds of open spaces, enterprises, and cultural projects. That synergy is becoming one of the overall movement's most promising assets.

Advocacy for Environmental Justice

The environmental justice movement grew out of the recognition that low-income communities of color have been the predominant location of many kinds of unhealthy and unsafe facilities, dumping grounds in a number of respects. The hazards included industrial sources of pollution such as power plants, incinerators, refineries, and toxic waste facilities, as well as sources rooted in transportation such as bus and truck depots and, increasingly, highways themselves. A more prosaic but no less damaging form of dumping took place on vacant lots and streets by unscrupulous contractors and haulers, fouling many neighborhoods with waste and debris, sometimes including toxic substances.

Those conditions reflected the relative lack of political and economic power in those communities, and the response has always required creating a stronger voice for residents. The environmental justice movement has drawn upon the legacy of previous dimensions of the civil right movement to combine strategies of grass-roots organizing, legal challenges, and political campaigns to force action from powerful public and private institutions. The most immediate charge has always been to obtain relief from the pollutants and hazards, battles that sometimes take several decades.[2] In the process of fighting such problems, some environmental justice groups have evolved into powerful forces for rebuilding and regreening their communities, developing new housing, businesses, open spaces, and environmental education facilities.

The Dudley Street Neighborhood Initiative (DSNI) in Boston is a prime example, and its choices of enterprises have made it a prominent exponent of green businesses and urban parks. The initiative grew out of residents' frustration in the 1970s with the dumping and other dangers associated with vacant lots and abandoned buildings, many of which had arisen from extensive arson-for-profit schemes common to many cities in that era. They wanted to do more than simply stop the immediate destruction and danger, and therefore organized to gain influence and formal authority over the redevelopment of the neighborhood. Over more than 20 years, the residents developed two organizations, the DSNI membership organization and a complementary community land trust, and these groups have gained control of 650 vacant lots. In addition to creating 850 permanently affordable housing units, DSNI also brought into being six public green spaces and a community center

("Greenhouse Helps" 2005). John Barros, executive director of DSNI, describes the motivation for these development and open space projects as fundamentally that of environmental justice; that in a sense, it all stems from the initial intention to redress the problems of dumping and abandonment.[3]

The next step in this urban environmental renaissance is a commercial greenhouse, built in 2005 on the site of a former auto body shop and financed in part by funds provided by the state highway department "to compensate the city for salt and oil pollution it caused 10 years ago" ("Greenhouse Helps" 2005). The greenhouse will produce green garlic and eventually other niche crops for the urban market, and will generate revenue for other DSNI projects. The business will employ local residents and is intended to be the anchor for a new commercial cluster.

DSNI is more accomplished than most community-based developers that began with environmental justice grievances, but the trajectory the group has taken is not out of reach for some others. The residents and organizations in Bayview-Hunters Point in San Francisco who persisted for 25 years to get a power plant closed are now playing major roles in the redevelopment of their neighborhood and the adjacent former Naval Shipyard, itself a source of contamination. Groups that have battled toxic releases in refinery-dominated Richmond, California, are now playing a proactive role in the city's general plan revision process. They are bringing to that process not only a strong focus on the environmental health concerns of minority and immigrant communities, but also a powerful voice in the overall development of the city's commercial, transportation, housing and open space priorities. These are typical of the growing number of environmental justice advocacy groups that have added planning and action in the realm of urban greening to their array of activities.

Community Economic Development

As the Dudley Street Neighborhood Initiative illustrates, community economic development has never been just about the financial performance of properties. It has always been centrally concerned with how new development can improve the economic status of individuals and families and enhance the viability of not only individual businesses but entire commercial districts. The field is diverse, and there are always vigorous debates about the effectiveness of public subsidies, the best ways to harness private market forces, and the right organizations to carry out the work, but there is a common understanding that the goal is to achieve economic and social outcomes that can be seen at the community level, not just at the level of individuals, firms, and developments.

A focus on the community means that development projects are not conceived, planned, funded, or implemented as standard business deals, nor is their success measured in the same way. The engagement of residents, merchants, neighborhood groups, community-based service providers, and other interests is a central element of the development process. This engagement can take on an almost infinite variety of forms and levels of intensity and consequence, from routine bureaucratic, often ineffectual hearings and notices all the way to deep, fundamental transfers of ownership, authority, and power. While every economic development project has its unique story of community engagement, there are some useful patterns and lessons that have emerged from history and current practices.

COMMUNITY ECONOMIC DEVELOPMENT TODAY

The field of community economic development is maturing, if not flourishing, in many respects. In contrast to several decades dominated by urban disinvestment and abandonment, there is a rapidly growing recognition and body of evidence that lower-income neighborhoods in central cities represent viable retail markets and business locations. Most cities are home to at least a few savvy community-based organizations and private developers capable of completing sizable projects in low-income communities. New sources of private capital aimed at financing commercial projects in lower-income communities have proliferated, not only due to the impetus provided by the Community Reinvestment Act but also through the growth of socially responsible private investment portfolios, the emergence of foundation program-related and mission-related investments in Community Economic Development (CED) projects, an increasing interest of pension funds in community development, and other trends. A range of government incentives, tax credits, loans, and regulatory changes, many of which the CED field had long been seeking, have been enacted to draw in capital and facilitate deals. At the broadest level, there is in many cities a sense of expanding investment activity, greater technical proficiency, and a sense that the revival of the economy of neighborhoods is under way. Whether it is the debate over the causes and consequences of the retail renaissance in Harlem, the recognition of an annual "Inner City 100" award for successful business start-ups around the country,[4] or the message of well-received books with upbeat titles like *Comeback Cities* (Grogan and Proscio 2001), there is an optimistic spirit around community economic development, especially compared with a decade or two earlier.

The big picture shows serious challenges as well. Many low-income communities have not shown this new appeal to investors or retailers. A substantial divide exists between so-called hot market and weak market cities, and the latter still face daunting challenges in completing viable neighborhood commercial development projects. In many older industrial cities, even ones in which the number of neighborhoods of highly concentrated poverty declined from 1990 to 2000, the trend of disinvestment and outward migration has continued to the point where most families with stable incomes have left whole neighborhoods of these cities, and in some instances have left the central city entirely for its first ring of suburbs (Kingsley and Pettit 2003; Jargowsky 2003). So far such trends leave the remaining populations and community organizations in the poorest neighborhoods unable to generate or support much new economic activity, even while nearby parts of their city may be gentrifying rapidly. Many of the new sources of potential capital still require rates of return or collateral that cannot be met by small firms or inexperienced community developers. Many government incentives are not targeted correctly or sufficiently compelling to generate market activity. Most of the available public redevelopment funding gets locked up by large-scale signature projects that may do little for neighborhoods. Independent neighborhood retailers face daunting cost challenges competing with category killers and big box chains. And the supply of experienced, proficient local community economic development is still very small in some cities and regions, and their accomplishments are dwarfed by the magnitude of the task ahead.

Both the optimistic and sobering perspectives on the field are driving an important aspect of current practice: community economic development is undergoing unprecedented scrutiny and facing greater pressure to inform and perform. New investors, traditional supporters of CED, and residents of underserved communities are all asking challenging questions. Projects that recycle land or buildings in underserved neighborhoods are significantly different from straightforward, by-the-book suburban greenfield shopping malls or downtown high-end developments. There is an increased focus on identifying the right market niches, projects, and partners, assessing risks realistically, estimating costs comprehensively, measuring and using a community's assets, avoiding potential pitfalls, and systematically evaluating process and results.

In this challenging context, urban greening projects can become critical components to a successful project, creating the environment in which more people are comfortable shopping, working or living, and in which they feel their community's identity is expressed. Public art becomes one of the main ways by which the local history, character and color of the neighborhood and its residents are reflected in the new properties. Effective design and landscaping of streets, walkways, gathering places, and small parks become not just amenities but necessary to encourage walkability, safety, and a sense of community. These and other aspects of greening a project and its immediate surroundings are more than something the developer simply contracts to have designed and built: they are often as important as vehicles for resident engagement as they are for their aesthetic features. As more community developers take an active role in the greening of their projects, they are becoming more sophisticated in their management of the process of planning and design with residents.

THREE TYPES OF COMMUNITY ENGAGEMENT

Neighborhood interests have organized in a number of ways that in turn shape the nature of community engagement in economic development. To admittedly simplify a complex field, we will identify three strands of activity, which we call community organizing, community development, and community building.

Community Organizing. People in low-income neighborhoods have been confronting powerful institutions in order to protect and advance their interests since at least the Great Depression, following myriad variations of the basic concepts tested and popularized by Saul Alinsky. The models usually call for building organizational structure and power in small increments, beginning with immediate victories (the archetypal issue being a new stop sign) and gradually moving toward more substantial policy-focused efforts, always remaining true to the residents' priorities. There is always a priority on resident leadership and decision making and the development of a power analysis that seeks to direct effort toward the levers of political and economic influence. Many grass-roots issue-based organizing groups are nonideological as well as nonpartisan, and will deal only with the immediate issues their members bring up, while others are linked to broader social movements and systematic political-economic analyses. They are often more suited to applying pressure on government or developers than to managing the implementation of that change once the demand has been won.

Community Development. Local development corporations arose from the need to go beyond protests and demands and directly engage in rebuilding. Today's community development corporations have their roots in civil rights and political activism of the 1960s melded with philanthropic initiatives to rebuild inner city neighborhoods. Many of the community development corporations (CDCs) came over time to focus mainly on affordable housing and commercial development and, to a lesser extent, workforce development, child care, and other services. In the 1980s and 1990s, as the urban development business became relatively depoliti-cized and the rigors of building and managing properties monopolized the time and energy of most CDCs, such projects became more of an end in themselves rather than a means to broad social change. Many CDCs drifted away from an activist orientation and lost contact with comprehensive approaches to neighborhood revitalization. The hun-dreds of CDCs around the United States vary tremendously in their size and capacity to complete projects. The current environment is shaking out many of the smaller ones while the larger and more sophisticated CDCs are taking on commercial and mixed-use projects far beyond the scale that what they would have imagined a decade ago.

Community Building. The inherent limitations of protest-oriented grass-roots organizing and the narrowed, property-focused vision of most CDCs left a vacuum that was addressed by the growth of the community-building movement beginning in the late 1980s. A new type of group emerged that aspired to span the boundaries among the different styles of community work, not only organizing and physical development, but also human services, health care, education, and other aspects of the lives of poor families. The groups researched issues from a community perspective, proposed policies, played an ongoing role in the reform of government systems, and served as the intermediaries for philanthropic initiatives. They work at increasing the capacity of neighborhood groups to affect the local policy process and often adopt a consensus-based rather than conflict-based style of organizing. From a group of six local projects to address persistent poverty established by the Rockefeller Foundation in the late 1980s, the National Community Building Net-work grew to 600 members by 2003.[5] Many of the community building organizations have been active in economic development and planning efforts, often facilitating collaboratives of neighborhood groups and shaping alternatives to the proposals of government or development companies.

Adherents of these three ways of working in communities can sometimes be skeptical of the other approaches. Issue-based community organizers sometimes see community builders as too quick to compromise on basic issues of power and control, to mistake their own access to powerful institutions for genuine popular power. Community developers make the case that without tangibly building a neighborhood and creating a constituency with a genuine economic stake in its future, other efforts will be incapable of bringing about sustained revitalization. Community builders contend that without continual innovation and access to new ideas, partners, and resources, community development will remain a small-scale niche business that will not make a sizable difference in the neighborhoods that need the most help.

Community development entities are increasingly incorporating elements of urban greening into their project design plans, their resident organizing strategies, and their business models. In addition to Dudley Street, three other cases illustrate the range and depth of these innovations.

In Chicago, the Bethel Center, a mixed-use transit-oriented development at an elevated train station on the West Side, was completed in 2005 by Bethel New Life, a faith-based CDC. The project took a decade of organizing (including, first, a campaign to keep the transit station open), planning, and development. The project, built on a former brownfield site, incorporates the latest in green building technology, including photovoltaic cells, energy-conserving and nontoxic construction, and a roof garden. In 2006 the Bethel Center was the winner of the first national award for Equitable Development from the EPA Smart Growth Network.

The Spanish Speaking Unity Council of Oakland, one of the country's oldest CDCs, created the Fruitvale Open Space and Recreation Initiative with several partners in the mid-1990s when its leaders recognized that its mission of bringing about the economic revitalization of the neighborhood could not be realized without directly improving parks, recreation, and community beautification. The project was one of a number of local urban initiatives supported by the Trust for Public Land. Unity Council resident organizers who had focused on public safety expanded their range of issues to draw in immigrant parents and children into an interactive process of designing one new and one rebuilt park. A coalition of community developers, university-based designers, parks policy specialists, and foundations created the momentum to ensure that the last large piece of open space on the city's waterfront was set aside for a new park, and then raised the federal, state, and local funds to see it through to completion.[6]

The open space initiative was complemented by a Main Street program that upgraded the design of storefronts and public spaces of the shopping district, as well as the keystone project: a transit village that transformed a parking lot into shops, housing, and offices around a significant new *paseo* and public square. In all Unity Council activities, the "greening" projects were intrinsic to the overall strategy for the commercial and residential sectors, and the relationship between resident organizing, community building, and property development was largely seamless.

The creation of Market Creek Plaza, a recently constructed shopping and cultural center in a lower income area of San Diego, also illustrates the centrality of resident engagement in art and design to the success of a community development project. The Jacobs Family Foundation purchased a vacant former factory site in the midst of the neighborhood and began a multiyear process of engagement with residents to determine what should be done with it. The residents decided that a shopping center anchored by a supermarket was the highest priority, along with facilities for expression of the diverse cultures of the area, which included residents with roots in African American, Mexican, Vietnamese, Laotian, Samoan, and other communities. The design and construction of that center featured an array of resident teams taking important decision-making responsibility for all aspects of the project.[7] These teams included construction contracting, employment, retail strategies, programs for youth, and resident ownership of the development, as well as art and design.[8]

The adults and young people of the neighborhood played a key role in shaping the physical spaces and overall design of the retail projects. The Market Creek process illustrates the uses of design as an expression of ethnic cultures and the accountability of the design professionals to the residents. Community art has played an extremely significant role not only in the overall look and feel of the shopping center and the adjoining creek-side amphitheater, but as a means for engaging residents in selection of themes and artists, paying tribute to local leaders (whose portraits adorn the exterior walls) and uniting the diverse cultures represented in the neighborhood. Art is, in short, a fundamental aspect of the community building as well as the commercial development. The foundation has almost certainly taken more time and spent more funds than a typical shopping center developer on art-related staff and volunteer activities, materials, and commissions, but its leaders consider the money well spent given that it is so intertwined with their mission of "resident ownership of neighborhood change." The challenge for the field, which must often operate with fewer assets or less patient capital, is to put the opportunities for resident engagement in public art, architecture, and landscape design within reach for more community economic developers.

Health Disparities and Community Factors

Perhaps the greatest recent source of new energy and outside support for the urban greening movement has come from advocates of creating more healthy communities in order to prevent chronic diseases and eliminate racial and ethnic health disparities. Chronic conditions such as diabetes and heart disease, which are closely linked with obesity and lack of fitness, have become enormous public health concerns in recent years, and that concern has brought the attention of health professionals to a wide range of urban planning and development issues. The issues are both universal and specific. On the one hand, problems related to weight, fitness, and diet are endemic, and people in all types of communities or levels of income need healthy environments for these reasons. On the other hand, the rates of the related chronic diseases significantly higher among lower income communities and among African Americans, and the challenges of improving their neighborhood environments and opportunities for nutritious food, are inextricable from their larger economic circumstances.

The definition of a healthy community includes the opportunity for residents to have the resources and supports needed to sustain a sense of safety and wellness. This involves the physical, social, and economic dimensions of community life and access to a wide range of opportunities. Among the most critical ingredients required to have healthy communities are decent employment and business opportunities, quality health care and social services, healthy foods, safe recreational facilities, easily navigated transportation systems, high levels of public investment to sustain good schools and other local infrastructure, clean air and water, and affordable high quality housing. Residents also benefit from being connected to others, rather than isolated, so that strong social networks that reflect diverse cultural needs are also a key element of a healthy community.

The relationship between how American communities are built and the health of their residents has been the focus of concerted public action for at least a century, but not always with the same high level of intensity. In the early 1900s, the dangers and inequities of rapid industrialization, immigration, and growth of slums led to efforts by pioneering public health experts, housing reformers, and urban designers to improve tenement conditions, create sanitary water and sewer systems, establish city parks accessible to the working class, and otherwise counter the most serious deficiencies of urban neighborhoods. The link between land use and public health was obvious and formed the basis for a wide range of policies that greatly reduced communicable diseases and improved living conditions. The reformers and scientists of the time made the connection between health and the built environment in many ways. One example: "Exposure to sunlight [a result of the tenement reforms] and the addition of green spaces at the turn of the 20th century led to a decrease in rickets" (Hanna and Coussens 2001: 49).

The functional connection between urban development, open space, and public health was far less powerful for much of the twentieth century, as public health and medicine became more focused on specific diseases facing individuals and families and less on environmental conditions, while land use planning became more thoroughly driven by market-based property development priorities. The predominant trends in metropolitan land use after World War II were sometimes justified by broad references to "health," as when urban slum clearance was portrayed as the removal of contagious blight conditions or when suburban single family, lower-density development was characterized as best for the development of children.

While there were some important economic if not social advantages to urban renewal and automobile-dependent suburbia as they emerged from the 1950s to the 1970s, these approaches were based in two fundamental problems. First, they were designed and carried out in a fundamentally inequitable way, with African Americans and other low-income communities of color displaced by the redevelopment process left in increasingly disinvested neighborhoods with poor community health conditions, and systematically excluded from most of the suburban options. As a leading source on suburban development and health puts it, "Cities became places of crowding and social dislocation, home to a whole range of problems that came to be understood as the 'urban crisis of the twentieth century'" (Frumkin, Frank, and Jackson 2004: 61). Lack of safety, inadequate public services, and neglected physical environments, combined with economic and social segregation, led to growing health disparities. As noted earlier, such neighborhoods also became the dumping grounds for a disproportionate level of society's environmentally dangerous byproducts. Children began to suffer from the effects of lead poisoning and respiratory illnesses such as asthma. Second, the dominant pattern of land use and development sowed the seeds of its own dysfunction, such that suburban sprawl is now itself seen as a prime contributor to ill health, as has been documented across a rapidly growing range of issues and conditions (Frumkin, Frank, and Jackson 2004).

These problems have recently become much more widely recognized, and we are now in a period where land use and the built environment are once again being known as central to improving health outcomes and reducing health disparities (PolicyLink 2002). To take full advantage of that growing level of awareness, public health professionals need to integrate into their work a practical knowledge of land use planning and policies—how communities are built, maintained, and improved through regulation, design, financing, and the overall property development process. The metropolitan landscape is far more variegated these days, with suburbia having become much more demographically and economically diverse, some cities and neighborhoods experiencing an economic rebirth while others languish, and all types of communities experiencing a level of immigration not seen in many decades. Opportunities for greening will arise in all of these settings, and the increased attention the health impacts of physical activity may hasten the creation of these new or revitalized spaces.

The revived connection between health and community development is being made at the levels of research, of professional interchange and collaboration, and of community-based organizations and local institutions such as schools or health departments. Issues such as how to increase the chances that children could walk or bicycle to school or play safely in a nearby park, or that nutritious foods could become a truly viable option in neighborhoods and schools, are receiving attention at all these levels.[9]

There is an emerging field of research into the consequences of various physical development patterns on such factors as walkability or access to healthy food, and of the community factors on such problems as diabetes and obesity (Flourney and Yen 2004). A number of national and regional foundations have sponsored a decade of research and documentation of emerging best practices, and government health agencies such as the Centers for Disease Control and Prevention have raised the medical importance of community factors.[10] At the same time that complex questions of causality and attribution are still being sorted through with long-term studies, and while debates over the relative role of "personal responsibility" and government action continue, a growing consensus of health researchers and clinicians seems to agree, at least, that community design factors play a large and growing role in the practical opportunities Americans have to exercise, keep fit and eat right, and that most of those factors are currently aligned so as to make good habits difficult.

The interprofessional collaboration between public health and urban planning and development has grown dramatically. Summaries of issues, broad conceptual frameworks, and conferences have begun to get many public health and urban planning development professionals talking to each other.[11] Some technical assistance manuals and briefing papers on specific aspects of land use, zoning, local economic development, park design, and other features of the metropolitan landscape have been published.[12] National trade associations are making the issues a staple of their meetings and information outlets. A small number of cities have formally introduced health factors into their land use planning processes.

Local efforts to create new ties have benefited from the increased interest on the part of health professionals, advocates, and residents in parks, school playgrounds and athletic facilities, trails, and food retailing. Initiatives such as Healthy Eating, Active Communities, a six-city project of the California Endowment, create local partnerships of residents, schools, and health departments in lower-income communities to address neighborhood factors, and these groups are emblematic of many others around California that have taken the lead in creating safe places for young people to play. While they may not necessarily change the design or function of a new park or facility from what would have been proposed, the health activists and professionals bring a new constituency, a new sense of urgency, and new sources of financial and political support to these local urban greening campaigns.

The varied activities in this domain have grown quickly and have generated a great deal of new interest in urban greening priorities. Given that solid beginning, it appears to need to soon develop a higher level of coherence and a common language and regular settings in which complex issues can be worked through, in order for the nascent partnerships to thrive and have maximum impact on their respective fields. Also, the particular issues and perspectives central to health disparities, social and economic equity, and environmental justice, which have sometimes been lost in the broader framing of the issue of "suburban sprawl," need to be reinforced and fully integrated into this work. The rates of many chronic conditions influenced by neighborhood factors are much higher in lower-income communities of color, and it will take new types of partnerships in health and land use to significantly address them.

Advancing Equity in Urban Infrastructure

The urban greening movement, insofar as it requires sizeable public capital investments, is part of an emerging set of efforts to restore and enhance the infrastructure of America's cities, and to do so in a way that advances social and economic equity. This is not as tightly defined or well recognized as a unified domain of organizing or action as the other three areas discussed in this chapter, but it is becoming both more visible and more widely discussed every year. In older core cities, the infrastructure challenges are often about how to replace aging and substandard systems. In rapidly growing metropolitan regions, the highest profile debates are about the infrastructure needed to support new housing and commercial development, and what such expansion will do to the environment or the water supply. Whatever the economic circumstances, though, provision and maintenance of parks and open space, restoration of waterfronts, linking of school buildings and grounds with surrounding neighborhoods, implementation of energy-efficient building technology, and many other issues central to urban greening are becoming more prominent, and more people are addressing the basic equity questions: who pays, who benefits, and who decides?

A 2006 brief from PolicyLink on the concepts of equity in infrastructure laid out the context in which attention to these concerns will be discussed:

Infrastructure is the skeletal support of communities and regions, and it requires effective, transparent government policies to guide its planning, spending, building, and maintenance. Growing populations, resource-intensive development patterns, new technology requirements of a rapidly changing economy, and several decades of underinvestment have combined to create a large backlog of infrastructure projects all over the country—in urban, suburban, and rural areas. Over the next two decades, the need for substantial infrastructure investments is expected to increase. Building or maintaining schools and colleges, water systems, highways, roads, mass transit, telecommunications systems, and parks require infusions of financial support that compete with other services for limited federal and local funds.

The networks, roads, sewer systems, pipelines, facilities, and properties that comprise public infrastructure define neighborhoods, cities, and regions: where housing is located, the kind of housing that can be built, transportation to jobs, the quality of schools, and the maintenance of basic public health and safety. . . . Sometimes the construction of new infrastructure, or the failure of an existing one, brings intense public scrutiny. Most often, however, critical and expensive infrastructure decisions are made in settings removed from public questioning and media scrutiny, and thus lack the informed debate and attention that supports equitable decision-making. Advocates need to be aware of the impact of infrastructure on a variety of issues and be prepared to bring them before the public.[13]

This political environment pertains to urban parks as much as to other forms of infrastructure. There is a continual struggle to find financial support for the maintenance and expansion of park systems, their refurbishing and rebuilding, and for programming and staffing; the issues of fair distribution of these scarce resources can be intense as well. Parks advocates and experts know what is at stake:

Successful parks are markers of healthy communities: children play; families spend time together; people of all ages exercise and relax; the environment adds to the beauty, security, and economic value of the neighborhood. On the other hand, neglected, dangerous, poorly maintained, or badly designed parks and recreation facilities have the opposite effect: families and young children stay away, illicit activities proliferate, and the property becomes a threatening or discouraging eyesore. To remain community assets, parks and recreation facilities need adequate budgets, good management, and a strong connection with residents. . . . Few cities provided adequate maintenance staffing and budgets, and most deferred critically needed capital investments. Parks and recreation are primarily the responsibility of local government, with no mandates to maintain services and relatively minuscule funding from the state or federal government. Often labeled as "nonessential" at budgeting time, parks and recreation departments consistently absorb larger budget cuts than most other local departments. (Raya et al. 2007)

The infrastructure of urban greening typically does not fail in ways that generate the high-profile disasters and emergencies associated with other types of infrastructure. Broken levees, collapsed tunnels and high-way overpasses, sinkholes in streets, electric power outages and other more dramatic challenges to normal life and the conduct of a city's business tend to galvanize public attention, at least for a while. Nonetheless, even if it is not driven by response to crises, the capital funding of parks and open space, waterfronts, trails and other green infrastructure is not only a multibillion dollar public investment—it also faces the same needs to address equity issues in order to address social justice and build political support. Principles for allocating infrastructure funds equitably include distributing funds fairly across communities and among public purposes, making the economic opportunities that flow from the investments available to all communities, using the investments to promote sustainable metropolitan growth, and making decisions in a democratic and transparent manner.[14]

A growing number of local governments and advocates have been undertaking promising equitable practices in support of parks and open space. They have raised significant amounts of new capital for land acquisition, repairs, and operations, and directed it to areas that were most in need. A number of new urban parks have been created to meet the needs of a changing population, even in districts where conventional planning had slated underutilized land for industrial purposes. They have greatly improved the capacity to measure, document, and report access and quality in parks and recreation, leading to more equitable distributions of funds. They have created venues in which residents of all kinds of communities can have a significant voice in decisions about parks policies and budgets. They have also overcome long-standing bureaucratic divisions to bring about the creative use of vacant and sometimes contaminated properties for green projects. As with the environmental justice activism described earlier, and from whose roots some of these parks projects have sprung, they include a combination of grass-roots organizing, legal advocacy, and policy changes. A report from PolicyLink describes several cases of each type of practice, with examples from Seattle, Portland, Los Angeles, San Francisco, Philadelphia, Chicago, Nashville, New Jersey, Colorado, and other cities and states (Raya et al. 2007). The organizations that have developed these practices represent an important resource for leaders in other communities. They have shown that even with the challenges posed for urban greening projects by the demands of seemingly more urgent "big ticket'' infrastructure, new resources can be raised in a way that also enhances social equity.

The Contribution to Greening

Urban greening efforts are firmly rooted in complementary movements for social, environmental, and economic change, and they appear to be growing stronger and more diversified in their methods and sources of support as a result of connections to those movements. Furthermore, these movements are not so much independent as they are increasingly interconnected, as environmental justice campaigns lead to community development projects, and activities by health professionals and advocates lead to campaigns for more equitable public investment in parks and other green infrastructure. The conceptual frameworks and examples explored in this paper suggest four overarching themes about the nature of these activities.

Resident organizing brings its own rewards as well as tangible results for the community environment. The involvement of low-income residents in issue definition, project and campaign planning, and other decision-making and action is not only a means to an end for many of the organizations profiled here, but also a highly valued process in its own right. Whether through the design of a public space or of a strategy for pursuing an advocacy campaign, for example, the engagement of residents and the growth of their capacities as leaders are central to the endeavor. These efforts are not, for the most part, movements driven by technocratic or political elites, but rather projects with significant commitments to grassroots empowerment.

Organizing for projects can lead to advocacy for policy change. Neighborhood greening efforts are notably tangible, localized, and rewarding in their direct results and rewards: a park is built, a waterfront is cleaned up, an eyesore or hazard is removed. This immediacy is essential and compelling, yet when these efforts are successful, they can also lead residents and organizers deeper into the realm of broader policy change. When community developers such as those profiled here succeed with innovative projects, this raises the prospect of those projects, or elements of them, becoming models for legislation or other more generalized programs. When local activists succeed in winning funds for their own park, they could thereafter become part of broader citywide or statewide coalitions to obtain more resources for their kind of work. This transition from project to policy advocacy does not happen as frequently as it probably should. Many community developers eschew policy in favor of working only in their own neighborhood, and resident activists are still relatively less involved in many areas of state policy that affect the prospects and budgets for urban greening. The potential for building the policy capacity of activists should be further explored.

New public attention can bring new sources of support. It is hard to overestimate the value of an issue becoming front and center in the public eye as something of universal concern. As with concerns with global warming, concerns about the "epidemic" of obesity have made that leap in public awareness in recent years. The focus by health professionals and advocates on community factors that can reduce obesity has been a boon to the long time supporters of parks and, more generally, urban design that promotes walking, running, bicycling, and recreation. The heightened attention shows signs of being translatable into increased resources for local projects. If the general public awareness of an "infrastructure crisis" grows over the next several years, it too may redound to the advantage of advocates for urban greening.

Urban greening reasserts the humanity and solidarity of lower income communities. The so-called deficit model of community development requires that problems, shortcomings, and deficiencies be highlighted to attract outrage, attention, and resources to an underserved neighborhood and its families. The deficit approach has been widely derided (though it is necessarily still a staple of many processes of applying for government funds) and succeeded by various ways to focus on neighborhood assets. Urban greening activities are intrinsically asset-oriented; they bring out the best in individuals and groups, celebrating local culture, facilitating collective volunteer action, and restoring or reclaiming community landmarks. They have significant power to build social bonds, and once forged or strengthened, these bonds can often be applied to other pressing issues.

The convergence of so many strands of community action and policy reform should continue to be valuable to the efforts to bring about the true greening of all kinds of neighborhoods in American cities. A more effective movement may well arise from the intersection of so many contributions.

References

Barros, John. 2006. Comments at a panel at the Growing Greener Cities: Symposium on Environmental Issues in the 21st Century, Philadelphia, October 16. Recorded by panel moderator Victor Rubin.

Flournoy, Rebecca, and Irene Yen. 2004. *The Influence of Community Factors on Health: An Annotated Bibliography*. Oakland, Calif.: California Endowment and PolicyLink.

Frumkin, Howard, Lawrence Frank, and Richard Jackson. 2004. *Urban Sprawl and Public Health: Designing, Planning, and Building for Healthy Communities*. Washington, D.C.: Island Press.

"Greenhouse Helps Drive Growth in Roxbury—Group's First Commercial Project Takes Root in Facility to Produce Green Garlic—and Bring Jobs to the Neighborhood." 2005. *Boston Globe*, May 11.

Grogan, Paul, and Tony Proscio. 2001. *Comeback Cities: A Blueprint for Urban Neighborhood Revival*. Boulder, Colo.: Westview Press.

Hanna, Kathi, and Christine Coussens. 2001. *Rebuilding the Unity of Health and the Environment: A New Vision of Environmental Health for the 21st Century*. Washington, D.C.: National Academy Press.

Jargowsky, Paul A. 2003. *Stunning Progress, Hidden Problems: The Dramatic Decline of Concentrated Poverty in the 1990s*. Washington, D.C.: Brookings Institution.

Kingsley, G. Thomas, and Kathryn S. L. Pettit. 2003. *Concentrated Poverty: A Change in Course*. Neighborhood Change in Urban America Series 2. Washington, D.C.: Urban Institute.

Pastor, Manuel, Jr., and Deborah Reed. 2005. *Understanding Equitable Public Infrastructure Investment for California*. San Francisco: Public Policy Institute of California.

Pastor, Manuel, Jr., James Sadd, and Rachel Morello-Frosch. 2007. *Still Toxic After All These Years: Air Quality and Environmental Justice in the San Francisco Bay Area*. Santa Cruz: Center for Justice Tolerance and Community, University of California.

PolicyLink. 2002. *Reducing Health Disparities Through a Focus on Communities*. Oakland, Calif.: PolicyLink.

Raya, Richard et al. 2007. *Promising Practices in the Advancement of Equity in Infrastructure*. Oakland, Calif.: PolicyLink.

Robinson, Lisa. 2005. *Market Creek Plaza: Toward Resident Ownership of Neighborhood Change*. Oakland, Calif.: PolicyLink.

Rubin, Victor. 1998. "The Roles of Universities in Community Building Initiatives." *Journal of Planning Education and Research* 17, 4: 302–11.

———. 2006. *Safety, Growth, and Equity: Infrastructure Policies That Promote Opportunity and Inclusion*. Oakland, Calif.: PolicyLink.

Chapter 11

Leveraging Media for Social Change

Harry Wiland and Dale Bell

Greening is a topic receiving ever greater media attention. The press is covering it in new ways—from its ability to play a role in the responses to climate change and its use in local communities' economic development to its identification in people's health, recreation, and well-being. Leaders ranging from city mayors to corporate leaders are increasingly making public statements and implementing policy and programs that support greening in a myriad of ways. Recently, we, as documentary filmmakers, have focused a new communication strategy on the topic and in this chapter we explore how people like us can have an impact on public policy. We use two examples, our first project focusing on the elderly, for which we created a new media strategy, and the other on urban greening, in which we replicated the approach.

Over the years, as media professionals, we have seen how many social entrepreneurs lacked the ability to *communicate* their knowledge to the right kind of audience to make a real difference. Committed to the presentation of public policy issues, we faced this challenge on a daily basis. While we knew that the goal was to leverage media for maximum results, we also began to question current approaches, asking, "What is the good of working years on a project if the same viewers always tune in and nothing really changes? How do we expand and deepen the audience beyond the 'choir'?"

We have known each other since the late 1960s, having met in New York where Dale produced *Woodstock* and Harry produced *Johnny Cash: The Man, His World, and His Music,* but we did not work together until 1999. Between us, we have produced hundreds of hours of national and international programming and have won our share of awards, including an Academy Award, a Peabody Award, four Emmys, and two Christophers. We had a strong working relationship with PBS. But new broadcast developments brought us together and forced us to rethink a number of assumptions. The advent of cable and its relentless 24-hour competition threatened our methods, especially our reliance on PBS. It diluted our audience and sources of funding. The proliferation of lower-budgeted cable programming forced us to fight for our professional survival. We asked ourselves some hard questions. What were our long-range goals? Was broadcast programming enough to accomplish these goals? Could we craft a new approach to fit into the equation? Would we find funders? What would our relationship with PBS and other documentary film outlets look like?

We had a number of brainstorming sessions to come up with a strategy that combined our old broadcast production skill-set with the use of new digital online media. We knew we wanted to fulfill our lifelong desire to pursue a social entrepreneurial mission—one that created a brand name for such targeted public policy issues as social welfare, education, environment, and health and motivated people to lobby for change. We realized we needed a clear vision and innovative, compelling tactics that would encourage full and meaningful debate and participation across the political, social, and economic spectrum. To do so, we created a new media model that packaged television and multimedia products aimed at piercing the hearts of our audiences. Our goal was to erase their skepticism, strengthen their empowerment, ignite their curiosity, and offer hope that change is possible. We have experimented with this model on two projects; the first, undertaken in 2002, focused on aging, a critical issue as baby boomers get older and the second, begun in 2003, looked at urban greening, equally compelling in the face of climate change. The first grounded the model for the second. Since we have more results from the earlier project, we will detail it and show how we transferred our model to the second one that remains ongoing.

A New Media Model

In crafting the new media model, we realized that we could not rely on the production of a single film or television program, or even a series or the publication of a well-researched book. We needed a suite of media tools that was comprehensive, universal, dynamic, and scaleable. We viewed digital online media, based on a website, as creating an enormous opportunity because it offered on-demand, readily accessible 24/7 support for our broadcast programming. Our television program would be the "rock in the water," but our website would provide the ripple effect, offering ongoing waves of information that we could refresh after an initial broadcast. For example, our website would offer downloadable action guides, teachers' guides, coalition-partner activity schedules, best practice profiles, film clips, book reviews, interactive blogs, and links to informational databases. Equally important to our approach was our inclusion of two other components: local community outreach with associated educational elements and a national promotion campaign with strategic partnerships. Together, these components would transform a "program" into an *initiative*. They would extend the scope of a project across socioeconomic and ethnic lines, geopolitical borders, and time. Our new media model includes a special television broadcast, project website, locally televised town hall meetings, and symposia along with a variety of other materials ranging from academic curricula and video resource libraries to community outreach programs, companion books, DVDs, action guides, and a speakers bureau.

We realized that the only place for our new media model was PBS because no other broadcast outlet would have the airtime, funding possibilities, or interest in an in-depth examination of public policy issues. We presented our plan to PBS with an asterisk. Since at least a third of our project budget would be devoted to the creation of other media and outreach, we proposed to PBS that we would raise 100 percent of the required program funding in exchange for retention of the copyright of the intellectual capital we created. The only condition was that, in exchange, we would need a written contract with PBS, guaranteeing network primetime broadcasts for the project. This would allow us to go directly to funders—corporate sponsors and foundations—with firmly committed airdates. PBS agreed. This new way of working together has enabled us to carve out an important and unique programming niche.

We knew that to be successful, our public policy campaigns would have to be well-funded, well-researched, well-produced, and well-distributed in order to reach our intended targeted audience. To increase our effectiveness, we formed a 501(c)3 social entrepreneurial funding vehicle, the Media and Policy Center Foundation. Having a foundation allowed us to attract support that we otherwise would not receive.

In 2002, we began our first project, And Thou Shalt Honor: Caring for Our Parents, Spouses, and Friends. It was a two-hour primetime PBS broadcast focused on caregiving and what to do about the impending health care crisis resulting from the graying of America. Over the next four years, we screened the documentary on the national 340-station PBS network, reaching 16 million viewers.

At the same time, we developed our website, www.mediapolicycenter .org, where we showcased our Caregiver Resource Center Video Library and other materials, crafted outreach and educational programs, and assembled an extensive network of community coalitions that organized local activities around the series. Our efforts resulted in the formation of more than 1,500 community coalitions, built with the help of our national partners described later in this chapter. In each location the groups produced print tools (including a flier/brochure describing the series, viewers guide, and branding materials such as electronic logos, letterhead, and web icons); interactive websites with downloadable materials including a community action guide, K-12 materials, press releases and electronic newsletters to coalition partners, and public policy papers to promote legislation. These text-driven and electronic outputs help to support and create a network of concerned and committed citizens.

Our local partners sponsored other activities, ranging from town hall meetings to brown-bag lunches in the workplace to organized discussion groups in libraries, hospitals, schools, and church halls in order to give "legs" to the broadcast and focus attention on local efforts to improve care for caregivers and build community support. Most important, these efforts let others know that they were not alone in meeting the challenges of providing caregiving to an aging parent.

The second wave of our community outreach campaign was spearheaded by the organization and execution of a series of regionally based televised "care-giving town hall meetings," three-hour interactive events. We put these meetings together in partnership with our local coalitions. Each had approximately 150 to 300 participants, including professionals, government officials, business leaders, students, educators, NGO volunteers, community activists, and citizens. For our part, we recorded and edited the meetings, giving them to local PBS stations to broadcast as one- or two-hour specials. One, held in conjunction with the 2004 midsummer National Governors Conference, was in Seattle. Another appeared in the midst of the Democratic National Convention in Boston. We produced a National Town Hall Meeting in 2005, marking the 40th anniversary of the signing of the Older Americans Act by President Lyndon Johnson. These meetings have appeared on local and statewide PBS stations in more than 15 states.

We also undertook a number of other follow-up activities. For example, we wrote a companion book, *And Thou Shalt Honor: The Caregiver's Companion* (2002, with a Foreword by Rosalynn Carter) to provide information and practical support essential for caregivers. It has action plans and checklists for key issues, plus a comprehensive directory of essential caregiving resources. It was a best seller on the PBS website store and, to date, has sold more than 25,000 copies. We also produced a follow-up half-hour film, *Getting Around*, a community outreach project dealing with the elder driver issue that PBS screened in April 2007 (Figure 1).

With each new project, we continue to evolve our new media model. In 2003 we applied it to a new and even more ambitious interest, promoting environmental change through the adoption of sustainable best practices. We conceived of a four-program series, *Edens Lost & Found*, set in Chicago, Los Angeles, Philadelphia, and Seattle. Each one-hour

Figure 1. Rally in support of caregivers.

segment profiles residents who confronted the challenges of urban restoration through the creation of sustainable urban ecosystems. The series explores urban forestation, watershed management, air pollution control, mass transit, renovation of infrastructure, expansion and management of open lands, community gardening, and environmental justice. While each segment shows different approaches characteristic of each place, each also resonates with an appreciation of the common goal: making neighborhoods, cities, and regions greener.

With *Edens Lost & Found* we replicated and expanded our new media model. We contracted with the PBS, with the first two programs appearing in May 2006 and the second two airing in January 2007. We developed a website, wrote a companion book (Wiland and Bell 2006), and developed community outreach programs with associated educational materials and a national promotion campaign with strategic partners (Figure 2).[1]

Our million-dollar outreach campaign for *Edens Lost & Found* incorporated the earlier features but expanded on the new media model. We put together a video library that includes documentaries of specific subject matters as well as films of events related to the PBS series, such as

Figure 2. The people responsible for the production of *Edens Lost & Found*.

university-based symposia associated with our airings (see Appendix 1). For the community outreach and educational programs, we wrote a high school-community college curriculum, crafted a certificate program for university extension students, and provided materials for school children (Figure 3). In Philadelphia, for example, we distributed customized print materials that included action guides, viewers' guides, and U.S. Forest Service materials to thousands of students and community volunteers through our partner organizations. In addition, we secured additional local NPR and PBS programming; provided *Edens Lost & Found* footage for local town hall meetings; offered the full PBS documentary as a premium for fundraising to Pennsylvania Horticultural Society, Philadelphia Green, and the local area PBS station, WHYY; put a special Philadelphia section on the *Edens Lost & Found* PBS website; and cosponsored, along with the Pennsylvania Horticultural Society and the Penn Institute for Urban Research, the two-day symposium, Growing Greener Cities, in fall 2006.

We are now tailoring outreach programs for the other three cities. Table 1 outlines our Chicago efforts. Here we began to work (and continue to work) with several local partners well before the first screening

Figure 3. Promoting educational outreach: Harry Wiland speaking at the Conservation Learning Summit in 2005.

of the Chicago segment. Our partners include Chicago Wilderness, OpenLands, Eden Place, Friends of the Chicago River, the city of Chicago, and the Illinois Sustainability Education and Training Program (ISTEP).

Due to a last-minute shortfall in funding from two of our key outreach funders, the table represents more a proposed than a realized program. Nonetheless, it serves as a guide to future outreach activities and also shows how to use a documentary to galvanize a broad coalition to reach different ages and interest groups. For example, Chicago Wilderness continues to work with the city of Chicago in transforming school campuses. The Mighty Acorns program promotes the elementary school environmental stewardship seen in the Chicago segment. Friends of the Chicago River partners with schools to promote stewardship of the Chicago River. The Center for Neighborhood Technology created low-cost local area Internet networks that offer conservation software showing how to reduce energy consumption to residents of Chicago's working-class neighborhoods.

Our foundation received an important grant for educational outreach from ISTEP to develop a 20-lesson high school curriculum devoted to environmentally sustainable best practices. Our academic team, headed by Deb Perryman, Elgin High School Environmental Studies instructor

TABLE 1. *EDENS LOST & FOUND* PROPOSED OUTREACH ACTIVITIES IN CHICAGO

Outreach activity	Intended outcomes
1. Transforming School Campuses	• Five schools will work with Chicago Area Schools/ Chicago Wilderness in this program, and 60 teachers will train in the Campus Forestry Program. • Of the expected 3,000 student participants, our goal is 100 volunteers for Chicago Wilderness. • Of the 60 teachers, our goal is 20 volunteers for Chicago Wilderness. • Of the 100 trees planted, at least 95% will survive because they are receiving proper care as directed through the program. • The story of each school's transformation will be uploaded on the *Edens* website, and/or to local Chicago media.
2. Elementary Environmental Stewardship	• Students and teachers will be asked to volunteer for Chicago Wilderness events. Of the 1,600 students, our goal is that 100 return as volunteers. Of the 100 adults involved in this program, we expect 30 to volunteer at a later date. • PowerPoint presentations of each field trip will be documented on the *Edens* website, or presented to the local media.
3. Nurturing Volunteers in their Neighborhoods	• 100 students, teachers, and community volunteers will be trained to conduct on-going tree inspections of the trees in their neighborhoods. • We will do a pre- and post-test, and we expect participants will be able to correctly answer 75% more questions on the post-test. • Students, teachers, and community members will continue to assess the health of the trees for a time period of 5 years (there may be student turnover, but core adults will remain the same). • Each volunteer will be required to keep and submit data to CPS. CW will then make all data available on the *Edens* website. • Of the 200 participants, we hope that 50 will volunteer for another CW program.
4. Teacher Training Related to Rain Gardens	• As schools are selected to have a rain garden installed, teachers will also be selected for this training program. • Our goal is to have 4 teachers from each school participate.

TABLE 1. (CONTINUED)

Outreach activity	Intended outcomes
Center for Neighborhood Technology (CNT)	• Of the teachers who enroll in the program, we hope 3 of 4 will remain active in the program for a minimum of five years. • Teachers will be asked to reflect on the curriculum, teacher training, and the application of their new skills to the classroom. • Teachers will continue to help us revise the program and recruit additional participants. They will recruit one colleague into the program for the following school year. • Each student participant's learning will be evaluated as well, with a desired outcome of 75% more questions answered correctly on the post-test.
5. Teen Podcast (CNT)	• Our goal is to have 10 teens from each neighborhood podcast for the first season. • Our goal is to add 10 teens from each neighborhood each month until we reach a program capacity of 50 teens. • Our goal is to select excellent podcasts to be uploaded onto the *Edens* website. We will gauge program effectiveness by monitoring the number of podcast downloads from the site. • The participating teens will be required to write a reflective essay detailing what they learned about themselves and their communities during the podcast program. The students will then apply what they learned to increase sustainability in their communities by proposing a systemic solution to the issues they studied.
6. Alternative Transportation: Car Sharing (CNT)	• Increase I-Go usage in low-income households by 50% at the end of the first 6 months. • Increase I-Go usage in low-income households by another 25% at the end of the second 6 months. • Provided outreach materials will be used to teach these residents about environmental and health impacts involved in transportation issues. We will evaluate the effectiveness of the program by reaching our I-Go usage goals. • All materials developed will be available on the *Edens* website. Profiles of families who have benefited from the I-Go program will be featured each month on the *Edens* website, and submitted to the media for possible feature stories.

TABLE 1. (CONTINUED)

Outreach activity	Intended outcomes
Web-Based Interactive Community Action Games Using the Online Action Guide at edenslostandfound.org. (CW)	• Our goal is to have 100 classrooms participate in the "Green Chicago Game." • We also want 50 community-based groups to use the game for their members to learn more about sustainability efforts in their community. • The guide offers 101 ways an individual can take action in Seattle. We will highlight one real-life example of each opportunity to put a human face on the issue.

and 2005–2006 Illinois Teacher of the Year, created it (see Appendix 2). She tested the curriculum at Elgin High School and elsewhere throughout the state. She has also conducted more than a dozen *Edens Lost & Found* teacher workshops in Illinois. In October 2006, Deb and Harry presented this curriculum at the annual meeting of the North American Association for Environmental Studies (NAAEE). Deb has enlisted other national Teachers of the Year to try out the curriculum in their classrooms before it becomes more widely available.

Workshops are the latest addition to the outreach program and reflect the flexibility of our media model. As a result of the workshops Deb had conducted, thousands have been introduced to *Edens Lost & Found*'s set of environmental best practices. Notably, neither the curriculum nor the workshops formed part of the initial media model but evolved when we identified this outlet.

In Los Angeles, we are working with Andy Lipkis and TreePeople to expand our message. With local coalition partners, sponsors, and representatives of Los Angeles city government we held our first *Edens Lost & Found* town hall meeting in fall 2007, with 150 to 300 attendees, including business leaders, community activists, academics, students, experts, and government officials. The agenda focused on 12 to 15 topics, each introduced with a short film clip and then followed by a no-holds-barred discussion. We recorded the multihour event, yielding more than enough footage to create a compelling 60- to 90-minute local PBS program. We made a second longer version for nonbroadcast educational and community use.

Our new media model also incorporates a national promotion campaign to broaden recognition of and support for the issue. We invite membership organizations and educational institutions to become outreach partners. They engage in online viral marketing, using the Internet and coalition partner mailing lists to expand the PBS broadcast

TABLE 2. WHAT DOES BECOMING A NATIONAL PARTNER INVOLVES

Whether you represent a National Partner or a local community-based coalition, we hope that you will pick an action from one or more of the following:

- distribute our material—publicity, promotion, outreach—to your constituencies, either through email, print, or otherwise;
- participate in the organization of our town hall meetings when they take place in your community;
- designate someone on your team who could serve as liaison/organizer;
- suggest new partners or coalitions that we—or you—might pursue to ask them to join;
- recommend new ways for us to spread the word throughout your constituencies;
- propose ways that we might get our educational curricula materials into the hands of those agencies/institutions with whom you already work at the high school and college levels;
- suggest where we might be able to obtain new lists of people who would be interested in our shared goals;
- recommend new marketing strategies that we might pursue and implement jointly;
- indicate which elected officials at the municipal, state, and federal level we might contact to present our materials;
- indicate who on your team might serve as "adviser" for the second season of cities and subjects, domestically and internationally;
- recommend how you might modify our materials to better serve your constituencies;
- think of new potential funders who might want to be associated with the project in the PBS neighborhood in subsequent years.

audience. This allows us to reach millions of interested parties in a cost-effective manner. Not only did the partnerships enhance our audience ratings, but they also enabled us to reach our preselected target audiences.

What is required of our partners? In short, whatever they can afford to do. We created a "Partners Action Plan" listing suggested activities. As in the case of many volunteer programs, the response varies greatly. What every partner did do was to provide us with their membership email lists. This guaranteed online access to millions of pre-selected individuals who were concerned about the state of greening in this country. Table 2 illustrates the range of expectations for national partners.

For *Edens Lost & Found*, our national partners include the National Outreach Center (PBS), TreePeople, U.S. Forest Service, Project for Public Spaces, Environment Now, and Keep America Beautiful. They contribute content, publicity, and ongoing outreach. Many other government and NGO organizations are involved in certain substantive or local outreach aspects according to their interests and concerns so we have locally based or regional partners as well. Examples are the Pennsylvania Horticultural Society, University of Pennsylvania Institute of Urban Research, and University of Southern California Center for Sustainable Cities, as well as public and charter schools across the country.

Some of our national partnerships are special. Ashoka and Google, who are strongly committed to social entrepreneurship, are two examples.[2] Both are content advisers and underwriters. A key partner, Ashoka, is dedicated to promoting social good through the support of fellows—individual and partnership teams that work in six broad fields: learning/youth development, the environment, health, human rights, economic development, and civic participation. In 2006, Ashoka selected us as fellows, adding tremendous leverage to the new media model. It funded our vision with a three-year grant, introduced us to other potential social venture sponsors, and offered us the incalculable moral and spiritual support social entrepreneurs need to truly be effective.

One of the initial benefits of our Ashoka fellowship was a significant in-kind grant from Google Grants. Through GoogleAdwords, we are now reaching an audience in the many millions. In addition, we are registered in Google Analytics, a tool that shows us how people find and explore our website and how we can enhance their visitor experience. This helps us to continually update and improve our site.

Our next project, *Edens Overseas*, will apply our new media model to identify international best practices and their application to the United States. We anticipate airing this series of programs globally, significantly increasing the impact of the message. We have never undertaken a project of this scale nor tried to promote an outreach and educational program in other countries. We can only guess what its effectiveness will be. The experiment with the new media model continues.

Outcomes of the New Media Model

In measuring the effects of our new media model on local and national policy, we are gauging direct impact in terms of attracting audience attention. For *And Thou Shalt Honor*, we know that between August and October 2002, when we were engaged in heavy outreach and publicity activities, along with the actual national airdate on October 9, the number of visitors accessing the website dramatically increased. They came from 45 of the 50 states. Most were first-time visitors who reported that they heard about the website from many sources, including television, community meetings, organizations, relatives, friends, workplace colleagues, and electronic formats (for example, other websites, emails, mailing lists or surfing the Internet). Market researchers Kelly & Salerno reported that our aggressive market-by-market publicity push resulted in more than 600 print placements generating an estimated circulation of almost 100 million in 23 of the top 25 media markets. Radio and television satellite tours increased the total media impact to more than 107 million and helped drive ratings exceeding the PBS primetime average of 1.7 million households in 19 markets. The average Nielsen rating for *And Thou Shalt Honor*'s October 9 broadcast was 1.6, with an average share of 2 million households (compiled by Nielsen Media Research). Ratings and shares were higher for KOPB of Portland, Oregon (3.8 rating/6 share) and KLRU of Austin, Texas (3.3 rating/6 share). Considering there were also large amounts of outreach for *And Thou Shalt Honor* in these two cities, the higher rating values may be correlated with the higher level and the success of outreach efforts.

While we do not yet have the complete results for *Eden's Lost & Found*, we believe that the broad outcomes from the PBS national broadcast and outreach efforts will be similar to those of *And Thou Shalt Honor*. Our Nielsen ratings for the *Edens Lost & Found* airings were 1.4, or 1.4 million households, which averages to a first night viewership per hour program of approximately 3 million individuals. We also have seen that the four programs provided greatly heightened awareness in each of the featured cities around the local greening and an increased level of civic commitment, resources, and activities from the public and private sectors to address these issues. They gave exposure to representatives from the featured organizations in these cities who are now serving as spokespeople and consultants to other cities and municipalities across the country about green revitalization and restoration efforts. They strengthened and publicized the work of national organizations, whose purview already addresses these issues, and opened new avenues of financial support to underwrite additional programming for subsequent broadcast seasons.

A Sustainable Media Model

When we started this work we knew that we had to create not only a new media model but also a sustainable social entrepreneurial model. The effort has been challenging but ultimately successful. We can outline two key steps necessary for such an effort. The first is to gain control of the intellectual capital through copyright. This allows the repurposing of content. For example, we can create customized digital and online accessible products to meet the demands of our other goals, including developing community outreach and educational programs that include not only books and DVDs, but also streaming video clips for various uses including town meetings and distribution to other outlets. (We are in discussions with two national newspapers that have expressed interest in carrying these short clips devoted to environmental best practices on their websites.)

The second is to enlist local and national partners to enhance dialogue about our topics. Through their networks and existing and new programs they have disseminated the messages of our PBS programs, giving them the long lives and wide circulation that will lead to civic consciousness and action.

We and others can apply our new media model to projects that similarly require the time and intellectual effort to present public policy not only in healthcare and greening but in other critical subjects before a global audience. We believe that presence and growth of this interactive audience will make our new media model even more sustainable as greater numbers of people have access to the Internet. In the short run, we have accomplished our goals. In the long run, we aspire to see the development of public policy that addresses the issues we have engaged.

Appendix 1. *Edens Lost & Found* Video Library

1. *The Importance of Watershed Management*
2. *IRP*: Integrated Resource Planning and Management
3. *The Green Building Revolution*
4. The next economic wave: *Green Collar Careers*
5. *Greening: The New Urban Crimefighter*
6. The quest for *Environmental Justice*
7. Urban sprawl and *Mass Transit Solutions*
8. Re-greening the city: *Planting and Harvesting the Urban Forest*
9. Alternate fuels: Finding *Renewable Energy Sources*
10. Community service and *Environmental Stewardship* with Illinois Teacher of the Year Deb Perryman and Michael Howard, Executive Director of Eden Place, Chicago.
11. *Portrait of a Farmers Market*: Creating sustainable and profitable agricultural markets.
12. A city tradition: Portrait of the *Philadelphia Flower Show*
13. One tree at a time: A portrait of *Andy Lipkis & TreePeople*
14. Restoring Chicago's ecosystem: *Chicago Wilderness*
15. Reclaiming a great city through the blood, sweat, and tears of volunteers: *Pennsylvania Horticultural Society*
16. Academic Symposium #1—Los Angeles, 2004
17. Academic Symposium #2 with *Keynote Speaker Wangari Maathai*—University of Pennsylvania, October 15–17, 2006

18. *Restoring Our Urban Rivers*: Chicago River; Schuylkill River, Philadelphia; the infamous Los Angeles River
19. *Successful Urban Planning*: The Olmsted/Burnham Legacy in Chicago and Philadelphia; missing an Olmsted opportunity in Los Angeles
20. *Youth Reclaim the Environment*: Girls Today, Women Tomorrow in Los Angeles; Lily Yeh's Village of Arts and Humanities in Philadelphia; Michael Howard's Mighty Acorns in Chicago; Deb Perryman's high school students in Elgin, Illinois.
21. *Sustainable Living Practices*: What individuals can do in their everyday life with Ed Begley.
22. *The Plight of Indicator Species*: Salmon of Seattle
23. *Creating Great Public Spaces*: Millennium Park in Chicago; Grand Avenue Project, Los Angeles; Mural Arts Program and Lilly Yeh, Philadelphia; restoration of Seattle waterfront.
24. The importance of the *Neighborhood Park*. Doris Gwatney and Caroll Park, Philadelphia; Jennifer Wolch and the New Neighborhood parks of Los Angeles, including Jackson Park restoration in Pasadena and Stella's dream to build a park for her kids in El Monte.
25. *Transforming Brown Fields into Environmental Treasures*: Calumet project in Chicago; Hydroponic farming in Kensington, Philadelphia; Hansen Dam, Sun Valley, Emerald Necklace in Los Angeles.
26. *Transforming School Environments: From Cement to Green*: Greater exercise using new permeable surfaces for the play yard with Howard Neukrug; Andy Lipkis plants trees to keep kids from getting skin cancer.
27. *Jane Jacobs and the New Urbanism*: Creating walkable communities where you live, work, go to school, and shop within walking distance or nearby public transportation.
28. *Rebuilding Sustainable Communities from the Ground Up*: High Point in Seattle.
29. *Restoring Your Own Eden*: sustainable practices in your own backyard.

Appendix 2. High School Curriculum: *Edens Lost & Found* Curriculum, Grades 9–12

The *Edens Lost & Found Curriculum* is divided into the following 20 topics, all of which are discussed in the *Edens Lost & Found* book and documentary series. Each topic will be covered in approximately 8 to10 pages, depending on the subject matter, extension activities, and reproducibles provided. In addition to the science and social studies standards addressed throughout the curriculum, we also highlight various cross-curricular activities, such as literature, math, and art tie-ins. We provide assessment guidelines for teachers and thorough instructions on how to use the curriculum in the classroom to complement existing materials.

Activity lengths will be varied and flexible. This will allow teachers to pick and choose activities that correspond not only to the topic being covered and standards that need to be met, but also to work with the time they have available. Some activities can be done in as little as 20 minutes, while other lengthier extension activities may carry on over several weeks.

Service Learning

This section provides the basics on getting started with the teaching strategy known as service learning.

Building and Defining Communities

This discussion explores the art of community and why community-based support is so important to urban restoration. Every day, young people move freely between different social circles: the community of their families, their close friends, their school campus, and their cities, towns, or neighborhoods. Though they belong to each of these communities, they may not take any action to cement their standing in that group. Active participation goes a long way toward making a person feel happy, productive, and connected to others in his or her group. By pitching in to clean up a dilapidated park, plant a garden, or clean up a local river, people make friends and are rewarded with a greater sense of community.

Acting Together and Decision Making

How do citizens make decisions? What are the different strategies and activities that can be used to help young people make decisions about issues that affect their school and community? Using topics raised in *Edens Lost & Found*, this section fosters critical thinking skills through the exploration of relevant sustainability debates. It shows students how to engage local legislators and businesses and how to develop a community-based resource guide and website that will focus on the specific needs of the students' region.

Understanding Sustainability

How is sustainability defined for a society and its environment? This topic introduces and defines the resources that contribute to a sustainable ecosystem and explore best practices across the United States and in other parts of the world.

URBAN PARKS AND OPEN SPACE

Eighty percent of our population live in cities. But too few have access to open space and public parks. City parks and open space improve our physical and psychological health, strengthen our communities, raise property values, and make our cities more attractive and desirable places to live and work for everyone. This section highlights cities that have put open space to good use for the betterment of not only their environmental health, but their economic viability as well.

URBAN FORESTRY

In the battle to save our cities, urban forestry stands guard on the front lines. Tree-lined streets not only beautify, but also help to moderate city temperatures and fight air pollution—in addition to raising property values. Trees hold water and prevent run-off and erosion. Tree planting and maintenance also fosters community spirit and strengthens neighborhoods.

WATERSHED MANAGEMENT

Watershed management involves more than just water storage and purification. It is also about land management and delivery systems. This chapter also includes the basics of water quality monitoring, water pollution, developing watershed plans and the Clean Water Act.

WASTE MANAGEMENT AND RECYCLING

Here the long-term impact of waste disposal and the importance of environmentally conscious alternatives to landfills are explored. This chapter address the need to reuse natural resources and upgrade our urban infrastructure in order to reduce waste and conserve energy. We give students practical information on the history and execution of one of the country's oldest environmental practices: recycling. What has recycling accomplished and how have laws changed over the last 20 years in order to make recycling a part of our everyday lives?

ENERGY

What are the different types of energy sources used in the United States? What are the pros and cons of each of these sources? What is energy conservation and how do we promote it in our communities? This topic examines the politics and science involved in the energy conservation movement as well as the future of alternative sources of fuel.

Green Building

Creating sustainable structures has become the goal of many citizens, architects, and governments. This topic's activities show just how some cities have used the best practices available for green building and landscaping, and explores the science, community action and, political success behind their stories.

Mass Transportation

Of course, New York, Washington, D.C., San Francisco, Chicago, and many other older cities have had mass transit for years. But now automobile-centered cities such as Los Angeles, Houston, and even Orange County, California, are beginning to become believers in the benefits of mass transit. As freeways become increasingly choked, other cities across the country are turning to mass transit alternatives. How can cities change their ways and what effect will it have on their environmental health? This section looks at success stories and the stories of those fighting for change in their communities.

Soil Quality

Applying scientific innovation to protect our nation's soil for future food production and the reduction of contaminants.

Air Quality

This topic explores the social, economic, and scientific implications of our air quality. This will include, but not be limited to, the Kyoto Accords and current U.S. Clean Air legislation.

Urban Agriculture and Community Gardens

This section delves into all of the social, economic, and environmental implications of the growth and distribution or our nation's food. Whether through corporate or family-owned farms, how are chemicals used, how do they affect our communities and health, and how can the growing neighborhood garden movement change the quality of the food we eat and bring communities together?

Population Growth and Integrated Resource Management

This section shows the dangers of the exploding global population as explored through the social, economic, and scientific lens. As America's population grows past 300 million inhabitants, the issues of energy use, resource management and waste disposal take on new and monumental importance.

Biodiversity

Here we discuss the social, economic, and scientific elements involved in protecting animal species, habitats, and plant life.

Understanding Public Policy

The Clean Water and Clean Air Acts, as well as many other pieces of environmental legislation, are federal laws that rely on citizen participation for their successful implementation. This section will discuss model ordinances that can be put into place to assist municipalities in becoming more sustainable, and the role that students and teachers can play in that process. This section will also explore citizen willingness to pay, through bond issues, for public improvements such as parks and the acquisition of public lands.

Urban Planning

Throughout history, the design of a city has been a monumental task left to the most skilled of professionals—architects, engineers, designers—many of them visionaries who have left lasting, if abandoned, legacies. This section examines the history and foresight of some of America's most renowned city planners and how many of their ideas are again inspiring cities seeking to rejuvenate their urban centers.

Environmental Justice

Access to nature should be a human right. The best that nature has to offer should be readily available to people of all backgrounds and all economic groups. Similarly, human waste, refuse, and poisons—those byproducts that are damaging our natural habitat—should not be made the burden of the economically disadvantaged. This section explores modern social issues surrounding the topic of environmental justice and shows how ordinary citizens are fighting for it.

GROUNDWORK FOR THE FUTURE: SUSTAINABLE COMMERCE AND
ENVIRONMENTAL EDUCATION

This section tackles the long-held myth that environmental stewardship
is at odds with industry and with economic development. Companies
and organizations are increasingly proving this perspective to be wrong;
the growth potential for innovative organizations and governments that
choose to employ sustainable business practices is beyond measure. In
this section we examine these issues and shine light on some of the voca-
tional advantages to embracing environmental education in schools and
stewardship in communities.

References

McLeod, Beth Witrogen. 2002. *And Thou Shalt Honor: The Caregiver's Companion.*
Foreword by Rosalynn Carter. Emmaus, Pa.: Rodale Press.
Wiland, Harry, and Dale Bell. 2006. *Edens Lost & Found: How Ordinary Citizens Are
Restoring Our Great American Cities.* White River Junction, Vt.: Chelsea Green.

Chapter 12

Transformation Through Greening

J. Blaine Bonham, Jr., and Patricia L. Smith

The Vacant Land Crisis

In the years following World War II, Philadelphia and its residents experienced an unprecedented loss of businesses and employment, resulting in a crushing wave of depopulation. Since its zenith as the "workshop of America" in the first half of the twentieth century, the nation's first capital saw its population of 2.1 million people plummet by 600,000, reducing the number of residents in some neighborhoods by half or even two-thirds to 1.5 million (Bonham, Spilka, and Rastorfer 2002). This decline resulted in an economic slump as factories closed, leaving vacant hulks throughout the city. Residential property owners neglected or abandoned housing, and formerly robust commercial corridors became the sites of boarded-up buildings. The loss of tax-paying businesses and people meant a drastic decline in revenue for basic municipal services and improvements, further contributing to the downward spiral in the afflicted neighborhoods. As the once proud homes, shops, and offices deteriorated, property values dropped, and the morale of residents fell.

In 2000 the Brookings Institution announced that in a comparison of 83 cities, Philadelphia had the highest level of vacant properties (Metropolitan Career Center 2001: 41). A year later, the Philadelphia Department of Licenses and Inspections reported 31,000 vacant lots and 26,000 abandoned houses—many of which were structurally unsafe and required demolition. While major changes were needed to address this depressing picture, attempts at redevelopment seemed risky and appeared overwhelming; skepticism ran high.

City government was by no means blind to the distressing situation, and through the years had tried to rectify it. Similarly, the nonprofit Pennsylvania Horticultural Society (PHS) had accumulated several decades of experience countering blight through its urban greening program, Philadelphia Green. In 2001, when newly elected Mayor John F.

Street launched the Neighborhood Transformation Initiative (NTI), a $250-million program to remove blight and renovate the city's distressed neighborhood, he also announced a partnership with Philadelphia Green to create a broad-scale vacant land management program.

For Street, this partnership emanated from a deep-seated conviction that vacant lots were a cause for great public concern. They made neighborhoods look desolate and forgotten, diminished the quality of life for residents, and sent a message to outsiders that the community was in decline. Beyond economics and aesthetics, abandoned properties collected trash and attracted illegal activity. While Street and his advisers knew that a half century of urban deterioration and blight would not be remedied quickly, they also hoped that major change would occur if city agencies, community organizations, and environmental nonprofits combined their resources to work toward common goals. Prior to his election, Philadelphia's downtown district, Center City, had experienced an impressive rebirth under such a formula. In addition, PHS's innovative vacant land work had led to marked improvements in many distressed neighborhoods. This chapter details the NTI's transformative effects, focusing on its vacant land management program from the combined perspective of the Philadelphia city government and PHS.

The Formative Years of Philadelphia Green

PHS, formed in 1827, is a membership-based horticulture network that has, in the past three decades, developed an extensive nationally recognized urban greening program. It began as a society for those interested in botany and gardening to share information and socialize. In 1829, it sponsored the first Philadelphia Flower Show, an annual tradition that continues to the present. By the early 1970s, the flower show had become so popular that PHS was generating more income than needed to support basic operations. PHS leaders decided to apply the surplus to address the lingering pattern of urban blight. In 1974, they organized "Philadelphia Green" by teaming with the city's Department of Recreation to sponsor 10 resident-built community vegetable gardens on vacant lots. The gardens were an immediate success, largely because many of the gardeners had come from the South and had farming experience.

By the early 1980s, Philadelphia Green expanded this effort with its Green Countrie Towne program (taking its name from William Penn's 1682 label for Philadelphia), an effort that not only aimed at greening urban areas but also aspired to build neighborhood social capital by using greening to heighten organizational capacity among residents. With funding from local foundations—notably the Pew Chartable Trusts and the William Penn Foundation—along with city government through the City of Philadelphia Community Development Block Grant, it concentrated on eight low-income neighborhoods and worked with local social services organizations to craft an intensive greening approach. It organized residents to build community vegetable and flower gardens and plant street trees, window boxes, and wine barrels. The aim was to create sustainable greening projects that would require minimal ongoing support from Philadelphia Green once the initial landscaping was complete. The program helped stem years of neighborhood decline by promoting community self-awareness and pride. Many of the Green Countrie Townes were able to leverage their greening projects and attract new community-development funding from corporations and government that supported programs ranging from housing to illegal drug market elimination.

Iris Brown, from North Philadelphia's Norris Square neighborhood, witnessed the salubrious effect of the program: "Through community gardening, things started to change and our neighborhood changed. If a person planted a tree, then another person wanted to plant one. . . . We cultivate more than gardens—we foster hope. And with aid from other agencies we're able to tackle other issues like vandalism, crime, and drugs" (Bonham, Spilka, and Rastorfer 2002: 76–79).

By the 1990s, the success of the Greene Countrie Town program led Philadelphia Green to work with well-established community development corporations (CDCs) to promote open space planning. For example, it partnered with the Associación de Puertorriqueños en Marcha (APM), a CDC located in a depressed section of eastern central Philadelphia in the mid-1990s. Together the organizations established 25 community gardens, planted 202 trees, and acquired and developed 2.42 acres for new housing and a shopping center. Philadelphia Green, in reinforcing the role of landscaping for the refurbished properties, taught the residents of new homes how to plant and maintain their front yards. The results were transformative. "Since these lots were reclaimed, the community has participated in maintaining their appearance," reflected APM's Director for Development, Rose Gray. "Something is different—you can sense that the neighborhood has taken an interest" (Bonham, Spilka, and Rastorfer 2002).

In 1995, Philadelphia Green embarked on an even more ambitious project by partnering with the New Kensington Community Development Corporation (NKCDC) to establish a program to manage some of the 1,100 vacant lots in three neighborhoods. By 2002, the partnership had "cleaned and greened" nearly 700 parcels. Most of the properties became tree lots—sites stripped of unsightly concrete barriers and adorned with as many as 65 trees. Other lots were converted to gardens or parks, and still others were transferred to adjacent homeowners as "sideyards" (Bonham, Spilka, and Rastorfer 2002: 94–98). "Our vacant land work with Philadelphia Green has been an amazing success. When we first started the project, people were moving out of the area and the land had little to no value," Sandy Salzman, executive director of NKCDC, said. "Today it's a totally different picture. People are buying into the neighborhood, vacant land is being sold for considerable prices, and people feel good about the remaining open space."

Building on the success in New Kensington, Philadelphia Green next linked up with the federally funded American Street Empowerment Zone (ASEZ). Working with four local CDCs to clear vacant lots of trash and debris, Philadelphia Green developed an efficient, cost-effective plan for cleaning and planting large vacant lots with trees and grass. By 2003, it had restored more than 13 acres, making a dramatic change in the participating neighborhoods.

Despite the success of Philadelphia Green's community greening efforts, the number of trash-filled vacant lots continued to mushroom and threatened to overwhelm these accomplishments. Community organizations and residents were not equipped to address the enormity of the situation. In order to have a continuing impact, Philadelphia Green needed to persuade city government to address the vacant land problem as part of its community development strategy.

In 1999, Philadelphia Green had anticipated this problem and commissioned Fairmount Ventures Inc., a consulting firm to nonprofits and philanthropy (www.fairmountinc.com), to assess whether proactively addressing the problem at a citywide scale would be more effective than the current practice of reacting to vacant land crises as they arose. The results revealed that the city government had an insufficient budget to clean and maintain vacant land regardless of the strategy it pursued (Kligerman et al. 1999: 27). It found that to decrease the number of vacant lots, city government would have to make a substantial investment, one that would provide lasting aesthetic and quality-of-life benefits to residents and would, long-term, increase property values and add to the tax base. While the study offered sound proposals, it premised success on a sympathetic mayoral administration, one that would find and dedicate the required resources.

A New Direction

When John F. Street ran for mayor in 1999, he pledged to turn his attention to neighborhoods while moving forward with several large-scale economic development projects, including the expansion of the Pennsylvania Convention Center and the construction of new stadiums for

Philadelphia's professional baseball and football teams. He promised to raise at least $250 million to invest in Philadelphia neighborhoods, contending that, given the right conditions, the capital markets would invest in the revitalization of neighborhoods just as they did in sports arenas.

Once elected mayor, Street laid the foundation for the promised citywide neighborhood revitalization strategy. He held town meetings in each of Philadelphia's 10 City Council districts to solicit citizens' views about improving their neighborhoods. Participants in these meetings identified abandoned cars, unsafe buildings, debris-filled lots, and dead and dying street trees as key issues. Street also appointed a task force called the Blight Elimination Subcommittee for Neighborhood Revitalization that involved community members, civic leaders, and nonprofit organizations (PHS included). The task force recommended a four-pronged approach to transform Philadelphia neighborhoods, including a comprehensive planning process, a financing strategy, an implementation plan, and creation of a cabinet-level position to oversee the program. With his cabinet, departmental commissioners, and members of City Council, Street toured the city's 10 council districts to potential projects for city-supported neighborhood reinvestment.

To gain a better understanding of neighborhood conditions, the Street administration retained The Reinvestment Fund (TRF) during the fall of 2000 to study Philadelphia's housing markets. TRF analysis of key data (home sale prices, housing tenure, presence of subsidized housing, vacancy rates, land use, mortgage foreclosure rates, and the ratio of prime to subprime lending) led to its identification of six distinct market clusters. They ranged from neighborhoods of regional choice (strong housing markets due to distinct architecture, well-maintained housing, proximity to rivers and parks, bountiful tree canopies, landscaped streetscapes, and public spaces) to transitional neighborhoods (dynamic markets where housing values are trending either up or down) to reclamation neighborhoods (weak housing markets due to high levels of abandonment, low home values, and poorly maintained houses) (see Plate 8).

Building on the strengths and community assets of each cluster, TRF outlined individualized roles for public sector investment, identifying specific strategies, programs, and services and devised a plan to target government resources to provide maximum benefit. For example, for strong, stable neighborhoods TRF recommended public actions to promote their special qualities and amenities to attract new residents to the city. For transitional neighborhoods, it suggested tactical approaches, including code enforcement. For reclamation markets it outlined asset development strategies to produce new, economically diverse communities (City of Philadelphia 2004; Nowak, this volume).

Street unveiled the Neighborhood Transformation Initiative (NTI) in April 2001, listing six objectives:

- facilitate and support community-based planning efforts that reflect both a citywide and neighborhood vision;
- address the blight caused by dangerous vacant buildings, trash-filled lots, abandoned cars, graffiti, and litter to improve the appearance of Philadelphia streetscapes;
- advance the quality of life in neighborhoods with a coordinated and targeted code enforcement program;
- improve the city's ability to assemble and develop vacant land;
- stimulate and increase investment in Philadelphia neighborhoods through a comprehensive approach that stresses partnerships among civic, public, and private sectors;
- leverage scarce public resources to the fullest extent and strategically invest these resources in neighborhoods.

Street also listed specific goals for NTI. They were: eliminating the backlog of dangerous buildings by demolishing 14,000 vacant houses and stabilizing an additional 2,000; cleaning the city's 31,000 vacant lots and instituting a program to keep them reasonably free of debris; establishing a land bank to facilitate the acquisition of vacant land for redevelopment and permanent open space; and investing in the construction or repair of 16,000 housing units. Finally, he also called for changing government operations by stressing coordination and collaboration among city agencies, use of improved technologies, and developing partnerships to deliver neighborhood services. He emphasized leveraging private investment with public funds to create opportunities for redevelopment.

The NTI required a commitment of more than $1.6 billion by 2007, with most of that money dedicated to eliminating the backlog of dangerous vacant buildings, providing home repair grants and loans, and financing the assembly of land for market-rate and affordable housing (City of Philadelphia 2001). The complex NTI financing relied on several bond issues plus targeted operating budget funds. It employed tax-exempt governmental purpose bonds for the demolition of dangerous buildings, qualified redevelopment bonds for land assembly activities in blighted neighborhoods, and taxable bonds to fund home improvement loans. In addition, the mayor dedicated $10 million of city operating funds for a minimum of five years to pay for blight abatement activities, including cleaning and greening vacant lots, targeted code enforcement, and removing unsafe street trees. Finally, he deployed federal public housing and community development funds to support the NTI.

The Philadelphia Redevelopment Authority (RDA) bonds, issued in multiple series, formed the main funding source. Under an agreement with the RDA, the city agreed to pay up to $20 million annually to cover the debt. Favorable interest rates and full use of the $20 million pledge generated more than $296 million in bond proceeds for NTI.

Taking Care of the Basics

From the beginning, Street viewed the reclamation and management of vacant land as a key aspect of the NTI. Although not the legal owner of the land, the city had responsibility for the health, safety, and general welfare concerns that stem from abandoned property.

The PHS work undertaken in the 1990s had underlined the situation. In a 1995 study funded by the Pew Charitable Trusts, reseachers Blaine Bonham and Gerri Spilka showed how debris-filled vacant lots decreased the quality of life for residents, discouraged investment in the city, and contributed to depopulation trends (Bonham and Spilka 2005). Conversely, they demonstrated that greening strategically located lots preserved (and often raised) nearby property values and spurred redevelopment activity. Further, when involving open space planning and community management of urban vacant land, these efforts strengthened the social fabric of neighborhoods. It also established that sustainable greening and beautification projects required public/private partnerships and the active participation by, and commitment of, community stewards.

In June 2001, Street initiated the Vacant Lot Clean-up Program (VLCP), located in the Office of the Managing Director, to tackle the problem of unmanaged vacant land. With an initial $4-million budget, VLCP aimed to clean 31,000 lots in a year and implement a maintenance program to keep the lots reasonably clear of debris. Philadelphia (or any other city, for that matter) had no precedent for a lot-cleaning initiative of this scale. In undertaking the program, the managing director assigned staff (140 municipal employees and 75 temporary workers) and augmented existing equipment with $500,000 worth of purchases (used pick-up trucks, trailers, wood chippers, clippers, and mowers). The VLCP manager worked with the Department of Licenses and Inspections to issue citations for violations of the city property maintenance code that allowed city workers and contractors to gain access to the vacant lots.

The VCLP met its goal and cleaned 31,000 vacant lots in one year. As of March 2007, the managing director's office has completed 85,476 lot cleanings. The city also expanded efforts to abate graffiti, combat littering, promote recycling, and curb illegal dumping. It eliminated the backlog of dead street trees and pruned more than 20,000 others. In a parallel program, it removed 279,134 abandoned cars from the Philadelphia's streets.

Philadelphia Green Recruited for NTI

From the onset of NTI, it was apparent that government action and funding alone would not enable the fledging program to realize its full potential. Street knew that the lot cleaning was not the complete answer to Philadelphia's vacant land problems. In launching the VLCP, he declared the city's intention to partner with Philadelphia Green to turn abandoned vacant lands into community assets. In response, Philadelphia Green developed a new approach to urban greening, the NTI Green City Strategy. Incorporating successful elements of its Green Countrie Towne program from a decade earlier, Philadelphia Green now had municipal resources to address these issues at scale. Combined with foundation funding, it proposed to upgrade and expand the city's green infrastructure through the development of community gardens and gateways, major tree plantings, and the restoration of neighborhood parks and civic spaces (Figure 1).

By coupling the resources of city government with Philadelphia Green's community presence and years of hands-on revitalization work, the new strategy had the ability to make a lasting change. The NTI Green City Strategy provided interim management of existing lots and also allowed planning for new open space as a way to retain residents and businesses and attract new housing and commercial investment. Although Philadelphia Green planted grass and trees to stabilize vacant land, it viewed these efforts not as permanent open space but as attractive placeholders until another use could be determined. "By simply clearing trash and debris and creating a more park-like setting we were able to transform the land into something of use, revealing its potential to become something more," Michael Groman, the senior director of Philadelphia Green, observed. As with all its work, the implementation of the new enterprise required the support of community groups, municipal agencies, and private and public entities.

When the Street administration adopted the NTI Green City Strategy, it initially allocated $4 million of budgetary support, and in continuing funding though June 2007 brought the total of the city's investment in the program to more than $12 million (City of Philadelphia 2003). With these funds, Philadelphia Green targeted six neighborhoods for intensive treatment. Collaborating with community partners, the NTI staff and local political leaders picked properties for improvement that would create a positive visual impact on well-traveled corridors.

Figure 1. Chart created by PHS to illustrate the process of the NTI Green City Strategy. Pennsylvania Horticultural Society.

The idea was to select neighborhoods that had a high likelihood of developing into future "hot spots"—communities on the rise, perhaps five to ten years away from significant growth.[1] "When you start concentrating vacant land improvements and maintenance in a very visible way, it is not only the individual sites that become attractive to buyers, but the whole neighborhood becomes transformed," Philadelphia Green Associate Director Bob Grossmann said. "We strive for what we call a 'tipping point,' which is the degree of stabilization that causes private investment and development to start entering the community and begin utilizing the land."

Beyond the six target areas, Philadelphia Green leveraged the city's significant investment by enhancing its ongoing programs. It had an

inventory of more than 80 neighborhood parks that were part of Philadelphia Green's Parks Revitalization Program, an effort that helps local
friends groups work with the Department of Recreation and Fairmount
Park Commission to reclaim the land as community spaces. It also created a City Harvest program funded by the Albert M. Greenfield Foundation, in which inmates of the Philadelphia prison system grow
produce that is donated to local food cupboards. Finally, Philadelphia
Green strengthened its educational initiatives for city residents with its
Tree Tenders and Garden Tenders training projects, and the City Gardening Series held at branches of the Free Library of Philadelphia.

The "Clean & Green" Model to Stabilizing Land

Although Philadelphia Green had several years of vacant land work
experience, going to scale required a revamped and expanded system
implementation program. To accomplish this, it began the Vacant Land
Stabilization Program, a "clean and green" model based on the earlier
New Kensington and American Street Empowerment Zone efforts. The
program focused on individual lots and involved disposing of litter,
grading soil, planting grass seed, and installing trees and simple wood
fences to establish park-like settings. Landscape contractors, most of
whom are Philadelphia-based, performed all the stabilization work. But
before Philadelphia Green could put a shovel in the ground, the city
and Philadelphia Green had to deal with ownership issues. Although,
more often than not, the property belonged to a private owner, the city's
Department of Licenses and Inspections certified the selected sites as
blighted and gave Philadelphia Green permission to enter the properties to remediate the blight as a contractor to the city (Figures 2 and 3).

By August 2007, Philadelphia Green had stabilized more than 6 million square feet of land. It also developed a maintenance program for
the reclaimed sites. Reasoning that volunteers could manage only a few
spaces in their neighborhoods, it established a competitive bidding
process for contractors to provide ongoing care. The program expenses
included an initial cost for cleaning, grading, and planting that averaged
about $1.50 per square foot. Additional seasonal maintenance (April
through October) cost about 17 cents a square foot. To date this project
has had substantial quality-of-life benefits, as noted by Philadelphia
Green director Joan Reilly: "It is almost unbelievable that a waist-high
wooden fence and a couple of saplings would deter the destruction that
used to occur on the exact same spot. It shows that criminal activity is
drawn to places that seem neglected, so stabilizing the land becomes a
harbinger of hope."

Evidence of the success of the Vacant Land Stabilization Project has

Figure 2. Intersection of Third and York Streets (from Bodine Street) before stabilization work. Pennsylvania Horticultural Society.

emerged in communities across the city. For example, Philadelphia Green partnered with Project HOME and other likeminded organizations to address the blight and economic decline in North Philadelphia's "Ridge on the Rise" area. Focusing on the commercial corridor within the boundaries of Ridge Avenue, Brown Street, and Thirty-Third Street, the team transformed abandoned office buildings and notorious dumping sites into clean safe open space. Coupling the stabilization with colorful art installations (courtesy of the City's Mural Arts Program), gateway improvements, and street tree plantings, the conversion was profound. As a result, the decline of the old commercial strip has been halted. Also, the area south of Girard Avenue is beginning to experience more investment activity as the increasing real estate values of Center City push development northward.

Community Land Care, Keeping Lots Clean

As Philadelphia Green and its partners worked to clean and green vacant lots, the city was busy demolishing thousands of dangerous buildings. Although the NTI demolition program provided seeds and fenced

Figure 3. The intersection after stabilization work. Pennsylvania Horticultural Society.

the lots, maintaining the growing inventory of such spaces threatened to overtax the city's capacity. In 2003, NTI officials asked PHS to devise a pilot program to engage community service organizations in the basic housekeeping—trash collection and weed removal—of newly cleared lots. The resulting program, Community Land Care, involving the maintenance of 3 million square feet, had two purposes. It improved the physical appearance of the neighborhoods and provided employment for local residents—creating more than 80 jobs (Figure 4).

One participating group was Ready, Willing and Able (RWA), which strives to employ, empower, and support homeless individuals in their efforts to achieve self-sufficiency. Although primarily a street-cleaning organization, RWA is a perfect fit for Community LandCare and employs a work crew of 5 to 10 people each season. Kate Houstoun, RWA deputy director for community affairs, says, "Our trainees are often in awe of the transformative power their work has on their community. In turn, the work has transformative power in their lives; it helps them get back on their feet."

Figure 4. A Ready, Willing and Able team onsite in the American Street Empowerment Zone. Pennsylvania Horticultural Society.

Finding New Use for Vacant Land

As part of the NTI Green City Strategy, Philadelphia Green partnered with the Philadelphia Water Department's Office of Watersheds on a low impact development (LID) demonstration project to use vacant lots for storm-water management. This green infrastructure reduces runoff that causes flooding and pollutes waterways (see Kennedy, this volume). Funded by the Pennsylvania Department of Environmental Protection's Growing Greener program, the project involved transforming five vacant sites in North Philadelphia by grading the land to form shallow trenches and berms and planting trees and shrubs to capture rainfall and allow for its absorption into the ground. This LID approach of detaining, filtering, and infiltrating runoff by mimicking natural processes works hand-in-hand with efforts to enhance open spaces in urban neighborhoods. A Temple University evaluation study reported a 30 percent reduction in stormwater runoff from June 2005 to May 2006 (Yung and Myers 2007: 8). Philadelphia Green is now working with the Water Department to use similar methods on a variety of other green spaces, including an urban farm, recreation centers, and gardens (see Brown, Vitiello, this volume).

Why It Works

Under NTI, the city has spent more than $53 million in operating budget dollars to combat blight and beautify neighborhoods, allocating nearly 25 percent, or $12 million, to the Green City Strategy. In addition, local businesses and foundations, such as Citizens Bank and the William Penn Foundation, contributed funding to the NTI Green City Strategy. In six years, the NTI Green City Strategy has improved 9 million square feet of vacant land (6 million through vacant land stabilization plus an additional 3 million through the Community LandCare maintenance program).

Several key factors contributed to this progress. The initiative is large-scale but targeted, has substantial public sector support, yet leverages private or donor funds. It employs the experienced PHS for implementation and involves community participation from start to finish. Notably, the deeply rooted alliance between PHS and city government allowed the city to share work normally seen as a government function with a nonprofit partner. The collaboration between the two maximized each partner's strengths. For example, while PHS provided the single-minded focus and technical experience required to organize projects, the city marshaled the resources to implement them. While PHS has a civic reputation and established community standing that rallied support for the greening and undertakings, the city supplied the necessary funding to realize the revitalization efforts.

The Benefits of a Clean and Green City

Today's Philadelphia neighborhoods do not look the same as they did in 2000. As of March 2007, public and private investment funded 23,935 units of affordable and market-rate housing and 28,019 home repair grants. The city had demolished 5,444 dangerous buildings, and erased graffiti from 567,932 walls. There is no longer a backlog of 8,500 hazardous street trees that need attending, and 6 million square feet of vacant land in key locations has been cleaned, greened, and secured with post and rail fencing (Table 1).

The benefits of infusing a city with pockets of clean and green open space are many and varied, witnessed when one walks through Fairmount Park, visits a community garden, or attends a concert at a neighborhood square. The most obvious advantage is visual. Open spaces create an appealing atmosphere that provides relief from congested

TABLE 1. NTI: SUMMARY OF ACCOMPLISHMENTS

	2000	2001	2002	2003	2004	2005	2006	1st–3rd Q FY07	Total
Quality of Life Programs									
Abandoned Cars Removed	62,762	53,033	53,813	38,540	27,403	21,626	17,835	4,122	279,134
Graffiti Abated	34,464	54,533	74,720	90,876	91,100	92,375	93,272	26,592	557,932
Cleanings of Vacant Lots			35,787	12,186	11,270	9,367	10,014	6,843	85,467
Buildings Demolished			1,040	573	1,380	984	1,056	411	5,444
Buildings Cleaned and Sealed			1,769	1,475	1,515	1,456			6,215
Affordable Housing Programs									
Special Needs Rental Units Completed		71	122	136	74	115	66		584
Rental Units Completed		781	324	143	302	492	371		2,413
Homeownership Units Completed		192	166	125	116	92	140		831
Total Affordable Housing Completed		1044	612	404	492	699	577		3828
Housing Preservation Programs									
Basic Systems Repair Program					14673	7503	3364	2479	28,019
Homeownership Rehab Program (HRP)					154	37	18	46	255
Settlement Grants					3545	954	995	656	6,150
HELPP Loans					13	7	1		21
Phil-Plus and Mini-Phil					70	41	48	47	206
PHIL-Loans closed			77	80	207	168	141	154	827
Total PHIL-Loan Amount in Millions			$1.30	$1.60	$4.10	$3.50	$2.90	$3.10	$17
Other Housing									
Large-Scale Market Rate Planned & Underway					8731	4374	3144		16,249

Source: Office of the Mayor, Neighborhood Transformation Initiative

urban surroundings. A second value is environmental. Trees and other plants improve air quality, absorb storm water and slow the formation of ground-level ozone. A third value is social. Community greening helps build social capital, reduce crime, provide neighborhood gathering places, and improve health by offering recreational opportunities. A fourth value is economic. Investment in greening yields significant financial returns. Two pioneering studies by Susan Wachter at the Wharton School, University of Pennsylvania, are demonstrative. The first, focused on the New Kensington neighborhood, found that an approximately $1 million investment "translated to property value gains of $4 million through tree plantings and $12 million through lot improvements." The second, *Public Investment Strategies: How They Matter for Neighborhoods in Philadelphia—Identification and Analysis,* analyzed the citywide effects of greening and associated public investments. The findings showed that derelict vacant land *decreased* the value of neighboring houses by 20 percent while green and well-maintained formerly vacant land not only recaptured the initial decrease, but increased the worth of adjacent homes by 17 percent, for a total 37 percent gain. Additionally, improvements to streetscapes (tree plantings, container plantings, and small sitting parks) added 28 percent to the value of nearby houses.[2]

With these positive results, the city and PHS anticipate ongoing collaboration. They plan to continue to expand the inventory of stabilized land by at least 600 parcels a year and to enlarge the Community Land-Care program by incorporating more neighborhoods and thus, more community-based groups. In addition, PHS is one of many local nonprofits working with 14 city agencies to develop a long-term roadmap for creating quality open spaces called GreenPlan Philadelphia. GreenPlan Philadelphia includes an inventory of the city's natural resources, recommendations for future greening and funding strategies for the plan's implementation.

This case study of pairing a nonprofit intermediary and government, the Pennsylvania Horticultural Society and city of Philadelphia, can serve as a template for other cities seeking to remedy the devastating effects of abandoned vacant land. It shows how each can build on the strengths of the other. Although change may not occur overnight, tremendous revitalization can and will happen when likeminded organizations strive for the same goal.

References

Bonham, J. Blaine, Jr., and Gerri Spilka. 1995. *Urban Vacant Land: Issues and Recommendations.* Philadelphia: Pennsylvania Horticultural Society.
Bonham J. Blaine, Jr., Gerri Spilka, and Darl Rastorfer. 2002. *Old Cities/Green*

Cities: Communities Transform Unmanaged Land. Chicago: American Planning Association.

City of Philadelphia, Mayor's Office of Communications. 2001. "Mayor Street Launches $1.6 Billion Neighborhood Transformation Initiative." Neighborhood Transformation Initiative Press Release.

————. 2003. "Urban Greening and Land Stabilization Efforts Receive $4 Million Boost from NTI." NTI Press Release, 2003.

City of Philadelphia, Neighborhood Transformation Initiative (NTI). 2004. *A Vision Becomes Reality.* NTI Progress Report.

Kligerman, Don et al. *Vacant Land Management in Philadelphia Neighborhoods: Cost Benefit Analysis.* Philadelphia: Fairmount Ventures, 1999.

Metropolitan Career Center. *Flight or Fight: Metropolitan Philadelphia and Its Future.* Philadelphia: Metropolitan Career Center, 2001.

Wachter, Susan, and Kevin C. Gillen. 2006. *Public Investment Strategies: How They Matter for Neighborhoods in Philadelphia—Identification and Analysis.* Philadelphia: Wharton School, University of Pennsylvania.

Yung, Jan, and Mary Myers. 2007. "Study of Stormwater Runoff Reduction by Greening Vacant Lots in North Philadelphia, PA." Ambler, Pa.: Department of Landscape Architecture and Horticulture, Temple University.

Chapter 13

Community Development Finance and the Green City

JEREMY NOWAK

The relationship between community development finance, the revitalization of distressed, former industrial American cities, and the importance of environmental investments can be seen in the work of The Reinvestment Fund (TRF), a community development financial institution that supports residential and commercial projects in mid-Atlantic cities.[1] TRF's investments in an environmentally degraded section of Philadelphia illustrate that environmental investments are critical to rebuilding certain cities and a dual interest in social and financial returns facilitates the connection.

This examination of TRF's work in one part of Philadelphia provides an opportunity to discuss the historical context of environmental degradation and the investment rationales of real estate developers and social entrepreneurs such as TRF. It also introduces the concept of *smart subsidy allocation* as part of the process of market building and civic organization (the term smart subsidy refers to non-market investment inputs that lead to short- and long-term market outcomes).[2]

This discussion of TRF's work and its implications aims to contribute a policy perspective that recognizes environmentalism as foundational to the revitalization of many older industrial cities and towns. While contemporary urban and regional policy supports this view, environmental activity still remains a conceptual adjunct in urban economic development practice. We must change this perspective if we are to rebuild obsolete industrial infrastructure and rethink postindustrial design and social function.

Postindustrial Cities and the Environment: Connections and Disconnections

The second half of the twentieth century brought dramatic change to many American cities, particularly those in the Northeast and Midwest industrial belt. Social and economic decentralization escalated, resulting in a decline in urban jobs and population (and a concomitant increase in both in the suburbs), a widening disparity between urban and suburban per capita income, and profoundly higher rates of poverty within cities (see Rusk 1993). These changes occurred as the structure of American manufacturing significantly shifted; firms decentralized to U.S. suburban and sunbelt locales (a trend that actually predates World War II) and later moved offshore. Advances in communications and information technology, growing transnational production and exchange, and increases in manufacturing productivity stimulated this phenomenon.

This changed the function and image of many American cities. They were no longer the center of economic growth and innovation—the industrial design and manufacturing workshop identified with late-nineteenth- and early-twentieth-century industry—but became the homes of marginalized communities, characterized by population and job loss, fiscal crisis, and the decline of public institutions.

In some places urban decline had stronger effects than in others. For example, Baltimore, Philadelphia, and Detroit lost 30 percent or more of their population within 50 years, leaving acres of deteriorated factories and abandoned housing stock. Smaller cities like Gary, Indiana, Youngstown, Ohio, Chester, Pennsylvania, and Camden, New Jersey suffered even more dramatic declines because they lacked economic diversification and had limited capacity for resource, firm, and demographic agglomeration.

While older industrial cities declined, others (particularly in the South and Southwest) grew. Cities that could annex suburban growth, serve as immigrant gateways, and avoid the costs of retrofitting deteriorated infrastructure had substantial growth advantages (see Rusk 1993). Nonetheless, by the end of the twentieth century, these places also experienced social and economic slowdowns in the face of suburban expansion.

In combating these challenges, American cities implemented strategies to stimulate growth and respond to the political problems and economic anxiety caused by poverty and global competition. They encouraged investment in central city offices and in housing and tourism; enterprise development or attraction efforts; place-based neighborhood initiatives; job training and social welfare programs; and public policy and service delivery reforms. Well-documented and controversial histories relate federal, state, and local innovations in support of these efforts.[3]

By the last decade of the twentieth century, urban fortunes began to show signs of change, especially in older industrial cities. Recently, three market trends fueled this burgeoning movement: renewed demand for urban space by immigrants and elderly or childless adult households; the rise of suburban land scarcity due to zoning and environmental pressure; and the growth of urban research institutions—universities and health related facilities—providing postindustrial employment and innovation.[4]

Today, many older cities are a remarkable amalgam of decline and revival, exhibiting dynamic and problematic trends, often in close proximity. By 2000, many had strengthened or redefined their economic bases, stabilized population losses, demonstrated increased ethnic and income diversity, and experienced the strongest real estate market in decades. Nonetheless, many still experienced high poverty levels, aging infrastructure, and a low-quality workforce. In addition, they had needs for environmental reclamation that have become inextricably linked to the potential for future growth. Their postindustrial functions required land recovery, physical space redesign, upgraded amenities, ecological improvements for infrastructure systems, and retrofitted natural assets.

Cities with built environments and land use patterns meant to accommodate more manufacturing and larger populations have been especially challenged by these demands. Philadelphia is a case in point. In the past 50 years it lost more than half a million residents, which is a 25 percent reduction from its high point of 2 million people.[5] Zoning codes mirrored a 1950s industrial city. In 2001, it had 26,000 vacant residential buildings, 31,000 vacant lots, and 2,500 abandoned commercial and industrial sites.[6] Its riverfronts displayed an uneven patchwork of industrial, warehousing, residential, and entertainment uses. Its underutilized parks, designed in an earlier era, reflected the idea of being refuges from the city, not places integrated into the city's residential life. Most important, vast areas of the city where housing stock was small, old, and costly to renovate were increasingly being abandoned and acres of brownfields were left fallow.

While many believe that the obsolescence and abandonment experienced by Philadelphia indicate a lack of economic competitiveness, bolstered by specific policy choices and macroeconomic forces, the pulls and pushes of the city's decentralization and economic change are more complex and controversial. And whatever the history and structural rationale, the results represent an environmental crisis for all Philadelphians, residents, workers, and consumers, that, unchecked, will serve as a barrier to ongoing economic and community development efforts. To the extent that a city is not being actively rebuilt through ongoing investment, it is actively deteriorating, creating material hazards and accruing the costs of deferred maintenance.

We do not have comprehensive policy language that fully connects the dots between community development and environmental recovery. While important elements exist, they are fragmentary. A larger developmental framework still needs to be articulated. Central to the framework is our current brownfield legislation. This legislation is a development resource. But while it recognizes the environmental predevelopment costs to market recovery, similar to public infrastructure costs as highways or water and sewer connections, it is transaction-based. It does not point to a longer-term change in a city's environmental system. Its grants, tax incentives, and liability reforms are helpful in removing costs and risks but its application is limited to specific sites whose selection criteria have no reference to a city's broader revitalization aims.

A hopeful trend that contributes to an integrated development and environmental perspective is the smart growth planning perspective. Although its advocates have concentrated more on land preservation in suburbia than urban environmental reclamation, it offers a systems approach within which brownfield projects can be understood: limit exurban growth; bolster first suburbs and then rebuild older core cities (Katz 2000). It assumes that various preservation and development levers in a regional system will have interactive effects on the other parts.

The environmental justice movement may be another lever to promote better integration between community development and environmentalism. Throughout the country the recognition of the racial and social class dimensions of environmental degradation is aiding advocacy campaigns calling for remedial funding and rethinking of overall development policy (Pellow and Brulle 2005). Activists are challenging the concentration of toxic infrastructure and the location of new public and private projects that have the potential for environmental hazards. They are energizing residents of towns like Chester, Pennsylvania, and Camden, New Jersey, recipients of uses nobody else will have, to demand political mediation of land uses that will make their neighborhoods healthier and more economically attractive.

Other areas in which to link community development and environmentalism are energy and public health. Concerns about energy efficiency and the cost of energy have been an important part of urban community development for many years. For example, disadvantaged communities often participate in government-funded urban weatherization programs. Also, in poor urban neighborhoods, understanding the place-based effects of utility shutoffs has become more topical recently as our ability to track and geocode information has improved. We are now able to get a better sense of the impact of large-scale utility shutoffs and their effect on residential abandonment (Hillier et al. 2003). With these tools we can intervene proactively to prevent housing losses. Finally, the emergence of green building design as a mainstream part of the building industry has animated community development. What was once a marginal interest is now an accepted consumer product with important ramifications for urban investment and development, especially given the long-term maintenance costs of older buildings. Likewise, innovations in affordable housing design are also centering on energy issues.

A final example is in the public health arena. Some cities' public health departments and universities are identifying the relationship between environmental degradation and the incidence of disease (including childhood cancer) and neurological impairment.[7] While public health research remains dramatically underfunded, it is a source to be rallied for the cause of community development.

These disparate and thin strands of legislation, research, planning, technological innovation, and political advocacy are yet to be integrated with community and economic development practice. Nor have they led the environmental movement in the United States to speak for a new wave of urban reform. Although the tide is changing, the rebuilding of old cities is not yet viewed—fully enough—as an environmental project.

The absence of an environmental perspective in urban development runs counter to earlier urban-based social movements. In the progressive era, housing, planning, and slum eradication reformers used the language of public health in advocating their causes. They did have an environmental mooring linking infectious diseases and poverty to community development issues of the day: substandard infrastructure and the place-based effects of the unhealthy "slum."[8] While naive in methodology and deterministic in approach, these reformers understood the unity of human behavior, economic livelihoods, and environmental (social and biological) circumstances. Today, we need to return, in a more sophisticated way, to reestablish these linkages.

Real Estate Development, Environmental Risks, and the Smart Subsidy

The private sector is key to linking community development and environmentalism. While many businesses benefit from not having to account for the cost of environmental distress, there is nothing inherent to maximizing returns that would necessarily lead anyone to be for or against a particular environmental perspective. The shorter the time horizon of investor returns and the more disconnected investors are from the products into which they invest, the more this kind of neutrality is institutionalized. Investors worry about risk, return, and liquidity and (if they think about it at all) assume that consumer demand for environmental quality will drive the appearance of businesses and products into which they can invest and make returns. Investors use environmental products as a market niche, like other business markets.

For real estate developers in cities and suburbs, interest in an environmental perspective is contextual and transactional. In general, they view quality environmental amenities as creating market value and opportunity. They assess the circumstances in which the costs of environmental amenities do not matter. They also have strong beliefs about which environmental issues are a barrier to development and financial returns.[9]

Certain ingredients are necessary for real estate success: cost and regulatory predictability, and market and price knowledge. These factors enable investors to calculate the costs of doing business, including those associated with production, distribution, and regulations associated with particular products, circumstances, and jurisdictions. Similarly, investors need the best possible market knowledge to make judgments about their ability to reach the market given competition and demand. Market knowledge is critical to the pricing model, which ultimately drives profitability. The better the knowledge of these issues, the better the capacity to make decisions, manage risk, raise capital, and implement projects.

The difficulties of calculating risk in an uncertain market is precisely why environmental factors are so important to the revitalization of distressed real estate markets in older industrial cities. Extensive environmental damage represents exceptional costs (development barriers) and high-quality environmental amenities represent the potential for a market premium (development entry). While real estate developers in parts of a city like Philadelphia are confronted with more than 150 years of industrial history, they are also faced with the opportunities of a vast park system, miles of riverfront, and the potential for acres of developable land from torn-down housing that can be reincorporated into new urban design possibilities.

For the Philadelphia real estate developer, environmental factors add uncertainty to development costs and financial value. These are direct and indirect costs. They involve the price of the remediation of damaged land and physical plant and the potential devaluation of a product due to its proximity to damaged land or buildings that may not be slated for near-term development. Environmentally damaged land costs are but one part of a package of uncertainties related to investing in older industrial cities, including the cost of rehabilitating obsolete buildings, labor and regulatory expenses, and the need to reorient street grids.

Not surprisingly, during the past 40 years the explosion of new housing, retail, and office construction in the United States has largely been a suburban—green fields—phenomenon. Calculations of costs and market demand and the "footprint" for living, working, and shopping spaces in suburban commodity formats are relatively uniform and certain. Recently, investors have entered urban markets. These investors tend to be smaller-scale niche developers who have particular market knowledge and civic capacity. But they have less access to patient capital than large-scale developers.

The right environmental amenities can create a sufficiently strong development asset or market sign to catalyze all types of investors. As seen in even the most distressed cities, park and river reclamation is certainly important and commonly tried as a means to redefine an urban future (see Economics Research Assistants 2005). The potential of parks and rivers to create real estate value varies depending on how former uses are addressed, the capacity to provide quality public management, the costs of environmental reclamation, the development value of proximate areas, and the spatial design and location of the existing built environment.

Beyond rivers and parks, developers and investors are interested in other environmental features. Landscaped street ways, well-kept lots, and public gardens represent a longer-term guarantee of value from the public and civic realm. The instinctive reaction of any investor and developer who approaches a historically declining distressed market is to identify areas of relative strength that still provide an opportunity for market entry and the creation of new products. Well-managed natural amenities on a street, in a park, along a river, as an entryway to a community, or along a retail strip provide evidence of market viability. While these features are only one of many other data points, they count. They show not only that somebody is investing, but that somebody has the civic capacity to manage public and private behavior and accountability.

This last point is analogous to the "broken window" syndrome, used to explain modern policing policy (see Wilson and Kelling 1982). Walk down a street of broken windows, abandoned cars, trash, and boarded up homes and you have one impression of where the market is going. Moreover, you feel free to contribute to the downward spiral of the area; if you want to commit a crime, the area seems unprotected. Now consider a street with well-maintained homes, with belongings left on porches, plantings along the pavements, and no trash in sight, and you draw a different conclusion.

While visual markers affect investment conclusions, the developer calculus regarding neighborhoods also depends on the scale of a potential development. In a large site, such as a Hope VI project, the development may create enough of its own quality to lessen the influence of nearby areas.[10] While large-scale development creates protected assets, in most instances sizable projects are difficult to execute because of their complexity and, if gated, because they are undesirable. Moreover, most real estate development occurs in and around an existing built environment where there is inevitably a strong mutual exchange of value from one place to the next, thus making the surrounding visual and larger environmental conditions critically important.

In conjunction with political, economic, and civic issues, the environmental dimension to rebuilding a distressed real estate marker is clear. You have to remediate environmental barriers and accentuate environmental amenities and market signals. Distressed (and therefore uncertain) markets require public subsidy at the early stage of development to mitigate costs from clean up, remediation, and other development, and the costs of accentuating environmental maintenance and management in areas surrounding new development sites. Given limited resources and the overwhelming problem of distressed markets, the question is how to best allocate subsidy most effectively. In the vocabulary of development finance, how do you make subsidy *smart*?

The allocation of public, private, or civic subsidy to environmental remediation and amenity development is smart if it follows four rules: (1) the application of the subsidy does not mask or facilitate operating inefficiencies by the developer or investor; (2) the subsidy is limited (not open ended), diminished, or eliminated in either a defined time period or in conjunction with project execution; (3) the subsidy will have multiplier effects, thus justifying the choice of one location over another; and (4) the subsidy will not function as a surrogate for what any profit-maximizing investor or developer would efficiently achieve.

A smart subsidy is efficient, transparent, productive, and necessary. Its application will yield the greatest market and civic leverage. While smart subsidies are difficult to manage in political terms, they are increasingly important to cities such as Philadelphia; these cities have significant infrastructure costs but limited financial resources requiring careful assessment of the best use of public investment in order to maximize market activity.

While it may be easier to calculate market leverage, civic return is equally important; indeed, one feeds off the other. While market leverage has to do with a project's future economic benefits from a subsidy, civic return assesses how a subsidy reinforces existing civic qualities, which, in the long term, assist in the informal management of community assets, resulting in ongoing consumer demand. This latter assessment requires nuance; even in the most distressed communities, some choices make more sense than others as they relate to the projection of civic and market multiplier effects.

In sum, the recovery of urban land and environmental quality requires a blended approach: public subsidy, market investment, and civic organization. The allocation of subsidy must occur with the discipline and clarity of purpose that emphasizes long-term market productivity, reinforces the self-organizing qualities of the civic infrastructure, and sees the funding as diminishing over time. While the need and use of public infrastructure investment always exists, as the market accrues value investors and developers can incur more of that cost.

A TRF Case Study in Lower North Philadelphia

To see how these issues play out in a concrete case, I will turn to Brewerytown, a recently redeveloped section of Philadelphia in lower North Philadelphia. Brewerytown is a 45-acre area of severely distressed property where, in the past seven years, The Reinvestment Fund has invested more than $20 million in debt, equity financing, and federal New Market Tax Credits.

In making its investment in distressed markets, TRF sought to use its funds to overcome four types of barriers to private investment: the uncertainty of market demand; the absence of liquidity for certain financial products; the existence of extra-market costs that cannot be internalized by developers and businesses; and difficulties reconciling the interests of competing civic and political constituencies.

TRF aims to establish market acceptance, knowing that such an effort sometimes involves establishing the viability and standards for a new borrower type (for example, charter schools), having patience (for example, the redevelopment of large section of East Camden during the 1990s),[11] or allocating a high-risk product (land acquisition) to borrowers with limited balance sheet capacity. In all cases, it is absorbing early entry risk and providing a smart subsidy, as defined earlier.

Overcoming barriers as an early entrant into a market represents a real cost to the core business of lending and investing and explains why many investors are absent from hard-to-penetrate urban contexts. Simply stated, if the value proposition—the cost of the transaction versus the economic return, given the risk profile—does not work, mainstream investors and developers stay away. They leave the market to niche investors and developers who, by mission, market knowledge, cost of capital, or limitations in options, are willing to invest. Once the barriers are lowered and it appears that the market is moving, a flow of consumer and institutional development capital follows.

When TRF financing is successful in early entry circumstances, its capital is followed by other lenders, who often function as a source of liquidity for TRF. In other instances the market simply takes off on its own and TRF either can leave that market or play a new role in it as provider of underwriting knowledge, planner, purchaser of bank participations, or subordinate lender. In all cases, success should lead to increased financing predictability and the declining need for subsidy in various forms, including infrastructure, price, and information subsidy.

In real estate, TRF's highest-impact early entry role is as a provider of predevelopment financing for land acquisition and development planning or as subordinated debt in projects that have narrow operating margins or high loan-to-value ratios. Land-acquisition and predevelopment financing has a significant environmental impact when it involves holding land with environmental liabilities, paying for environmental studies and remediation, and managing risk prior to the period when project feasibility is certain. The TRF investment is particularly effective in instances where land values are uncertain due to general market volatility or a lack of comparable projects.

The simplest way to mitigate early entry risk in these markets is to invest in knowledgeable entrepreneurs and developers who have a demonstrated track record in managing cost and risk in that market and have the financial capacity to share risk. The absence of these entrepreneurs increases the risk for an investor such as TRF and curtails the flow of high-quality customer (consumer demand) information.

The capacity to analyze market and civic information is key. For these reasons, and to project longer-term development opportunities in distressed communities, TRF invests in high-quality data analysis that details the strengths, weaknesses, and inflection points in a real estate market. This too represents an early-stage investment (subsidy) that could be done by public entities, but is rarely done in such a way as to facilitate market recovery analysis.

TRF's approach to understanding the potential of distressed urban real estate markets is to collect and analyze urban and regionwide data to gain a sense of the patterns of the city's overall real estate market while zeroing in on smaller areas to provide more intensive investment planning informed by the macrolevel data. Understanding both the macro and micro pictures simultaneously is an important way to identify places of investment opportunity and the best use of subsidy.

At the macro level, TRF collects an array of housing market data (housing values, vacancy rates, public housing, mixture of commercial and residential units, homeownership and rental levels and location, and permit data), geocodes the information at the census block group level, and uses a statistical cluster analysis to see which places share like characteristics and how various market types interact. This method provides a complex ecology of a city that informs the micro analysis. It reveals the location of areas of strength and helps explain the overall nature of market strength or weakness at a single point in time. While the method employs time-series data (especially for housing values), there is nothing about a cluster analysis of this kind that in and of itself is predictive. But like a financial balance sheet, it is a suggestive accounting of current conditions that can be used to construct future development scenarios.

While an analyst can identify as many market clusters as he wants, determining what number is useful is difficult. The task of choosing and verification is as much art as science and as much ethnography as statistics. The best verification method requires the firsthand knowledge that comes from driving the streets, visually checking statistical trends, speaking with residents, realtors, investors, and public officials, and thus moving back and forth from sidewalk to computer screen to challenge the reliability of data and everyday perceptions.

Based on the statistical analysis and firsthand qualitative research in Philadelphia, in 2000 TRF identified six clusters (as noted in Plate 9). They ranged from the highest-end regional choice clusters to the lowest-value reclamation markets. (At that time, the lowest-end reclamation markets in Philadelphia had residential vacancy levels of about 22 percent.) Each of the six market types needed public investments ranging from relatively minor interventions of marketing, code enforcement, and preservation assistance to major land assembly activities and environmental remediation. The TRF typology provided a gross way in which to construct public allocation parameters and priorities. In fact, the Philadelphia city government used this information to guide its Neighborhood Transformation Initiative (see Bonham and Smith, this volume).

In pursuing its full planning methodology, TRF undertook three additional steps, moving from the macro to the community planning and project investment level.

First, TRF placed additional layers, containing a full array of social, economic, and environmental data, over the cluster maps. This enabled zeroing into any community for the purposes of planning and analysis, pulling up block-level indicators that included population, income, crime, and environmental information. Second, after identifying points of interest, it engaged in rigorous "on the ground" discussions with local civic groups and other constituencies in the selected area. Third, it used the data and discussions to identify potential projects for investment and to assess the requisite public, civic, and private actions that must occur to realize project success.

As a social investor, TRF cares deeply about the reclamation of obsolete land and buildings and the repositioning of natural assets. Through its analysis of Philadelphia, TRF concluded that some of the strongest and weakest markets come together along parks and riverfronts. The presence of a park or river does not inherently lead to a strong community; a variety of other factors over and above the existence of the natural asset are necessary. However, under the right conditions, natural assets are critical.

Above all, with the TRF analysis identifying opportunities that were at the right intersection of market strength and unrealized development potential, it observed that in distressed markets, points of potential market strength are often associated with five situations. They are the presence of (1) natural assets; (2) major institutional or employment hubs; (3) transportation hubs; (4) clusters of strong residential and commercial activity; and (5) proximity to areas of empirically significant reinvestment. Unrealized development potential exists when there is the ability to leverage, connect, or assert any of those points of strength into the more distressed market through the right combination of civic, public, and private economic activities.

In addition to identifying sites for investment projects, the TRF market typology assists in establishing the sequence and structure of public and private investment in and around areas of strength where the right or wrong actions could tip the market in one direction or the other. Again, this evaluation cannot be based only on the aggregate mapping of urban market data. The typological analysis provides a bird's-eye view that must be verified and concretized through smaller area planning and analysis.

As a case in point, let's examine Brewerytown, circled in Plate 9. Its western edge was comprised of old industrial warehouses and abandoned factory buildings within walking distance of Fairmount Park, one of the nation's largest and most beautiful urban parks (8,500 acres). In its southern portion, market demand and activity was strong and growing as a natural extension of the downtown real estate market, indicated in blue in Plate 10. These sections bordered the weakest markets in the city. To the west and north were pockets of stable low- and moderate-income (largely African American) row home blocks interspersed with streets that had abandonment rates of 50 percent or more.

The western section of Brewerytown with its abandoned industrial site was pivotal. Either it could block development from the south, resulting in the depression of working class housing values to the east and north; or it could catalyze market change and have broad ecological significance for the park and adjacent neighborhoods. The problem in Brewerytown was how to connect the park and the adjacent neighborhoods simultaneously. From its discussions with community groups and others in the area, TRF uncovered nascent developer interest in the area. But it also realized that this interest would vanish in the absence of a means to manage the costs of land assembly, environmental remediation, and the complex politics of place emanating from park commissions, civic groups, labor unions, and many other constituencies.

TRF concluded that the western section of Brewerytown could be an important demonstration site for its inner city real estate investment strategy. As smart subsidy, it would take advantage of the adjacent stronger markets, remove industrial blight that contained significant contaminants, and establish a precedent for park-related development that had eluded that part of the city for decades. Moreover, despite the significant levels of abandonment, the north and east had a significant number of strong blocks where the civic quality of the community showed great development potential.

Starting in 2000, TRF worked with a half-dozen developers and community groups—for profit and nonprofit—to move development forward in what, at times, has been a controversial process. The controversies of development are typical in situations where low- and moderate-income residents welcome its positive effects (increased housing equity, better services and retail) but are also understandably nervous about its potential negative consequences (increased property taxes and a scarcity of affordable rental units).

To help mediate these issues and support an equitable approach to development in the area, TRF employed a six-pronged, multidimensional approach. First, it added funds to public allowances for early-stage demolition costs and the remediation of environmentally contaminated land. (In the absence of this subsidy, no private investment would have occurred because real estate values were particularly uncertain.) Second, it provided early, high-risk land financing for two developers prior to the demonstrated viability of projects. (This investment resulted in the mixed-income development of more than 400 housing units, with several hundred additional units now planned.) Third, it provided planning assistance to local nonprofit groups for the preservation of affordable homeownership and rental units. (These civic groups wanted to get ahead of the market and identify ways to preserve longer-term affordability.) Fourth, it added support for public subsidy to demolish dangerous properties and landscape vacant lots until the point at which development opportunities emerge. (This was key to presenting a sense of order and organization and also to demonstrating the civic and political will to catalyze change.) Fifth, it secured philanthropic assistance—grants from the William Penn Foundation—to provide façade treatments for existing housing units contiguous to the construction of new housing units. (These preservation investments had the effect of both increasing the value and marketability of new developments and making it clear to existing homeowners that existing property owners had a stake in change.) Sixth, it supported the development of a new supermarket and other commercial developments on vacant land in the area.

These initial TRF investments leveraged an additional $50 million in other private capital and millions in public subsidies and tax credits, giving new momentum to the area. More than $100 million in other projects are in the planning stage. Among the future projects are park-related infrastructure investments by public sources, additional housing units, an upgraded recreation center, a plan for an Audubon nature site, higher-quality lighting and fixtures, and additional development of vacant land along the park edge. To take advantage of the growing residential and park connections, more significant infrastructure investments will have to be made. As the residential population grows and organizes its civic power, these investments will likely follow (see Plate 11).

The efficient use of smart subsidy spurred the initial success of the area's redevelopment. TRF and other investors have followed the subsidy with market-disciplined financing that is resulting in the reclamation of dozens of acres of industrial wasteland and is beginning a new process of park-neighborhood integration. This approach recognized that the public sector, private sector, and civic interests all have important roles to play in redevelopment. It also understood that market change in a complex urban setting relies as much on civic consent as on the mitigation of financial risk. But it also recognized that early-stage costs of redevelopment would have to be covered either by the public or by a socially motivated financing entity such as TRF. Finally, a key element in Brewerytown and adjacent developments is an active program to remediate brownfields, build green lots, refurbish parks, and pay attention to the fact that both existing and new residents care about living in high-quality environmentally sound surroundings.

Between Decline and Renewal

Twenty-first-century cities, especially older industrial cities, are at a volatile intersection of *decline and renewal*. Their transformation is not only a matter of the conversion of their employment bases but also of marshalling investments based on quality data-based analysis to retrofit their industrial ecologies. These investments have three purposes: (1) remediate environmentally hazardous sites resulting from decades of industrial and commercial use; (2) reclaim and reposition natural assets (particularly river and lake fronts), converting them from obsolete industrial uses to residential, commercial, and recreational functions; and (3) reconnect areas of market strength and decline.

The Brewerytown case study exemplifies how a community development financial institution can information and a market orientation to negotiate changes in the marketplace. It represents one of many examples of how to knit an environmental perspective into community and economic development and a development perspective into environmentalism, critical to achieving an integrated practice that will result in sustainably redeveloped cities.

References

Birch, Eugenie L. 2007. "Hopeful Signs: U.S. Urban Revitalization in the Twenty-First Century." In *Land Polices and Their Outcomes*, ed. Gregory K. Ingram and Yu-Hung. Cambridge, Mass.: Lincoln Institute of Land Policy.

Development Finance Network. 2004. *Capital Plus*. Chicago: Shorebank Corporation.

Economics Research Assistants (ERA). 2005. *Real Estate Impact Review of Parks and Recreation*. Report submitted to Illinois Association of Park Districts. Chicago: ERA.

Hillier, Amy E., Dennis P. Culhane, Tony E. Smith, and C. Dana Tomlin. 2003. "Predicting Housing Abandonment with the Philadelphia Neighborhood Information System." *Journal of Urban Affairs* 25, 1: 91–106.

Katz, Bruce, ed. 2000. *Reflections on Regionalism*. Washington, D.C.: Brookings Institution Press.

Katz, Michael B., and Mark J. Stern. 2006. *One Nation Divisible: What America Was and What It Is Becoming*. New York: Russell Sage Foundation.

Manhattan Institute. 1998. *The Entrepreneurial City*. New York: Manhattan Institute.

McGovern, Stephen J. 2006. "Philadelphia's Neighborhood Transformation Initiative: A Case Study of Mayoral Leadership, Bold Planning, and Conflict." *Housing Policy Debate* 17, 3.

Norquist, John. 1998. *The Wealth of Cities: Revitalizing the Centers of American Life*. Reading, Mass.: Addison Wesley.

Pellow, David Naguib, and Robert J. Brulle, eds. 2005. *Power, Justice and the Environment: A Critical Appraisal of the Environmental Justice Movement*. Cambridge, Mass.: MIT Press.

Popkin, Susan, Bruce Katz, Mary K. Cunningham, Karen D. Brown, Jeremy Gustafson, and Margery Austin Turner. 2004. *A Decade of Hope VI: Research Findings and Policy Challenges*. Washington, D.C.: Urban Institute. www.urban.org/url .cfm?ID = 411002.

Rusk, David. 1993. *Cities Without Suburbs*. Washington, D.C.: Woodrow Wilson Press.

———. 1999. *Inside Game, Outside Game: Winning Strategies for Saving Urban America*. Washington, D.C.: Brookings Institution Press.

Smith, Marvin M., and Christy Chung Hevener. 2005. *The Impact of Housing Rehabilitation on Local Neighborhoods: The Case of St. Joseph's Carpenter Society*. Philadelphia: Federal Reserve Bank.

Wilson, James Q., and George L. Kelling. 1982. "Broken Windows: The Police and Neighborhood Safety." *Atlantic* 249, 3: 29–38.

Winkelstein, Warren, Jr. 2000. "Interface of Epidemiology and History." *Epidemiologic Reviews* 22, 1.

Chapter 14
Growing Edible Cities

DOMENIC VITIELLO

Many ecologists argue that industrialized agriculture's dependence on fossil fuels is unsustainable. Rising energy costs and expected declines in oil production are not the only causes: oil- and gas-based fertilizers and pesticides have also depleted the world's soil fertility. The solution, they claim, lies in localizing food production at the regional scale and shifting to organic farming methods that revive soils and conserve water.[1] Growing greener cities thus requires growing more of what we eat locally and regionally. Decisions and actions at the level of individual households and firms will help transform markets for food. Yet collective initiatives are arguably even more significant, as they will enable the effective management of the broader restructuring of food systems. Herein lies a vital role for community and regional planners, who must evolve new forms of urbanism to sustain metropolitan societies in the third millennium.

Planning for sustainable food supply takes different forms—and has different implications—in different parts of metropolitan America. Developing sustainable food-sheds means something different in downtown, ghetto, and suburban environments, and in high-wealth versus low-wealth communities. As in all facets of urbanism, tackling the problems and opportunities of sustainable food supply in cities and regions requires a diversified set of planning strategies that are applied appropriately in context.

This chapter surveys debates about regional food systems, especially urban farming and its relationship to community and economic development. It uses the greater Philadelphia area's emerging urban agriculture sector as a case study exploring the challenges, opportunities, and emerging best practices for U.S. cities and regions. As featured in the multimedia project *Edens Lost & Found*, the city is home to groundbreaking farms on sites from brownfields to greenfields. More ephemeral experiments in inner city agriculture and aquaculture offer an opportunity to explore ambitious ideas and market failures that can promote better understanding of how to make urban farming viable. In addition to these producers, Philadelphia institutions are building a robust regional infrastructure of distribution, processing, and marketing of food grown in the greater Delaware Valley region. Finally, a variety of public health, education, community gardening, open space preservation, and stormwater management initiatives in the city and region raise important questions about the role of urban farming in connecting environmental planning and community and economic development in an era of climate change and shifting energy use.

Energy, Climate Change, and Food Systems

Urban agriculture constitutes a local response to global problems. The Green Revolution of industrialized agriculture increased worldwide food production threefold between 1950 and 1990 while expanding the area of farmland just 10 percent. Cheap oil has meant cheap food for much of the world. But this increased productivity has come at a price. It resulted in a cycle of dependence on oil- and natural gas-based pesticides, herbicides, fertilizers, and irrigation systems, which, while making soils more productive in the short term, depleted soils for the long term. Since the early 1990s, crop yields have stopped rising. In the United States today, it takes roughly 10 calories of hydrocarbon energy to produce 1 calorie of food consumed at the table (Pfeiffer 2006; Brown 2006).

The global industrial food system directly accounts for about 21 percent of worldwide fossil fuel consumption, and indirectly for more than that. In the United States 21 percent of all energy used in the food system goes to agricultural production, 14 percent supports bulk transportation, 23 percent for processing and packaging, 11 percent of energy is in retailing and restaurants, and 32 percent in home refrigeration and preparation. This latter figure underscores the importance of lower-energy appliances.

The energy-intensive nature of the U.S. food system results largely from its dispersed geography. The average ingredient in a meal in the United States is grown over 1,500 miles away. America's dependence on foreign produce, from Chilean cherries to New Zealand strawberries, only perpetuates its dependence on foreign energy sources (Brown 2006; Pfeiffer 2006). Meanwhile, residential and commercial development has reduced the supply of farmland on the fringe of North America's metropolitan areas. Moreover, the increasing distance between homes and supermarkets results in increased driving.

Local organic food production has a role to play in diminishing energy consumption in virtually all parts of the food system. It reduces the use of fossil fuel-based pesticides and fertilizers, limits the need for long-distance transportation, and typically requires a low level of processing, packaging, and refrigeration. Indeed, many Americans have embraced these and other benefits of local, organic food in recent years. The number of farmers' markets in the United States expanded from 1,755 in 1993 to 3,100 in 2002, yet they still only accounted for 0.3 percent of food sales, leaving room for growth (Murray 2005; Quinn 2006).

Urban Farming and Community Development

At the local level, urban agriculture has a role in community development. Minority urban households suffer from disproportionately high levels of child obesity and poor nutrition—18 percent of Latino households and 22 percent of non-Hispanic black households in the United States are unable to purchase sufficient food (Chen 2006). As an economic development and environmental justice strategy, local organic farming has the capacity to address issues of public health, poverty, and food security.

City planners and everyday train riders regularly compare the ghettos of Detroit, Baltimore, East St. Louis, and Philadelphia to third world slums. And urban agriculture is one area in which urbanists in North America and Europe's low-wealth communities can profitably learn from the developing world. Inner city farming is already employed as a large-scale community development strategy in Kinshasa, Harare, and Havana.[2]

Cuba provides some lessons. With the loss of Soviet economic support in 1991, the island's oil imports collapsed. The country's GDP fell by more than one-third, while its highly industrialized agricultural sector was decimated by the lack of fuel for farm machinery and factories making fertilizers and pesticides. The nation survived by shifting to a system of decentralized permaculture, a system developed by Australians in the 1970s that applies organic growing methods to the particular ecology of specific regions according to an ethic of social and environmental sustainability.[3] Cubans turned rooftops, patios, and virtually all open land in and around cities into labor-intensive (not capital- or energy-intensive) organic gardens and farms. In Havana, residents grow more than half their vegetables inside the city limits. Farmers' markets in every neighborhood constitute a decentralized system of distribution and sales. Cubans learned to breed worms and oxen, to erect drip irrigation systems that conserve water, and to make organic pesticides and fertilizers that they now export to other parts of Latin America. In the process, they restored soils that had been depleted by earlier industrialized farming, and they brought yields back to pre-1991 levels.[4]

While Cuba's experiences provide limited lessons for industrialized *nations*, they have much to offer to local low-wealth *communities* and community development institutions. In the United States, some communities have already adopted these techniques. In South Central Los Angeles, for example, people's poverty impels them to seek improved access to nutritious food. They have adapted unused land into community gardens, yet lack of site ownership by gardeners often makes these temporary land uses, as highlighted by the June 2006 eviction of the gardeners (and Darryl Hannah) from South Central Farm. Among middle-class communities, Ithaca, New York, Davis, California, and Vancouver, British Columbia, for example, have made lifestyle choices to support local organic agriculture. Communitarian organizations such as the Community Solution in Yellow Springs, Ohio, and local groups affiliated with the Post-Carbon Institute's international Re-Localization Network and the Global Ecovillage Network have created largely self-sustaining intentional communities.[5] Although these groups preach inclusion and widespread adaptation of their methods, to date they represent the lifestyle choice of relatively few individuals. More important, from the perspective of planners, developers, and service providers in low-wealth communities, their experiments in living are typically affordable only to middle-class and affluent Americans.

For low-wealth communities, scholars and advocates argue that urban agriculture represents an important form of asset-based development, especially in inner cities with ample supplies of vacant land. Cornell agricultural sociologist Thomas Lyson calls such collectivized efforts "civic agriculture."[6] Residents, often immigrants, leverage their knowledge of their environment, as well as years of gardening, farming, and craft traditions from their places of origin, into full-scale farming (which is distinguished from gardening by its greater scale and more formal relationships between producers and consumers). In addition to private and third sector initiatives, the public sector can play important roles through strategies such as land banking, economic development support programs, and tax policy and fiscal incentives that apply environmental economics to local markets for food (Pothukuchi and Kaufman 1999).

Like other urban greening initiatives, urban farming can bring people together to achieve a variety of planning and community building goals.[7] For example, urban farms can improve storm water and waste management as well as local air quality.[8] Where they increase food security, place the means of production in local hands, and restore the ecology of polluted neighborhoods, city farms can advance social, economic, and environmental justice. In this sense, urban agriculture may be viewed as a movement. In its most radical forms, it promotes "guerilla gardening" in which farmers squat on previously unproductive land. In a more mainstream vein, urban farming has received support from the Slow Food movement, which has helped spread the popularity of organics and inspired a backlash against industrial agriculture and highly processed foods.[9]

Demand for locally grown organic food has indeed expanded rapidly in recent years, as the *Wall Street Journal* and Wal-Mart have recognized (see, e.g., Gray 2006). As an economic development strategy, small-scale organic urban farming holds some promise, though also significant limits. It involves relatively low start-up and overhead costs, and is not land- or capital-intensive. Though labor-intensive, in most cases it does not create a large number of jobs per farm, and, in most regions, many of the jobs are seasonal. That said, urban agriculture can help communities attain modest workforce development goals, providing low- and semi-skilled training and work. Moreover, it offers summer jobs for young people that are an important source of individual and household income in low-wealth communities. Finally, with careful business planning, opportunities exist for the development of value-added processing that serves specific niche markets, in addition to the opportunities in production, sales, and restaurant and catering enterprises that specialize in local organic food (Lazarus 2000; Ferguson 2000; Silva 1999).

Localized food systems necessarily include more than the farms, gardens, and greenhouses where growing takes place. Community tool sheds, seed harvesting, and agricultural education programs help sustain production and the labor force. The institutional infrastructure of distribution and marketing includes farm stands and farmers markets as well as community-supported agriculture (CSA) programs and other sorts of buying clubs that connect producers to consumers. In low-wealth communities, food cupboards play important roles in fighting hunger, though mostly on a short-term basis.[10]

What can make these systems sustainable? Beyond effective business planning that makes farms, CSAs, and markets financially viable year-to-year, localizing a city or community's food supply requires fostering production and distribution year-round. Canning and drying local food can meet some of this need. In temperate climate zones, indoor cultivation and other measures to extend the growing season can expand production temporally. Many urban farmers have adopted methods of permaculture. Architects Katrin Bohn and André Viljoen have applied this concept to the metropolitan scale, at least in theory, advocating the design of "continuous productive urban landscapes." Their designs integrate year-round food production into urban spaces, including residential yards and rooftop greenhouses, public parks and sidewalks, the broad roofs of big box stores, and land that buffers infrastructure, such as the vast swaths of vacant land that line the railroads through Philadelphia and other formerly industrial cities.[11]

How might U.S. cities develop such landscapes and self-sustaining food systems? This is clearly a more feasible task in warmer and wetter regions, while in other places farmers must address issues of temperature, water supply, and sunlight. Philadelphia offers an example of a temperate region at the border of an intercoastal plain and a piedmont zone. Questions of adaptation to climate may not be transferable to Dallas, Los Angeles, or Boise. Yet in terms of land use, growing techniques, distribution, and marketing, the Philadelphia region's evolving local food system fairly represents the current initiatives, limits, and potential of urban agriculture in U.S. cities more broadly.

Farmadelphia

The Philadelphia region appears to be in a relatively advantageous position with regard to food supply. SustainLane ranks it third among U.S. cities with the best local food and agricultural capacity, after Boston and Minneapolis, primarily since it "draws upon a healthy network of in-state farmers."[12] Philadelphia is home to recent success stories in urban agriculture, but also to cases of failure that likewise hold important lessons.

Philadelphia's local food system consists of two basic parts. The first part includes producers who operate a range of farms in different parts of the region, on inner city brownfield sites, greenfields within and outside the city, and larger farms in the hinterland of Lancaster, Berks, and Bucks counties in Pennsylvania, as well as southern New Jersey and the Delmarva Peninsula. The second part is a set of organizations that foster distribution, marketing, and some processing of food grown in the city and region. This institutional infrastructure effectively ties together the local—or, more accurately, regional—food system.

Philadelphia's largest institution explicitly focused on food security is the Food Trust, founded in 1992 as a nutrition education program for inner city children. That year, it opened its first farmers market at Tasker Homes, a public housing project located amid the oil refineries and junkyards of southwest Philadelphia. In a region of approximately 5 million residents, the Trust estimates that some 475,000 people suffer from hunger and malnutrition, including more than 200,000 children. Philadelphia is the poorest large city in the nation, with nearly one-quarter of all residents living in poverty. Today, the Trust runs a series of school-based programs that educate students about personal and community health and offers healthy, locally grown snacks to kindergarteners. It has worked with the School District of Philadelphia to raise the nutritional value of food available in cafeterias and vending machines. The Trust's neighborhood-based campaigns support the development of supermarkets in underserved communities and improve snack food choices at corner stores for adolescents. Finally, it operates 19 farmers markets in affluent and low-wealth city and suburban neighborhoods, including two that are open year-round. Sales for these markets have doubled from $500,000 in 2002 to $1 million in 2006.[13]

Another 11 farmers' markets in the city and suburbs are run by Farm to City (www.farmtocity.org), which touts these markets as "providing a civilized and democratic gathering place" whose community-building functions are as important as their health and environmental impacts. Farm to City manages CSAs and buying clubs, including the Winter Harvest program that extends the traditional season of CSAs in temperate regions. It fosters the growth of these local food networks through its website and administrative assistance for CSAs and buying clubs starting up in the Greater Philadelphia region. Farm to City casts this as an effort through which expanding urban markets help preserve family farms in the rural hinterland. Its farmers' market sales more than tripled from $200,000 in 2001 to $625,000 in 2005, while its Winter Harvest program has grown 800 percent; it will open four new markets in 2007 (Karlen 2007).

The third institution connecting farms in southeastern Pennsylvania and New Jersey with the metropolitan market is the Fair Food project of the White Dog Cafe Foundation. Fair Food's restaurant project links family farmers to chefs, caterers, and grocers. It also publishes a *Wholesale Guide to Local Farm Products* and provides consulting services that build business relationships between farmers and buyers. Its PIG (Pigs in Grass) Alliance operates a statewide network of farms and organizations supporting humane pork production. It uses its farm stand in downtown Philadelphia's historic Reading Terminal Market to promote artisanal foods from ethical producers, such as raw milk cheeses, organic fruits, and free-range meats. Like the Food Trust school programs, the Fair Food Farm-to-Institution project is working to help local food producers break into the cafeterias of hospitals, universities, and corporate office parks.[14]

The Food Trust, Farm to City, and Fair Food have joined in a regional consumer campaign, "Buy Fresh, Buy Local," which mirrors similar efforts across the country. Their Local Food Guide lists more than 70 farmers' markets, grocery stores, farm stands, restaurants, caterers, and CSAs where the region's residents can access locally grown food. Beyond consumer education, Farm to City, Fair Food, three cooperative grocery stores, and four other partners are developing the Common Market, a local food distribution center. With its 30,000-square-foot warehouse in North Philadelphia, this partnership aims to attract caterers, buying clubs, and a canning operation that will further expand and establish the markets and institutional infrastructure of local food supply. The directors of Farm to City and Fair Food view this project as a key step in building the region's capacity to expand local food supply (Pierson and Karlen 2006; Bolesta 2006).

Two of the partners in the Common Market are also food producers. Weavers Way Co-op, a community-owned market, has operated its own farm since 2000. It returned a portion of the Awbury Arboretum in the Germantown and Mount Airy neighborhoods of northwest Philadelphia to something resembling the historic land arrangements of nineteenth-century farms and country estates. The store's produce manager designs crop plans to complement its purchases from other producers in the region and elsewhere. Co-op members supply the bulk of the labor by performing required yearly work hours. Students from a local public elementary school, an environmental education charter school, and the Pennsylvania School for the Deaf help with planting, weeding, harvesting, and growing seedlings in the spring.[15]

The Urban Nutrition Initiative (UNI) of the University of Pennsylvania Center for Community Partnerships, another Common Market partner, is building on the work of the Food Trust with more intensive public school programs in West Philadelphia. At University City High School, it has integrated food and nutrition lessons into social studies, language arts, and math and science classes. It offers cooking classes during lunch period. After school and during the summer, it runs job training programs in urban agriculture through which students learn to manage schoolyard gardens, farm stands, and a mobile produce market operated out of UNI's delivery truck.[16]

On a much larger scale, the city is the improbable home to the largest agricultural secondary school in America, Saul Agricultural High School. Saul has 130 acres in northwest Philadelphia used for cattle, horse, and sheep pastures. However, its curriculum concentrates on industrial farming methods, limiting the school and its graduates' contributions to the region's sustainable agriculture sector. Another public school, Abraham Lincoln High School in Northeast Philadelphia, runs a Horticulture Academy preparing students for careers in landscaping, arboriculture, greenhouse production, and retail flower sales.[17] Like other urban districts, Philadelphia's public schools confront regular crises of funding and dropouts, but their existing programs offer the capability to educate future generations of urban farmers.

Perhaps the greatest latent capacity for urban farming in the region lies in the over 500 community gardens in the city, most of which are supported by the Pennsylvania Horticultural Society's Philadelphia Green Program. As noted earlier, although community gardens are not farms, they feed many people on a seasonal basis and are vital parts of the urban food system. Through its Garden Tenders program and other workshops, Philadelphia Green constitutes the most pervasive horticultural education program in the region. Its ability to rally communities to gardening and greening, coupled with material support for gardens and its partnership with the Neighborhood Gardens Association land trust, make the organization a powerful force for mobilizing and stabilizing communities and their local food supply. In just its first year (2006), Philadelphia Green's City Harvest program marshaled the energies of inmates working in the Philadelphia Prison System's "Roots to Reentry" garden as well as more than 200 community gardeners to supply almost 8,000 pounds of fresh produce to food cupboards in low-income neighborhoods (PHS 2006).

In the late 1990s, Philadelphia Green explored the possibility of investing more seriously in urban farming. It took some of its leading community gardeners to Cuba to study the permaculture systems developed during the "special period." And it commissioned a report on the feasibility of urban agriculture, which included eight case studies of North American urban farms. Published in 2000, when a gallon of regular gasoline in the United States cost around $1.50, it found that "Philadelphia does contain some key ingredients required for these ventures, namely the availability of vacant, unused land . . . and the entrepreneurial spirit of a core group of organizations and individuals who support the growth of urban agriculture in Philadelphia." However, it noted that "other factors, such as the acquisition, quality, and location of land—as well as the ability to secure the necessary funds to both start and initially sustain these businesses—represent formidable obstacles" (PHS 2000: 18). Of the eight farms profiled, three were only "marginally profitable," one was breaking even, one had closed, and two were too new to tell. One was turning a decent profit, employing 100 people, but only after incurring $20 million in start-up costs (PHS 2000: 6–8). For the time being at least, PHS concluded that urban farming did not appear a promising investment.

The only local Philadelphia farm profiled in this report was Greensgrow, which had started in 1997–98 in the former factory district of Kensington. Mary Seton Corboy, a former chef, conceived it as a supplier for high-end restaurants, including the White Dog Café. The farm's three-quarter-acre site was the former home of a steel galvanizing plant, so it grew everything above ground: basil and lettuce in hydroponic systems, heirloom tomatoes in raised beds sealed at the bottom, and potted plants in greenhouses donated by farmers in rural Pennsylvania.

Figure 1. Greensgrow Farm, showing its farm stand and greenhouses. Domenic Vitiello.

In 2000 Greensgrow struggled to remain viable, sustained by grants as much as sales. Its experiment in hiring employees from a welfare-to-work program failed, as Corboy learned she needed to maintain a staff of no more than two or three people to sustain manageable labor costs. The farm began to turn a profit only in 2003, as it diversified its product line, expanding its nursery business, developing a CSA, and becoming a broker for Philadelphia restaurants seeking organic produce from nearby Pennsylvania and New Jersey farms. In Kensington, it collaborates with Pennsylvania State University's Integrated Pest Management program to adopt biocontrols such as lady bugs that help keep its production pesticide-free. Today, Greensgrow is a nationally celebrated leader in urban farming, an important model for farms located on brownfield sites (Figure 1).[18]

Greensgrow is a singular success story among a larger number of failed inner city farms in Philadelphia. In north central Philadelphia, Seachange, Pennsylvania's first accredited organic urban farm and CSA, was displaced by a cinema and student housing project for nearby Temple University. Philaberry Farms in lower North Philadelphia supplied blackberries and raspberries to a handful of local grocery stores and restaurants for about eight years. It was a sideline venture for a real estate entrepreneur who held the site until the market became favorable for residential development in the early 2000s. Since the mid-1990s, various proposals have surfaced to cultivate mushrooms in some of the city's many vacant industrial buildings, which seem well suited for the dark, dank growing environments enjoyed by fungi. Kaolin Farms, a leading grower from Kennett Square, Pennsylvania, the "mushroom capital of the world," was one such proponent but was forced to abandon its plan due to the cost of importing and exporting growing medium in an area without ready supplies of manure (Goodman 1997; Kaufman and Bailkey 2000).

Even more complex schemes have been attempted in aquaculture. In 2000, consumer advocate Lance Haver established Phoenix Foods with about $2 million in public and private funds on tax-free land in the West Philadelphia Empowerment Zone. Workers in this employee-owned company installed an innovative system to raise fish and basil together in a symbiotic "aquaponic" relationship wherein fish effluent fed the plants and the plants cleaned the water for the fish. Technical glitches and insufficient productivity left the venture bankrupt four years later (Schimmel 2004). A more cautious $450,000 research project funded by the Delaware River Port Authority was conducted by the University of Pennsylvania's School of Veterinary Medicine to test the viability of commercial fish farming in plastic tanks at the Philadelphia Navy Yard. The venture was deemed impractical, however, and not pursued (Goodman 1997; Murray et al. 2003).

On a more positive note, tanks of another sort have been the scene of the city's most important experiment in making urban farming financially viable. At the foot of two large storage tanks operated by the Philadelphia Water Department (PWD), the Institute for Innovations in Local Farming has operated the Somerton Tanks Farm since 2003. This Northeast Philadelphia site was not contaminated, so cultivation has taken place on a half acre of in-ground beds just wide enough for farmers to straddle as they plant, weed, and harvest crops of carrots, watermelons, and especially salad mix. Like Greensgrow, Somerton's outlets have been diversified between its CSA, farm stand, Food Trust and Farm to City farmers' markets, and restaurants and caterers.

Somerton is primarily a demonstration project aimed at providing a prototype for subacre urban farming using the Institute for Innovations in Local Farming patented Small Plot Intensive (SPIN) method of "highly sophisticated rotational planting patterns [that] raise yields, reduce pest pressure, and build soil fertility." With two farmers working the site, its gross sales rose from $26,100 its first year to $52,200 in 2005 and close to $70,000 in 2006. It is extending the season by growing winter produce in a hoophouse, expanding these sales into the colder months. The institute promotes SPIN as "a method uniquely suited to entrepreneurs" who can use its "precise revenue targeting formulas [to] push yields to unprecedented levels."[19] For the PWD, Somerton demon-

Figure 2. Somerton Tanks Farm, with beds of lettuce in the foreground. Tomatoes and the produce preparation tent are at the right. Domenic Vitiello.

strates that stormwater management can take profitable forms. "This shows that you can earn a living farming in the city. It provides economic development," says the PWD's Nancy Weissman.[20] Somerton's two farmers have been convinced, deciding to buy and build equity in their own farm (Figure 2).[21]

In 2006, the Institute for Innovations in Local Farming commissioned a feasibility study examining potential sites on which others might replicate the Somerton model, with market and financial projections that will aid in future business planning. It sells a detailed SPIN farming manual on its website and, with its Canadian partner and co-originator of the model, is offering a "SPIN Cities" summer workshop in Wisconsin. Weissman and the institute's director, Roxanne Christensen, spent much of 2006 meeting with landowners and aspiring farmers in greater Philadelphia; in 2007 they are focusing on land and farm policy recommendations to support the growth of city farming.

One group picking up on Somerton's model is the Schuylkill Center for Environmental Education in the upper Roxborough section of northwest Philadelphia. Its 340 acres include several nineteenth-century

Figure 3. Manatawna Farm, one of several nineteenth-century farms that remain in the upper Roxborough section of Philadelphia. Owned by Fairmount Park and operated as a hay farm for Saul Agricultural High School, it borders other historic farms that are part of the Schuylkill Center for Environmental Education. If preserved, this farmland inside the city could accommodate more intensive agriculture that would make significant contributions to the local food system. Domenic Vitiello.

farms, much like the Awbury Arboretum where Weavers Way Co-op has developed its farm. As issues of peak oil and local food supply gain attention from a broader public, this preserved farmland becomes attractive as more than just open space. Indeed, in 2006 the Schuylkill Center added a farmer to its staff, who proceeded to plow long fallow fields. The center is working with neighbors who own adjacent historic farms to explore the possibility of tapping further capacity for local production in a collaborative community project. Even if they have little time to toil in the fields themselves, lawyers and architects with large properties might offer their land for cultivation by others, gaining rent and fresh produce from their own backyards (Figure 3).

While this upper Roxborough effort presents a model for middle-class neighborhoods with ample private and institutional open space, the Mill Creek section of West Philadelphia is home to a promising model of community development through urban farming for low-wealth communities. Like Somerton, Mill Creek Farm began in 2005 as a stormwater management project supported by the PWD. Located in a neighborhood long plagued by sinking homes and sinkholes that are

Figure 4. Visitors on the "living roof" of Mill Creek Farm's vernacular green building. Domenic Vitiello.

the legacy of a buried stream, the site had been vacant for some 3 decades, though part of it has been a community garden for 15 years.[22]

Mill Creek Farm is a nonprofit community development initiative, combining its environmental mission with educational, nutrition, and community-building programs aimed at improving food security. Run by two young women, Johanna Rosen and Jade Walker, who previously worked with the Urban Nutrition Initiative, it partners with local schools and its neighboring community gardeners to "facilitate intergenerational exchange between school age groups and elders." Its toolshed is an example of "vernacular" green building, with cob walls, solar-powered electricity, a living roof, gray water collection, and compost toilet. Its pickup truck, donated by the local transit authority, is being converted to run on biodiesel and used vegetable oil.[23] Produce from the farm is sold at the local Mariposa Co-op and Mill Creek's own farm stand, where neighbors pay below market rates for garlic, tomatoes, and okra, its most popular crop (Figure 4).

Supported by the Philadelphia Green program, Mill Creek Farm is also a model for how some existing community gardens might spawn more formalized community and economic development through agriculture. One group of gardeners celebrated by *Edens Lost & Found*, Iris Brown, Tomasita Romero, and the women of Grupo Motivos from the Norris Square section of Kensington, is exploring the possibility of building a greenhouse. This kind of initiative would not only extend the season, but also enable Grupo Motivos to grow some plants native to their homeland of Puerto Rico, which in turn could help expand their catering and cultural education programs.

Urban agriculture has, in fact, attracted a great deal of interest in Philadelphia recently. The Urban Voids international design competition for reusing vacant land in the city, organized by the City Parks Association in collaboration with the Reinvestment Fund, Pennsylvania Horticultural Society, and Pennsylvania Environmental Council, attracted approximately 40 entries proposing some form of inner-city farming. Some of these included wind, solar, and other renewable energy to power the farms. In 2007, community economic development pioneer Paul Glover founded a new group, the Philly Orchard Project, to assist neighborhood-based organizations in stabilizing vacant lots and establishing less labor-intensive agriculture as a permanent part of the urban fabric. These plantings of fruit and nut trees, berries, and perennials can take many different forms, from fruit-bearing street trees and neighborhood orchards with free harvest for low-wealth residents, to "edible community centers" with greenhouses, to small business ventures.[24]

Clearly, there is no shortage of ideas for the future of urban agriculture in Philadelphia and other regions. Existing farms such as Greensgrow, Somerton, Mill Creek, and Weavers Way offer replicable models for different sorts of urban and suburban sites, for-profit and nonprofit organizations, and diverse programming goals. The Institute for Innovation in Local Farming has shown that strategic business planning and Small Plot Intensive Farming can foster effective economic development. Greensgrow has proved that brownfields can become productive, profitable, organic farms. The Common Market and the region's growing networks of farmers' markets and CSAs represent an emergent alternative distribution and marketing system to the far more wasteful and fossil fuel-intensive systems of traditional food distribution and supermarket chains. Some wastes are being recycled from and into the local food system (the Philadelphia Energy Cooperative Fry-o-Diesel venture, for example, collects and reprocesses restaurant trap grease into biodiesel).

Overall, however, Farm to City director Bob Pierson estimates that less than 1 percent of all food consumed in Greater Philadelphia is "locally" grown within a half-day's drive of the city.[25] It will take planning and development on a far larger scale to meaningfully localize the region's food supply. In the inner city, issues of soil fertility and contamination, land ownership and site control, and organizational capacity all represent challenges, as they do in much redevelopment.

Yet emerging best practices in Philadelphia and other regions hold enormous promise. In cities with large supplies of vacant land, like Baltimore, Detroit, and New Orleans, urban farming presents great opportunities for environmental remediation, education, and community revitalization. If farmed intensively and supported by food processing and preservation efforts, these areas with ample land could produce a majority of their fruit and vegetables, as well as some grains.[26] In denser areas such as New York City, even an act as small as planting fruiting street trees can make a difference in the nutrition and air quality of an inner city block.

Toward an Edible City

We can live without oil, but we cannot live without food. Meeting the environmental and economic challenges of the twenty-first century will require dramatically reducing the global food system's dependence on oil and natural gas. Metropolitan "food sheds" must be relocalized—for example, reducing East Coast cities' dependence on lettuce from California and clementines from Spain. But can urban farming really make regional food sheds self-sufficient?

The answer in Phoenix and Las Vegas is probably not. But the answer in Philadelphia, Atlanta, Seattle, and Chicago is closer to yes. Localizing even half a region's food supply would cut fossil fuel dependence immensely, not to mention the benefits to public health. In any metropolitan area, this will not be achieved by inner-city growers alone. The institutional infrastructure fostering connections between urban markets and farmers in their rural hinterlands are at least as important as developing city-based farms. Household and community gardens likewise remain critical venues for individual and collective actions that increase local food supply.

In recent years, pioneer urban farmers have experimented with various types of agriculture and aquaculture. Most of these endeavors have failed to turn a profit. Yet the market context of these ventures is changing, on both the demand and supply sides. In the early twenty-first century, urban farming is an important avenue for community and economic development, much more so than even just a few years ago. With rising energy prices and the specter of peak oil, urban agriculture will be more than viable. It promises to become a vital part of community development that addresses a great variety of social, economic, and environmental imperatives in the twenty-first century.

References

Bolesta, Katy. 2006. "Market Forces." *Philadelphia Weekly*, August 23.

Brown, Lester. 2006. *Plan B 2.0: Rescuing a Planet Under Stress and a Civilization in Trouble*. New York: Norton.

Chen, Michelle. 2006. "Nearly One in Five U.S. Latinos 'Food Insecure.'" *New Standard*, December 20.

Christensen, Roxanne, and Nancy Weissman. 2006. Interview, August 28.

Corboy, Mary Seton. 2005. Interview, March 30.

Deffeyes, Kenneth. 2005. *Beyond Oil: The View from Hubbert's Peak*. New York: Hill and Wang.

Díaz Peña, Jorge, and Phil Harris. 2005. "Urban Agriculture in Havana: Opportunities for the Future." In *Continuous Productive Urban Landscapes: Designing Urban Agriculture for Sustainable Cities*, ed. André Viljoen. Burlington, Mass.: Architectural Press.

Ferguson, Beth. 2000. "Urban Aquaculture: Ethnic Markets Sustain New Business." *New Village Journal* 2.

Flores, Heather. 2006. *Food Not Lawns: How to Turn Your Yard into a Garden and Your Neighborhood into a Community*. White River Junction, Vt.: Chelsea Green.

Flynn, Kathleen. 1999. "An Overview of Public Health and Urban Agriculture: Water, Soil and Crop Contamination and Emerging Urban Zoonoses." Cities Feeding People Report 30. Ottawa: IDRC.

Food and Agricultural Organization (FAO). 2004. *The State of Food Insecurity in the World*. Rome: FAO.

Food Matters. 2006. 2, 2 (Fall).

Glover, Paul. 1983. *Los Angeles: A History of the Future*. Los Angeles: Citizen Planners.

Goodman, Howard. 1979. "Sowing the Seeds of Change: Down on the Farm in Philadelphia." *Philadelphia Inquirer*, October 12.

Gottlieb, Robert, and Andrew Fisher. 1996a. "'First Feed the Face': Environmental Justice and Community Food Security." *Antipode* 28, 2: 193–203.

———. 1996b. "Community Food Security and Environmental Justice: Searching for a Common Discourse." *Agriculture and Human Values* 13, 3: 23–32.

Gray, Steven. 2006. "Organic Food Goes Mass Market." *Wall Street Journal*, May 4.

Greenhow, Timothy. 1994. "Urban Agriculture: Can Planners Make a Difference?" Cities Feeding People Report 12. Ottawa: IDRC.

Hammel, Laury, and Gun Denhart. 2006. *Growing Local Value: How to Build Business Partnerships That Strengthen Your Community*. San Francisco: Berrett-Koehler.

Heller, Martin, and Gregory Keoleian. 2000. *Life Cycle-Based Sustainability Indicators for Assessment of the U.S. Food System*. Ann Arbor: Center for Sustainable Systems, University of Michigan.

Holmgren, David. 2002. *Permaculture: Principles and Pathways Beyond Sustainability*. Hepburn, Australia: Holmgren Design Services.

Jacobi, Petra, Axel Drescher, and Jorg Amend. 2000. "Urban Agriculture—Justification and Planning." *City Farmer*. cityfarmer.org.

Johnson, Lorraine. 2005. "Design for Food: Landscape Architects Find Roles in City Farms." *Landscape Architecture* (June).

Karlen, Ann. 2007. Presentation at the Urban Sustainability Forum, January 18.

Katz, Sandor. 2006. *The Revolution Will Not Be Microwaved: Inside America's Underground Food Movements.* White River Junction, Vt.: Chelsea Green.

Kaufman, Jerry. 1999. "Exploring Opportunities for Community Development Corporations Using Inner City Vacant Land for Urban Agriculture." University of Wisconsin-Madison, February.

Kaufman, Jerry, and Martin Bailkey. 2000. "Farming Inside Cities: Entrepreneurial Urban Agriculture in the United States." Lincoln Institute of Land Policy working paper.

Koc, Mustafa, Rod MacRae, Luc J. A. Mougeot, and Jennifer Welsh, eds. 2000. *For Hunger-Proof Cities: Sustainable Urban Food Systems.* Ottawa: International Development Research Centre.

Lawson, Laura. 2005. *City Bountiful: A Century of Community Gardening in America.* Berkeley: University of California Press.

Lazarus, Chris. 2000. "Urban Agriculture: A Revolutionary Model for Economic Development." *New Village Journal* 2.

Lyson, Thomas. 2004. *Civic Agriculture: Reconnecting Farm, Food, and Community.* Medford, Mass.: Tufts University Press.

Mill Creek Farm. 2006. Brochure.

Mollison, Bill, and David Holmgren. 1990. *Permaculture One: A Perennial Agricultural System for Human Settlements.* Tyalgum, Australia: Tagari.

Mougeot, Luc J. A., ed. 2005. *Agropolis: The Social, Political and Environmental Dimensions of Urban Agriculture.* London: Earthscan.

Murphy, Pat. 2006. "Plan C—Curtailment and Community" *New Solutions* (September).

Murray, Danielle. 2005. "Oil and Food: A Rising Security Challenge." Earth Policy Institute.

Murray, Link et al. 2003. "A Review of Operating Economics and Finance Research Needs." Aquaculture White Paper 4. Northeast Regional Aquaculture Center.

Nelson, Toni. 1996. "Closing the Nutrient Loop." *WorldWatch* 9, 5 (December): 10–17.

Patel, Ishwarbhai C. 1996. "Rutgers Urban Gardening: A Case Study in Urban Agriculture." *Journal of Agricultural and Food Information* 3, 3: 35–46.

Pennsylvania Horticultural Society (PHS). 2000. *The Feasibility of Urban Agriculture, with Recommendations for Philadelphia.* Philadelphia: PHS.

———. 2006. "PHS Launches 'City Harvest,' a Program to Feed the Hungry." Press release, June.

Pfeiffer, Dale Allen. 2006. *Eating Fossil Fuels: Oil, Food, and the Coming Crisis in Agriculture.* Gabriola Island, British Columbia: New Society.

Pierson, Bob, and Ann Karlen. 2006. Interview. July 10.

Pimentel, David, and Mario Giampietro. 1994. "Food, Land, Population and the U.S. Economy." Carrying Capacity Network.

Pollan, Michael. 2006a. *The Omnivore's Dilemma: A Natural History of Four Meals.* New York: Penguin.

———. 2006b. "The Vegetable-Industrial Complex." *New York Times,* October 15.

Pothukuchi, Kameshwari, and Jerome Kaufman. 1999. "Placing the Food System on the Urban Agenda: The Role of Municipal Institutions in Food Systems Planning." *Agriculture and Human Values* 16, 2: 213–24.

The Power of Community: How Cuba Survived Peak Oil. 2006. Documentary.

Premat, Adriana. 2000. "Moving Between the Plan and the Ground: Shifting

Perspectives on Urban Agriculture in Havana, Cuba." In *Agropolis: The Social, Political and Environmental Dimensions of Urban Agriculture*, ed. Luc J. A. Mougeot. London: Earthscan.

Quinn, Megan. 2006. "Peak Oil and the Case for Local Food Systems." Ohio State University, January 11.

Quon Soony. 1999. "Planning for Urban Agriculture: A Review of Tools and Strategies for Urban Planners." Cities Feeding People Report 28. Ottawa: IDRC.

Ratta, Annu, and Jac Smit. "Urban Agriculture: It's About Much More Than Food." 1993. *World Hunger Year* 13 (Summer): 26–29.

Rodriguez, Harahi Gamez. 2000. "Agriculture in the Metropolitan Park of Havana, Cuba." In *For Hunger-Proof Cities: Sustainable Urban Food Systems*, ed. Koc Mustafa, Rod MacRae, Luc J. A. Mougeot, and Jennifer Welsh. Ottawa: International Development Research Centre.

Rose, Gregory. 1999. "Community-Based Technologies for Domestic Wastewater Treatment and Reuse: Options for Urban Agriculture." Cities Feeding People Report 27. Ottawa: IDRC.

Rosen, Johanna, and Jade Walker. 2006. Interview, September 24.

Schimmel, Bruce. 2004. "Phoenix Falling." *Philadelphia CityPaper*, May 13.

Schurmann, Franz. "Can Cities Feed Themselves? Worldwide Turn to Urban Gardening Signals Hope." 1996. *Pacific News Service*, June 3.

Shuman, Michael. 2000. *Going Local: Building Self-Reliant Communities in a Global Age*. New York: Routledge.

———. 2006. *The Small-Mart Revolution: How Local Businesses Are Beating the Global Competition*. San Francisco: Berrett-Koehler.

Silva, Beth. 1998–1999. "Urban Farming: Making Metropolitan Market Revenue." *AgVentures* 2, 6 (December–January): 40–45.

Smit, Jac, and Joe Nasr. 1992. "Urban Agriculture for Sustainable Cities: Using Wastes and Idle Land and Water Bodies as Resources." *Environment and Urbanization* 4, 2 (October): 141–52.

———. 1995. "Farming in Cities." *In Context: A Journal of Hope, Sustainability, and Change* 42 (Fall): 20–23.

Smith, Jesse. 2006. "The Plot Thickens." *Philadelphia Weekly*, July 19.

Sommers, Paul, and Jac Smit. 1994. "Promoting Urban Agriculture: Strategy Framework for Planners in North America, Europe and Asia." Cities Feeding People Report 9. Ottawa: IDRC.

SPIN Overview. 2005. Institute for Innovations in Local Farming.

Spirn, Anne Whiston. 2005. "Restoring Mill Creek: Landscape Literacy, Environmental Justice and City Planning and Design." *Landscape Research* 30, 3 (July): 395–413.

Steele, Jonathan. 1996. "Growing Good News in Cities—UN Habitat Summit." *Observer*, May 5.

Stix, Gary. 1996. "Urbaculture: Cities of the Developing World Learn to Feed Themselves." *Scientific American* (December).

Tansey, Geoff, and Tony Worsley. 1995. *The Food System: A Guide*. London: Earthscan.

United Nations Development Program (UNDP). 1996. *Urban Agriculture: Food, Jobs and Sustainable Cities*. New York: UNDP.

"Urban Food Production—Neglected Resources for Food and Jobs." 1992. *Hunger Notes* 18, 2 (Fall).

Van Allen, Peter. 2004. "Back to Basics: Farms Sprouting in Philadelphia" *Philadelphia Business Journal* (July).

Viljoen, André, ed. 2005. *Continuous Productive Urban Landscapes: Designing Urban Agriculture for Sustainable Cities*. Burlington, Mass.: Architectural Press.

Viljoen, André, and Joe Howe. 2005. "Cuba: Laboratory for Urban Agriculture." In *Continuous Productive Urban Landscapes: Designing Urban Agriculture for Sustainable Cities*, ed. André Viljoen. Burlington, Mass.: Architectural Press.

Part III
Measuring Urban Greening

Chapter 15
Ecosystem Services and the Green City

Dennis D. Hirsch

Many recognize that natural ecosystems can produce commercial goods such as timber or seafood, yet few are aware that ecosystems also provide valuable *services* to human society.[1] Wetlands and natural floodplains can protect cities from destructive floods. Trees, plants, and soils can filter and purify a city's water. Insects pollinate crops. Forests absorb carbon and stabilize the climate. Despite the importance of these and other ecosystem services, many of us take them for granted.[2] The vital effort to green our cities can, at times, suffer from the same narrowness of vision. Those who advocate the greening of cities rarely focus on the economic services that natural environments can provide. They thereby miss an important policy argument for investing in the natural environments in and around cities.

This chapter seeks to fill this gap. It proceeds in three sections. The first part explains how natural ecosystems can provide valuable services to cities. It describes the upstate watershed lands that filter the New York City water supply, and the gulf wetlands that historically protected New Orleans against storm surges. From these examples, it concludes that cities benefit greatly from healthy ecosystems and that, when it comes to investing in ecosystem services, environmental and economic goals can converge. The second part asks who should be responsible for the protection and enhancement of ecosystem services. Using a public goods argument, it asserts that government should be in charge, even though the market may also have a role to play in this area. The third part evaluates four government mechanisms that can be used for this purpose and assesses their strengths and weaknesses.

Economic and Environmental Values of Ecosystem Service Investments for Cities

Ecosystems provide important services for cities as demonstrated by the upstate watershed lands that cleanse New York City's drinking water, and the coastal wetlands that have the potential to protect New Orleans and its environs from hurricanes.

NEW YORK CITY AND UPSTATE WATERSHED LANDS

New York City's nearly 9 million residents and thousands of businesses consume approximately 1.4 billion gallons of water daily (Salzman 2005: 100 n.25). The Catskill/Delaware watershed, an expanse of forested and rural lands to the north and west of the city, provides 90 percent of this water supply (Daily and Ellison 2002: 68). The Croton watershed contributes the rest. The system, construction of which began in 1837, currently stores more than 500 billion gallons of water in 19 reservoirs and three controlled lakes and employs more than 6,000 miles of conduits and pipes to bring water to the city. Until recently, the water had been so clean that the city did not have to treat it, other than to add a bit of chlorine as a disinfectant and some fluoride to prevent tooth decay (68).

This had begun to change by the 1990s. Increased development of watershed lands took a toll on the city's drinking water as contaminated runoff from golf courses, driveways, lawns, construction sites, and other similar land uses degraded water quality. Farm runoff and leaching from residential septic systems further contributed to the problem. In the meantime, the regulatory requirements were growing stricter. Acting under the authority of the Safe Drinking Water Act, the Environmental Protection Agency (EPA) in 1989 issued a rule requiring all cities with surface water drinking supplies to build a filtration plant, unless the city could demonstrate that it was acting to protect watershed lands in a way that would preserve water quality (EPA 1989, 1998). New York City acknowledged the need to build a filtration plant for the smaller Croton system. However, it was reluctant to do so for the larger Catskill/Delaware system, since the plant would cost between $6 and $8 billion.

In January 1991, the New York State Department of Health, acting as the delegated enforcer of the federal Safe Drinking Water Act, presented the city with a stark choice for the Catskill/Delaware system: either undertake a watershed restoration effort capable of meeting the minimum water quality requirements, or build the filtration plant. The city's Department of Environmental Protection chose to restore the watershed. It made this choice largely for economic reasons. In contrast to the water filtration plant's $6 to $8 billion price tag, watershed restoration was projected to cost $1.5 billion (Daily and Ellison 2002: 68). Investing in the ecosystem service, the city reasoned, would save it billions of dollars.

New York City's Watershed Protection Program calls for a variety of measures, such as improvements to septic and sewer systems, upgrades to local wastewater treatment plants, and enhanced monitoring of water quality (EPA 2006). It also calls for spending $300 million on the acquisition and preservation of important watershed lands or, alternatively, on the purchase of conservation easements that will prevent these areas from being built on (EPA 2006: 11). Such undeveloped lands contribute to the water cleaning effort by slowing the progress of stormwater runoff, thereby allowing contaminants to settle out and enter the soils. Soil particles and living organisms absorb these contaminants before they pass downstream. In this way, forests, wetlands, and riparian lands serve as "living filters" that remove sediments, metals, oils, excess nutrients, and other contaminants from the water supply. New York City's watershed restoration policy thus relies, in part, on the ecosystem service of water filtration. As of 2006, the city had spent $174 million on the acquisition of fee title or conservation easements for 71,000 acres of watershed land (USEPA 2006: 11). The EPA has continued to authorize the city to use watershed restoration in place of the much more expensive filtration plant (see Plate 12 for a map of the New York City watershed).

As this story shows, New York City's investment in ecosystem services produced (and continues to produce) both environmental gains and important economic benefits for the city and its taxpayers. This success suggests that, in some instances at least, cities can achieve environmental and economic goals together. It also shows that the greening of cities should not stop at city limits, but should extend beyond. Cities need to widen their vision to encompass ecosystem lands outside their borders that may be providing them with important services. In the 1990s, EPA estimated that more than 140 cities were considering watershed conservation as a means of protecting the quality of their drinking water (Salzman 2005: 109). New York City's experience shows that these cities should seriously examine such a policy.

New Orleans, Coastal Wetlands, and Hurricane Katrina

The case of the coastal wetlands outside of New Orleans shows another way in which cities can derive great value from ecosystems, and the dire consequences that can result when society neglects these resources. For many years, Louisiana's millions of acres of coastal wetlands have slowed down hurricanes and other storms, reduced storm surges, and protected the city of New Orleans (Zwerdling n.d.). The wetland system owes its origin to thousands of years of Mississippi River soil deposits, and relies on the river's periodic floods for replenishment. Without this nourishment, the wetlands naturally subside and turn into open water. Beginning in the late 1800s, the U.S. Army Corps of Engineers constructed an extensive levee system to protect human development along the Mississippi River from destructive floods. The Corps largely achieved this aim. However, its levee system had the unintended effect of depriving the wetlands of their needed nourishment (Louisiana Coastal Wetlands Commission 1998: 2). Instead of bringing new soils and nutrients to the wetlands, as the river's periodic floods had done, the levees directed almost all this material out into the gulf's deep waters and beyond the continental shelf, where it was of no use (Zwerdling n.d.). Starved of their essential soils, floodwaters, and nutrients, the wetlands began to sink and lose vitality with each passing year (see Plate 13 for a map of the Louisiana coastal lands).[3]

This left the wetlands vulnerable to a second assault, the cutting of navigation canals. In the 1940s, the discovery of major oil and gas deposits beneath the coastal wetlands led energy companies to cut thousands of channels through the wetlands in order to drill and transport the petroleum and gas resources (Zwerdling n.d.; Louisiana Coastal Wetlands Commission 1998: 2). The channels allowed saltwater to penetrate freshwater marshes. They also altered the natural flow of water in the wetlands and so inhibited the dispersion of soil and nutrients. These injuries further degraded the wetlands (Louisiana Coastal Wetlands Commission 1998: 40). The combined effect of the levees and the energy canals has been devastating. Since 1930, more than 1,500 square miles of Louisiana coastal wetlands have turned into open water, and an additional 25 to 35 square miles—roughly the size of Manhattan—are lost every year, thus robbing New Orleans of its protective shield (Louisiana Coastal Wetlands Commission 1998: 31; Zwerdling n.d.). As one Louisiana scientist observed, "in effect, the city is moving closer to the gulf as each year goes by" (Zwerdling n.d.). Actions by the Corps and energy companies have dangerously depleted the essential ecosystem service of storm and flood protection.

Scientists and policymakers have known of this phenomenon for years and have predicted that a major hurricane could devastate New Orleans. Nearly 40 years ago, a team of scientists called for cutting seven openings in the levee system to allow controlled flooding that would bring new sediments and nutrients to the wetlands; government officials and others largely ignored the proposal (McKay 2005). By the 1990s, as the hurricane threat became more apparent, a broad group of stakeholders, including federal, state, and local government representatives, landowners, environmentalists, wetland scientists and others, turned their attention to the problem, issuing an insightful report, *Coast 2050: Toward a Sustainable Coastal Louisiana* (Louisiana Coastal Wetlands Commission 1998). The report argued forcefully for immediate action. It set out a $14-billion, 30-year strategic plan to build a 60-mile channel to divert a portion of the Mississippi to replenish the parched wetlands (125, 144).

The drafters presented the report to the White House and Congress, each of which largely failed to act. The White House Office of Management and Budget asked Louisiana to come up with a cheaper, shorter-term plan. Then Congress sat on the revised $2 billion proposal, which was pending when Hurricane Katrina hit New Orleans (McKay 2005).

While Katrina's human toll remains foremost, its economic costs of $200 billion are staggering (Wolk 2005). Furthermore, evidence suggests that wetlands restoration could have reduced, if not prevented, the flooding of New Orleans. A drafter of the *Coast 2050* report asserted that if, at the time of Katrina, the coastal wetlands east of New Orleans had been as extensive as they were in 1965, the hurricane's storm surge would have been 20 percent lower, some of the levee failures would not have occurred, and much of the flooding would have been prevented.[4] The failure to invest in ecosystem service protection represents one of the greatest missed opportunities in the nation's history. Once again, the lessons are that investments in natural ecosystems can make economic sense, and that cities can benefit from greening efforts outside their jurisdictional boundaries.

Who Should Pay for Ecosystem Service System Protection and Enhancement?

If it makes economic sense to protect ecosystem services, why does the market not generate more investment in them? Should we leave it to the market to maintain ecosystems, or does the public sector have a role to play here? The answers lie in the fact that most ecosystem services are what economists call "public goods," the type of goods that if provided to one, must be provided to all (Menell and Stewart 1994: 54). The Louisiana coastal wetlands are a good example. Even if some New Orleans residents were willing to pay to restore the wetlands, in order to benefit from the resulting storm surge protection it would be impossible to parcel this service out to these individuals and deny it to other city residents A wetlands protection program reduces or prevents flooding for all residents regardless of who pays. Other classic public goods are national defense and clean air. The market system cannot provide public goods because those who do not pay for a good can still enjoy its benefits, which leads many to decide to consume the good for free (Salzman and Thompson 2007: 18). This leaves the private sector with little incentive to invest in the production of public goods because it cannot obtain sufficient payments to cover production costs (Menell and Stewart 1994: 55). It also allows wasteful use, and fails to signal scarcity. In short, the inability to fence anyone off from a public good makes it impossible to charge for such benefits, and so prevents the market from providing them. Wasteful consumption of the coastal Louisiana wetlands by energy companies, and the absence of any private investment in the wetlands, demonstrate the inexorable logic: the wetlands provide a public good and so the market failed to protect them.

Four Government Strategies for Protecting Ecosystem Services

Where the market fails, the public sector has an important role to play. But how, exactly, should government protect and enhance valuable ecosystem services? This question is fundamental for those in city administration, or at other levels of government that seek to implement effective policies for preserving and expanding ecosystem services. Government can protect ecosystem services in four ways. It can (1) fund and implement projects that directly restore and enhance ecosystems; (2) charge a fee for the destruction of ecosystem services; (3) subsidize the preservation and enhancement of ecosystem services; or (4) establish market-based programs for the trading of ecosystem services. This section examines each of these strategies and offers some preliminary thoughts about their relative strengths and weaknesses.

Option 1: Government-Funded Restoration Projects

Under the first approach, government undertakes the restoration project itself. The Coast 2050 project, with its plan for a $14-billion government investment, exemplifies this method. New York City's purchase of upstate watershed lands provides another example.

A third leading example is the Napa, California, "living river" flood control project. While Napa County is widely known for its wineries and tourist crowds, the city of Napa has not shared in much of this success. In part, this is due to the floods that have periodically devastated the town, leaving streets, residences, and businesses inundated with water and mud (Daily and Ellison 2002: 92). In 1986, Napa experienced a particularly damaging flood that left three residents dead, caused 5,000 more to evacuate their homes, and created $100 million in property damage (95). The U.S. Army Corps of Engineers responded with a plan to put a "concrete straitjacket" around the river—high walls on either side that would beat a straight line through the center of town (95, 88).

A group of residents who took the name Friends of the River objected. The Friends believed that the concrete structure would make downtown Napa even less attractive to tourists and businesses. They were also concerned that the concrete channel, like the other levee systems that had come before it, would eventually prove unreliable and fail to protect the town. As an alternative, the Friends suggested a "living river" approach to flood protection. They argued that any solution had to get at the root cause of the flooding, which was human development on floodplain lands. This had led to the removal of the trees and tall grasses that had served as natural sponges for rainwater, and to the destruction of the wetlands and plains that had served to absorb flood waters (Daily and Ellison 2002: 92). Moreover, the levees intended to channel and control the river had, instead, increased its force and velocity and so its destructiveness. To gain real and lasting protection from floods, the city would need to reverse these actions and restore the river ecosystem with its natural flood protection properties.

The Friends proposed to achieve this through a "living river" flood protection project that would include acquisition of floodplain lands, restoration of wetlands and grasslands, and the removal of bridges and levees. The project would create an open space in the city of Napa that would serve as a river floodplain during the wet months and recreational parkland during the dry ones (Daily and Ellison 2002: 100). This would provide an environmental amenity, rather than a concrete wall, in the heart of downtown. The project would, however, cost $194 million, as compared to only $44 million for the corps' proposed levee approach, and would require a tax increase for county residents. The Friends argued that these additional expenditures would be offset by much larger economic gains associated with enhanced tourism and business development in the city, higher property values, and lower flood insurance rates.

Ultimately, the corps approved the living river approach and the citizens of Napa County passed their largest tax increase ever to support it. By 2001, when the project was still in its early stages, commercial real estate values in the city of Napa had increased by 20 percent and new hotels and a wine-oriented museum were in the works. Anticipating the completion of the project, flood insurance rates in the city had gone down by 20 percent (Daily and Ellison 2002: 103). One study concluded that county residents would see a seven-to-one return on their sales tax investment (102). Delegations from Australia, Argentina, and China came to Napa to observe the ecosystem-based approach to flood protection, and numerous cities in the United States have begun to emulate it (106).

The Napa experience suggests that direct government investment can be an effective approach to the protection and enhancement of ecosystem services. Such projects operate on the premise that ecosystem services are public goods, that the market will not provide them, and that the government must accordingly act to do so. One virtue of this approach is that it shares the burden of restoration fairly among the affected citizenry. It also spreads the cost among many different contributors (taxpayers), thereby making even large-scale, expensive projects economically feasible.

These benefits notwithstanding, the direct investment approach often faces political hurdles for two reasons. First, major public investments generally require tax increases like the one that the citizens of Napa County passed. Voters often resist new taxes and so make it difficult to fund a direct investment approach. Second, political and natural systems operate on very different timelines. Election cycles and term limits define the political time-scale. Natural systems, and the attempts to restore them, follow natural cycles that occur over much longer periods. This means that many of the politicians of today will not be in office to reap the political rewards of investing in the restoration of ecosystems (Lazarus 2004: 41). This may explain why one of the other direct investment approaches mentioned earlier—the Coast 2050 proposal for Louisiana—languished in Congress in the years prior to Hurricane Katrina. The politicians being asked to act on the project would not be in office in 2050 when its full benefits would materialize.

OPTION 2: FEE SYSTEMS

Government can also protect ecosystem services by requiring those who damage ecosystem services to pay a fee for doing so (Salzman 2005: 115). For example, many cities have imposed stormwater utility fees based on the amount of a property's impervious surface.[5] Such surfaces—for example, rooftops, driveways, parking lots, tennis courts—pave over the soils and vegetation that would otherwise provide the valuable ecosystem service of rainwater absorption. This contributes directly to stormwater runoff, flooding, and pollution in local waterways. By basing the fee on the amount of impervious surface, governments are essentially charging landowners for the destruction of an ecosystem service. A similar approach could have been used in the gulf wetlands by requiring those energy companies that cut channels through wetlands to pay for the harm they have caused. This kind of approach sets a price on the destruction of ecosystem services. Parties that would otherwise exploit ecosystems for free now have to pay for the privilege. If the government sets fees high enough, it will provide landowners and others with an incentive to minimize the damage that they cause to ecosystems.

This approach may yield more efficient outcomes than the direct investment method described above. Regulated parties often have a better sense than the government of the benefits derived from their exploitation of a given ecosystem. Assuming that the fee accurately reflects the damage caused by the behavior, it would force the party to assess whether the value of the behavior outweighs the cost. In theory, this arrangement should lead to choices that benefit society. One drawback of the approach is the difficulty in assessing accurately the value of the damage and setting correct fee levels. Ecosystem services are especially difficult to value because of their complexity. More often than not, government sets the fee too low, allowing destructive behavior to continue. To avoid this problem, governments should use the fee approach only when they can accurately estimate the costs of ecosystem damage.

OPTION 3: SUBSIDY PROGRAMS

Governments can also subsidize private actions to preserve and enhance ecosystem services (Salzman 2005: 116, 121–27). For example, the city of Sydney, Australia pays landowners to improve privately held lands bordering the rivers and streams that supply Sydney's reservoirs (Sydney Catchment Authority 2007: 9–10).

These 110,000 kilometers of "riparian" lands have the capacity to filter pollutants and sediments out of the city's drinking water. However, landowners have allowed their livestock to enter these lands, where they contribute fecal matter and pathogens to the waterways, and damage the vegetation and soils that provide the filtering function (9). Sydney's Riparian Management Assistance Program seeks to address this problem. It awards money to landowners who fence off their riparian lands, adopt erosion control measures, and/or plant vegetation along river and stream banks. During its first year, the program awarded $909,000 for projects that will protect 35 kilometers of streams and gullies and will plant over 23,000 trees in riparian locations (10). While these accomplishments are small in comparison to the overall length of the waterway, the program demonstrates how subsidies can be employed to leverage private ecosystem protection efforts. Returning to the example given at the beginning of this chapter, New York City could potentially have employed a subsidy approach to improve land management along the Catskill/Delaware watershed. However, land development pressures in that region may have rendered subsidies ineffective. New York's decision to use direct investment in fee titles and conservation easements was likely a wise one.

Subsidy programs, much like fee systems, overcome the public goods problem by charging a price for the destruction of ecosystem services. Here, the "price" is the loss of the subsidy that the party would otherwise have obtained had it acted to preserve the ecosystem (Wiener 1999: 726). Thus, landowners in the Sydney catchment area who fail to fence their riparian lands forgo the award that they would otherwise have received. Subsidy programs are essentially another way of putting a price on ecosystem destruction and they share many of the strengths and weaknesses of fee systems, as described above.

How should the public sector choose between the fee method and the subsidy approach? Two factors favor the fee approach. Fees raise revenue that can be used for further ecosystem restoration, to reduce taxes on beneficial behavior, or for other governmental purposes. In contrast, subsidy programs deplete the government treasury. Furthermore, some subsidies can actually encourage parties to undertake destructive behavior in order to get paid for taking steps to mitigate the damage. Designers of such programs should seek to minimize the risk of such "moral hazards." Subsidies have the advantage of being easier to achieve politically. And, as was noted, many voters react negatively to any new fees or taxes.

The choice between fees and subsidies can also turn on baseline expectations for social behavior (Salzman 2005: 160). Consider a farmer who has the power either to drain a wetland or to preserve it. If we expect the farmer, as a publicly minded citizen, to preserve the wetland and its water purification service, then we are likely to view his decision not to do so as the act of a polluter. This might make us more disposed to charge for his polluting actions then to subsidize his refraining from them. In contrast, if we assume that the farmer is entitled to drain his land, then we are likely to view his decision not to do so as the act of one who is providing a water purification service to the rest of society. Viewed in this way, we will probably be far more willing to pay the farmer for continuing to provide this valuable service to the rest of us. Social expectations are likely to vary depending on the context. The attractiveness of fees, versus subsidies, will likely vary with them.

OPTION 4: TRADING SYSTEMS

Trading systems provide another mechanism for putting a price on ecosystem services, and so for creating an incentive to protect and enhance them. They do this by allocating a property right in the ecosystem service and then allowing regulated parties to meet environmental requirements by purchasing this right. In 1995, the city of Eugene, Oregon entered into an agreement with state and federal authorities that established a trading system for the protection of the city's wetlands (City of Eugene 2007). Wetlands provide valuable ecosystem services such as water filtration, flood control, and species habitat. The federal Clean Water Act accordingly requires private developers who build on existing wetlands to "mitigate" the impact by creating and/or protecting other wetlands, often at a greater than 1:1 ratio in terms of acreage (Memorandum of Agreement 1990).

A developer who wants to build on a wetland can meet this requirement by creating new wetlands. Alternatively, a developer can comply by purchasing the right to wetlands produced by someone else.[6] The Eugene program facilitates these trades. Under the program, the city certifies those wetlands whose ecosystem functions meet performance standards and assigns to the owner of the property a "certified credit" for that wetland (City of Eugene 2007: 3). It also establishes a "wetlands mitigation bank" in which the owner can store that credit. Developers who want to build on wetlands, and who need to mitigate the damage they are causing, can meet this requirement by purchasing credits from the bank. This regulatory approach creates two types of incentives for wetlands protection: one for entrepreneurs to create new wetlands, and one for developers to avoid building on existing ones so as to reduce their mitigation costs. Since its first transaction in 1994, the Eugene wetlands mitigation bank has sold 86 mitigation credits at an average price of $50,000 per credit, for a total market value of $4,300,000. This demonstrates the potential of such systems to generate private investment in wetlands and their ecosystem services.

Wetlands mitigation and banking programs, like other trading systems, force those who have harmed the environment to pay for restoration. The developer who builds on a wetland—not the public as a whole—pays for the replacement. This kind of approach is fair when discrete entities or individuals are responsible for the damage to the ecosystem but is ill-advised for large-scale problems that call for collective funding solutions. The approach has some efficiency advantages when compared to direct governmental investment. It pushes the regulated entity to make a choice between investing in the ecosystem service or avoiding harm to the environment. In these cases parties assess the relative costs of the alternatives and choose the one that achieves the desired environmental goal at the least expense. In contrast, the government may have less incentive to engage in such an analysis when it is deciding whether to directly fund and implement an ecosystem restoration project.[7] One downside to this approach is the difficulty in measuring equivalence of ecosystem functions between the wetland being built upon, and the one replacing it.[8] If this equivalence is not assured, the trade may appear environmentally beneficial on the surface but may actually deplete important ecosystem functions such as water filtration or habitat. The city of Eugene certifies wetlands based on compliance with performance standards. This step is critical if such trades are to benefit, not hurt, the environment.

On Not Draining the Swamp

In recent decades, society has come to understand ecosystems and their important services better. Those who might once have spoken of "swamps" that should be drained as quickly as possible, are now likely to talk of wetlands and their valuable contributions to habitat, water purification, and flood protection. The same change of perspective applies to other ecosystems as well. This enhanced appreciation of the beauty and function of ecosystems, and of the services they provide, has led to an increased desire to protect them. To achieve this goal will require effective regulatory tools designed for the purpose. Far less progress has been made on this front. Society urgently needs more experimentation with, and study of, the various policy approaches.

Cities can play a significant role in this effort. They operate on a smaller scale than state or federal governments, and are well suited to policy experimentation and innovation. Moreover, they have many opportunities to make productive investments in ecosystem services, especially if they look outside their own jurisdictions to the natural environments on which they rely for clean water, flood control, and other such services. Cities should seek opportunities to preserve and protect ecosystem services. In so doing, they will add to the base of knowledge regarding how governments can best achieve this important goal.

References

City of Eugene Public Works Department. 2007. "West Eugene Wetlands Mitigation Bank: Annual Report 2006." March.

Costanza, Robert et al. 1997. "The Value of the World's Ecosystem Services and Natural Capital." *Nature* 387.

Daily, Gretchen C., and Katherine Ellison. 2002. *The New Economy of Nature.* Washington, D.C.: Island Press.

Lazarus, Richard J. 2004. *The Making of Environmental Law.* Chicago: University of Chicago Press.

Louisiana Coastal Wetlands Commission and Restoration Task Force and the Wetlands Conservation and Restoration Authority. 1998. *Coast 2050: Toward a Sustainable Coastal Louisiana: An Executive Summary.* Baton Rouge: Louisiana Department of Natural Resources.

McKay, Betsy. 2005. "Moving the Mississippi." *Wall Street Journal,* October 29–30.

Memorandum of Agreement Between Department of the Army and the Environmental Protection Agency Concerning Clean Water Act Section 404(b)(1) Guidelines. 1990. *Federal Register* 55 (March 12): 9211–12.

Menell, Peter S., and Richard B. Stewart. 1994. *Environmental Law and Policy.* New York: Little, Brown.

Salzman, James. 2005. "Creating Markets for Ecosystem Services: Notes from the Field." *New York University Law Review* 80.

Salzman, James, and J. B. Ruhl. 2000. "Currencies and Commodification of Environmental Law." *Stanford Law Review* 53: 648–57.

Salzman, James, and Barton H. Thompson, Jr. 2007. *Environmental Law and Policy*. 2nd ed. New York: Foundation Press.

Salzman, James, Barton H. Thompson, Jr., and Gretchen C. Daily. 2001. "Protecting Ecosystem Services: Science, Economics and Law." *Stanford Environmental Law Journal* 20.

Sydney Catchment Authority. 2007. "Report on Catchment Management and Protection Activities for 2005–2006." Sydney, Australia.

U.S. Environmental Protection Agency (EPA). 1989. "Surface Water Treatment Rule." *Federal Register* 54 (June 29): 27486.

———. 1998. "Interim Enhanced Surface Water Treatment Rule." *Federal Register* 63 (December 16): 69390.

———. 2006. EPA Region 2. *Report on the City of New York's Progress in Implementing the Watershed Protection Program, and Complying with the Filtration Avoidance Determination* (August 21).

Wiener, Jonathan Baert. 1999. "Global Environmental Regulation: Instrument Choice in Legal Context." *Yale Law Journal* 108.

Wolk, Martin. 2005. "How Hurricane Katrina's Costs Are Adding Up: Insurance Industry Costs Plus Federal Outlays Could Equal '$200 Billion Event.'" MSNBC (September 13).

Zwerdling, Daniel. n.d. "Nature's Revenge: Louisiana's Vanishing Wetlands." Transcript. *American RadioWorks*. http://www.americanradioworks.org/features/wetlands/index.html.

Chapter 16
Metro Nature: Its Functions, Benefits, and Values

KATHLEEN L. WOLF

A family leaves its urban row house on a sunny morning. Family members say goodbyes under the branches of a street tree. Mom walks the children through the neighborhood park to the schoolyard, recently landscaped by students to create a butterfly garden. She continues on, glancing at emerging seedlings when passing the community garden on her way to the bus stop. She boards a bus to get to work, and fellow riders peer into a green belt along the route. Dad walks down the street, shaded by overhead canopy, past small but well-tended yards. A few minutes later he arrives at his workplace, entering a building with a green roof.

Metro nature inhabits the places where people live, work, learn, and play in cities. The urban forest, community gardens, parks and open space, and public landscapes provide green backdrops for the daily routines of millions. Where not planned or planted, the inexorable energy of volunteer seeds and plants eventually interrupts the grip of pavement. If encouraged, metro nature seeps into the lives of urbanites through beauty and curiosity. But metro nature is not necessarily the nature of America's cultural identity or idealism. City green often does not fully measure up to what many consider to be "natural." Consequently, many overlook and often take it for granted.

Metro nature poses many quandaries for a society that favors individualism and private property rights. It is a civic resource that does not respect intentions of possession or exclusion. Gated gardens exist, providing joy and beauty to a nature hoarder. But urban greening is often a civic natural resource, with attendant tensions of who is to receive benefit and who is to steward the resource to sustain its generosity.

This chapter has two purposes. First, it traces the historical roots of American attitudes toward nature. Second, it takes up a key pragmatic concern of contemporary times: how to justify public expenditures for natural resources that offer little promise of generating marketable goods. It presents a set of valuation concepts that place metro nature in the realm of economics, a major driver of contemporary decision-making in public policy and budgeting. Concepts are drawn from a wide range of social research.

Looking Back: Americans and Nature

At its most fundamental, nature is the source of human sustenance and livelihood. Yet many perceive the processes of productivity as far removed from urban centers. Certain cultural biases preclude thinking about nature in cities as anything more than a means of urban beautification, as a way to mask or screen sensory offenses. While there are notable exceptions as more city leaders employ ecology to enhance the sustainability and efficiencies of cities, historical and cultural precedents continue to shape American perceptions and expectations of everyday nature. Nature is a work of the mind, and people build images on strata of shared memory and ideals.

Agrarian Society

Thomas Jefferson's visions of an agrarian-based society provide the earliest American perceptions of nature. An outspoken proponent of a new republic made up of communities of small family farms, Jefferson imagined an America where agriculture-dependent citizens owned and worked their own plots of land, making them free and beholden to no one. He believed the qualities of the hard-working, self-sufficient farmer were essential for the creation and maintenance of a democratic self-governing nation.

Jefferson held that manufacturing and associated practices of commerce distorted relationships among men, bred dependence and servility, and spawned greed and corruption (Jefferson 1982: 165). While later recognizing the economic need for factories in an emergent economy, he always retained a high regard for the honorable, hard-working farmer. He believed that the nation's moral security rested in its agricultural community: "Corruption of morals in the mass of cultivators is a phaenomenon of which no age or nation has furnished an example." He saw farmers in communion with nature's beneficial influence and close to divine laws and moral principles: "Those who labour in the earth are the chosen people of God," endowed by the Creator with "substantial and genuine virtue"—to keep alive the "sacred fire" (1982: 164–65).

American geography made Jefferson's political vision credible. The frontier extended unimaginable distances, providing an ongoing supply of land for settlement and for creating livelihood through labor. This phenomenon supported an evolving theme in the American consciousness, a sense of the country being a new and different society, premised on a model of democratic self-government and nurtured by a bountiful landscape that afforded a regenerating influence on its inhabitants.

These beliefs became embedded in American political rhetoric. While particularly pervasive in the 1800s, the image of the good American farmer persists today. Marketing and public imagery continues to tap a sentimental connection to the land, as images of the country farm deep in the national collective consciousness.

WILDERNESS RECKONINGS

Wilderness constitutes another deeply rooted image in American culture. Initially, wilderness was the unknown, the disordered, and the uncontrolled. The compulsion to understand, order, and transform the environment in the interest of survival and, later, success has been central to civilization. American colonists regarded wilderness as a wasteland to be conquered in the name of progress and civilization. They were so surrounded by wilderness that they lacked appreciation. But they built a civilization from the raw materials of the physical wilderness. Soon, wilderness taming became a symbol of strength, identity, and meaning for an emergent America (Nash 1982: xii).

This symbol became even more potent as the exploration and settlement of the continent made pristine wildlands scarce. By the nineteenth century, Americans saw the wilderness as an asset, not a liability. Once threatening the very survival of individuals and communities, wilderness now served as a peaceful sanctuary.[1] Henry David Thoreau captured the changed attitude, asserting that "in wildness is the preservation of the world." He associated a sense of ethical and moral renewal with wilderness encounters. Nonetheless, a universally shared definition or image of wildness remains elusive. Some assume that wilderness is "out there," and its very existence is the antidote for the poisons of industrial society (Schama 1995). Others regard the "healing wilderness" attitude as a romantic notion, a cultural anachronism that locks up the resources needed for enterprise and commerce.

CONSERVATION OR PRESERVATION?

Between 1850 and 1920, a new consciousness emerged in the United States as Americans developed a growing appreciation for nature as an economic, aesthetic, and spiritual resource, together with an emergent conviction that nature's resources were increasingly imperiled. In 1893, historian Frederick Jackson Turner put forward the "frontier thesis," arguing that the pioneer encounter with the wilderness forged the fundamental American identity, its sense of exceptionalism and power. Lamenting the loss of the frontier, he was writing just as the U.S. Census proclaimed that the frontier was "closed." Turner's concerns also intersected with major national transformations: the emergence of industrialization, rapid urbanization, full-fledged commercial agriculture, and large-scale natural resource extraction.

In this environment, a number of activists and writers crafted new philosophical perspectives on nature. These ideas and ensuing political action would ensure preservation of wildlife and landscapes of great natural beauty, and encourage the wise and scientific use of natural resources (Heckscher 1996). Yet, an enduring tension crystallized between preservationists and conservationists, and has shaped American attitudes into contemporary times.

Some advocates proclaimed the spirituality and virtue of untrammeled nature, and were alarmed by the dramatic changes on the landscape associated with the voracious appetite for land ownership that was a hallmark of America's maturing democracy. Bold, dramatic landscapes came to typify sublime aesthetics, and a sense of divinity that was not limited to predemocratic traditions of church authority. Naturalist John Muir articulated preservationist values, seeing the wilderness as a place of personal renewal and solace (Worster 2005). Preservationists claimed that certain wild places were irreplaceable natural and historic treasures. Distinct landscape settings merited reserve status to assure that current and future generations had opportunity for appreciation and respite. Political action resulted in the formation of the National Park Service to dedicate special landscapes for that appreciation and for recreation and scientific study.

Others urged conservation of natural lands "for the greater good for the greatest length." They called for the regulated use of nature for public activities and commercial endeavors. Their efforts yielded the U.S. Forest Service, an agency first headed by Gifford Pinchot (Pinchot 1919: 48). Inspired by George Perkins Marsh's *Man and Nature* (1864), conservationists forged a new way of looking at the natural world, issued ominous warnings about man's altering and exhausting the land, and inspired practical correctives, including reforestation, watershed management, soil conservation, and controlled grazing (Lowenthal 2000). Conservationists aimed to exploit natural resources, while putting in place effective stewardship and indefinite provision of goods and services. Their view blended natural resource management with the nation's economic well-being. They recognized the potential of applied science harnessed to provide public good and reoriented public policy to resource use and allocation to maintain productive enterprise by avoiding resource depletion.

ECOLOGICAL REACTIONS

Within the writings of the early conservation movement were hints of another perspective on nature and society that would gain prominence in the mid-twentieth century. In earlier works, be they about resource use or reserve status, nature was depicted as static. Landscapes not impacted by human activity were thought to remain largely intact. New insights recognized that nature is dynamic, and ongoing change is the consequence of interacting materials, organisms, and forces. Several key works nudged new thoughts. Nathaniel Shaler's *Man and the Earth* (1905) called for future human relationships with the natural world to be characterized by a new consciousness and ethical responsibility based on ecology and biodiversity loss. Frederic E. Clements's *Plant Succession* (1916) proposed a dynamic model of the growth of vegetation that moved toward an eventual condition of equilibrium and Aldo Leopold's *Sand County Almanac* (1949) pushed the idea of an evolutionary ecology to the forefront of public awareness. By the 1960s, Rachel Carson's best-selling *Silent Spring* (1962) shocked readers with descriptions of the horrendous effects of pesticides on animal and human life. Together these works ushered in a broader set of attitudes about the deleterious consequences of human industry in nature. Nature was cast as an inherently bountiful yet fragile public good, and technology as an evil destroyer that debased nature and endangered its benefits. By the 1970s, reformers enacted public policy, including the Clean Air and Water Acts and the Endangered Species Act, to restore nature and regain environmental stability.

METRO NATURE REALITIES

In this brief history of public policy concerning nature in America, a consistent antiurban, antimodernism message lies just below the surface. The views of writers, activists, and reformers are associated with "wide open spaces"—farm fields, bold panoramic landscapes, or vast stands of managed forests—not urban greenery. Most insistent is the assumption that nature is a physical place that is "unspoiled" or not threatened by human activity. American Romantic writers perpetuated this theme when they "took nature to mean, . . . what man has not made, though if he made it long enough ago—a hedgerow or a desert—it will usually be

included as natural" (Coates 1998: 3).Thus, preservationists, conservationists, and ecologists may have disagreed on the values and uses of pristine landscapes, but generally considered urban landscapes to be
tainted, if not unnatural.

Nevertheless, nature occupies a special place in the human spirit.
Even as wilderness advocates directed public attention to the purity and
sacredness of wild nature, they recognized the inseparableness of cultural nature in place and mind (Schama 1995). John Muir actually characterized Yosemite as a "park valley" and celebrated its resemblance to
"an artificial landscape garden . . . with charming groves and meadows
and thickets of blooming bushes." Henry David Thoreau wrote in his
journal in 1856 that "it is vain to dream of a wildness distant from ourselves. There is none such. It is in the bog in our brains and bowels, the
primitive vigor of Nature in us, that inspires that dream. I shall never
find in the wilds of Labrador any greater wilderness than in some recess
of Concord, i.e. than I import into it."

Over time America's population became increasingly urban. Only one
in ten Americans lived in cities in Jefferson's time. By the early 1900s,
only one in ten lived on farms. Today, nearly 85 percent of the U.S. population lives in urbanized areas. While large natural landscapes are the
places of people's imaginings, the reality is that most spend their time
in and around everyday nature in metropolitan natural areas. With few
exceptions these are leftover spaces, isolated parks and open spaces that
have little interconnection. While some cities have formal parks, products of an earlier era's civic-minded organizations or individuals, or
green belts, pocket parks, and community gardens, many do not have
such resources in adequate supply. In addition, many green spaces suffer from overuse and inadequate maintenance efforts. Most elements of
the urban nature palette are less than adequately cared for.

Despite a historic trend of public indifference to urban greenery,
some voices have called attention to the importance of nature in cities.
The most historically significant is Frederick Law Olmsted (1822–1903),
the designer of New York's Central Park. An enthusiastic advocate for
urban parks and boulevards, Olmsted left extensive written commentary
on the implementation, modification and maintenance of park designs.
He also imbedded social commentary about the value of urban greening
in these writings. He wrote:

Such a scheme [for a Philadelphia park] should, in the first place, provide
ample opportunity for comparatively private walking exercise in the fresh air; . . .
its next, and in many respects, its most important object should be to appropriate the best series of beautiful landscape pictures that can be included in a
tract of ground of not unreasonable extent; and its last main purpose, . . . should
be to secure ground which . . . delicate and refined in general character and

abounding in suggestions, at least, of seclusion and tranquility, should also be recognized as offering an opportunity and occasion for constantly recurring public gatherings of a lively and festive character. (Olmsted 1992a: 231)

Most local parks and open spaces are in the purview of municipal governments that aim to satisfy local recreational and aesthetic needs. However, a few federal or state initiatives address urban natural areas, but not systematically. The USDA Forest Service distributes funds to encourage urban forestry programs and the Environmental Protection Agency has programs that address urban lands or waters that pose public health risks, such as brownfields, that may be restored to serve as public green space. But few agencies have considered a full picture of urban nature, in its various inceptions and expressions, as an integral component of city systems, and worthy of sustained dedicated staff and budget. One barrier to such an approach has been a lack of appreciation of the economic values of urban nature.

Ironically, Olmsted foretold the economic value of metro nature investment that merited greater policy attention:

The multiplication of large towns, and the increase in population of many old towns . . . has led to a careful investigation of the causes of degeneration and demoralization to which men, when living in dense communities, are known to have been subject, and to the experimental trial of certain means intended to prevent acts and discourage habits, among the people of towns, which have been found harmful, and to facilitate acts and habits of a different kind.

The result of these trials has been such, that various measures are now generally regarded as in the highest degree economical, which, not a very long time ago, would have been deemed wildly extravagant, such for instance, as the general provision under municipal governments of street lights and side-walks, water works and sewers.

Provisions for attracting dwellers in towns to air, refresh, and recreate themselves at frequent intervals, in grounds preserved against the conditions which prevail in the streets and wherever buildings are closely associated, have been latterly classed, by all who have given much intelligent attention to the subject, among these established requirements of a sound municipal economy. (Olmsted 1992b: 293)

While earlier generations understood the economic benefits of nearby nature, can today's leaders translate metro nature benefits into economic terms?

The Economics of Metro Nature

While the discourse on the humanistic contributions of nature to individuals, communities, and society was once prominent in public debate, today's decision makers are more inclined to pursue observed facts and economic valuations as the bases for public policy. Even though they may privately acknowledge the experiential aspects of human encounters with nature, they premise their public actions on empirical sources.

Until recently, analysts regarded the reported benefits of urban greening concerning human health, happiness, functioning, and spirit as important, but not quantifiable. However, in recent decades, researchers have employed science to explore the extent and quality of the "human services" of urban greening. This application of scientific methods to this issue has had two outcomes. First, the observed benefits of restorative experiences and social renewal due to time spent in gardens and parks have been intuitively noted for centuries, and are now confirmed. Second, and more important, the systematic, critical approaches of science have revealed greater texture and dimension in the human relationship to nature. We can describe benefits in terms of psychology, physiology, and sociology, and recognize variability across place, time, and human groups. This critical mass of knowledge provides urban greening advocates with undeniable evidence about the importance of green spaces in cities.

Much of the current urban research centers on the value of ecosystem services and green infrastructure. Ecosystem services are the processes by which the environment produces essential resources for fundamental human life-support, such as clean air and water, fisheries habitat, and plant pollination. Green infrastructure involves using landscape systems to provide biotechnology services and grey infrastructure alternatives on a metropolitan or regional scale. Because they are fairly new in application, both concepts entail two sets of understandings. First, they require identification of the character of the resource or service being supplied by a natural system, and the "consumer" unit of society—community, city, nation, or planet—being served. Second, their economic valuation is based on public goods theory, a mode of thinking that explains behaviors surrounding the use and exchange of nonmarket goods and services.

Public goods differ from market goods in several ways. First, their consumption by one does not reduce the amount available for another.[2] Second, their consumption is nonexcludable—that is, it is nearly impossible to exclude any nonpaying individuals from consuming the good. Here is an example of public good/market good differential applied to nature: any number of people who walk under a street tree will enjoy its shade and beauty irrespective of who pays for the planting and maintenance of the tree. This contrasts with trees grown for timber harvest; owners of such a forest can legally exclude others from using it, and once consumed, the forest will not be used again for many years.

Most forms of urban greening—community gardens, the urban forest, parks, greenbelts—are public goods. Unlike private goods and services that are valued through market prices, public goods do not have a pricing vehicle. Private land owners and managers neither receive a readily calculated return on investment for creating or conserving metro nature, nor do they have any incentives to include consideration of metro nature in land-use decisions, market transactions, and capital investment allocations.

Government authorities are the ones who regularly invest in public resources that members of society intuitively accept as providing value; examples include education, emergency response systems, and transportation. Often, proposals that incur public costs or affect private development bring forward advocates with evidence on how much (market) value will be gained or lost should the proposal go forward. Often, those who favor conserving or creating noncommodity nature are at a disadvantage in political debates because they cannot forward similar arguments. A lack of a monetary estimate of value for metro nature suggests that nature has zero value, or more commonly, that costs of urban nature are not offset by any economic gains (Boyer and Polasky 2004). For public officials, it would be helpful in knowing when to invest in a public good like metro nature if there were some way to estimate the values of nature's services in order to weigh this against economic returns from development or foregone payments for other municipal infrastructure. It is useful to be able to express the gains or losses in values in metro nature in monetary terms to equalize local land use debates.

A fair comparison of policy alternatives requires that all the consequences of a proposal be weighed, not just those that are easily measured and valued in monetary terms because they are bought and sold in a market. To fill this void, economists and others have attempted to supply monetary estimates of value created by nature. To this end, they have developed a number of methods for estimating nonmarket benefits and applying such methods to a variety of ecosystem services. However, most have applied their measures to rural land or forests, not urban settings. Nonetheless, as is seen later in this chapter, they can use the same methods to estimate values of metro nature public goods.

Valuation Methods

In instances when nature is a source of renewable, tangible products, conservation-oriented resource managers can measure "direct market value" because the output can be bought and sold in a market. Or when direct extraction of a good from a nature setting is possible, analysts can measure the exchange value of trade "goods." Examples include fruits harvested from ornamental street trees, milled wood from removed hazard trees, or wood chip mulch from wind-felled park trees. These products may be intentional yields or circumstantial goods exploited by opportunistic individuals. While there are exceptions, such as some community gardens, market productivity is rarely a primary objective of metro nature planning and management.

When markets do not exist for a nature resource, analysts can use two other measures: "nonconsumptive use" and "indirect use" values (Boyd 2006). They can calculate nonconsumptive use values for many of the human services provided by metro nature. A nature class for elementary students, conducted in a greenbelt is an example. They can also calculate indirect use values: the benefit of a patch of nature experienced at a location removed from the actual site. Improved water quality in an urban stream due to a bioswale installation in a nearby parking lot is an example. They quantify nonconsumptive and indirect use values using nonmarket valuation techniques. Some examples of the use of nonmarket valuation techniques follow.[3]

Travel Cost. When experiencing metro nature involves travel and spending, the calculation of such expenditures supplies an indication of the implied value of the nature service. The method typically sums costs across a population of visitors or users. An example is a tally of visitor spending to visit a floral display in a park, including transportation and incidentals such as meals or souvenirs. Such values can only be calculated if detailed information is available about the characteristics of users and their visitation patterns to a single park or across an entire park system. Travel cost method has been used extensively in wildland recreation valuations (such as national parks) but less so in urban applications.

Hedonic Pricing. Demand for services may be reflected in prices that people pay for associated goods. Hedonic pricing is defined as the observed market prices for goods having multiple attributes that can be statistically pulled apart to uncover the value of a particular characteristic for which there may not be an overt indicator of value. Analysts commonly use residential sales prices to estimate the value of various aspects of environmental quality. Real estate sales data typically include structural and neighborhood characteristics. Employing Geographic Information System (GIS) locational data on environmental conditions and quality allows estimates of the relationship between variability on one characteristic (such as number of trees in a yard or building floor space) and property value by holding other characteristics constant. One drawback of the method is that it only measures the perceived value of nearby property owners, but not of people who are some distance away and may benefit (such as occasional visitors to a regional park).

Avoided Costs. Nature services create savings on services otherwise required if such services were not available. Such savings accrue as a result of actions that reduce expenses for materials, human resources, treatments, or mitigation. In other words, they allow communities to avoid costs. Examples related to metro nature usually involve avoided costs to a municipal government or other public agency rather than expenditures for individuals. For instance, retaining urban forest canopy is likely to reduce storm-water quantity, which means that a city public works department would not have to install larger pipes to manage peak rainfalls.

Replacement Costs. Human-constructed production systems can replace the services provided by a metro nature system, and the resulting costs provide a value estimate for foregone functions and benefits. For instance, if a long-standing community garden is converted to a building site, then the costs of purchasing produce from a store can be tallied across user households. Urban wetlands serve as flooding buffers, expanding and contracting with seasonal precipitation. If removed those functions must be replaced by an engineered system and capacity costs can be estimated.

Factor Income. In rural or wildland settings, healthy ecosystems can enhance incomes by improving the condition of a resource. Incomes of fishermen, for example, can be increased if watershed management improves the condition of a commercial fishery. This approach has rarely been applied to metro nature.

Contingent Valuation. In the absence of observable behavior (such as travel or house prices), survey-based or stated-preference methods can yield monetary values of metro nature. Typically, a survey poses hypothetical scenarios that have descriptions of alternatives. Respondents express their willingness to pay for a proposed nature improvement (such as a new park or restoration of an existing park), or willingness to accept payment for the loss or decline of a natural element (such as loss of a scenic view). The responses produce an estimate of the mean willingness to pay by a selected population of people for an environmental amenity.

Contingent valuation can raise questions about reliability because people may not respond carefully to hypothetical situations. Adding conjoint analysis to the survey supplements and helps validate the data. Here, a survey asks people to respond to different sets of choice attributes (such as the recreational facilities of a park). If one of the choice attributes is a cost (such as a user's fee) then results of conjoint analysis can indicate whether the public prefers hiking trails over play lots, for instance, and what they are willing to pay for park use. Contingent valuation and conjoint analysis studies have been used to estimate the value of many wildland and rural environmental amenities, and are now being applied more widely in metro nature situations.

VALUATION EXAMPLES

Some progress has been made in understanding the economics of metro nature. Well-planned and -maintained nature elements, ranging from a single tree to parks, are associated with higher prices and payments. One well-documented effect on residential property values is the "proximate principle." Numerous studies have shown that appraised property values of homes that are adjacent (or proximate) to naturalistic parks and open spaces are typically valued at about 8 to 20 percent more than comparable properties (Crompton 2001). Variability is dependent on the usage rate of a park, quality of care and upkeep, and distance of the property from a park boundary. In addition, the presence of trees has been found to increase the selling price of a residential unit from 1.9 percent to 4.5 percent to 7 percent.[4]

Views of natural features, particularly trees and forests, also affect market value. The natural vegetation of urban parks is judged to enhance scenic value while manmade objects decrease visual quality (Schroeder 1982). Visual quality and property value have been documented to a limited extent in urban settings. Residential housing prices vary from 4.9 percent with a forest view (Tyrvainen and Miettinen 2000) to 8 percent with a park view (Luttik 2000).

Such assessments are typically made using hedonic valuation methods. Urban areas are ideal for application of this approach because there is a wealth of data available on house and property sales. Arguably, hedonic values can be capitalized on by local government to increase property tax assessments or excise taxes paid on a property sales. The incremental value across all properties influenced by a natural feature can be aggregated, and the case may be made that the sum is adequate to pay for annual debt and maintenance of a metro nature site or feature.

These patterns of economic valuation are consistent with public judgments of visual quality and aesthetics. The presence of old, large trees has been shown to increase the attractiveness of town streets (Schroeder and Cannon 1987) and positively affect the psychology of residents (Sheets and Manzer 1991). Cognitive responses to the presence of vegetation may enhance economic activity in communities. A study found that rental rates of commercial office properties were about 7 percent higher on sites with a quality landscape, including trees (Laverne and Winson-Geideman 2003). The contingent valuation method has been used to explore consumer response. Multiple studies of retail behavior show that shoppers say that they are willing to pay about 9 to 12 percent more for products in downtown business districts with trees versus comparable places without trees. Customer service, merchant helpfulness, and product quality are all judged to be better by shoppers in areas with trees (Wolf 2005). Drivers viewing commercial settings (such as auto sales and motels) from a high-speed highway had more positive impressions of a community with roadside landscape that included trees and said they would be willing to pay from 7 to 20 percent more for goods and services there (Wolf 2006).

The Economic Valuation of Human Benefits and Services

Studies about the psychosocial benefits of the human experience of urban nature provide a broader basis for the economic valuation of metro nature. Emanating from public health, environmental psychology, sociology, urban planning, urban forestry, and geography, these studies display a consistent pattern of positive outcomes associated with nature contact. The theoretical underpinnings of the results are quite varied, however.

Disciplines use different methods to assess benefits outcomes, from the quantitative to the qualitative. They include rigorous correlation and experimental approaches. The data ranges from stated preferences for city scenes, from which categories of nature content and perception are statistically distilled, to physiological measures (such as blood pressure and heart rate) that indicate remarkably rapid response to views of nature. Qualitative data-collection methods include systematic and formal prompts (such as journals or in-depth interviews) to urge people to reflect on what provides meaning, solace, and wonder in their lives, and nature experiences are often important factors.

The categories of human benefits typically listed for ecosystem services include aesthetic, recreation, and (eco)tourism, cultural and artistic inspiration, spiritual and historic, and scientific and educational. These concepts capture important functions but their descriptions often imply a distancing of nature from the everyday, suggesting that nature provides respite only when one is active within a nonurban setting. Perhaps this outlook reflects historic preservation and conservation attitudes. Today approximately 85 percent of the U.S. population lives in urbanized landscapes. The studies that follow suggest that nature experiences should be integral to life's routines in cities and towns. The research on the human dimensions of urban greening confirms Olmsted's observations that intentional pursuits of nature experience not only provide benefits, but that a ubiquitous backdrop of nature settings within urban areas mitigates many of the harsh consequences of urban living. "Nearby nature" is essential nature.

PHYSICAL HEALTH

The relationship between health and nature offers a significant path for metro nature valuation. An enormous body of work has emerged in recent years. For example, hospital patients who have a view of nature recover faster from surgery and require less medication for pain (Ulrich 1984). Obesity research is another rich source of qualifying data for the valuation of metro nature. This research has documented the dramatic rise in the percentage of people who are overweight or obese, conditions that contribute (over the life of the average person) to increases in diabetes, cancer, and heart disease. Economic consequences of routine, mild exercise, when aggregated across entire cities or the nation, are striking. Medical expenses are lower for people who do routine physical activities and exercise. Studies suggest that when inactive adults increase their participation in regular moderate physical activity, annual mean medical costs are reduced by $865 per person (in 2000 dollars) (Pratt, Macera, and Wang 2000). In addition, researchers have recently calculated the implications of rising obesity rates in relationship to the workplace. Over the last decade the state of California has experienced one of the fastest rates of increase in adult obesity in the United States. Researchers found that the combined cost of physical inactivity and obesity reached an estimated $21.7 billion in 2000 (CDHS 2005: 65). This health trend impacts the business sector, since costs include direct and indirect medical care ($10.2 billion), workers' compensation ($338 million), and lost productivity ($11.2 billion).

Currently, the Centers for Disease Control (CDC) and various federal resources agencies are collaborating on studies of how urban form (street layout and the presence of sidewalks) can encourage walking and biking. The CDC is also considering how community volunteerism and outdoor programs can boost activity levels. Having nearby trees and parks may help urban dwellers choose to walk to work or school. Physical comfort contributes to such decisions. Urban heat islands occur where impervious surfaces dominate, resulting in ambient temperatures that are 2 to 11F greater than surrounding landscapes (EPA 2004). Elevated temperatures contribute to such heat-related health problems as dehydration. Ground level heat also increases air pollution levels, leading to higher incidence of respiratory ailments. One of the most cost-effective means of mitigating urban heat islands is tree planting (Akbari, Davis, Dorsano, Huang, and Winnet 1992). Pavement under trees can be up to 34F cooler in arid climates, and every 10 percent increase in overall urban tree canopy generates approximately 2F reduction in ambient heat.

MENTAL HEALTH

Recent environmental psychology studies indicate that the presence of trees and nearby nature in human communities generates numerous and powerful psychological and cognitive benefits. A series of studies in Chicago have determined that trees in public housing neighborhoods lower levels of fear, contribute to less violent and aggressive behavior, and encourage better neighbor relationships and better coping skills (Kuo 2003). School-related studies show that children with ADHD show fewer symptoms (Taylor, Kuo, and Sullivan 2001), and girls show more self-discipline in academics if they have access to natural settings.

The effect of nature on workplace productivity is little understood. Metro nature may provide value in several ways. A study by Kaplan (1993) found that office workers with a view of nature are more productive, report fewer illnesses, and have higher job satisfaction. Some firms conduct team-building exercises through nature restoration projects. Group volunteering for the sake of civic ecology aids environmental sustainability, and may provide economic value for firms as work teams develop greater camaraderie and effective group dynamics.

The theory of restorative experiences underlies many of these positive responses (Kaplan and S. Kaplan 1989). The theory posits that modern work and learning demand extended periods of directed focus and attention. Such activity, particularly if sustained for long periods of time, can induce attention fatigue that results in irritability, loss of concentration, and inability to function effectively. Nature can provide restorative experiences, particularly if the setting contains these elements: being away (a sense of removal or separation from attention demands), fascination (being readily engaged in the features of the place), extent (the perception that there is adequate space for varied experiences), and compatibility (feeling that the space supports one's purposes or chosen activities). Notably, small parcels of well-designed urban nature as well as nearly wildland areas provide these conditions.

Investigators focusing on urban nature benefits are now considering the issue of "dosage." What are the elements of nature and the exposure times that most effectively influence psychosocial improvement? Additional knowledge in answer to this question will have economic consequences, since it is possible that nature experience doses may alleviate or reduce pharmaceutical treatments.

SOCIAL ECOLOGY

In response to ever increasing evidence about the environmental and psychosocial benefits of urban greening, some local governments are responding by creating and managing metro nature as comprehensive systems of parks, open space, tree canopy, and community gardens. While few cities have achieved green infrastructure systems that rival the integrity or completeness of grey infrastructure systems (such as transportation or utilities), a contemporary recognition of a need for nature and ecosystems that are systematically integrated with other urban systems represents a major change in public programs.

If comprehensively developed across an entire city, or at least subregions of the city, metro nature provides community-wide benefits. For example, urban sociology studies suggest that urban greening enhances interactions among individuals, within small groups, and across neighborhoods. It can increase perceptions of personal safety, and is associated with crime reduction. Public housing residents have reported that they would feel a greater sense of safety in their development if it had well-maintained landscaping including trees and grass (Kuo, Bacaicoa, and Sullivan 1998). A follow-up study found that greener public housing neighborhoods tend to be safer, with fewer incivilities and reported crime (Kuo and Sullivan 2001). Views of green space from homes are linked to greater perceptions of well-being and neighborhood satisfaction (Kaplan 2001). Active involvement in community greening and nature restoration projects can produce a range of social benefits that range from healthy food production to strengthening intergenerational ties and organizational empowerment (Westphal 2003). Improved community relations can translate into economic value if individuals and urban districts have less need for professional and public services and the costs associated with them.

An example of such savings in public services is the Crime Prevention Through Environmental Design (CPTED) program that was launched in the 1970s as an indirect means to deter crime. In its early iterations, CPTED participants altered physical conditions of public spaces to deter or inhibit activities that would facilitate crime. For instance, they thinned tall dense vegetation located adjacent to walkways used at night. In its second generation, CPTED, or Situational CPTED (Saville 1998), promotes a holistic approach to community dynamics and the conditions that foster crime. Its adherents encourage social monitoring of public spaces as a form of self policing in addition to modifying the physical characteristics of a place. For instance, encouraging after hours use of schools may increase the number of people moving about a neighborhood, providing more "eyes on the street" to deter crime. Research suggests that urban greening programs are one way to promote community organization and the formation of social capital, important conditions to help discourage criminal activity (Saegert and Winkel 2004).

Social scientists at Cornell University are exploring the intriguing idea that citizen involvement in urban greening promotes community resilience, which may enable more effective response to local disasters or security threats (Tidball and Krasny 2007). They hypothesize that urban community greening integrates natural, human, social, financial, and physical capital in ways that encompass diversity, self-organization, and adaptive learning and management. Ongoing activity and adaptive response in favorable conditions develops positive feedback loops that have the potential to play a key role in supporting urban community resilience before and after a disaster or conflict. Such ideas certainly complement the observed outcomes of Nobel Peace laureate Waangari Mathai's Green Belt movement in Kenya. While Mathai's programs were ostensibly to prevent landscape degradation with tree planting, the social outcomes included empowerment and social capital strengthening.

Looking Forward

Scientific understanding about how metro nature benefits people has expanded substantially. Nonetheless, there is a lag in policy response since many municipalities still regard urban nature as the "parsley around the pig." Some may object to the whole exercise of nonmarket valuation as applied to the environment since the process is fraught with uncertainty and assumptions. The point of valuation analysis is not so much to think in money or market terms, but to frame choices and make clear the tradeoffs between alternative outcomes (Boyer and Polasky 2004). How do the costs and benefits of investments in natural capital compare to investments in other urban services such as law enforcement or education? Is the tradeoff worthwhile? These are the types of questions for which even preliminary valuation can provide useful information. Looking forward, what are the next steps?

ECONOMIC MODELING

Ecological economists have merged valuations of ecosystem services into broader models of cost benefit analysis. Despite the high rate of human contact with even small bits of nature in cities, current models do not adequately include economic valuations of the human services of metro

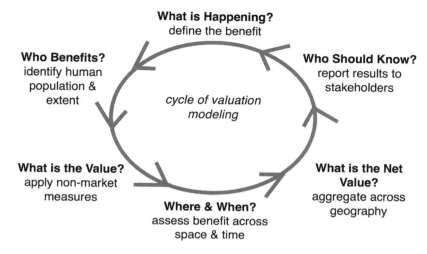

Figure 1. A valuation model.

nature. How might human dimensions be better represented in future efforts?

Building a valuation model, in a very general sense, includes four steps: first identifying benefits and then salient populations and context, next calculating valuations, and last aggregating benefits and values.[5] Figure 1 traces the process by which new information invites ongoing review and revision. First, benefits are determined and are expressed as components or units that can be counted, such as some measure of health improvement. Economic value per unit is then calculated, probably using nonmarket valuations. Next, specifics of who gains from the benefit, and the location in space and time of incidence of the benefit begins to connect the model to a place. Aggregation extrapolates a benefit that was probably conjured in a limited circumstance, and extends it to all suitable conditions. Reporting results enables ongoing review and use of the resulting economic information. Achieving complete precision in models will remain a challenge for some time. Nonetheless, the effort can provide compelling reasons for cities to justify continued and consistent investments in metro nature.

RESEARCH NEEDS

There are research activities that would help provide more robust valuation models. One approach would be to look comprehensively at the human services provided by metro nature over the human lifecycle.

What is the character, quality, and sequence of desirable nature experiences throughout an urban resident's life? Existing research suggests that benefits begin in childhood, extend through adolescence and early adulthood, continue during the active adult phase, and provide value for aging seniors. Relatively little is known about detailed response at different ages, or how such reactions dovetail together over the lifespan of a person, family, or extended group. Having such knowledge would enable urban planners and designers to create a diversity of "nature niches" in cities, including activity programs and visual elements that optimize the human services provided by public investment.

A second research program could fill in knowledge gaps about diversity in nature response based on cultural background. Studies over the past several decades indicate that different cultural groups have different preferences for the content and configuration of urban green spaces (Elmendorf, Willits, and Sasidharan. 2005). Some cultural groups prefer places and vegetation that enable experiences with small groups or in solitude, and that evoke more pristine nature settings. Other cultural groups prefer green spaces that have more open vegetation arrangements, creating spaces that are perceived to be safer, and are more conducive to large group gatherings. Attention to diverse and underserved populations would enable better benefits valuations and conclusions.

A third approach would be to focus research based on land use type. Most cities use similar land use demarcations, such as single and multi-family residential, industrial, retail and commercial, and transportation. Past research has focused on residential settings. Yet urbanites spend significant amounts of time in other land use contexts as they work, learn, and travel. A grove of trees in a schoolyard probably generates a host of public goods that differ from those generated by a grove of trees around the lunch room of industrial workers. Valuation modeling could be particularly effective if linked to geospatial distributions of human activity and responses that are associated with mapped land uses. Land use interventions that encourage greater physical activity across all places where people concentrate offer opportunities for substantial valuation gains, as the deferred costs of medical treatment for obesity are now some of the greatest public costs of our society.

For the Good of the City

This essay introduced historic yet persistent American perceptions of nature that are grounded in the large landscapes of the nation's early history, including agriculture, natural resources tracts, and wilderness preserves. It showed that today the majority of the U.S. population lives in urbanized areas. It also traced how scientists are coming to understand better how fundamentally important the presence of nature is in everyday life, and how it serves far more significant purposes than mere beautification and aesthetics. Nearby nature contributes to improved mental functioning, better physical health, more positive community dynamics, and general quality of life.

The essay argued that monetizing such benefits assists decision makers in public policy. It showed how some headway has been made to value the human services of metro nature but asserts that more should be done. Economists have developed nonmarket valuation techniques for lands and resources beyond the city limits, while others have looked at health relationships. Effectively integrating metro nature into the city by using the tools of scientific understanding and economic valuation will allow it to become the true inspiration for the good city.

References

Akbari, Hashem, Susan Davis, Sofia Dorsano, Joe Huang, and Steven M. Winnet, eds. 1992. *Cooling Our Communities: A Guidebook on Tree Planting and Light-Colored Surfacing.* Washington, D.C.: U.S. Environmental Protection Agency.

Anderson, Linda M., and H. Ken Cordell. 1988. "Influence of Trees on Residential Property Values." *Landscape and Urban Planning* 15: 153–64.

Boyd, James W. 2006. "The Nonmarket Benefits of Nature: What Should Be Counted in Green GDP?" Discussion Paper 06–24. Washington, D.C.: Resources for the Future.

Boyer, Tracy, and Stephen Polasky. 2004. "Valuing Urban Wetlands: A Review of Non-Market Valuation Studies." *Wetlands* 24, 4: 744–55.

California Department of Health Services (CDHS). 2005. "Obesity Costs California $21.7 Billion Annually." *Physician Law Weekly* (May 4).

Carson, Rachel. 1962. *Silent Spring.* Boston: Houghton Mifflin.

Clements, Frederic E. 1916. *Plant Succession: An Analysis of the Development of Vegetation.* Washington, D.C.: Carnegie Institution of Washington.

Coates, Peter A. 1998. *Nature: Western Attitudes Since Ancient Times.* Berkeley: University of California Press.

Crompton, John L. 2001. *Parks and Economic Development.* Washington, D.C.: American Planning Association.

de Groot, Rudolf S., Matthew A. Wilson, and Roelof M. J. Boumans. 2002. "A Typology for the Classification, Description and Valuation of Ecosystem Functions, Goods and Services." *Ecological Economics* 41: 393–408.

Dombrow, Jonathan, Mauricio Rodriguez, and C. F. Sirmans. 2000. "The Market Value of Mature Trees in Single-Family Housing Markets." *Appraisal Journal* (January): 39–43.

Elmendorf, William F., Fern K. Willits, and Vivod Sasidharan. 2005. "Urban Park and Forest Participation and Landscape Preference: A Review of the Relevant Literature." *Journal of Arboriculture* 31, 6: 311–17.

Heckscher, Juretta Jordan, ed. 1996. *The Library of Congress. Evolution of the American Conservation Movement, c.1850–1920.* Preface. http://memory.loc.gov/ammem/amrvhtml/cnchron2.html.

Jefferson, Thomas. 1982. "Query X1X." *Notes on the State of Virginia*. Ed. William Peden. New York: Norton.

Kaplan, Rachel. 1993. "The Role of Nature in the Context of the Workplace." *Landscape and Urban Planning* 26: 193–201.

———. 2001. "The Nature of the View from Home." *Environment and Behavior* 33, 4: 507–42.

Kaplan, Rachel, and Stephan Kaplan. 1989. *The Experience of Nature: A Psychological Perspective*. Cambridge: Cambridge University Press.

Kuo, Frances E. 2003. "The Role of Arboriculture in a Healthy Social Ecology." *Journal of Arboriculture* 29, 3: 148–55.

Kuo, Frances E., Magdalena Bacaicoa, and William C. Sullivan. 1998. "Transforming Inner-City Landscapes: Trees, Sense of Safety, and Preference." *Environment and Behavior* 30, 1: 28–59.

Kuo, Frances E., and William C. Sullivan. 2001. "Environment and Crime in the Inner City: Does Vegetation Reduce Crime?" *Environment and Behavior* 33, 3: 343–65.

Laverne, Robert J., and Kimberly Winson-Geideman. 2003. "The Influence of Trees and Landscaping on Rental Rates at Office Buildings." *Journal of Arboriculture* 29, 5: 281–90.

Leopold, Aldo. 1949. *Sand County Almanac*. New York: Oxford University Press.

Lowenthal, David. 2000. *George Perkins Marsh: Prophet of Conservation*. Seattle: University of Washington Press.

Luttik, Joke. 2000. "The Value of Trees, Water and Open Space as Reflected by House Prices in the Netherlands." *Landscape and Urban Planning* 48: 161–67.

Nash, Roderick. 1982. *Wilderness and the American Mind*. New Haven, Conn.: Yale University Press.

Olmsted, Frederick Law. 1992a. Report on Plans of the Park Commission of Philadelphia, December 4, 1867. *The Papers of Frederick Law Olmsted*, vol. 6, *The Years of Olmsted, Vaux & Company*. Ed. David Schuyler and Jane Turner Censer. Baltimore: Johns Hopkins University Press.

———. 1992b. Report on the Proposed City Park in Albany, N.Y., December 1, 1868. *The Papers of Frederick Law Olmsted*, vol. 6, *The Years of Olmsted, Vaux & Company*. Ed. David Schuyler and Jane Turner Censer. Baltimore: Johns Hopkins University Press.

Payne, B. R. 1973. "The Twenty-Nine Tree Home Improvement Plan." *Natural History* 82, 9: 74–75.

Pinchot, Gifford. 1910. *The Fight for Conservation*. New York: Doubleday.

Pratt, Michael, Caroline A. Macera, and Guijing Wang. 2000. "Higher Direct Medical Costs Associated with Physical Inactivity." *Physician and Sportsmedicine* 28, 10: 63–70.

Saegert, Susan, and Gary Winkel. 2004. "Crime, Social Capital, and Community Participation." *American Journal of Community Psychology* 34, 3–4: 219–33.

Samuelson, Paul A. 1954. "The Pure Theory of Public Expenditure." *Review of Economics and Statistics* 36, 4: 387–89.

Saville, Gregory. 1998. "New Tools to Eradicate Crime Places and Crime Niches." Paper presented at the Conference on Safer Communities: Strategic Directions in Urban Planning. Convened jointly by Australian Institute of Criminology and Victorian Community Against Violence. Melbourne, Australia.

Schama, Simon. 1995. *Landscape and Memory*. New York: Vintage.

Schroeder, Herbert W. 1982. "Preferred Features of Urban Parks and Forests." *Journal of Arboriculture* 8, 12: 317–22.

Schroeder, Herbert W., and William N. Cannon, Jr.. 1987. "Visual Quality of Residential Streets: Both Street and Yard Trees Make a Difference." *Journal of Arboriculture* 13, 10: 236–39.

Shaler, Nathaniel Southgate. 1905. *Man and the Earth.* Chautauqua, N.Y.: Chautauqua Press.

Sheets, Virgil L., and Chris D. Manzer. 1991. "Affect, Cognition and Urban Vegetation: Some Effects of Adding Trees Along City Streets." *Environment and Behavior* 23, 3: 285–304.

Taylor, Andrea Faber, Frances E. Kuo, and William C. Sullivan. 2001. "Coping with ADD: The Surprising Connection to Green Play Settings." *Environment and Behavior* 33, 1: 54–77.

Tidball, K. G., and M. E. Krasny. 2007. "From Risk to Resilience: What Role for Community Greening and Civic Ecology in Cities? In *Social Learning: Towards a More Sustainable World*, ed. Arjen E. J. Wals. Wageningen, The Netherlands: Wageningen Academic Press. 149–64.

Tyrvainen, Liisa, and Antti Miettinen. 2000. "Property Prices and Urban Forest Amenities." *Journal of Economics and Environmental Management* 39: 205–23.

Ulrich, Roger S. 1984. "View Through a Window May Influence Recovery from Surgery." *Science* 224, 27: 420–21.

U.S. Environmental Protection Agency (EPA). 2004. *Heat Island Effect.* www.epa.gov/heatisland/

Westphal, Lynne M. 2003. "Urban Greening and Social Benefits: A Study of Empowerment Outcomes." *Journal of Arboriculture* 29:3: 137–47.

Wolf, Kathleen L. 2005. "Business District Streetscapes, Trees and Consumer Response." *Journal of Forestry* 103, 8: 396–400.

———. 2006. "Assessing Public Response to the Freeway Roadside: Urban Forestry and Context Sensitive Solutions." *Transportation Research Record: Journal of the Transportation Research Board* 1984: 102–11.

Worster, Donald. 2005. "John Muir and the Modern Passion for Nature." *Environmental History* 10, 1.

Chapter 17
Green Investment Strategies: How They Matter for Urban Neighborhoods

SUSAN M. WACHTER, KEVIN C. GILLEN, AND CAROLYN R. BROWN

Urban greening is an important component of the broader category of "place-based investments." The mobility of global capital has transformed the rules for local economic growth, increasing the role of place based investments and local quality of life. These have joined traditional business location factors—such as availability of raw materials or port access—as important determinants of urban economic growth. In cities and their neighborhoods place-based investments are impacting the quality of life and long run sustainability of communities.

Because of the new role of quality of place, such investments are now critical public policy tools with the potential to turn around the decline of cities and their neighborhoods. Although the importance of place-based investments[1] is recognized, there is little empirical evidence directly quantifying their impact. Researchers have only begun to measure how specific place-based investments, such as new community gardens or newly landscaped commercial corridors, affect neighborhoods.

The purpose of this study is to describe a methodology for quantifying the economic benefits of green investment and to use the methodology to measure gains from recently implemented green investment initiatives in the City of Philadelphia. The methodology, which deploys precise, time-based spatial data to identify when and where investment occurs, permits the identification and measurement of the neighborhood-level effects of public investment.

The measurement of these gains can justify public spending. Place-based investments depend on public spending decisions rather than private action, due to the "collective action" problem. Individuals tend to underinvest in goods that provide benefits to others (positive externalities) since these gains to others are not accounted for in their investment decisions. It is up to the public sector to provide public goods. This means that place-based investments must rely on scarce public resources in order to be procured. Thus it is important to demonstrate that such strategies produce measurable improvements to neighborhood quality.[2]

We also can use this methodology for gaining a deeper understanding of the process of neighborhood change. Urban economists[3] and others have long discussed how physical signs of deterioration and distress accelerate the progression of neighborhood decline by inducing out-migration and abandonment. Transforming blighted vacant lots through greening activities may reverse this process through changing percep-tions of neighborhood distress, arresting rates of housing abandonment, and restoring the local property tax base. This can result in a "virtuous" cycle of lower tax rates which helps in the revitalization of older commu-nities.

Nonetheless, evidence identifying the impact of specific place based and additional growth investments has been limited due to data and technological barriers. This study benefits from advances in geographic information systems (GIS) technology which enables the merging and analysis of large spatial datasets.[4]

Most important, as discussed in detail below and in the chapters by Smith and Bonham in this volume, we take advantage of specific public initiatives on place-based green investment in Philadelphia and the availability of data on the place and timing of these investments. Using these data and methodology, we demonstrate that greening activities and place-based investments are responsible for considerable gains in the value of homes and the desirability of neighborhoods throughout the city of Philadelphia.

Urban Greening and Place-Based Investment in Philadelphia

Philadelphia, as a former manufacturing center, experienced a major population decline due to deindustrialization from approximately 2 mil-lion people in 1950 to 1.5 million in 2005. As a result, many neighbor-hoods show signs of disinvestment and blight.

The city currently has an estimated 40,000 vacant lots comprising upward of 1,300 total acres of land and 71,887 units of vacant housing (Census 2000), often a precursor to vacant land.[5] Blighted lots are dis-tributed throughout the city. With the exception of the center city busi-ness district, no neighborhoods are entirely exempt, although some are especially hard hit. In these neighborhoods, vacant lots and vacant and abandoned housing are sporadically distributed among semi-intact blocks of row houses, creating an irregular pattern of vacancy, with few large tracts appropriate for redevelopment. Given the spatial pattern of intermittent vacancy and occupancy, urban greening has emerged as a potentially key land management strategy in Philadelphia.

Philadelphia and similar declining cities are faced with the challenge of countering the effects of neighborhood decline and uneven development. Vacant lots are points of blight that can undermine the social fabric of neighborhoods. They contribute to crime and render neighborhoods unattractive, unhealthy, and unsafe for residents, particularly families with children, and they contribute to further disinvestment as they discourage maintenance of the existing housing stock.[6]

Philadelphia as a city of neighborhoods has the potential to deliver attractive housing in pleasant communities, but this potential is undermined by the pervasive disamenity of untended, blighted land. Throughout the city, green infrastructure has been neglected with the loss of trees, greenways and the neglect of streetscapes in major commercial corridors that are entryways to the city and its residential neighborhoods. The potential to reverse this and enhance the quality of life in Philadelphia neighborhoods is recognized but difficult to carry out. To do this requires collective will and funding.

Green investment is often an individual undertaking. People can and do plant their own trees in order to enhance the attractiveness of their homes when the benefits of doing so exceed the costs. However, without collective action, similar public investment may or may not occur, even when clearly desirable. The result is that worthy investment that can reverse neighborhood blight may not be undertaken. This also means that successful collective action can have large returns—indeed, far larger returns than undertaking individual greening investments.

This chapter shows a method to value the quality of life improvements in neighborhoods undertaking green investment strategies. These quality of life improvements are measured by estimating the increased willingness to pay for neighborhood amenities, including tree plantings, community corridor improvements, and vacant land clean-up and maintenance.

In a precursor to the city-wide study of these investment strategies, we first analyzed the impacts of vacant land cleanup in a specific area, New Kensington, which pioneered this strategy in a multiyear vacant land management program run jointly by the New Kensington Community Development Corporation (NKCDC) and the Pennsylvania Horticultural Society (PHS).[7] The NKCDC- and PHS-sponsored Vacant Land Management Program was launched in 1995 to address the growing crisis of vacant land caused by a cycle of abandonment, demolition, and neglect in this formally heavily industrialized community.

During the first year of the program, PHS planted street trees and established community gardens with organized block groups. By 1996,

NKCDC and New Kensington residents had implemented the first large-scale tree planting on six vacant lots. Following these initial plantings, joint efforts between NKCDC and PHS resulted in the ongoing establishment of community gardens, street-tree plantings, and stabilization of vacant land. NKCDC also began administering a side-yard program in 1996 that facilitated transfer of vacant property to adjacent home-owners.

The Vacant Land Management Program served as a pilot project for the city's Neighborhood Transformation Initiative (NTI)—a comprehensive campaign begun in 2002 to eliminate the blight caused by long-term vacant structures, abandoned automobiles, and trash strewn vacant lots. The city worked with PHS to design a citywide greening strategy to treat both existing vacant lots and new lots created through ongoing vacant property demolition. Vacant lots were cleared of debris, seeded, landscaped with tree plantings, and enclosed with rustic wood post fencing. Between 2000 and 2003, the program was responsible for cleaning, improving, and maintaining 12,186 lots. Another 18,800 lots were cleared of trash and debris.

NTI also supported improvements of commercial corridors that serve the city's low- and moderate-income neighborhoods. Besides NTI, BIDs also set out to improve commercial corridors. BIDs are geographically defined quasi-public agencies that provide collective public services (including improvements to public spaces) within their jurisdiction. Typical services offered within a BID include enhanced security, street cleaning, trash removal, and streetscape improvements such as landscaping, lighting and coordinated signage.

Special service districts such as BIDs are strategies often used by fiscally strapped cities that may not be capable of providing the high-quality public services required to improve failing neighborhoods and attract new residents and investment. Commercial establishments within the BID boundary pay an annual fee that covers the costs of the enhanced services provided within the BID, with the understanding that the improvements are likely to lead to increased foot traffic and greater commercial revenues in the district. The oldest and most successful BID in Philadelphia is the Center City District, started in 1991 to improve tourism and quality of life in the downtown area. The dataset employed for this research evaluated the impact of the nine BIDs located in neighborhoods across the city.

An Approach to Measuring the Economic Benefits of Green Investment

Despite the importance of efforts to revitalize communities, there is little dynamic research on the potential for new public investment and reinvestment to improve neighborhood quality. Increases in property values occur through "capitalization"—a process in which any asset gains in value when the per period returns on that asset increase. Thus, when neighborhoods become more satisfactory places to live, "returning" more quality of life, neighborhood housing prices increase.

Most studies of house-value capitalization deploy a traditional "hedonic" specification,[8] in which variables of interest, such as adjacency to a park, are added to a basic specification of house size, location, and other characteristics. Such a static approach, while quite useful, does not capture the gains from new investments and may underestimate the benefits of the amenity. Parks like other amenities may be associated with other positive housing characteristics. The correlated attributes may make it difficult to identify separately the positive impacts of the park.[9]

Here we not only enter the greening variables into the specification, but also include the timing of the greening initiative.[10] The methodology deploys an econometric analysis of both spatial and time-based data, and integrates separately collected datasets into one database. These include data on city of Philadelphia property sales and more than fifty attribute characteristics for over 120,000 properties and over 200,000 sales for the period from 1980 to 2005. Additional datasets on neighborhood attributes such as public safety, public transit accessibility, commercial-corridor quality, and schooling, as well as place-based investment data, were collected and integrated with the property database. The datasets permit the tracking of the quality and quantity of these investments by specific geographical location and, where available, the precise timing of public investments. In particular, the PHS provided data on the location and timing of new tree plantings, streetscape treatments, and vacant lot stabilization efforts. As a result, we are able to compare neighborhood values before and after these investments based on an analysis of nearby property sales.

These data are used to construct a larger spatial database that combines value and attribute data (such as property parcel price, square footage, and unit amenities) with basic geographic information (for example, street address, latitude and longitude, distance from central business district), and information on the property's relation to various public service areas, including the school district and police precinct where the property is located, and whether the property is in a business improvement district. The spatial database and GIS technology allow us to estimate a measure of the impact on values of many place-based variables defined at different geographical scales for individual neighborhoods and for the city as a whole.

These data also allow us to control for the many attributes that contribute to property values. Hedonic pricing models deconstruct a good or service traded in the marketplace into a bundle of distinct attributes. These attributes constitute the essential physical features demanded by consumers and can be valued individually.

In this study, as expected, we find that physical attributes associated with higher house prices include more square footage; larger lot size; better physical condition; amenities such as fireplaces, central air conditioning, or a garage; and being either in or relatively near downtown. Factors associated with lower house prices include a street-corner location, being renter-occupied, or being in a depreciated condition.

A time trend variable is incorporated into the model in order to control for the state of the overall housing market, which is highly dependent on the availability and cost of financing. Except for a period from 1988 to 1995, overall housing prices have gone up in Philadelphia over time through 2004, a period in which the cost of financing for home purchase declined.[11]

We also include measures of neighborhood public services. While we lack direct data on new investment in these services, we have some outcome measures, specifically a measure of school quality (high-school dropout rate) and a measure of public safety (index of local crime). We find again, as expected, that the quality of schools and public safety in a neighborhood also matter a great deal.[12] Our results indicate that higher crime rates are associated with lower home values on the order of about −14 percent for every 1 percent increase in the overall crime index. Furthermore, a high dropout rate in high schools, after controlling for the high poverty rate of the student body, is also shown to be negatively correlated with house prices, by approximately −5 percent.

Finally, location matters as measured not only by the distance to the central business district but also as measured by access to public transit. The results suggest a positive relationship between house values and proximity to subway stops. Homes within walking distance (less than 1/8 mile) of subway stops carry a price premium of 3 percent over those farther away.[13]

Findings on Place-Based Investment

The potential benefits of place-based investment are identified by measuring the additional value people place on living in neighborhoods where and when such investments have taken place. We test for the impact of public investment by identifying when and where they occur and their effect on the transaction prices of nearby properties. We include data on and discuss results separately for commercial-corridor improvements, vacant land management, neighborhood greening strategies, and BID initiatives.

COMMERCIAL GREENING

We use the phrase "commercial greening" to denote improvements to public spaces that are commercial in nature, for example, commercial streets or shopping centers. For a corridor rated as in "excellent" condition, being within a quarter mile of the corridor imparts an additional 23 percent to a home's value, while being beyond a quarter mile but within a half mile imparts an additional 11 percent. Being located within a BID service district, by contrast, is estimated to impart an additional 30 percent of value to house values. The value of the BID is higher than the value of an "excellent" commercial corridor because—presumably —a BID is already a commercial corridor in very good condition, plus BIDs offers additional public services—for example, extra signage, police, cleaning, seasonal decorating—that commercial corridors do not.

VACANT LAND MANAGEMENT

As we have discussed, vacant lots left in the wake of housing abandonment and demolition often have significant and adverse effects on a neighborhood's quality of life, attracting refuse and vandals and creating a perception of impaired public safety. Our findings indicate that adjacency to a neglected vacant lot subtracts 20 percent of value from a home relative to comparable homes farther from the site. Recent public initiatives have worked to "stabilize" these sites by cleaning and greening. This process involves removal of discarded trash; grading and amending the soil; planting grass, trees, and shrubbery; and even adding such amenities as benches, sidewalks, and fences. Our results indicate that these efforts almost entirely reverse the negative impact of adjacency to neglected vacant lots resulting in a gain in value of 19 percent.

NEIGHBORHOOD GREENING

Investment in "neighborhood greening" is a general term to denote everything from adding parks to improving streetscapes to planting new trees in public spaces. As the results listed in Table 1 suggest, proximity to a greening event positively affects home values. Proximity to a new tree planting is associated with an overall increase in house prices of 9 percent.

Streetscapes are part of the "green infrastructure" of the urban envi-

TABLE 1. SUMMARY OF GREEN INFRASTRUCTURE FINDINDS, PHILADELPHIA, 2004

	Percent impact	Dollar impact
I. Commercial greening		
≤¹/₄ mile to commercial corridor in "excellent" condition (net impact)	23	19,021
¹/₄–¹/₂ mile to commercial corridor in "excellent" condition (net impact)	11	9,097
Located in a business improvement district	30	24,397
II. Vacant lot managment		
Adjacent to vacant lot	− 20	(16,540)
Adjacent to stabilized, green lot	17	14,059
III. Neighborhood greening		
Near tree planting	9	7,443
Improvements to streetscapes	28	23,156

Magnitude of various estimated effects on house values from public investments, based on 2004 median house value of $82,700. "Percent impact" = expected percent change in value; "dollar impact" = "percent impact" times median house value.

ronment. A streetscape project represents horticultural treatments to a sidewalk or roadway that improve the appearance of the area, making it a more attractive and pleasant place. Treatments can include tree plantings, container plantings, small pocket parks, parking lot screens, and median plantings. Streetscapes tend to focus on commercial corridors with high visibility and high levels of pedestrian or vehicular traffic. Our results indicate that streetscaping imparts a considerable increase in surrounding home values as well, on the order of a 28 percent gain in value relative to similar homes in comparable areas without streetscape improvements.

In Table 1 we summarize the magnitude of the various estimated effects on house values from different public investments. The column "Percent Impact" shows the expected percent change in value from the base price.

Implications for the Effect of Greening and Place-Based Investment on Neighborhood Quality

The purpose of this chapter is to discuss a methodology for quantifying the economic benefits of green infrastructure. We identify key place-based green infrastructure public investments and demonstrate their potential impact using "willingness-to-pay" data as indicators of changes in the overall neighborhood quality of life. Overall, the empirical results suggest large-scale positive impacts from investment in public spaces.

Using these data and methodology, we confirm that greening activities and place-based investments confer additional value to homes and to the desirability of neighborhoods. Among the key findings are that (1) clearing and greening a vacant lot lead to a 17 percent rise in value for adjacent properties; (2) improvements to streetscapes increase the value of homes in proximity to the corridor by 28 percent; and (3) homes located within BIDs are valued 30 percent higher than comparable homes not in BIDs. By employing a contingent valuation method, which assigns a dollar value to the geographically distributed benefits of new place-based community amenities, our results can help to translate (abstract and theoretical) concepts such as "quality of life" or "sense of place" into measurable economic terms.

Such research as this contributes to our understanding of the determinants of how people value their neighborhoods by identifying the effects of place-based investments on property values in surrounding areas. While the importance of neighborhood effects of community investment seems intuitive, most studies fail to find empirical evidence of such neighborhood effects. Deploying a place-based methodology for evaluating the impact of place-based investments, making use of precise time-based, spatial information to identify when and where the investment occurs (while controlling for other property and neighborhood characteristics) can quantify the benefits of green investments. Since the focus is on investment strategies rather than static characteristics of neighborhoods, the information is relevant to community and city decisions on whether and which investments are supported.

The primary focus of the place-based investments studied here has been greening of public spaces. The methodology used is especially pertinent to studies of greening because the specific time- and space-based nature of greening events are both observable and measurable. As such, green investments in particular are a particularly apt subject category to measure the returns from place-based investments in public spaces. For policymakers, these results can assist in determining the expected return from place-based investments, as well as identifying the specific types of investments that yield the highest returns.

References

Bowes, David R. 2001. "Identifying the Impacts of Rail Transit Stations on Residential Property Values." *Journal of Urban Economics* 50, 1: 1–25.

Bradbury, Katherine, Christopher Mayer, and Karl Case. 2001. "Property Tax Limits and Local Fiscal Behavior: Did Massachusetts Cities and Towns Spend Too Little on Town Services Under Proposition 22?" *Journal of Public Economics* 80, 2: 287–312.

Case, Bradford, Henry O. Pollakowski, and Susan M. Wachter. 1991. "On Choosing Among House Price Index Methodologies." *American Real Estate and Urban Economics Association Journal* 19, 3: 287–307.

Correll, Mark R., Jane H. Lillydahl, and Larry D. Singell. 1978. "The Effect of Greenbelts on Residential Property Values: Some Findings on the Political Economy of Open Space." *Land Economics* 54, 2: 207–17.

Crompton, John L. 2000. "The Impact of Parks and Open Space on Property Values and the Property Tax Base." Ashburn, Virginia: National Recreation and Park Association.

Ellen, Ingird G., Michael H. Schill, Scott Susin, and Amy Ellen Schwartz. 2001. "Building Homes, Reviving Neighborhoods: Spillovers from Subsidized Construction of Owner-Occupied Housing in New York City." *Journal of Housing Research* 12, 2: 185–216.

Florida, Richard. 2003. *The Rise of the Creative Class, and How It's Transforming Work, Leisure, Community, and Everyday Life.* New York: Basic Books.

Gillen, Kevin, Thomas Thibodeau, and Susan Wachter. 2001. "Anisotropic Autocorrelation in House Prices." *Journal of Real Estate Finance and Economics* 23, 1.

Hammer, Thomas R, Robert E. Coughlin, and Edward T. Horn, IV. 1974. "Research Report: The Effect of a Large Park on Real Estate Value." *Journal of the American Institute of Planners* (July): 274–77.

Lee, Chang-Moo, Dennis P. Culhane and Susan M. Wachter. 1998. "The Differential Impacts of Federally Assisted Housing Programs on Nearby Property Values: A Philadelphia Case Study." *Housing Policy Debate* 10, 1: 75–93..

Lutzenhiser, Margot, and Noelwah R. Netusil. 2001. "The Effect of Open Spaces on a Home's Sale Price." *Contemporary Economic Policy* 19, 3: 291–98.

Mills, Edwin S., and Bruce W. Hamilton. 2004. *Urban Economics.* New York: HarperCollins.

Philadelphia City Planning Commission. 2005. *Vacant Land in Philadelphia: A Report on Vacant Land Management and Neighborhood Restructuring.* Philadelphia: City Planning Commission.

Rosen, Sherwin M. 1974. "Hedonic Prices and Implicit Markets: Product Differentiation in Pure Competition." *Journal of Political Economy* 82.

Rothenberg, Jerome. 1991. *The Maze of Urban Housing Markets: Theory, Evidence, and Policy.* Chicago: University of Chicago Press.

Thibodeau, Thomas, Kevin Gillen, and Susan M. Wachter. 2001. "Anisotropic Autocorrelation in House Prices." *Journal of Real Estate Finance and Economics* 23, 1.

Wachter, Susan M. 2005. "The Determinants of Neighborhood Transformation in Philadelphia—Identification and Analysis: The New Kensington Pilot Study." Report to the William Penn Foundation.

Wachter, Susan M., and Kevin Gillen. 2006. "Public Investment Strategies: How They Matter for Neighborhoods in Philadelphia—Identification and Analysis." Philadelphia: Wharton School, University of Pennsylvania.

Wachter, Susan M., and Grace Wong. 2007. "Green Cities Strategies, Home Values and Social Capital." *Real Estate Economics.*

Chapter 18

Measuring the Economic Impacts of Greening: The Center for Neighborhood Technology Green Values Calculator

Julia Kennedy, Peter Haas, and Bill Eyring

The natural resources that keep cities alive—clean air, water, land, and energy sources—are finite. The perception that these materials are free and limitless, however, has undermined the actual value of healthy natural resources.

In recent years this perception has begun to change. The high prices of petroleum and natural gas are invigorating the market for alternative energy technologies and products. The recently established CO_2 trade community has brought economic value to reducing emissions. A similar identification of the value of clean water sources and reliable water infrastructure is needed to promote stronger water resource management practices. According to the World Bank, water should be thought of "as a commodity, and full cost should be recovered for its supply, which would then, one hopes, amount to some kind of financial accountability in terms of supply costs, and presumably lead to improved efficiency" (Mau and Leonard 2004). If the costs and benefits of water infrastructure are known and are accurately quantified and compared, then users and decision-makers will be better able to make profitable decisions.

The Center for Neighborhood Technology (CNT), a Chicago-based nonprofit corporation that promotes the development of environmentally and economically equitable and sustainable communities, is supporting "green" or alternative stormwater management methods that can capitalize on the hidden assets of the urban environment by creating working landscapes in spaces that would be otherwise bare or would be green, but designed for aesthetic value alone. To this end, CNT has developed a quantitative tool, the Green Values Calculator, to compare the hydrologic and financial costs and benefits of green infrastructure to those of conventional stormwater management. With the value economics of stormwater management clear, determining and electing the improvement method that yields the maximum ecological and financial benefit can follow.

Knowing the economic value of green infrastructure can lead to policy and behavior change. The Green Values Calculator provides a tool to inform the full spectrum of stormwater management decision-makers from elected officials to citizens. The calculator can be used to produce specific quantitative data desired by government officials and civil servants, support the implementation of green infrastructure on a municipal scale, and develop qualitative information that explains the benefits of green infrastructure to the citizens considering green infrastructure features for their individual properties.

Stormwater and Pollution

Management of stormwater is not a new endeavor and, in fact, has been "problematic to some extent for as long as there have been cities, but the volume of stormwater continues to grow as development replaces porous surfaces with impervious blacktop, rooftop, and concrete" (Kloss and Calarusse 2006: 1). In the past, the primary threats to water quality were identifiable point sources, such as factories and wastewater treatment plants. However, under the Clean Water Act, the federal Environmental Protection Agency (EPA) and state environmental agencies have rigorously regulated the polluted effluent released by point sources.

Today's water pollution emanates from nonpoint sources: greater volumes of stormwater runoff and increased volumes and varieties of pollutants in the runoff. The modern U.S. urban landscape "with its large areas of impermeable roadways and buildings has significantly altered the movement of water through the environment. . . . [W]ith development and sprawl increasing at a rate faster than population growth, urbanization's negative impact on water quality is a problem that won't be going away" (Kloss and Calarusse 2006: v). Along highly developed coastlines, urban stormwater runoff is already the largest source of ocean shoreline water pollution (Kloss and Calarusse 2006: 5). Researchers have conclusively established the link between urbanization and negative hydrologic impact on rivers and streams, demonstrating that as little as 10 to 15 percent impervious cover in a watershed can degrade the quality of receiving waters (Stormwater and Runoff Pollution n.d.). However, relatively few studies have documented how this process occurs, or how much urbanization needs to be reversed to result in ecological improvements.

Stormwater that used to be absorbed in a landscape composed of nat-

Figure 1. Runoff: from streets to sewers to streams. Lynda
Wallis/Freelance Illustrations.

ural vegetation and soils has become a high-speed, high-velocity conduit
for pollution into rivers, lakes, and coastal waters. Traditional stormwater management has treated water flows as a nuisance to be quickly duc-
ted (when local ordinances insist) to detention basins or treatment
plants and then to streams (Figure 1). These management systems fall
into two groups, each with its own efficiencies and failures. One is separated storm and sanitary sewers found in newer cities. The runoff flowing through separated systems, largely untreated, dumps directly into
waterways with a full load of pet waste, road pollutants, trash, pesticides,
and fertilizers and scours and erodes stream banks with its high-velocity
arrival. The other is the combined sewer system, found in older cities,
where stormwater flows into the same pipes as sewage. While this water
typically flows into sewage treatment plants, rainfall events, even small
ones, can cause these systems to overflow, dumping untreated human,
industrial, and commercial waste, mixed with stormwater, into waterways. In Washington, D.C., as little as 0.2 inches of rainfall can cause
the combined sewer system to overflow (Kloss and Calarusse 2006: 4).
Washington's precipitation rate is 3 inches of rain per month (city-
data.com).

Most municipalities face staggering challenges in complying with federal water quality standards. Although the EPA National Pollutant Discharge Elimination System generally regulates municipalities with
separate systems, their large volumes of stormwater render impractical
the usual methods of treatment and control of point sources. Compliance with these permits does not result in improved water quality under
federal rules, requiring municipalities with combined sewer overflows

(CSOs) to implement short- and long-term improvement strategies. Although many major projects are under way and producing results, many more have yet to be built. CSO mitigation is an expensive undertaking: the 2000 Clean Watersheds Needs Survey (CWNS) estimated that $56 billion in capital investment was needed for CSO control. In addition to these investments, the EPA estimates that meeting federally mandated stormwater management regulations and successfully controlling urban runoff would require another $11–22 billion (Kloss and Calarusse 2006: 11).

The financial pressure on local governments, combined with the growing multidisciplinary interest in sustainability, have created a broad audience for alternative forms of stormwater management, ones that provide a greater flood prevention, environmental protection, and economic value. "Capturing, retaining, and trying to improve the quality of vast quantities of urban stormwater runoff is often more difficult and expensive than reducing the amount of stormwater generated from the outset through strategies to reduce imperviousness and maximize infiltration and filtration" (Kloss and Calarusse 2006: 7).

Public officials at all levels of government, engineers, the environmental community, real estate developers, and urban planners are increasingly realizing that the adoption of green infrastructure is a necessary step toward environmentally and economically sustainable cities.

What Is Green Infrastructure?

Green infrastructure on the regional scale usually means an interconnected network of open spaces and natural areas (such as greenways, wetlands, parks, and forest preserves) that naturally recharges aquifers, improves water quality, and provides recreational opportunities and wildlife habitats. Green infrastructure on the municipal, or even neighborhood scale, refers to best management practices (BMPs) comprising such landscape features as rain gardens, vegetated swales, and permeable pavements that mimic the natural capacity of the landscape to manage and absorb precipitation where it falls. These solutions manage stormwater through infiltration, filtration, evaporation, and detention. Ultra-urban landscapes can handle green infrastructure by constructing new features or incorporating BMPs into existing green spaces.

The green infrastructure approach uses stormwater as a resource that, combined with other natural features of the landscape, creates value for communities while reducing damage due to pollution and flooding. Green infrastructure, as adopted around the country has varied names: low-impact development around the Chesapeake Bay, natural drainage systems in Seattle, sustainable stormwater management in Portland, and high-performance infrastructure in the urban Northeast. Often BMPs are part of a "treatment train" or a system integrating green and conventional stormwater technologies. The most common BMPs are

- rain gardens (more formally, bio-retention cells), which are man-made depressions in the ground planted with native vegetation and sometimes filled with engineered soils that collect and store water runoff, often directed from roof downspouts or curb cuts, infiltrating the runoff into the soil over 48 hours or less, and filtering out many pollutants on the way;
- disconnected downspouts that decrease runoff quantity and speed by keeping stormwater out of the sewer system and direct water to a rain garden, other vegetated area, or rain barrel;
- rain barrels that collect runoff from rooftops for reuse, for watering lawns and gardens, or in gray water recycling systems for the buildings;
- green roofs, which are layers of living vegetation and a growing medium installed over a waterproof membrane on a roof that retains and filters rainwater, capturing and slowing down the smaller quantity of runoff that will eventually be created and insulating buildings from excessive heat and cold;
- permeable paving materials (concrete, asphalt, stone, or plastic) designed with void spaces that absorb rainwater, filter pollutants and recharge groundwater;
- tree plantings that reduce the volume of runoff through water uptake and evapotranspiration;
- native vegetation whose long roots (3 to 10 feet as opposed to 34 inches for turf grass) absorb and filter runoff;[1]
- vegetated swales, which are broad, planted channels used for the movement and temporary storage of runoff that conveys water while simultaneously infiltrating it;
- planter boxes located adjacent to buildings and along sidewalks to accept water routed from roofs and streetscapes and store runoff in the soils to be evapotranspired by plants or infiltrated slowly into underdrains;
- filter strips, which are vegetated areas designed to receive runoff from adjacent impervious surfaces that slow runoff speed, trap sediments and other pollutants, and provide some absorption; and
- naturalized detention basins that temporarily store runoff and release it gradually into the downstream drainage system, allowing the settling of pollutants and constituents as well as the biological uptake by vegetation and microorganisms (Figure 2).

Multiple studies show that green infrastructure techniques can remove from 50 to 95 percent of the common harmful constituents found in stormwater runoff (Schueler and Holland 2000: 375) and

Figure 2. Green infrastructure incorporated into an urban yard.
Lynda Wallis/Freelance Illustrations.

reduce runoff volumes by 90 percent (Barr 2006: 12). They also reveal
that BMPs can reduce construction costs significantly. In a landmark
urban retrofit effort, Seattle's Street Edge Alternatives (SEA) reduced
impervious area by 11 percent and added over a thousand new trees and
shrubs. This streetscaping reduced the quantity of stormwater runoff by
98 percent (Seattle Public Utilities n.d.). In Bellingham, Washington,
the city retrofitted two parking lots with green infrastructure resulting
in a 75 to 80 percent reduction of construction cost compared to the
projected cost (based on similar projects conducted by the city) of out-
fitting the parking lots with conventional in-ground storage and treatment infrastructure (LaCroix et al. 2004: 5).

While BMPs primarily offer flood protection and water quality
improvements, they also have secondary benefits, including improving
air quality, energy conservation, biodiversity, quality of life, and even
reducing crime. In 2001, researchers at the University of Illinois,
Urbana-Champaign, found that residents living in public housing whose
grounds had few trees and little grass reported more aggression and violence then did their counterparts living in buildings with more access to
nature (Kuo and Sullivan 2001: 543). Residents also reported increased
levels of mental fatigue, accompanied by aggression. These quality-of-
life issues are just beginning to be investigated, along with the public

Figure 3. The Green Values Stormwater
Toolbox provides the means to build green
infrastructure. Lynda Wallis/Freelance
Illustrations.

health impacts of environment and community design. However, the economic strength of green infrastructure techniques remains, and will most likely remain, the primary driver of a rapid shift to widespread implementation.

Knowledge regarding the financial benefits of implementing green infrastructure is just beginning to emerge. Many green infrastructure features are inexpensive to build and maintain, while reducing the cost of treatment by decreasing stormwater volume entering sewer systems. Researchers in Portland, Oregon, have shown that the use of swales, as opposed to conventional stormwater pipes, curbs, and gutters, can result in savings of up to $4,000 to $5,000 per acre of developed area (City of Chicago 2003: 19). Conducting a cradle-to-grave cost-benefit assessment of infrastructure components reveals the accumulating economic benefits of green infrastructure. For example, creating a conventional infrastructure system includes the expense of manufacturing, transporting, and installing it as well as costs related to its operation, maintenance, and eventual replacement. The materials for BMP construction are readily found in nature, require minimal transportation, and have low operating and maintenance costs and indeterminate life spans. A green infrastructure landscape feature can replenish itself and exemplifies the new sustainable design paradigm: cradle-to-cradle (Figure 3).

The Green Values Stormwater Toolbox

Despite recent studies demonstrating the efficiency and cost-effectiveness of green infrastructure, its widespread adoption faces barriers due to a lack of information about its use and design, performance, costs, and benefits. To fill this gap, CNT is working on four fronts: technology, policy, practice, and outreach. First, it is constructing multiple demonstration sites, installing and monitoring green infrastructure features in an effort to help engineers and municipalities predict the performance of BMPs. CNT's headquarters building is one such demonstration. It is a platinum LEED building, the second in Chicago and thirteenth in the nation to receive this rating. The building features a rain garden as part of the 100 percent native plant garden maintained by CNT staff. Native vegetation and several new trees surrounding the building's parking lot work with an infiltration trench in the lot's low point to absorb runoff that previously created a large puddle partially blocking the way to the office.

CNT's ongoing research and advocacy projects review the current standing of legislative and regulatory policies related to stormwater management. This research identifies opportunities to encourage implementation and remove outdated barriers to the use of green infrastructure techniques. Also, CNT has developed an active public outreach and education program, encompassing schools, churches, and municipalities to accompany its demonstration projects. In addition, it has placed its Green Values Stormwater Toolbox on its website (greenvalues.cnt.org). The toolbox has clear, illustrated explanations of the different forms of green infrastructure and describes their ability to manage rainwater and runoff. The toolbox also includes the Green Values Calculator, a program that compares the costs of green infrastructure and traditional stormwater management.

The Green Values Calculator employs specifications defined by the user, such as size, impervious cover, vegetation, soil type, and life cycle, to model the quantity and intensity of runoff produced by a given site. The user can select up to six BMPs to model a "green" scenario. The Green Values Calculator then presents a financial analysis of green and traditional management systems, revealing the hydrologic and cost differences between the two. A unique feature of the Green Values Calculator is its capacity to quantify the full life-cycle cost and benefit factors (first-time construction costs and operating costs) for the green scenario. For example, the calculator attributes dollar values for the carbon sequestration capacity of increased green area, the per acre foot of groundwater recharged, and the rise in property value resulting from the increased number of trees on an individual lot. It also explains benefits that cannot be calculated—for example, the aesthetic value added to an urban setting by increasing its natural nontree cover.

The Green Values Calculator Methodology

In comparing the hydrologic profile of a site with a fully conventional system with that of the same site with BMPs used in lieu of, or in collaboration with, conventional technologies, the Green Values Calculator applies the standard hydraulic equations and coefficient values used by engineers in designing stormwater systems. The difference in quantities of runoff that require management and the cost differences for the installation, maintenance, and replacement needs over the user-defined life span become the parameters for assessing the financial benefits or losses that result from BMP implementation. The cost data for this analysis is derived from industry sources and transparently presented on the website in a tabulated format. The details of the methodologies used in the hydrologic and economic analyses are presented below.

User Interface

Users can either choose a neighborhood configuration from a set list or enter specifics about their own neighborhoods and yards. The previously configured neighborhoods, ranging from "Dense Urban Neighborhood" to "New Development, Suburban," have default values assigned to the various fields and have the optimal set of BMPs applied. These scenarios are meant for users without a specific place in mind who want to explore the differences in the stormwater management options based on general scenarios. Those wishing to analyze a defined location enter the following parameters: area of the site, number of lots, roof size, number of trees on the lot, driveway sizes (if applicable), garage/impermeable deck size (if applicable), sidewalk width, street width, soil type, real discount rate, and life cycle.

These parameters determine the impervious-to-pervious ratio of the land cover to establish the appropriate value for the hydraulic coefficients (curve numbers and C-values). The user then applies any of the six green infrastructure techniques, individually or in combination, including such BMPs as roof drains to raingardens at all downspouts, half of lawn replaced by garden with native landscaping, porous pavement used on driveway, sidewalk and other nonstreet pavement, green roofs, tree cover provided for an additional 25 percent of lot, and use of drainage swales instead of stormwater pipes. The Green Values Calculator then uses the site parameters to generate the conventional and hydrologic green profiles.

Green Values Calculator: Hydrologic Analysis

The analysis assumes a 10-year storm that lasts for 24 hours based on precipitation data for the northwest suburban area of Chicago. Conceptually, the Green Values Calculator models the flow from raindrop to detention. It routes the runoff from the lot to the street, and through the community, measuring volume, and peak flow rate.[2] Benefits can be seen on an individual lot scale, which highlight the runoff reductions an individual can create, and on the neighborhood scale, identifying the results that municipalities can achieve.

In every case, when the user applies BMPs the volume, speed, or detention required for the runoff is significantly reduced. The annual recharge of groundwater is also higher with green infrastructure. Users can experiment with different BMPs to determine which combination produces desired results. They can then look at the cost analysis that occurs simultaneously in order to make development design decisions.

While the Green Values Calculator methodology uses widely accepted hydraulic analyses, it has one limitation: its basic assumption that the watershed is homogeneous. Thus the results of the different scenarios represent their effects averaged over a simulated area rather than a specific place. Nonetheless, this approach is reasonable for the purposes of providing a comparison of management practices.

GREEN VALUES CALCULATOR: AN ECONOMIC ANALYSIS

When the Green Values Calculator generates a cost-benefit comparison between the conventional and green infrastructure systems, it considers a user-defined life span, moving beyond initial construction costs. In assessing the investments, it takes into account the changing value of the dollar and the appreciating or depreciating value of the system. Finally, it includes often-overlooked components, such as property appreciation due to landscape features, to give a complete understanding of the economic value of the two types of systems.

To establish costs, the Green Values Calculator derives data from standard industry sources and clearly references them. The cost-benefit analysis of the full lifecycle of the system includes the first-time construction costs and the yearly maintenance and replacement costs of each component of the overall stormwater system. Each infrastructure component was assigned a middle-range value after establishing the high to low pricing range for construction cost, maintenance costs, and the average life cycle and replacement needs. (The middle values used are either direct sources or an average of the range, if the range is weighted to one side or the other.) Finally, the Green Values Calculator allows the user to define the interest rate and terms for authorizing this investment.

The results show that green infrastructure BMPs are often far less expensive than conventional systems. They are cheaper to maintain, last longer, appreciate in value and often, if properly maintained, incur minimal replacement costs. For example, trees newly planted or preserved during a site development, can greatly increase the property value of a site over its life cycle and need replacement only every 40 years if prop-

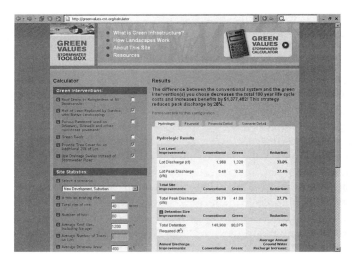

Figure 4. The top of the Green Values Calculator page provides a summary of the hydraulic and financial comparisons. The user can see the details of the results by referring to the four tabs: Hydrologic, Financial, Financial Detail, and Scenario Detail. The scenario detail provides specific comparisons and is the best tool for understanding the differences among systems.

erly maintained. A study of the factors that influence neighborhood transformations in Philadelphia found that new tree plantings increased the surrounding housing values by approximately 10 percent. In the pilot neighborhood of the study this translates into a $4 million gain in property value through tree plantings (Wachter 2004). Drainage swales planted with native vegetation increase in effectiveness as the plants are established and reach ecological balance. Swales require occasional cleaning, but if properly maintained, will never require replacement (City of Chicago 2003: 19).

The Green Values Calculator accounts for more than the cost of installing and maintaining a stormwater management system. It estimates the financial benefits of green infrastructure features, including property value increases for lots with numerous and well-established trees, and the dollar value of reduced air pollution, carbon sequestration, and ground water recharge (Figure 4).

The Green Values Calculator as a Scenario Builder

To understand the power of the Green Values Calculator, the following scenarios show how Joe Grant, a developer of suburban subdivisions, can transform his recently purchased parcel of agricultural land into a new community. Joe has purchased 40 acres and plans to divide it into 80 half-acre lots. He anticipates that the homes, driveways, and patios will be an average size: 1,200 square feett (sf) of roof, 400 sf of driveway, and 100 sf of deck or patio. The streets and sidewalks will be sized to standard, with 32-foot-wide streets and 5-foot sidewalks. Joe's subdivision should last for as long as a hundred years. But he has a problem. In order to gain a building permit he must comply with the town's recently passed zoning ordinances, which require conservation development: a site design that includes open space preservation, stream buffers, and a percentage capture of stormwater runoff onsite. To comply with the municipal regulations, Joe has assured public officials that his subdivision will release water from the site into the nearby stream at a rate of 0.25 cubic feet per second (City of Chicago Department of Water Management Regulations, n.d.). The town insists he meet the goal, and they recommend he do so through the use of stormwater BMPs. Joe turns to the Green Values Calculator and gets to work. He chooses six green infrastructure installations (rain gardens, disconnected downspouts, native vegetation, trees, vegetated swales, permeable pavement, and green roofs). Table 1 shows what Joe found.

The Green Values Calculator provided three important results. First, the conventional system accrued no benefits. Second, the permeable pavement, while successful as a runoff reduction strategy, is too expensive. Third, green roofs in a new suburban development do not make hydraulic or financial sense.[3]

The Green Values Calculator showed Joe that he could use green infrastructure, specifically a combination of rain gardens, native vegetation, tress, and vegetated swales, to meet the town's regulations and save over $300,000 in the process.[4] Joe decided to hire a professional engineering firm that specializes in conservation development to further explore the inclusion of stormwater BMPs in his site design.

The Green Values Calculator can also be used to make long-term planning decisions in ultra-urban environments. In urban environments the lot size will shrink considerably (from about 22,000 sf to 5,000 sf) but the impermeable areas, such as the roof size, the roads, driveways, patios, etc., change only marginally (for example 1,000-sf roof, 0 sf driveway, 100 sf patio). An urban site will likely be connected to existing infrastructure. The city authority may be taking steps to reduce the strain in the existing infrastructure and occurrence of CSOs by requiring that all new or re-developments adhere to strict guidelines for the volume of water that can be introduced into the sewer system after a rain. Table 2 describes how the cost/benefit analysis of green infrastructure works differently under this scenario.

TABLE 1. GREEN VALUES CALCULATOR RESULTS FOR A NEW SUBURBAN SCENARIO

Conventional technique	Green alternative	Green runoff reduction (cumulative benefit of all BMPs, %)	Cost-benefit analysis (for developer, public, and homeowner over 100-year life cycle)
Install turf grass on all lawns	Build rain gardens at roof downspouts and replace half lawn with native vegetation	27	Save $975,000
Plant no trees	Increase tree cover by 25%	36	Save $810,000
Construct curbs, gutters, and storm sewers	Install vegetated swales	36	Save $1,239,000
Pave driveways, sidewalks, patios with impervious materials	Use permeable pavement in low impact areas	40	Save $865,000
Build conventional roofs on all houses	Build green roofs on all houses	41	Spend $4,000,000

The green infrastructure alternatives perform less favorably as retrofits in a dense urban neighborhood. In this scenario, construction costs for comparable conventional infrastructure are not taken into account because they already exist.

It is still possible to find ultra-urban scenarios with positive runoff reduction and cost/benefit results. This analysis could be interpreted by city planners to mean that the best decision for decreasing stormwater runoff from an urban neighborhood is to encourage rain garden plantings and downspout disconnection, encourage homeowners to plant less turf grass and more native plants on their lots, increase native plantings in city-controlled open space (that is, parks and parkways), and plant more trees in parks and right-of-ways.

The use of permeable pavements or green roofs could be used only in cases where the existing infrastructure required replacement already—for example, streetscaping retrofits—in order to maximize cost/benefit comparisons. Also, the relative value of green or conventional approaches is determined in part by the pricing cities impose for stormwater management. Philadelphia, for example, has changed its stormwater charges from a flat fee to one based on a property's impervi-

TABLE 2. GREEN VALUES CALCULATOR RESULTS FOR A DENSE URBAN
NEIGHBORHOOD

Conventional technique	Green alternative	Green runoff reduction (cumulative benefit of all BMPs, %)	Cost-benefit analysis (developer, public, and homeowner over 100-year life)
Install turf grass on all lawns	Build rain gardens at roof downspouts and replace half lawn with native vegetation	37	Save $56,239
Plant no trees	Increase tree cover by 25%	44	Save $46,286
Construct curbs, gutters, and storm sewers	Not applicable, infrastructure already in place		
Pave driveways, sidewalks, patios with impervious materials	Use permeable pavement in low impact areas	48	Spend $13,554
Build conventional roofs on all houses	Build green roofs on all houses	48	Spend $2,389,784

ous cover, with a discount for landowners who implement green infrastructure on large paved areas such as parking lots. Philadelphia's policy is deliberately designed to encourage green infrastructure applications by internalizing the full stormwater service cost in fees. While urban retrofits cannot count avoided costs for local stormwater infrastructure, they may save on other public expenditures. Given that green roofs and permeable pavement may be the most feasible green applications in dense areas, Philadelphia also sees those installations as saving the high public cost of building additional storage to comply with Clean Water Act requirements to reduce combined sewer overflows (Neukrug 2007).

The Green Values Calculator in Action

While still undergoing revision, the Green Values Calculator has served to clarify several real-life situations for municipalities and engineers. In June 2006, the city of Chicago used it to determine where to install green infrastructure on a 151-acre city-owned property, North Park Village, a former tuberculosis sanitarium on the northwest side of Chicago. Now accommodating a senior citizen home, a 46-acre nature center, and

TABLE 3. OPPORTUNITIES AND ANALYSIS FOR NORTH PARK VILLAGE

Opportunity	Runoff reduction (%, total peak discharge, cfs)	$ Saved over 30-year life cycle
Peterson Park: A combination of constructing rain gardens at the field house, planting native vegetation along the fence line, and adding some trees would reduce ponding of storm water in the vicinity of the field house.	47	$9,500
Chapel and Main Lawn: Rain gardens to manage water around the chapel could reduce the problems due to poor drainage. There are many areas of the 12-acre lawn that would benefit from clearance of buckthorn under the trees and planting native vegetation.	19	$210,000
Health Center Building, Parking, Lot, and Lawn: A green roof is desired for the Health Center and might be feasible. Not many green roofs are visible from the ground, as is this one would be. The roof should be analyzed for its contribution to the mold problems that originally closed the building. The large parking area and driveway could be good locations for demonstrating porous pavement, but they should also demonstrate cheaper measures using attractive gardens to handle runoff from the existing pavement.	39	−$1,208,180

a public park, the city's Department of General Services is considering the potential of "greening" it. Here CNT analysts modeled a scenario that included rain gardens, native vegetation, green roofs, and permeable pavement (Table 3).

This analysis would suggest that the most effective and cost-friendly opportunities for green stormwater management in North Park Village are to include rain gardens at the downspouts of some of the larger buildings and replace large tracts of the facility's lawn (turf grass) with prairie (native vegetation). However, the human context of this scenario places a priority on the results that have less favorable cost/benefit results.

The city of Chicago is actively promoting green roofs for their stormwater and energy conservation benefits. As a result of innovative programs and incentives, Chicago now has more square footage of green roofs than any other city in the U.S.[5] The senior community that lives in North Park Village has made it a top priority to reopen the Health Center building that was closed as a result of mold problems. A new roof may be required to reopen it, offsetting some of the high costs of a green roof retrofit by the necessary construction required to replace the roof with a conventional model.

The flood risk posed by the proximity of the Old Hospital Complex downspouts to senior apartment patio doors could make the necessary small investment shown in the Green Values Calculator well worth it. The calculator shows the construction of rain gardens here to be a financial loss, but does not account for the potential cost that could occur should a large rain create enough flow through each downspout to flood over the patio and into the ground floor living rooms of many of the senior housing apartments. The resulting loss of goods and resources, particularly for a vulnerable population, would greatly outweigh the extra cost used to build and maintain the rain gardens. A relatively small amount spent in flood prevention through green infrastructure could save a large amount in potential damages.

The city of Chicago was pleased with the performance of the Green Values Calculator and interested in the greening opportunities it highlighted. The calculator's analysis provided a more informed framework for discussion of what green infrastructure practices would be appropriate for the site and where to install them. The city has submitted proposals to the Illinois EPA nonpoint source pollution program to build a green infrastructure demonstration park at North Park Village. If funded, it will become a site where the public can learn about the many forms of green infrastructure and the environmental and financial benefits they provide.

In addition, Chicago has turned to CNT for assistance in using the Green Values Calculator in pursuing other aspects of its widely publicized mayoral initiatives in greening, notably its new stormwater ordinance. Taking effect on January 1, 2008, this legislation requires all new developments over 15,000 square feet and all parking lots over 7,500 square feet to control the rate and volume of each site's runoff through BMPs or impervious surface reduction. Under contract to the city, CNT is tailoring the Green Values Calculator to accompany the ordinance's guidelines provided to developers and contractors. The city views the Green Values Calculator as a tool to demonstrate to the development community that green infrastructure is technically reliable and financially feasible.

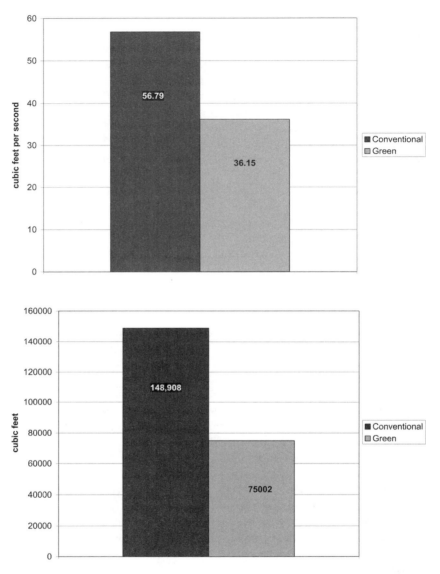

Figure 5. Reductions in runoff produced by a new suburban development site with these green infrastructure features incorporated: (top) total peak discharge (cfs); (bottom) total detention required (cf).

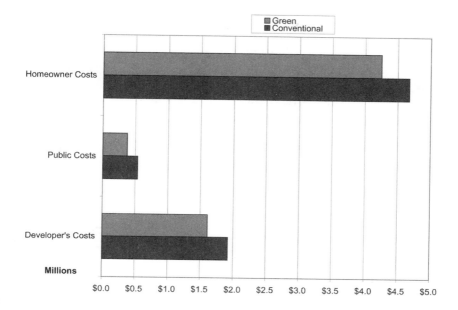

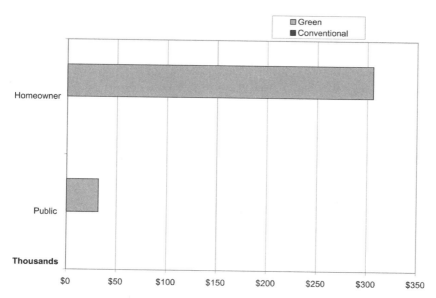

Figure 6. Reduced cost of building and maintaining the green stormwater management system, as well as benefits accrued by that system, over 100 years: (top) stakeholder costs; (bottom) stakeholder benefits.

Conclusion

Stormwater runoff poses a serious ecological threat to the development of new and existing cities. As metropolitan development spreads, and already urbanized areas support increasingly dense populations, cities must find ways to manage their natural resources efficiently, sensitively, and wisely. With the emergence of green development, encompassing buildings to business and water infrastructure, comes the need for rigorous environmental and economic analyses to show its advantages convincingly. In the case of green infrastructure, methods for this type of analysis are advancing rapidly as indicated by the development and use of such tools as the Green Values Calculator. The Green Values Calculator, while not perfect, is an important effort that addresses stormwater management alternatives by providing information for making optimal, reasonable, and well-informed decisions. These decisions are beginning to be made. A recently elected commissioner to the Metropolitan Water Reclamation District of Greater Chicago, one of the nation's oldest authorities in water resource management, brought a fresh view to its boardroom when she declared: "The sustainable cities of the future will be those that are most successful at changing their own culture, that make the transition from viewing stormwater as a problem to viewing rainwater as a liquid asset to be captured, treasured, saved and not squandered" (Shore 2007). With the environmental ramifications of inaction becoming increasingly urgent, and the financial motivations of applying green solutions increasingly compelling, the necessary cultural, social, and policy changes are not only possible, but within our grasp.

References

Barr Engineering. 2006. *Burnsville Stormwater Retrofit Study*. Prepared for city of Burnsville, Minnesota. Minneapolis: Burns Engineering.

City-data.com. Washington, District of Columbia. Precipitation. http://www.city-data.com/city/Washington-District-of-Columbia.html.

City of Chicago. 2003. *A Guide to Stormwater Best Management Practices*. Chicago: City of Chicago Departments of Environment, Planning and Development, Transportation, and Water Management.

City of Chicago Department of Water Management Regulations for Sewer Construction and Stormwater Management. n.d. Stormwater Management Ordinance Regulations. Chicago: City of Chicago Department of Environment http://egov.cityofchicago.org/webportal/COCWebPortal/COC_EDITORIAL/Stor mwate rRegulations.pdf.

"Green Roofs Keep on Growing." 2007. *A Fresh Squeeze: Chicago Edition*, October 1. http://www.afreshsqueeze.com/articleDtl.php?id = 47014843bd083.

Hollander, D. A., Bill Eyring, and A. R. Schmidt. 2006. "Developing a Comparative Tool for Both Conventional and Green Stormwater Management Techniques." Paper presented at the World Environmental and Water Resource Congress, May 2006, Lincoln, Nebraska.

Kloss, Christopher, and Crystal Calarusse. 2006. *Rooftops to Rivers: Green Strategies for Controlling Stormwater and Combined Sewer Overflows*. New York: Natural Resources Defense Council.

Kuo, Frances J., and William C. Sullivan. 2001. "Aggression and Violence in the Inner City." *Environment and Behavior* 33: 543–71.

LaCroix, Renee, Bill Reilly, Joy Monjure, Kim Spens, Mary Knackstedt, and Bruce Wulkan. 2004. *Reining in the Rain: A Case Study of the City of Bellingham's Use of Rain Gardens to Manage Stormwater*. Bellingham, Wash.: Puget Sound Action Team.

Mau, Bruce, Jennifer Leonard, and the Institute Without Boundaries. 2004. *Massive Change*. New York: Phaidon Press.

Neukrug, Howard. M. "Clean Waters . . . Green City: A Sustainable Approach to Water Utility Management." Presented at Stormwater Solutions That Hold Water meeting, Chicago, May 2007.

Schueler, Thomas R., and Heather K. Holland, eds. 2000. *The Practice of Watershed Protection*. Ellicott City, Md.: Center for Watershed Protection.

Seattle Public Utilities. Street Edge Alternatives Project. City of Seattle. 2001. http://www.ci.seattle.wa.us/util/About_SPU/Drainage_&_Sewer_System/Nat ural_Drainage_Systems/Street_Edge_Alternatives/index.asp.

Shore, Debra. 2007. "Changing the Culture About Our Liquid Asset." *Chicago Tribune*, January 17.

Stormwater and Runoff Pollution. n.d. Stormwater FAQs. Raleigh: North Carolina Department of Environment and Natural Resources. http://www.ncstormwater.org/pages/stormwater_faqspage.html#whyshouldicare.

Wachter, Susan. 2004. *The Determinants of Neighborhood Transformations in Philadelphia—Identification and Analysis: The New Kensington Pilot Study*. Philadelphia: Wharton School, University of Pennsylvania.

Chapter 19
What Makes Today's Green City?

WARREN KARLENZIG

The green city concept has ascended rapidly in public consciousness with the onset of concerns about global climate change, rising energy prices, and personal environmental health impacts. Today's green city now evokes not only a city that is physically greening its streets and its public and private spaces and byways, but also one that strategically embraces development of renewable energy, less-polluting fuels, widely available local food, efficient public transit, innovative treatment of wastes, polluted land and water, walkability, sufficient affordable housing, and green buildings.

As recently as the mid-1980s, a "green city" was thought of solely as a city with a high concentration of street trees, parks, lawns, and green spaces. Whether a city had significant contaminated industrial sites, street or sidewalk litter problems, or noticeable air and water pollution might be additional criteria for judgment. The actors responsible for managing such issues included a patchwork of unaffiliated organizations or individuals: horticultural societies for tree planting and public space greening; public works and recreation departments for street greening and park maintenance; the U.S. Environmental Protection Agency (EPA) for overseeing contaminated industrial site remediation and for penalizing air and water polluters; and city public works departments for litter control.

After 1987, a systems-based perspective of green or "sustainable" cities began to emerge in the wake of the work of the United Nations World Commission on Environment and Development (known as the Brundtland Commission after its chair, Gro Harlem Brundtland). The Brundtland Commission's definition of sustainable development— "development that meets the needs of present without compromising the ability of future generations to meet their own needs"—broadened thinking to include not only quality-of-life and environmental analysis, but also ushered in an era of sophisticated rating systems, employing scientific, technical and economic measures, and comprehensive and specific policy goals and planning initiatives ("Our Common Journey" 1987).

In addition, the recent findings of the fourth UN Intergovernmental Panel on Climate Change and Sustainable Development are prompting local assessments of greenhouse gas carbon emissions mitigation. These findings have also promoted localities to develop strategies to adapt to localized climate change effects that are expected to produce impacts on urban areas, including increased and more severe flooding, drought, and wildfires (WMO and UNEP 2007). Many states and cities are now involved in rigorous carbon emission inventories and carbon reduction action plans. The state of California and the cities of Portland, Oregon, Seattle, and New York are leaders in the practice of devising carbon greenhouse gas emissions inventories and mitigation action plans. The International Council for Local Environmental Initiatives (ICLEI), an organization with more than 650 local governments involved in the Cities for Climate Protection Campaign, has also been an important participant in helping local governments devise carbon emission inventory and reduction standards and practices.[1]

While defining a green city or sustainable city is becoming conceptually clearer, evaluating "greenness" or sustainability across cities on a comparative basis is more difficult. Differing approaches have advantages and limitations. The term "green city" continues to undergo evolution, complicating longitudinal measurements.

U.S. Sustainability or Green Ranking Systems: An Overview

The development of independent voluntary green ranking systems has recently accelerated in industry- or issue-specific areas. These rankings focus primarily on the articulation of a single element or indicator. For example, since 2000, the Leadership in Energy and the Environment (LEED) program of the U.S. Green Building Council (USGB) has certified green construction, an assessment that has enabled city-by-city comparisons of such activity.[2] By counting the number of LEED-certified and LEED-registered commercial buildings within a city, researchers can provide benchmarks through calculation per capita ratings. The USBG rollout of its neighborhood development standards, measuring residential density and access to public transportation, will add another potential indicator that can be normalized on a national scale.

The data for tracking specific city or county environmental performance are also available. For example, the EPA regularly reports air and tap water quality and the Census Bureau provides annual statistics on city residents' commuting patterns, including percentages of those who take public transit, walk, or bicycle to work. The Texas Transportation Institute maintains national data on urban freeway and surface road congestion rates, as well as overall public transit ridership miles for metropolitan regions.

Nongovernmental organizations, such as the Trust for Public Land, track park space as a percentage of overall city land area;[3] another NGO, Smart Growth America, has created an index ranking sprawl in 100 U.S. metropolitan areas ("Measuring Sprawl" 2002). Other sustainability metrics include state regulations requiring performance standards. For example, the California Integrated Waste Management Act of 1989 (AB 939), mandating communities to meet a minimum of 50 percent solid waste diversion from landfills, requires all cities and towns to report their performance annually.[4] Additionally, the California Renewable Portfolio standard (from California's 2002 Senate Bill 1078) requires utilities to measure the percentages of renewable energy use in providing electricity to each city.[5]

Beginning in the 1990s, numerous cities—including Jacksonville, Florida, along with Seattle and San Francisco—developed detailed sustainability indicator categories, often as part of comprehensive "sustainability plans." Devised by multistakeholder groups that include government officials, citizen organizations, business representatives, and unaffiliated individuals, indicators range across such broad areas as the environment, biodiversity, energy and climate change, human health, public information, and education.

Many of these proposed indicators have been difficult to measure or have limited use. In some cases, the gathering or creation of required data is not practical, cost-effective, or even possible, and thus most have not been maintained on a regular basis. Furthermore, as Kent Portney observed in *Taking Sustainable Cities Seriously*, "Unfortunately, virtually all the sustainability indicator projects have lacked extensive discussion concerning why specific indicators were selected, or more specifically, what aspect of sustainability they hope to measure" (Portney 2003: 48). Nonetheless, Seattle has been the most successful in selecting, updating, and tracking its initial indicators. Sustainable Seattle, a nongovernmental organization, first devised city indicators in 1993, and has been tracking them at a neighborhood level since 2003. In 2004 Sustainable Seattle appointed an Indicators Steering Council for King County, broadening its assessment.[6]

An Examination of Comprehensive Green City Indices

As recently as 2002, no studies were known to be available that measured green indicators across the nation's cities uniformly and comprehensively. Practitioners, policymakers, and industry specialists had general knowledge about which cities excelled or were deficient in certain areas (for example, public transit ridership or air pollution). None had the ability to examine cities as whole entities across these "siloed" pockets of knowledge and data. While "silos" of data combined with "farms" of localized indicators provided some information, there was no metric by which cities could be ranked against one another on an overall scale in order to identify leaders and laggards objectively.

Since 2003 three comprehensive green city indices for U.S. cities have emerged. Kent Portney's *Taking Sustainable Cities Seriously* (2003; see also 2006) provides an index of 25 to 40 U.S. cities "taking sustainable development seriously."[7] SustainLane, an Internet-based research organization, ranked sustainability in 25 U.S. cities in 2005 and expanded the list of the subjects of analysis to the 50 largest U.S. cities in 2006 (Karlenzig et al. 2007). *The Green Guide*, a website and newsletter, developed a "Top Ten Green Cities" list in 2005 and enlarged the ranking to the "Top 25 Green Cities" in 2006 ("Top Ten Green Cities" 2006).

TAKING SUSTAINABLE CITIES SERIOUSLY

Kent Portney, a professor of political science at Tufts University, published the first known comprehensive rankings for city sustainability. Using 34 indicators, he initially judged 25 cities ranging in population from 50,000 (Olympia, Washington) to more than 1 million (Phoenix, Arizona) (Portney 2003: 70). He later expanded the city list to 40 (Portney 2006). Among Portney's criteria are

- ecoindustrial park development;
- limits on downtown parking spaces;
- industrial recycling and green building programs (Portney 2003: 65–71).

Portney used a simple yes-and-no answer system, tallied the answers and ranked the cities with the highest number of positive responses. Seattle was number one in both years the survey was conducted (Portney 2006).

THE SUSTAINLANE U.S. CITY RANKINGS

SustainLane, a San Francisco-based Internet company, began to develop a peer-reviewed city sustainability index in 2004, releasing its first rankings for 25 cities in 2005 and expanding to 50 cities in 2006.[8] SustainLane used cities, not metropolitan areas, as the basis of analysis since this focus simplified data collection, narrowing it to inputs from 50 entities, not the thousands needed if it had used metropolitan regions as the primary geopolitical entity for analysis (Karlenzig 2007: 11–19). It also made feasible data normalization across the cities, particularly in areas such as tap water and air quality. Finally, since cities are discreet units of government with defined departments, roles, and budgets, they tend to be more accountable and responsive not only in providing information but also in finding the resulting aggregated benchmarking data useful.

In its peer-reviewed rankings, SustainLane evaluated primary and secondary data from public and nongovernmental organizations. In 2005, it gathered data on city residential commute-to-work rates from U.S. Bureau of the Census, solid waste diversion (including consumer and green waste recycling) rates from the cities, average air quality index from the EPA, number of farmers markets and community gardens per capita from the U.S. Department of Agriculture and the cities directly, per capita LEED-certified and -registered buildings from the U.S. Green Building Council, and percentage of city land used as park or open space from the Trust for Public Land and from the cities. In addition, it surveyed cities to assemble qualitative information about policies and programs on a Yes/No basis in the following areas: the city

- has conducted a climate change inventory within the past five years;
- has a clean technology incubation program;
- has a green fleet of scale (more than 10 percent of total city fleet using alternative fueled vehicles);
- has a sustainability/environmental office or role, and collaborates with university research institutions or government agencies on sustainability issues.

Not completely satisfied with its 2005 results, SustainLane adjusted its approach in 2006, using feedback from the public, government officials, sustainability experts, and peer reviewers to guide the revisions. In addition to enlarging the universe of cities (from 25 to 50), it added data on natural disaster risk, housing affordability and metropolitan area transit use and metro area road congestion categories. It incorporated the latter data because city resident commute-to-work figures alone did not adequately reflect contemporary urban-suburban travel.

Between the two years, SustainLane also revised its ranking methodology. In 2005, it assigned rankings based on an unweighted aggregation of 31 quantitative and qualitative factors across 12 categories; in 2006, it analyzed 36 indicators rolled into 15 larger categories (for example, the city resident commute category has 4 data inputs—transit ridership, carpooling, and walk-to-work and bike-to-work rates) and added a weighting system. Four categories out of the 15 larger categories had weights differing from the study's other 11 categories. These categories were transportation, natural disaster risk, housing affordability, and freeway/roadway congestion. SustainLane applied a 1.5 weight to the overall transportation category to reflect that transportation affects regional air and water quality, as well as roadway congestion and global climate change, and gave a .5 weight to the natural disaster risk, housing afford-ability categories, and roadway congestion categories so they would not be equally weighted with more critical sustainability categories such as air and tap water quality, green buildings per capita and energy supply/climate change policy.

SustainLane also changed is overall scoring. In 2005, the *higher* a city's cumulative numbers, the *lower* its rankings. For example, San Francisco, with a cumulative score of 4.875, ranked number 1 overall, while Hous-ton with a cumulative score of 18.93, ranked number 25 overall, or last. The average cumulative score for all 25 cities was 11.344.

In 2006, the study used a similar relativity scale to the 2005 study; being ranked number 1 or closest to number 1 was best and being ranked 50 was the worst. But, in contrast to the 2005 study, it inverted the overall scoring using a high of 100. Thus cities having the *highest* score received the *highest* ranking. Portland, Oregon with a score of 85.08 ranked the highest overall while Columbus, Ohio with a score of 32.50 had the lowest ranking. The average ranking was 54.42 (see Plate 14) (Karlenzig 2007: 1–10).

THE *GREEN GUIDE* "TOP 25 GREEN CITIES"

The Green Guide, a website and newsletter (acquired by the National Geo-graphic Society in 2007) published a third type of green cities ranking on its website in 2005 and 2006. As with SustainLane, it changed its approach in the two years. In 2005, it listed the top ten cities alphabeti-cally with no overall scoring provided ("Top Ten Green Cities" 2005). In 2006, it not only listed a larger number (25) drawn from cities with a population of 100,000 or more, but also ranked them according to a scale devised by a Yale School of Forestry graduate student. For its 2006 evaluation, it relied on surveys sent to mayors' offices in the nation's 251 cities with populations of more than 100,000 and data collected from the EPA, the Green Building Council, and other unspecified sources. It assessed and equally weighted 11 categories that included air quality, electricity usage and production, green design, green spaces, public health, recycling, social economic factors, transportation, and (drink-ing) water quality ("Top 10 Green Cities" 2006).

Assessing the Comprehensive Green City Studies

The three comprehensive green city rankings differ in their approaches, but also possess significant similarities. All three used surveys to gather information and data, and all three studies ranked cities, not metropolitan areas. Likewise all three gave credit for the presence of city environmental or sustainability policy. The analytical standards differed slightly and ranged from the *Green Guide*'s determining "whether the city has an environmental policy" ("Top 10 Green Cities" 2006). to SustainLane's determining whether the cities "have an environmental or sustainability management role or office" (Karlenzig 2007: 14) to Portney's surveying whether cities had a "single government or non-profit agency responsible for implementing sustainability programs" and whether "sustainability (was) an explicit part of a citywide comprehensive or general plan" (Portney 2003: 65).

Renewable energy use by city government was a criteria common to the three studies. Portney scored whether there was evidence of "renewable energy use by city government" (Portney 2003: 65). The *Green Guide* asked survey respondents "to note each city's energy mix from resources including coal, oil, biomass, geothermal, hydroelectric, nuclear, oil, solar and wind." SustainLane asked each city to disclose the percentage of renewable energy (solar, wind, geothermal, small-scale hydro, biogas) used to supply city electric power, and required a 2 percent renewable energy threshold to receive ranking credit (Karlenzig 2007: 14).

Other areas included inventorying green building programs, bicycle ridership programs, or bicycle commuting rates, recycling programs (recorded as part of waste diversion rates in the SustainLane study), and public transportation sponsorship or ridership rates. Water and air quality assessments made two of the three studies.

Both the SustainLane and the *Green Guide* studies supplemented survey information with data from such third-party sources as the EPA and the Green Building Council. In contrast, Portney's study relied solely on survey information; he stressed his study was used as an indicator of how serious cities were about sustainability, rather than how they *performed* as green cities. Notably, Los Angeles ranked number 3 in Portney's 2006 study, number 25 in the SustainLane study, and was unranked in the *Green Guide* results. It is difficult to determine whether the differences come from poor scores, lack of survey response, or some combination of the two.

Neither Portney nor the *Green Guide* study included such major U.S. cities as Dallas or San Antonio in their ranking (the eighth and ninth largest U.S. cities in population in 2004), nor did either explain why these major cities were not included. SustainLane's ranking included the largest 50 U.S. cities without exception.

The SustainLane study is the only one of the three studies to include local food indicators (community gardens and farmers markets per capita) as criteria for a green or sustainable city. Local food consumption reduces transportation impacts associated with the food industry. Food miles—the distance food travels from field to plate—increased 15 percent from 1992 to 2002 in the United Kingdom, according the British Department of the Environment. These activities contribute substantial amounts of carbon emissions associated with global climate change (Ellis n.d.). Asked author Helena Norberg-Hodge, "Is the global food system really a major contributor to greenhouse gas emissions? Yes, although the exact magnitude of its contribution is all but impossible to quantify. In the United States, for example, food transport totaled some 566 billion ton-miles in 1997, accounting for more than 20 percent of all commodity transport" (Norberg-Hodge et al. 2002: 31).

The *Green Guide* study was the only ranking of the three to include public health criteria. It relied upon "rankings of 125 healthiest cities as published in the 2004 *Organic Style* magazine" ("Top 10 Green Cities" 2006).

Following the "triple bottom line" philosophy advocating for social equity, the environment, and the economy, both SustainLane and the *Green Guide* included socioeconomic criteria, but Portney's study did not. Portney and SustainLane included economic criteria while the *Green Guide*'s did not.

Each survey exhibits significant differences among high-scoring cities. While Seattle scored first in Portney's ranking and third in the Sustain-Lane index, it ranked twenty-fourth in the *Green Guide* study. Portland scored number 1 in SustainLane, number 3 in the *Green Guide,* and number 10 in Portney. Austin, Texas, ranked second in the *Green Guide,* fourteenth in SustainLane, and twenty-second in Portney. These variations stem from the differing assessment standards employed by the ranking organizations.

The SustainLane Case Study: A Look at Three Cities

Understanding use and importance of city rankings requires a deeper look at what the studies are evaluating, their perceived weaknesses, and the reactions they evoke among national, state, and local leaders. A case study of SustainLane provides some insights into these questions.

The following is an analysis of the relative differences among three cities ranked high, medium, and low in the SustainLane 2006 rankings. It reviews performance among the various assessment criteria.

PORTLAND, OREGON

Portland, Oregon, ranked number 1 in the 2006 SustainLane U.S. City Rankings (see plate 15), with a total score of 85.08, succeeding runner-up San Francisco (81.82), which had been number 1 in 2005. Portland moved up from number 2 in 2005 to number 1 in 2006 after the addition of housing affordability, natural disaster risk, and other data categories to the index. It had multiple top ratings in the following categories or subcategories:

- City Innovation (tied for number 1): Included environmental purchasing program, $2.5 million in incentives for green residential and commercial building, carpooling, carsharing, and free downtown public transportation, for which it qualified in a bonus credit subcategory as part of overall city innovation.
- Energy/Climate Change Policy (tied for number 1): Included climate change inventory, climate change carbon reduction goals (Portland was the first U.S. major city to implement such goals in 1993) ("Portland/Multnomah County n.d.), green fleet of scale (above 12 percent was the 2006 threshold), and renewable energy of 10 percent of total, easily surpassing the 2 percent threshold for which study credit was given.
- Green Economy: The city had a high combined rating (number 2) based on green buildings per capita, number of farmers markets per capita (number 4), and the publication of city green business directories.
- Knowledge Base/Communications (tied for number 1): The city had a sustainability or environmental management department, published sustainability planning documents, had communications tools to provide public information on programs, policies, and performance, and was actively collaborating with research institutes and universities on sustainability programs and environmental research.
- Bike-to-Work: As a subcategory of the overall residential commute-to-work rate, the city had a 2.8 percent bike-to-work rate among residents, the highest of the 50 cities studied.

Portland ranked second in three categories: tap water quality, air quality, and LEED buildings per capita. It ranked fourth in planning/land use, having defined urban growth boundaries since 1980. Data from the

Smart Growth America Sprawl index and The Trust for Public Land determined the planning and land use ranking.

Portland's overall ranking excellence likely stems from multiple factors, including high levels of civic participation in sustainability planning. In particular, its success can be attributed to the city's leadership role in developing innovative programs reinforced by a system of city departments, agencies, commissions, citizen groups, and individuals. The city's top-ranking bicycle commute-to-work rate is the result of coordination among multiple public agencies and commuters. According to Mayor Tom Potter, the city has developed more than 700 miles of bicycle lanes.[9] Public transit systems allow bicycles to be transported at any time on light rail or buses, without restriction. Buses have bike racks and light rail rules allow bikes on any railcar. These amenities facilitate a greater number of options for cyclists who, for example, might ride their bicycles in the morning commute and might transport their bike on light rail or buses during their return trips.

During the survey period, Portland led the nation in its quantity of LEED-certified and LEED-registered buildings. Again, a combination of citizen and professional guidance, public policy, cash incentives, and a supportive real estate industry contributed to this high performance. The Portland green building movement began in 1994 with a pioneering citizen advisory committee-created green building action plan and gained strength in 2000 with the city's inauguration of an Office of Sustainable Development, which has a Green Building Division and Green Investment Fund ("Program History" n.d.). In 2001 Portland adopted its own green building rating system—"G-Rated"—and has applied its $425,000 million green building incentive fund widely (only Atlanta had a higher per capita number of green buildings in the SustainLane 2006 city rankings) ("Green Investment Fund" n.d.). A new real estate multiple listing service (MLS) developed in 2007 for the area's residential market combined with extensive residential building incentives and training material make Portland likely to continue being a leader in green activity.

Of the 15 major categories, Portland's lowest rankings were in housing affordability, at number 32 (U.S. Bureau of the Census), and in natural disaster risk, at number 30 (Risk Management Solutions and SustainLane primary research) (Karlenzig et al. 2007: 21–24).

Los Angeles, California

The middle-ranked Los Angeles (number 25), with a score of 52.28, had a mixed performance (see plate 16). On the higher side, it tied for number 1 in solid waste diversion, with an impressive 62 percent waste diversion rate and also scored well in energy and climate change policy, with 5 percent of its energy coming from renewable sources. (The city has conducted a recent climate change carbon emissions inventory and had the most aggressive carbon reduction goals of any city surveyed in the SustainLane city rankings.) Los Angeles also scored well or above average in areas in which it is typically not thought to excel, such as

- Metro public transit ridership: The Los Angeles region ranked number 8 (Texas Transportation Institute). The city has been adding numerous "Bus rapid transit" express lines since 2000 and added 60 miles of rail from the 1990s to 2005.[10]
- City residential commute rate: Los Angeles residents ranked number 17 with a respectable 9.5 percent daily public transit commute-to-work rate (U.S. Bureau of the Census).
- Land use/planning: Los Angeles ranked number 21 in planning and land use (Trust for Public Land and Smart Growth America). Although having multiple "city centers" and the highest density of any U.S. metropolitan region (Hardin 2005: A1), the Smart Growth index rated Los Angeles number 26 in terms of overall sprawl, measured by street connectivity, centeredness, mixed-use development, and density.

Los Angeles continues to face significant challenges in air quality (tied for last at number 49 with Long Beach) and tap water quality (ranked last at number 46, as four cities' data were unavailable in this category). In air quality, Los Angeles recorded "severe" ozone violations, "serious" carbon monoxide violations, and "serious" particulate matter violations, according to the EPA during the survey period for the 2006 city rankings.

Additionally, Los Angeles imports much of its tap water from outside the region, leading not only to high energy expenditures but also to a decrease in water quality because its open-air importation aqueducts spanning hundreds of miles are vulnerable to air pollution and water-pollution run-off. Los Angeles tap water, according to the Environmental Working Group (which gathered data from the EPA), contained 46 pollutants, with the levels of seven pollutants exceeding the EPA minimum standard. Notably, the city has developed water conservation programs that have kept water use equal to 1990 rates, despite a 15 percent increase in the area's population (Karlenzig et al. 2007: 99–102).

OKLAHOMA CITY, OKLAHOMA

At number 49, Oklahoma City, Oklahoma ranked second to last (see plate 17). The city's overall score, 32.92, was significantly below the average score, 54.42. The city ranked poorly in numerous areas, especially in transportation:

- Residential commute-to-work rates: Oklahoma City ranked number 49, with less than 1 percent of the city's residents using public transit to commute to work (U.S. Bureau of the Census).
- Carsharing and city-sponsored carpooling: The city reported no carsharing programs and offered no city-sponsored carpooling coordination.
- Metro public transit ridership ranked number 45 (Texas Transportation Institute).

Oklahoma City mayor Mick Cornett responded to the pre-release of the SustainLane city rankings data by confirming the city's lack of alternatives to the automobile: "I think from a public transit standpoint, we are not prepared [for an energy crisis]. We have designed and created a culture in this city for the automobile. The day when the automobile is no longer an option, this city is going to have to adapt quickly to the things other cities have done for a long time" (Wilmouth 2006).

Other areas in which Oklahoma City ranked poorly included

- Solid waste diversion, in which the city ranked number 41 (tied) for last place with several other cities. It has a reported diversion rate of 4 percent.
- Planning and land use: Oklahoma City ranked number 49 overall, with a number 44 ranking in city park land per total city acreage (Trust for Public Land) and a high sprawl rating, number 41, in the Smart Growth America study.
- Knowledge base: Ranking number 35, the city lacked an environmental or sustainability department or role and did not have a sustainability plan.
- Local food and agriculture: The city ranked number 41 overall, with a low rate of farmers markets (number 35) and community gardens (number 40) per capita.
- LEED buildings per capita: According to data from the U.S. Green Building Council, Oklahoma City ranked forty-fifth in certified and registered LEED buildings, having recorded only one LEED certified building during the survey period.

Two areas where Oklahoma City received high marks were air quality (number 12) and tap water quality (number 7).

Perceived Shortcomings of the SustainLane Rankings

The most significant negative feedback about SustainLane's 2006 city rankings research methodology concerned the lack of metrics on water conservation and per capita water consumption. These were absent because of the assumptions SustainLane built into its methodology. Those assumptions are (1) SustainLane employs data that is of relatively equal importance to cities across the United States. For example, water conservation programs are not included because they would be much more important for a desert city in the Southwest than for a city on the Great Lakes with a plentiful year-round local water supply; (2) Sustain-Lane uses standardized data in order to ease collection. Air quality data, for instance, is available in a standardized format freely available (Median Air Quality Index) from the EPA but water conservation and consumption are not (Karlenzig et al. 2007: 12).

One critic of the study asserted that "while this [absence of water conservation/consumption data] makes for a much cleaner comparison between urban centers, it also ignores one of the fundamental tenets of sustainable development: adapting to the natural environment as it is" ("SustainLane Releases" 2006).

Another issue with the SustainLane rankings is that some misconstrue the meaning of the rankings. Because they are not versed in reading study methodologies, some people have misinterpreted the ranking as being a list of the nation's "Top 50 Green Cities," rather than as a relativity ranking of overall sustainability for the largest 50 U.S. cities, with the top cities being leaders and the bottom cities being laggards.

The Effect of Sustainability Rankings

The release of the first city rankings in June 2005 included an award ceremony for the top ten ranking cities held in San Francisco. Five mayors and other public officials attended the ceremony. They came from Berkeley, San Francisco, and Santa Monica, California; Portland, Oregon; Seattle, Washington; Chicago, Illinois; Boston, Massachusetts; Minneapolis, Minnesota; and Austin, Texas. In receiving his city's number 3 ranking, Seattle mayor Greg Nickels remarked, "Thank you for coming up with a way to try to measure some of the things that we're doing in America's cities. . . . I'm a great believer in cities. I've worked in local government my entire adult life. Because it's a place where you can make a difference: you can roll up your sleeves every day and at the end of the day see the difference you've made. . . . I think it's appropriate that the cities of America are also the place where sustainability is talked about and really worked on every day."[11]

Media reaction to the 2006 SustainLane city rankings was substantial. National media outlets including CNN, CNBC, the *Wall Street Journal*, *New York Times*, and *Washington Post* covered the rankings or components of the rankings. Dozens of metropolitan area broadcast and print outlets also reported the results.[12] Considerable media coverage came from financial or real estate journalists with real estate section articles on the rankings published in the *Washington Post* (Gerencher 2006: F19), *New York Times* (Fessenden 2006), and *Wall Street Journal* (Shu 2006). Business media articles appeared on Marketwatch.com, in the *San Antonio Business Journal*, *Dallas Business Journal*, *Austin Business Journal*, and *Oklahoma Daily Journal*. This broad coverage gave an indication of how the media are beginning to align sustainability or green city stories with economic and environmental issues. Perhaps the economic threat of global climate change and energy supply disruptions has taken sustainability out of the exclusive domain of the environmental beat reporter.

City official reactions to the rankings ranged from prideful to angry. Portland's June 1, 2006, city news release, titled, "Portland Named Most Sustainable City," noted that Mayor Tom Potter would receive the SustainLane trophy at the city's annual Rose Parade. *Business First Columbus* (Ohio) headlined, "Columbus Ranked Least Sustainable City—Mayor Disagrees" ("Columbus Ranked" 2006).

Other city officials supervising city departments of sustainability or environmental departments reported that they would use the study to track internal sustainability initiatives with those in other cities. Since the 2005 city rankings appeared, cities have created sustainability or environmental management offices or special administrator roles (for example, New York City, director of long-term planning and sustainability; Washington D.C., director, district department of the environment; Denver, director, sustainable development initiative; Houston, director of environmental programming; Tucson, environmental planning manager).

These new city sustainability or environmental management offices joined the ranks of others in Portland, San Francisco, Seattle, Chicago, and Oakland (the top five cities in the 2006 rankings). San Francisco, which had established a three-person Department of the Environment in 1997, had by 2006 more than 60 Department of the Environment employees. Two cities, Chicago and San Francisco, also reported management roles for city "Street Greening" outside of the environmental department roles.

Of the most populous 50 U.S. cities, more than 60 percent had sustainability or environmental departments or roles by 2006, indicating that cities are dedicating personnel and resources to sustainability and environmental issues more than ever before.

The Intersection of the Conceptual and the Practical

What makes a green city and how do you measure it are topics of ongoing debate, analysis, and continual refinement. What is becoming clear from this study of ranking systems is that to be considered green or sustainable, cities must proactively manage policies that specifically address recycling, parks and open space, renewable energy, energy conservation, green building, public transportation, and bicycle ridership within an explicit sustainability plan or detailed environmental statement. They must not only track these programs but also communicate their goals, progress, and incentives to citizen groups, citizens, and business, while facilitating collaborative opportunities.

Major emerging green city elements include development of equitable local recreational opportunities, urban forestry and street tree programs, water conservation programs, local food access, socioeconomic factors such as improved housing affordability, alternative fueled fleets, and transparent quality of life indicators for clean air and water.

Exactly how cities implement and manage green city or sustainability policies and programs differs on a city-by-city basis. Some cities such as San Francisco, Chicago, Portland, and Boston have established environmental or sustainability departments as a separate managerial entity. Cities including Seattle, Denver, and Oakland have developed these offices as an entity residing within the mayor's office.

Significantly, in 2006, New York City mayor Michael Bloomberg appointed a Director of Planning and Sustainability, inculcating sustainability approaches into planning and city budgetary procedures. Mayor Bloomberg also established in his Office of Strategic Planning a high-level Sustainability Advisory Committee composed of industry experts, scientists, scholars, business leaders, and planners ("New New York" 2006). And in 2007 the mayor issued a wide-ranging plan, "PlaNYC: A Greener, Greater New York," to guide growth and development policy for sustainability planning in 10 areas through the year 2030.[13]

Portland, San Francisco, Chicago, and Minneapolis have published comprehensive sustainability plans and goals dating anywhere from the mid-1990s to the middle of the first decade of the twenty-first century, while in 2006 Denver announced the formation of a multistakeholder process called "Greenprint Denver."[14] Such goals and plans are likely to continue to draw on diverse stakeholders representing economics, business, real estate, social justice concerns, neighborhoods, education interests, traditional environmental community activists, and individual citizens concerned with improving the economy and quality of life in their community.

While methods and approaches for instituting green or sustainable cities vary, the drivers are common to all these efforts. Global climate change is emerging as the most significant catalyst. Global climate change inventories and carbon-emission reduction goals were common to all five of the top-ranking cities in the SustainLane study, though the study was the only one of the three examined that measured climate change policy indicators. Strong secondary concerns contributing to green city development include energy-related issues such as domestic energy security, energy economics and the possibility of the onset of so-called peak oil (Denver has already modeled impacts of peak oil on city purchasing and municipal operations),[15] food security, and New Urbanism.

Finally, it should be noted that the efforts of leading cities to become green or more sustainable is increasing significantly; states and counties are following the lead of these cities, or are initiating complementary efforts in developing renewable energy and global climate change policy, such as the 25 percent carbon emission-reduction goal put forth by California's AB 32.[16]

Many are openly characterizing the federal government as lagging in sustainability policy development and practices, particularly in the area of global climate change policy. A lawsuit against the Environmental Protection Agency by 19 private organizations, which were later joined by 12 states and local governments including the cities of New York and Baltimore, was settled in an historic April 2, 2007, Supreme Court 5-4 decision. The court found that carbon greenhouse gas emissions can be labeled and regulated as a pollutant just like any other pollutant covered under Clean Air Act regulations if the EPA finds that greenhouse gases "may reasonably be anticipated to endanger the public health or welfare" (see Yost and Maselli 2007).

The Republican governor of California, Arnold Schwarzenegger, addressed in his January 2007 State of the State speech the reluctance at the federal level to deal with global climate change: "One area where we definitely need the climate to change is the national government's attitude about global warming. It would not act, so California did. California has taken the leadership in moving the entire country beyond debate and denial . . . to action" (Schwarzenegger 2007).

How much the green city phenomenon influences the agenda in the 2008 federal elections and subsequent national policy remains to be seen. What is clear is that so-called big issues such as the environment, the economy, and social justice are no longer perceived as being the sole or primary responsibility of Congress and the Environmental Protection Agency and other entities of the federal government.

References

"Beyond Oil: Intelligent Response to Peak Oil Impacts." 2005. Denver World Oil Conference, Denver, Colorado, November 10–11. http://www.aspo-usa.com/fall2005/.

"California Owned Electric Utilities and the California Renewables Portfolio Standard." 2005. Report for California Energy Commission by KEMA, Inc. November. http://72.14.253.104/search?q = cache:l6nO-G3JmigJ:www.energy.ca.gov/2005publications/CEC-300-2005-023/CEC-300-2005-023.PDF + %22renewable + energy + percentage%22 + %22state + of + california%22 + %22utility%22&hl = en&gl = us&ct = c lnk&cd = 1.

"Columbus Ranked Least Sustainable City—Mayor Disagrees." 2006. *Business First of Columbus*, June 2. http://www.bizjournals.com/columbus/stories/2006/05/29/daily28.html?from_rss = 1.

Ellis, Hattie. n.d. "Food Miles." BBC website. http://www.bbc.co.uk/food/food_matters/foodmiles.shtml.

Fessenden, Ford. 2006. "Americans Head Out Beyond the Exurbs." *New York Times*, Week in Review, May 7. http://www.nytimes.com/2006/05/07/weekinreview/07fessenden.html?ex = 1304654400&en = ce20f029585f8c6a&ei = 5090&partner = rssuserland&emc = rss.

Gerencher, Kristen. 2006. "Making the Grade by Making the Most of Natural Resources." *Washington Post*, June 17: F19. http://www.washingtonpost.com/wp-dyn/content/article/2006/06/16/AR2006061600753.html?referrer = delicious.

Hardin, Blaine. 2005. "Out West, a Paradox: Densely Packed Sprawl." *Los Angeles Times*, August 11. http://www.washingtonpost.com/wp-dyn/content/article/2005/08/10/AR200508100211 0.html.

"Green Investment Fund." n.d. City of Portland, Oregon website. http://www.portlandonline.com/osd/index.cfm?c = 42134.

Karlenzig, Warren et al. 2007. *How Green Is Your City? The SustainLane US City Rankings*. Gabriola Island, British Columbia: New Society Publishers.

"Measuring Sprawl and Its Impact." 2002. Smart Growth America. http://www.smartgrowthamerica.org/sprawlindex/sprawlreport.html.

"The New New York." 2006. *Economist*, December 13. http://www.economist.com/world/na/displaystory.cfm?story_id = 8417954.

Norberg-Hodge, Helena, Todd Merrifield, and Steven Gorelick. 2002. *Bringing the Food Economy Home: Local Alternatives to Global Agribusiness*. Bloomfield, Conn.: Kumarian Press.

"Our Common Journey." 1987. Report of the UN World Commission on Environment and Development. New York: United Nations. http://www.iwahq.org/templates/ld_templates/layout_633184.aspx?ObjectId = 644589.

"Portland/Multnomah County Local Action Plan on Global Warming." n.d. City of Portland, Oregon website. http://www.portlandonline.com/osd/index.cfm?c = ebijg.

Portney, Kent. 2003. *Taking Sustainable Cities Seriously: Economic Development, the Environment, Quality of Life in American Cities*. Cambridge, Mass.: MIT Press.

———. 2006. Personal website. http://ase.tufts.edu/polsci/faculty/portney/sustainable-cities.asp.

"Program History." n.d. City of Portland, Oregon website. http://www.portlandonline.com/osd/index.cfm?c = 42248&a = 126515.

Schwarzenegger, Arnold. 2007. State of the State address, January 9. http://gov
.ca.gov/index.php?/press-release/5089/.

Shu, Catherine. 2006. "Telecommuting to Cope with Rising Gas Costs." *Wall
Street Journal*, May 9 http://www.careerjournal.com/myc/officelife/20060515-
shu.html.

"SustainLane Releases 2006 City Sustainability Rankings." 2006. Treehugger
.com. June 2 http://www.treehugger.com/files/2006/06/sustainlane_rel_1
.php.

"Top 10 Green Cities in the US." 2006. *The Green Guide*. http://www.thegreen
guide.com/doc.mhtml?i = 113&s = top10cities.

"Top 10 Green Cities in the US: 2005." 2005. *The Green Guide* http://www.the
greenguide.com/doc/107/cities.

Wilmouth, Adam. 2006. "Are We Ready for the Next Energy Crisis?" *Daily Okla-
homan*, April 18.

WMO and UNEP. 2007. "Climate Change 2007: Mitigation of Global Climate
Change." Intergovernmental Panel on Climate Change, Fourth Assessment
Report http://www.ipcc.ch/SPM040507.pdf.

Yost, Geoffrey H., and Smauel J. Maselli. 2007. "United States: U.S. Supreme
Court Issues Seminal Environmental Opinion in Massachusetts v. Environmental Protection Agency." http://www.mondaq.com/article.asp?articleid
= 48444&lastestnews = 1.

Afterword

NEAL PEIRCE

The early years of the twenty-first century have been ominous. Take any measure—potentially calamitous global warming, international terrorism, war in the Middle East, islands of genocide, fear of pandemics. Reasons abound to be deeply pessimistic about our times.

But there is an exception: life-generating, life-sustaining *green*. And it's not just the green of open field and forest, as critical as those "lungs of the world" remain. The new focus is how regenerative green can be expanded within the world of asphalt and concrete, the jungles of brick, steel, and glass that characterize the rapidly expanding growing urban regions of our time. The definition of "green" keeps growing as fast as morning glories race up a wall, embracing energy-saving and renewable resources, reduced burning of fossil fuels, cleaner air and water, more efficient water and wastewater systems, brownfields cleanup, community gardens, opportunities for better health.

The essays in this volume explore this new green landscape with fresh eyes. They look into historic antecedents, international comparisons, the effects on health, real estate, urban planning, and the essential social fabric of cities. Just glancing through the table of contents is heartening. A refreshing, clear message comes through: that the means, methods, and science to create sustainable green cities, places we would choose for ourselves and children and grandchildren, *do* exist and are within our power to effect. The question is not the possibility of green and livable cities in a more sustainable world; it is whether we have the collective imagination and will to make that world real in our place and time.

But this book will also make you impatient, and on many fronts.

Why, beyond Seattle, south Florida, Boston, and a few other locales, do we lack clear, statistically significant data on the greenness, the sustainability of our great metropolitan regions, the areas my colleagues and I choose to call the "citistates" of the today's world?

And what are we building? We now have a marvelous set of tools to judge the efficiency with which buildings use energy, water, construction materials. Those tools are known as LEED—the Leadership in Energy and Environmental Design—Green Building Rating System, put forth by the U.S. Green Building Council and now a the nationally accepted benchmark for the design, construction, and operation of high-performance green buildings. The issue's critical cause buildings are responsible for up to 60 percent of our greenhouse gas emissions. The price premium for LEED-level construction is roughly 2 percent, but that is easily offset by subsequent energy savings. So why aren't LEED standards already required for new buildings, public and private, in most American cities, and not just a handful of pace-setting communities such as Salt Lake City?

And what is the delay in expanding the standards beyond building form to the compactness and walkability of entire neighborhoods through the newly defined LEED-ND (neighborhood development) standards? America has been immensely fortunate to have the New Urbanist style of town and neighborhood planning introduced and expanded over the last 20 years. Now many developers who once scorned it are at least adopting some of its features of sociable front porches, alleys, and accessible town centers.

But more often than not, truly compact development violates the sterile, single-use zoning laws enacted from the early twentieth century onward. At the University of Pennsylvania Growing Greener Cities conference where many of the papers in this book were first presented, there seemed to be wide agreement that the time has come for state and local governments across America to make a priority of replacing outmoded zoning with modern and more flexible approaches including form-based codes, untangling obsolete building codes, and setting much more flexible new standards. Sadly, such reforms are viewed with skepticism by many materials manufacturers and unions and are low on most states legislatures' agendas.

An alluring new generation of "green blue" strategies—handling urban water (and runoff) in more sensitive, planet protecting ways—are celebrated in this book and are being introduced across the country. The tradition goes back to design of our great urban parks; today it is expanded to "daylighting" of once buried urban streams, ways to filter storm waters more slowly through swales, temporary retention ponds, and other landscaping that avoids big engineering solutions in favor of nature's more modest but ecologically sound green ways.

But "green blue" is spreading at very modest rates compared to the immensity of opportunity (and challenge) in building new communities and retrofitting old ones across America. The same can be said of the popular idea of green roofs and "living walls" that were also discussed in this book. Chicago Mayor Richard Daley gave green roofs major national credibility by converting the roof of City Hall to a blanket of grass and plants. It's true, green roofs cost more than regular ones, but their long-term payoff, from durability to building energy savings to reduced water runoff, are tremendous. So where are the new financial tools to let interested owners across America opt for green roofs with less upfront capital? Couldn't all these strategies be expanded much more rapidly?

And what of recycling urban lands more vigorously? Brownfields reclamation is proceeding, though often at a snail's pace. Beyond that, immense opportunities for urban infill are at hand across America's urban landscape, "wasted landscapes" ranging from old factory sites and parking lots to abandoned shopping malls. Added to that is the possibility of converting poorly designed cheap commercial roadways into tasteful boulevards with bike lanes, tree canopy and other greenery, and people-friendly design. Some of this is occurring throughout America. Waterfronts, especially, are enjoying a renaissance, widely converted from old industrial and railroading uses to esplanades and intense people uses. Still, in comparison to need and opportunity, we are far behind in recycling urban properties in and around our great urban regions. Why?

A heartening variety of "green city strategies," like Philadelphia's effort to recycle large swaths of partially abandoned residential areas for landscaping, redevelopment, and in many cases both, are cited in this book. The benefits can be enormous—for city economies, for bridging social divides, for erasing urban eyesores that repel reinvestment. But too few cities are thinking so green and entrepreneurially.

Chicago remains the nation's top example of turning natural green into higher quality of life *and* economic return. Just visit in spring or summer: You will see vast plantings of flowers and blossoming pots, starting along Michigan Avenue and around the Loop, and then along roadway medians extending out to the neighborhoods. No other American city may be quite so far along in converting asphalt schoolyards to grass, vacant lots into community gardens, in reinvesting in a vast system of 570 city parks, 31 beaches, and 16 historic lagoons. Turning the town green is a major, explicit priority of Mayor Daley and his administration. And the dramatic green Chicago waterfront created in the era of Dean Burnham has now been enhanced with the $475 million Millennium Park, an extravaganza of greenery, sculpture, fountain grass, and plantings that draws 4 million visitors a year.

As Chicago Alderman Mary Ann Smith told a parks conference in 2006: "We're creating places people want to be, not places people want to flee." A glance at the varieties of ages, sexes, races, and ethnicities rubbing shoulders in Chicago's new and refurbished public spaces proves the point. Green is *social.* You can even see it at a farmers market, a non-bar-coded world where the seller looks you in the eye and city folk get to meet produce growers directly. Green's not only fresher, it's more personal.

Add in the grand benefits of "green" schools so kids can learn better—and grow healthier—even while their schools consume less energy. The immense benefits for human health in greened, treed, and park-rich settings of greened cities. The "draw" of green cities in an era in which cities strive for a share of discerning, income-generating professionals. Green is not just cooling, beautifying, restorative to the human body, giving of joy, but a centerpiece of city hopes and success.

The Philadelphia conference opened a very unexpected aspect of green for me. The featured speaker was Wangari Maathai, the remarkable Kenyan environmentalist and social activist who in 1977 founded the Green Belt Movement that has planted over 30 million trees across Kenya to counter the serious soil erosion triggered by thoughtless and careless development. In 2004 she was awarded the Nobel Peace Prize for "her contribution to sustainable development, democracy and peace"—the first African woman to receive the award.

Maathai, in her remarks, painted the green issue as intensely personal. We are entering, she said, an era of potentially radical climate change with the prospect of dangerously rising waters and imperiled aquifers, scarcity of resources, and a likely "rising tide of environmental refugees."

The gross inequities of peoples and nations in the consumption of the globe's natural resources violates ideals of equity, fairness. So what is our responsibility? Start with the planting of a single tree, she counseled her listeners. Resolve to be "green masters," following Mahatma Gandhi's counsel to "Be the change you want to see." Accept the idea that the world's natural resources must be shared far more equitably than they are today. A green world and a world of peace, Maathai suggested, are inseparable; they must move forward in tandem, or neither will prevail.

And, said Maathai, we must "expand our concept of peace." The planting of trees, a truly "green" world, a more equitable sharing of the globe's natural resources are not separate issues.

Notes

Introduction: Urban Greening and the Green City Ideal

1. See www.thegreenguide.com/doc/113/top10cities; www.earthday.net/
UER/report/cityrank-overall.html.

Chapter 2. Growing Greener Regions

1. Each mode of transportation also has different implications for energy
usage and climate change. On the least intensive end of the spectrum one finds
the nonmotorized modes, including walking and bicycling, while at the other
extreme one finds the single-occupancy automobile.

2. Boston, Washington, D.C., and Babylon, New York, recently enacted new
mandatory green building codes. Boston's code requires all new commercial
structures over 50,000 square feet to meet a minimum of 26 of 69 criteria of
the U.S. Green Building Council. Improving market conditions will couple with
innovative regulatory techniques to limit the energy consumption of appliances
and lighting in our region's buildings, thereby limiting the need to generate
electricity.

*Chapter 3. The Inter-Regional Dimension: The Greening of London and the Wider South
East*

1. See *London Strategic Parks Project Report* (EDAW/Greater London Authority
2006) for a good discussion.

2. Mayor Livingstone argues that the world's major cities have a particular
responsibility to lead the efforts to mitigate and adapt to climate change. He is
spearheading a coalition of 20 of the world's largest cities (including Philadelphia and New York) committed to joint action. The coalition has recently
teamed up with the Clinton Foundation in order to use the purchasing power
of city governments as an instrument for more effective climate change practice.

Chapter 4. Greening Cities: A Public Realm Approach

1. Before then, this was a place familiar to lovers of American literature—the
ash heap featured in *The Great Gatsby*.

Chapter 5. Growing Greener, New York Style

This chapter is adapted from *New York City Mobility Needs Assessment 2007–2030* (Weinberger 2007), which the author wrote while serving in the Mayor's Office of Long-Term Planning and Sustainability as the senior policy advisor for transportation. Special thanks to Emily Yuhas of the Office of Long-Term Planning and Sustainability for her help in preparing the *Mobility Needs Assessment* and whose aid in preparing this article was invaluable. Thanks also to Mark Seaman of the Office of Long-Term Planning and Sustainability and to the members of the New York City Department of Transportation Office of Strategic Planning for their contributions to the *Assessment*.

1. The New York City Department of City Planning has forecast an increase of approximately 1 million residents by 2030.

2. Data for Boston were not available.

3. Even growing at a much faster rate, truck traffic will remain a low proportion of traffic, reaching 4.5 percent of total vehicle miles traveled in the city in 2030.

4. National Household Travel Survey New York City Supplement 2001 (http://nhts.ornl.gov/); 2000 U.S. Census; New York Metropolitan Transportation Council (NYMTC 1998).

5. Looking at just the shortest trips, less than one-half mile, gives insight to the challenges of pedestrian promotion. Of these short trips 84 percent are made by walking citywide, typically taking no more than 10 minutes. But walking trips are not distributed uniformly across the city. Walking accounts for 95 percent of trips less than a half mile in Manhattan, but only 46 percent of such trips in Staten Island; indeed, over 50 percent of these short trips are made by car in Staten Island, reinforcing the observation that where car ownership is high the car is the default mode. For Brooklyn, the Bronx, and Queens respectively, walking accounts for 84 percent, 75 percent, and 71 percent of such trips.

6. The MTA is a state agency that builds, operates, and maintains all New York City's public transportation systems, including the commuter rail lines that serve the eastern and northern suburbs. MTA also operates the toll bridges and tunnels within New York City and that connect New York City to Westchester County. As a state agency, however, the authority's goals are not perfectly aligned with the interests of the city.

Chapter 6. Greener Homes, Greener Cities: Expanding Affordable Housing and Strengthening Cities Through Sustainable Residential Development

1. See the McGraw-Hill Construction website, http://construction.com/AboutUs/2007/0326pr.asp.

2. LEED for Homes is designed to "recognize and reward the 25 percent of new homes that are the top performers in terms of resource efficiency and environmental stewardship," according to the U.S. Green Building Council. Responding to what the council calls "the unique needs of affordable housing," it established a special working group of industry leaders to determine the extent to which the LEED for Homes standard could better meet the needs of the affordable housing market.

3. See Tassos (2006: 5) and additional analysis by Enterprise (forthcoming).

4. As of July 2007, more than 600 mayors had committed to achieve a 7 per-

cent reduction in their cities' greenhouse gas reductions from 1990 levels by 2012 under the U.S. Mayors Climate Protection Agreement.

5. Specifically, the law requires residential properties over 10,000 square feet receiving 15 percent or more public financing to comply with the Green Communities Criteria as of October 2008. See the summary of the "District of Columbia Green Building Act of 2006, Bill 16–515," prepared by GreenHOME.

6. The benefits are speculative because of the limited data available on green affordable developments that have been in operation for a significant period of time.

7. In June 2007 the Internal Revenue Service issued proposed regulations that would substantially enhance the ability of housing agencies to calculate more accurate utility allowances for affordable housing developments financed with federal Low Income Housing Tax Credits. If adopted, these regulations would enable affordable housing developers to realize greater financial benefits from more energy efficient constriction, rehabilitation, and operations.

8. The Equator Principles are a voluntary set of guidelines based on International Finance Corporation standards for managing environmental and social issues in project finance lending. The principles initially applied to investments with capital costs above $50 million. On July 6, 2006, a revised version of the Equator Principles was adopted. The new Equator Principles apply to all countries and sectors, and to all project financings with capital costs above $10 million. See www.equator-principles.com.

Chapter 7. Urban Stream Restoration: Recovering Ecological Services in Degraded Watersheds

1. The research on which this chapter is based was supported by National Science Foundation Grant CMS 0201409. Related publications derived from the same study include Platt (2006) and Sievert (2006).

2. This case study is adapted from earlier studies by Timothy Beatley and Kurt Raskouskas on behalf of the University of Massachusetts Urban Watershed Study.

3. This case study is based on a seminar paper prepared by Beth Fenstermacher, a graduate student in landscape architecture at the University of Massachusetts, Amherst.

4. This case study is based on an unpublished report by Nancy Goucher and Dr. Sarah Michaels at the University of Waterloo School of Planning under a contract with the University of Massachusetts Urban Watershed Management Study. Ron Ormson at the city of Waterloo provided invaluable assistance in the preparation of the original study.

Chapter 8. The Role of Citizen Activists in Urban Infrastructure Development

1. The American Society of Civil Engineers (ASCE) lists 200 Landmark Projects on its "History & Heritage of Civil Engineering" website http://live .asce.org/hh/index.mxml.

2. John Muir established the Sierra Club in 1892 and focused much of its energy from the early 1900s to his death in opposition to the development of the Hetch Hetchy water system, a reservoir and aqueduct built to take water

from Yosemite National Park to the City of San Francisco (Brechin 1999: 108–17).

3. Alvin Alm, staff director for the President's Council on Environmental Quality from 1970 to 1973, summarizes the history of this period as follows: "Concurrent with the creation of NEPA was the founding of new environmental litigation organizations—namely the Natural Resources Defense Council and the Environmental Defense Fund. NEPA was like grain dust to the environmental litigators' match. These and other environmental and citizen groups used the NEPA tool to sue a host of federal agencies for noncompliance with NEPA. The courts generally came down on their side" (Alm 2007).

4. Independent Sector, a nonprofit organization representing charitable and volunteer groups, estimated in its report on *Giving and Volunteering in the United States 2001* that 83.9 million Americans contributed 15.5 billion hours of their time formally volunteering in their communities. They also identify "1.23 million charities, social welfare organizations, and religious congregations" as depending on giving and volunteering by community members. While these organizations cover the broad spectrum of health, human services, religion, education, the arts and other philanthropic activities, it is notable that 3 percent of Independent Sector's approximately 700 members are organizations focused on "Conservation and Ecology." If even half that percentage is applied to the overall population of groups (1.23 million), it suggests that there could be nearly 20,000 organizations and groups focused on environmental issues at work in America today (Independent Sector 2007). Furthermore, the U.S. Bureau of Labor Statistics reported that of a total 65.4 million volunteers, 1.8 percent have dedicated their time to "environmental or animal care" organizations—an interesting grouping of issues (BLS 2005).

5. Independent Sector, in *Measuring Volunteering: A Practical Tool Kit*, describes the issue succinctly: "despite the social and economic benefits of volunteering, empirical data about it is scarce in most parts of the world. Because few surveys have been carried out, little is yet known about how many people are involved in volunteering, what they do, what motivates them, and how valuable their contribution is. Obtaining reliable information about volunteering is essential if this valuable resource is to be developed to its full potential" (Independent Sector 2001).

6. The miniseries is comprised of four hour-long episodes, each focused on a major American city, Chicago, Philadelphia, Los Angeles, and Seattle. Each episode combines a brief historical profile with in-depth portraits of community activists, professionals, and government officials who are making a notable impact by improving their neighborhoods and cities. The series celebrates these individuals and tells the story of both their setbacks and accomplishments. As important, it is a call to action for others interested in getting more involved in their own communities.

Chapter 9. Blue-Green Practices: Why They Work and Why They Have Been So Difficult to Implement Through Public Policy

1. At the time Tourbier was an adjunct assistant professor of landscape architecture at the University of Pennsylvania and research director of the Center for Ecological Research in Planning and Design.

2. The R-WIN program was developed by Ingenieurgesellschaft für Stadtshydrologie mbH, in Hannover, Germany. This program is calibrated against data

collected at a green roof research station located south of Stuttgart. It is intended to be used by German municipalities to assess development proposals.

Chapter 10. The Roots of the Urban Greening Movement

1. The Fruitvale Recreation and Open Space Initiative (FROSI) encompassed all these elements in the revitalization of one city park, the creation of a second one, and the reviving of four open spaces managed by a community land trust. An account of the FROSI partnership can be found in Rubin (1998) and on the website of the Spanish-Speaking Unity Council. www.unitycouncil.org.

2. A 25-year campaign to close an exceptionally dirty power plant in the Bay-view-Hunters Point neighborhood of San Francisco is one of those described in Pastor, Sadd, and Morello-Frosch (2007).

3. Barros (2006).

4. Inner City 100, a "joint venture of Initiative for a Competitive Inner City and *Inc.* magazine, is the first-of-its-kind national listing of 100 fast growing companies located exclusively in America's Inner City." See www.innercity100.org.

5. See www.ncbn.org. The rapid growth of the network and a well-received annual conference did not ensure long-term stability, however. NCBN suspended operations in 2005, though most of the member organizations continue to operate.

6. See Rubin (1998) and the Unity Council website.

7. The process of resident engagement is described in Robinson (2005).

8. Residents can invest in the project and share in the developed assets and risks of Market Creek Plaza. Ownership can take the form of individual shares in the entity controlling the property on which the stores are located. These were recently purchased by 450 residents in the first such "neighborhood Initial Public Offering." A new philanthropic foundation focused on the community has also been formed and will grow in assets as the project expands and the family foundation sunsets and transfers its holdings to the community. For information about this process see www.marketcreek.com.

9. See, for example, the research and community-level innovations sponsored or documented by Active Living Research, based at San Diego State University, and Active Living by Design, at the University of North Carolina, Chapel Hill, two entities established by the Robert Wood Johnson Foundation. The annual New Partners for Smart Growth conference, www.newpartners.org, has become a significant meeting place for designers, planners, health professionals, and policymakers working on these issues.

10. Some leading foundations in the realm of healthy eating and active living include the Robert Wood Johnson Foundation, W. K. Kellogg Foundation, California Endowment, and Kaiser Permanente. The CDC division examining community factors, www.cdc.gov/healthyplaces, that includes 11 categories of health issues related to community design.

11. In addition to the New Partners for Smart Growth conference cited above, regional meetings such as those held in December 2006 by the Bay Area Planning Directors Association and the Bay Area Regional Health Inequities Initiative (representing county public health directors) are typical of a growing trend. Urban greening projects and other land use issues were the focal point of such meetings, and new collaborations at the local level are sometimes started as a result.

12. Several manuals for health professionals about urban planning and rede-

velopment have been produced by the Public Health Law Program, www.healthy
planning.org.
13. Rubin (2006); see also Pastor and Reed (2005).
14. The seven principles are discussed at length in Rubin (2006).

Chapter 11. Leveraging Media for Social Change

1. For more information see www.edenslostandfound.org.
2. In 2006, Harry Wiland and Dale Bell were elected Ashoka Lifetime Fellows,
the first media professionals to be so honored.

Chapter 12. Transformation Through Greening

1. Philadelphia Green's criteria for choosing target areas included the existence of many vacant properties; the presence of strong community organizations; a significant level of investment by private and public institutions; solid,
quality infrastructure, such as access to public transportation and proximity to
hospitals, schools, and other community institutions and geographic distribution across the city.
2. See Wachter and Gillen (2006).

Chapter 13. Community Development Finance and the Green City

1. For additional information on The Reinvestment Fund, refer to the fund
website, http://www.trfund.com/. Community development financial institutions allocate capital to achieve economic growth and opportunity with an
emphasis on restoring distressed places, assisting low-income populations, or tar-
geting resources to sectors with limited capital alternatives. They embody a dual
interest in achieving financial returns and social impact. The best information
on community development financial institutions is published by the Opportunity Finance Network, http://www.opportunityfinance.net.
2. The term originated in a TRF publication; see Development Finance Network (2004).
3. A critique of many of these efforts can be found in Norquist (1998). For
governance ideas from reform mayors, see Manhattan Institute (1999); for
urban revitalization between 1970 and 2000, see Birch (2007).
4. While much has been written about regional land issues and the role of
research institutions, see Katz and Stern (2006) for an interesting analysis of
urban demographic changes.
5. The population change in Philadelphia has remarkable 50-year symmetry:
1.4 million in 1900; 2 million in 1950; back to 1.5 million in 2000.
6. This information is derived from the city of Philadelphia's *Neighborhood
Transformations Initiative* report, which can be found on the city of Philadelphia
website. The NTI report was carried out in 2001 by the city of Philadelphia in
consultation with The Reinvestment Fund. McGovern (2006) discusses the NTI.
7. The National Center for Healthy Housing, http://www.centerforhealthy
housing.org/, is a great resource for this information.
8. For the historical connection between industrial development and epidemiology as a scientific practice, see Winkelstein (2000).

9. I am, of course, speaking of developers in an abstract sense, not about a particular developer who might have a perspective on environmental sustainability and the use of physical plant, land, or natural resources. Many people make investment and development choices that consciously prioritize, emphasize, or avoid some aspect of environmental quality or consequence. And, of course, increasingly, the *environmental* development niche is becoming a core part of many businesses, including national commercial and residential developers that specialize in green building design, the use of natural amenities, or the remediation of environmentally-damaged land. These businesses are successful to the extent to which there is consumer demand for their products. Market demand and profitability make conventional investors and developers into environmentalists.

10. For more on the Hope VI program, see Popkin et al. (2004).

11. An analysis of the East Camden work appeared in a Community Affairs Discussion paper published by the Philadelphia Federal Reserve Bank; see Smith and Hevener (2005).

Chapter 14. Growing Edible Cities

1. See Brown (2006); Pfeiffer (2006); Deffeyes (2005); Murray (2005); Pimentel and Giampietro (1994); Heller and Keoleian (2000: 40).

2. See UNDP (1996); FAO (2004); Koc et al. (2000); Mougeot (2005); Schurmann (1996); Steele (1996); "Urban Food Production" (1992); Stix (1996).

3. The classic text on permaculture is Mollison and Holmgren (1990); see also Holmgren (2002).

4. *Power of Community* (2006); Quinn (2006); Murphy (2006), Premat (2005); Rodriguez (2000); Diaz and Harris (2005); Viljoen and Howe (2005).

5. For ongoing localization efforts, see Post-Carbon Institute, www.postcarbon.org; its Re-Localization Network, www.relocalize.net; Community Solution, www.communitysolution.org; Global Ecovillage Network, gen.ecovillage.org. For more mainstream treatments of the values and best practices of localization, especially in economic development, see Shuman (2000, 2006); Hammel and Denhart (2006).

6. Lyson (2004); see also Koc et al. (2000); Mougeot (2005); Jacobi et al. (2000).

7. Ratta and Smit (1993); Kaufman (1999); Sommers and Smit (1994); Greenhow (1994); Quon (1999); Patel (1996).

8. Nelson (1996); Smit and Nasr (1995, 1992); Rose (1999); Flynn (1999).

9. See Flores (2006); Katz (2006); Gottlieb and Fisher (1996a, b).

10. Silva (1999, nn. 28, 30–31); Pollan (2006a, b); Tansey and Worsley (1995); Lawson (2005); Johnson (2005).

11. Viljoen (2005). For a phased plan to turn Los Angeles into such an agrotopia or ecotopia, see Glover (1983); http://www.ithacahours.com/losangeles.html.

12. http://www.sustainlane.us/Local_Foo_and_Agriculture.jsp.

13. See www.thefoodtrust.org; *Food Matters* (2006); Karlen (2007).

14. Pierson and Karlen (2006); see also www.whitedogcafefoundation.org/fairfood.

15. See www.weaversway.org.

16. See www.urbannutrition.org.

17. See www.phila.k12.pa.us/schools/saul; www.lincolnhs.phila.k12.pa.us/academies/hort.

18. Corboy (2005); see also www.greensgrow.org.

19. See www.somertontanksfarm.org.

20. Christensen and Weissman (2006); Institute for Innovations in Local Farming (2005); Van Allen (2004).

21. Correspondence with Nancy Weissman (December 1, 2006).

22. Spirn (2005); www.millcreekurbanfarm.org.

23. Interview with Rosen and Walker (2006); Smith (2006); Mill Creek Farm (2006); www.millcreekurbanfarm.org.

24. The Philly Orchard Project's web site includes links to comparable urban orchard programs across North America and the United Kingdom; see http://www.healthdemocracy.org/pop.html.

25. Interview with Pierson (2006).

26. For estimates of production in cities with existing and proposed local food initiatives, see Ratta and Smit (1993); Kaufman (1999); Sommers and Smit (1994); Greenhow (1994); Quon (1999); Patel (1996); Nelson (1996); Smit and Nasr (1995, 1992); Rose (1999); Flynn (1999); Flores (2006); Katz (2006); Gottlieb and Fisher (1996a, b).

Chapter 15. Ecosystem Services and the Green City

1. See Salzman, Thompson, and Daily (2001: 310–12), distinguishing between ecosystem "goods" and ecosystem "services."

2. Global ecosystem services are valued at $16–54 trillion annually; see Costanza et al. (1997: 259).

3. Ibid.; Zwerdling (n.d.); Louisiana Coastal Wetlands Commission (1998: 203); McKay (2005).

4. McKay (2005). According to this scientist, wetlands reduce storm surge by a foot for every three miles of wetlands that a hurricane crosses. A study of Hurricane Andrew in 1992 concluded that the wetlands reduced the storm surge by 6 feet between Cocodrie and the Houma Navigation Canal, some 23 miles to the north (Louisiana Coastal Wetlands Commission 1998: 55). "Clearly, the effect of storms on the human population and infrastructure in the coastal zone can be ameliorated by the maintenance of extensive coastal marshes and barrier islands" (56).

5. To cite but a few examples, such fees have been imposed in Lewiston, Maine, www.ci.lewiston,me.us/publicservices/stormwaterutility.htm; Lawrence, Kansas, www.ci.lawrence.ks.us/publicworks/stormwater-faq.shtml; Durham, North Carolina, www.durhamnc.gov/departments/works/stormwater_fees.cfm; Yakima, Washington, www.ci.yakima.wa.us.

6. For a helpful description of this program, see Salzman and Ruhl (2000).

7. New York City's direct investment in upstate watershed lands would appear to be a counterexample. However, it should be noted that the decision to make this investment was not entirely voluntary. The city was faced with a Safe Drinking Water Act requirement that it either build the filtration plant or restore the watershed. New York thus purchased the rights to upstate lands as a means of complying with a regulatory requirement. In this sense, the compliance situation had as much in common with trading systems as it did with the direct investment approach.

8. Salzman and Ruhl (2000) discuss this issue at length.

Chapter 16. Metro Nature: Its Functions, Benefits, and Values

1. A curious, parallel shift in attitude emerged regarding cities. Early in human history cities were refuges from threats by human and natural invaders. They were islands of security and order in a chaotic sea of wilderness. In the past century or so cities have acquired some of the apprehensions once reserved for the wild.

2. Paul Samuelson is credited as the first to address public goods, defining "collective consumption goods" as: . . . [goods] which all enjoy in common in the sense that each individual's consumption of such a good leads to no subtractions from any other individual's consumption of that good" (1954: 387–89). This property is known as nonrivalness.

3. See Boyer and Polasky (2004: 744–55); de Groot and Boumans (2002: 393–408).

4. Payne (1973: 74–75) found the 1.9 percent increase, Schroeder (1982: 371–22) the 4.5 percent increase, and Tyrvainen and Miettinen (2000: 205–23) the 7 percent increase.

5. Adapted from Boyd (2006).

Chapter 17. Green Investment Strategies: How They Matter for Urban Neighborhoods

1. See Florida (2003) on how quality of life makes a difference in attracting new knowledge workers to urban places

2. Identifying these gains enables the use of funding sources that would otherwise not be available. Anticipated growth in property tax revenues stemming from a proposed urban greening project can be used to demonstrate the feasibility of funding place-based investments through self-financing mechanisms, such as tax increment financing (TIF) or the establishment of a Business Improvement District (BID).

3. See Rothenberg (1991).

4. The database merges home sales with information on place-based public investments and neighborhood-level attributes, creating an integrated spatial database The dataset also includes information about value and additional variables that affect property values, such as the physical characteristics of specific houses, the location and density of the surrounding neighborhood, and the time of sale, as discussed below.

5. This is based on the smallest allowable residential lot size under current zoning (1,440 square feet) to conservatively estimate the total acreage of land due to demolished residential properties. See Philadelphia City Planning Commission (1995).

6. The concept of "Broken Windows" was used by the New York police to clean up the city's streets. http://www.nationalreview.com/comment/bratton_kelling200602281015.asp. The buildings whose windows were fixed no longer served as a refuge for criminals and drug dealers and thus helped in abating incidences of crime in the neighborhood. Wachter and Wong (2007) point out that green investment such as tree plantings can be viewed as a signaling event. If so, the event can have value above and beyond that of the investment itself. It indicates that investment in a neighborhood is occurring, social capital between residents is improving, and the neighborhood appears to be on a perceived "upswing." The authors measure the intertemporal dynamics of this effect

through an event-study methodology that measures how the capitalization of green investments varies with time from the event.

7. See Wachter (2005)

8. See Rosen (1974) for the classic discussion of the modeling of house prices. For a discussion on alternative price methodologies, see Case et al. (1991), Gillen et al. (2001), Lee et al. (1998) and Thibodeau et al. (2001).

9. See Mills and Hamilton (1994) for a good discussion of why it is difficult to identify neighborhood effects of amenities using traditional hedonics.

10. See Hammer et al. (1974) for an early hedonic study of the impact of parks. Correll et al. (1998), Crompton et al. (2000), and Lutzenhiser et al. (2001) show the impact of green investment using the hedonic methodology

11. For a further discussion of the results see Wachter and Gillen (2006).

12. Bradbury et al. (2001) and Bowes (2001) demonstrate the specific value of public services. Ellen et al. (2001) deploy a similar methodology to that employed here.

13. The availability of the required spatial and temporal information determines the extent to which this methodology can be used. This means that since the dates of tree plantings and vacant lot stabilization activities are known, we can separate home sales into "pre-upgrade" and "post-upgrade" periods. However, in the case of potentially important variables such as school dropout and crime rates, only one time period's worth of data was available. Areas with high dropout rates may also be areas with related variables we do not capture in our model. We are not able to categorize specific time-based changes in these variables as "upgrade" events and thus cannot as precisely measure their impact.

Chapter 18. Measuring the Economic Impacts of Greening: The Center for Neighborhood Technology Green Values Calculator

1. A site assessment in Chicago indicated that annual runoff volume could be reduced up to 65 percent by using swales and filter strips with native vegetation. The pollutant-removal capacity for these plants at the same site could be as high as 80 percent for suspended solids and heavy metals and 70 percent for nutrients. See City of Chicago (2003: 12).

2. The specific hydrologic indicators produced by the Green Values Calculator are: the volume of runoff produced by a single lot, the total volume of runoff produced by the entire site (all the lots combined), the maximum speeds at which runoff is leaving each lot and the site as a whole, the volume of detention required for the site to meet conventional government stormwater regulation, and the average volume of water that is annually absorbed into the ground and recharges groundwater due to green infrastructure implementation (Hollander et al. 2006).

3. The benefit in runoff reduction is insignificant compared to the enormously increased cost of installing green roofs instead of regular roofs. However, in an urban scenario, permeable pavements and green roofs make more sense. Although they are still expensive technologies, they can be incorporated into the urban landscape when no other open space is available. The runoff reductions these technologies can offer may eventually more then outweigh their costs when compared to the capitol investment required by large tunneling projects and other urban stormwater management measures.

4. Table 1 shows aggregate cost savings for developer, homeowner, and pub-

lic over full lifecycle. The $300,000 is solely developer first-time construction costs.

5. See "Green Roofs Keep on Growing" (2007).

Chapter 19. What Makes Today's Green City?

1. See International Council for Local Environmental Initiatives website, http://www.iclei.org/index.php?id=800.

2. See U.S. Green Building Council website, http://www.usgbc.org/Display Page.aspx?CMSPageID=220.

3. Park data indicating total land devoted to parks out of total city area are available from Trust for Public Land, Washington, D.C., from a 2002 report by Peter Harnik.

4. California Integrated Waste Management Plan of 1989 city requirements are summarized on the state of California website at http://www.leginfo.ca.gov/cgi-bin/displaycode?section=prc&group=41001–42000&file=41750–41751.

5. California Senate Bill 1078 is summarized in "California Owned Electric Utilities" (2005).

6. Sustainable Seattle's indicators were summarized on the group's website, http://www.sustainableseattle.org/Programs/RegionalIndicators/.

7. The expanded Portney study, published in January 2006, is on his personal webpage, http://ase.tufts.edu/polsci/faculty/portney/sustainable-cities.asp.

8. See Karlenzig et al. (2007). Also see online excerpts of the SustainLane U.S. City Rankings, http://www.sustainlane.us/overview.jsp. The complete 2006 city rankings and research methodology are available with additional updates and analysis in Karlenzig et al. (2007).

9. Author interview, April 2005.

10. Los Angeles city and county operate 10 bus rapid transit lines managed by the Los Angeles County Metropolitan Transportation Authority. http://www.mta.net/projects_programs/rapid/rapid.htm.

11. From video transcript, June 3, 2005, San Francisco.

12. A partial list is available at SustainLane government website, http://www.sustainlane.us/sl-media.jsp.

13. See "PlaNYC: A Greener, Greater New York." http://www.nyc.gov/html/planyc2030/html/plan/plan.shtml.

14. The website is http://www.greenprintdenver.org/.

15. See the proceedings of the Denver World Oil Conference ("Beyond Oil" 2005).

16. See Pew Climate Center website, http://www.pewclimate.org/what_s_be ing_done/in_the_states/ab32/in dex .cfm.

Contributors

Timothy Beatley is Teresa Heinz Professor of Sustainable Communities in the Department of Urban and Environmental planning, School of Architecture, at the University of Virginia, where he has taught for the last 20 years. Much of his work focuses on sustainable communities and creative strategies by which cities and towns can fundamentally reduce their ecological footprints while, at the same time, becoming more livable and equitable places. His most recent books on this topic are *Green Urbanism: Learning from European Cities* and *Native to Nowhere: Sustaining Home and Community in a Global Age*. He holds a Ph.D. in city and regional planning from the University of North Carolina at Chapel Hill.

Dale Bell is an award-winning filmmaker/activist whose productions have won the Academy Award for *Woodstock*, Peabody Award for the *Kennedy Center Tonight* series, two Emmys, two Christophers, and other awards and nominations. With Harry Wiland, he formed the nonprofit Media & Policy Center Foundation in Santa Monica to create PBS programming on eldercare, health care, and sustainable environments, all supported by many other media components, including books, websites, community action guides, symposia, academic curricula, and town hall meetings. He has been named an Ashoka Fellow, joining 1,700 other recognized social entrepreneurs in the world; he and Wiland are the first from media to be so honored.

Eugenie L. Birch is codirector at the Penn Institute for Urban Research and professor and chair of the Department of City and Regional Planning at the University of Pennsylvania School of Design. She has recently been awarded the position Lawrence C. Nussdorf Chair of Urban Research. She has done extensive work on how cities have incorporated greening into municipal policy and ordinances, and is currently engaged in a longitudinal study of downtown living.

J. Blaine Bonham, Jr., serves as executive vice president for the Pennsylvania Horticultural Society and leads its urban greening program, Philadelphia Green. Under Bonham's direction, Philadelphia Green has moved to the forefront of urban greening efforts in the United States and has served as a model for programs in other cities. Bonham joined the society in 1974 to develop an outreach program and has been executive vice president since 1998. He holds degrees in political science and horticulture and completed a Loeb Fellowship in advanced environmental studies at Harvard University in 1991. He was featured in the Philadelphia segment of the PBS series *Edens Lost & Found.*

Dana L. Bourland, AICP, LEED AP, is senior director of Green Communities for Enterprise Community Partners. Green Communities is a $555-million initiative to create 8,500 highly sustainable homes for low-income people and help make green practices the mainstream in all affordable housing. Dana directs all aspects of Green Communities, including strategic planning, capacity building, technical assistance, national partnerships, and delivery of project financing. She is widely recognized as a leading authority on sustainable solutions to affordable housing community development challenges. She received a Master of Planning Degree from the Hubert H. Humphrey Institute of Public Affairs at the University of Minnesota and is a former Peace Corps volunteer.

Carolyn R. Brown is a doctoral student at the University of Pennsylvania, Department of City and Regional Planning, with research interests in the areas of urban redevelopment and urban political theory. Her dissertation research will examine the nature of interest group conflict and public consensus in the planning and implementation of vacant property demolition initiatives. As a planning professional, she has consulted with local housing and community development agencies, nonprofit housing developers, and public housing authorities on affordable housing projects, housing preservation, and neighborhood planning initiatives.

Paul R. Brown is a member of the board of directors of CDM, a consulting, engineering, construction, and operations firm based in Cambridge, Massachusetts, dedicated to improving the environment and infrastructure for public and private clients worldwide. Brown has more than 30 years of experience in project development, project finance, and planning and management of public utilities and environmental facilities. He has also been a key leader in a number of water resource planning projects, emphasizing stakeholder involvement and multiobjective decision making.

Tom Daniels is a professor of city and regional planning at the University of Pennsylvania, where he teaches land use planning, growth management, and environmental planning. For nine years he managed the farmland preservation program in Lancaster County, Pennsylvania, where he lives. He is the author of *When City and Country Collide* and coauthor of *Holding Our Ground: Protecting America's Farms and Farmland*, *The Small Town Planning Handbook*, and *The Environmental Planning Handbook*. He frequently serves as a consultant to state and local governments and land trusts. He has a special interest in the land use and water quality connection.

Bill Eyring is a senior engineer for the Center for Neighborhood Technology (CNT) in Chicago. He has more than 35 years of experience in urban and water resource management, including 13 years on the staff at CNT. He has organized demonstration water management landscapes—green infrastructure—at schools, a utility corridor, and private homes. He cofounded three organizations that work to organize around different issues in the Des Plaines River Watershed. He worked with grassroots groups in two watersheds to develop and use report cards for their decision makers. He led the effort at CNT to develop the Green Values calculator, which provides a way to evaluate opportunities for low-cost and effective water resource management in neighborhoods.

Beth Fenstermacher holds a Master's degree in landscape architecture from the University of Massachusetts and a B.A. in environmental science from Boston University. She currently practices landscape architecture in Watertown, Massachusetts, with a focus on ecological and sustainable design practices.

Alexander Garvin has combined a career in urban planning and real estate with teaching, architecture, and public service. He is president and CEO of Alex Garvin and Associates, Inc. He was managing director of planning for NYC2012, New York City's committee for the 2012 Olympic bid, and was vice president for planning, design, and development at the Lower Manhattan Development Corporation, the agency charged with the redevelopment of the World Trade Center following 9/11. Over the last 35 years he held prominent positions in five New York City administrations, including deputy commissioner of housing and city planning commissioner. He is also a professor of Urban Planning and Management at Yale University.

Kevin C. Gillen, Ph.D., is a research fellow at Penn's Institute for Urban Research and a vice president with Econsult Corporation. A Wharton alumnus with a background in urban economics and real estate finance, his research interests are in analysis of real estate developments and operation of real estate markets, including their fiscal, economic, and financial implications. His research sponsors and clients have included the Philadelphia Housing Authority, Philadelphia Tax Reform Commission, Philadelphia Center City Owners' Association, Pennsylvania Housing Finance Authority, Pennsylvania Horticultural Society, Schuylkill River Development Corporation, William Penn Foundation, and U.S. Geological Survey. His research has been cited in the *New York Times, Philadelphia Inquirer, Philadelphia Daily News,* and *Philadelphia Magazine.*

Nancy Goucher has just finished her master of environmental studies degree in planning at the University of Waterloo in Ontario, Canada. Her thesis research focused on enhancing institutional organizational knowledge creation through adaptive capacity in water management organizations. Her research continues to explore the role of scientific knowledge in environmental decision making and policy development and specific water resource issues, including source water protection, flood damage reduction, and low-water response. She has coauthored nine publications. including journal articles in *Environmental Management* and *Review of Policy Research.*

Amy Gutmann is president of the University of Pennsylvania, where she also holds faculty appointments in Political Science, Communication, Philosophy, and Education. She has served at Princeton University as Provost, Laurance S. Rockefeller University Professor of Politics, Academic Advisor to the President, Dean of the Faculty, and Founding Director of the University Center for Human Values. Her recent books include *Why Deliberative Democracy?* (with Dennis Thompson), *Identity in Democracy, Democratic Education, Democracy and Disagreement* (with Dennis Thompson), and *Color Conscious* (with K. Anthony Appiah). Her reviews have appeared in the *New York Times Book Review, Times Literary Supplement, Washington Post,* and other general publications.

Peter Haas has been at the Center for Neighborhood Technology for 11 years, overseeing its nationally recognized GIS capacity, which helps communities map, model, analyze, and visualize the resources and opportunities available to them. He has developed analytic tools and applications for real estate markets and other community assets. In partnership with the Brookings Institution, he led research examining the relationship between the characteristics of places and household transportation costs, demonstrating that the former exhibited a much larger influence on costs than income and household size. He earned a Ph.D. in particle physics from Ohio State University.

Dennis D. Hirsch clerked for Judge John M. Walker, Jr., of the U.S. Court of Appeals for the Second Circuit upon graduating from law school. He then practiced environmental law with Sidley & Austin in Washington, D.C., and, subsequently, taught environmental law and property at Drake University Law School and Notre Dame Law School. Hirsch joined the Capital faculty in 1998 and teaches environmental law, advanced environmental law, and property. His scholarly writing includes a textbook on environmental law practice as well as several articles on environmental law and policy. He is a vice chair of the American Bar Association (ABA), Section of Environment, Energy, and Resources, Special Committee on Innovation, Management Systems and Trading, as well as vice chair of the ABA, Section of Environment, Energy and Resources, Task Force on Constitutional Issues.

Warren Karlenzig is president and founder of Common Current, a consulting firm working with business, government, and nongovernmental organizations on sustainable economic policy, collaborative stakeholder processes, and product development. He is former Chief Strategy Officer of SustainLane and primary author of *How Green Is Your City? The SustainLane US City Rankings*. He has consulted on sustainable economic policy for the White House Office of Science and Technology, the U.S. EPA, the California Department of Conservation, and the City of San Francisco.

Julia Kennedy is a natural resources engineer for the Center for Neighborhood Technology (CNT) in Chicago. Since earning a B.A. in engineering from Brown University in 2000, she has worked to promote environmental and community health and sustainability through use of appropriate technology and community organizing. She has written and designed a pocket guide to green infrastructure, performed research and community outreach to promote the use of green infrastructure, and made improvements to the Green Values online calculator and toolbox (greenvalues.cnt.org). She previously worked researching green infrastructure for the New Civic Works in New York City and served in the Peace Corps in the Islamic Republic of Mauritania.

David M. Kooris is senior planner for regional design at the Regional Plan Association. He manages a variety of community design and growth management projects in Connecticut and the Hudson Valley and on Long Island. Ranging from the region's rural fringe to its inner cities, his projects combine community involvement, visualization, and progressive implementation techniques to achieve smart growth and transit-oriented development throughout the region. He received an honors bachelor of arts in anthropology and geography from McGill University and a master's in city and regional planning and urban design from PennDesign at the University of Pennsylvania. A native of Fairfield, Connecticut, David has lived in Montreal, Vancouver, Sydney, Perth, and Philadelphia and has traveled throughout North America, Europe, and Australasia.

Sarah Michaels is a professor at University of Nebraska-Lincoln in the department of political science. She is author of numerous publications on water resources policy and management, knowledge gains in response to disasters, the science-policy interface, and comparative environmental policy. She has held positions in the Department of Geography, University of Colorado; Department of Urban and Environmental policy, Tufts University; and Department of Geography, University of Auckland, New Zealand. Prior to joining the University of Nebraska, she was associate professor and associate director of the School of Planning at the University of Waterloo. She routinely consults with government and private agencies related to her expertise.

Charlie Miller is founder and president of Roofscapes, Inc. His award-winning customized green roof designs integrate aesthetic and technical requirements, with an emphasis on thoughtful hydrologic engineering to sustain the living ecosystem. His interest in green roofs stems from his background in water resource engineering. Miller's research into the German success in using green roofs to treat urban runoff led him to form an alliance with Optigreen. Charlie is a member of the Technical Advisory Committees for the Center for Green Roof Research at Pennsylvania State University and the Green Roofs for Healthy Cities Coalition, a Toronto-based research and public policy organization. He is also a member of the ASTM Subcommittee on Sustainability—Buildings and the German Roof-Gardening Association.

Jeremy Nowak is director of The Reinvestment Fund (TRF), which he cofounded in 1985 after serving in a variety of community development and organizing positions. In addition to his leadership of TRF, Nowak chairs the board of directors of Mastery Charter School and Alex's Lemonade Stand. He also was on the Consumer Advisory Board to the Federal Reserve Bank and chaired the board of directors of the National Community Capital Association, the industry's trade association, from 1990 to 1994. Two years later Nowak was selected to receive the Philadelphia Award, the city's highest civic honor.

Neal Peirce is a leading American journalist on the national and global roles of metropolitan and multistate regions. In 1975 he began writing the country's first national newspaper column focused on state, local and federal system themes that continues today, syndicated by the Washington Post Writers Group. With Curtis Johnson he has authored newspaper series on strategic issues facing 24 U.S. metropolitan regions. They cowrote, *Citistates*, exploring the new regional phenomenon, and formed the Citistates Group, a network of journalists, speakers, and civic leaders focused on building competitive, equitable and sustainable twenty-first-century regions. Peirce was a founder of *National Journal*, and served in the 1960s as political editor of *Congressional Quarterly*.

Rutherford H. Platt is a professor of geography and planning law in the Department of Geosciences at the University of Massachusetts, Amherst. He specializes in public policy concerning urban land and water resources and natural hazards. Platt also directs the Ecological Cities Project, a program of research, teaching, and outreach based at the University of Massachusetts, Amherst. He has served on many national and regional panels, including the National Research Council Water Science and Technology Board and several of its committees. In 2002, he was designated a Lifetime National Associate of the National Academies. His latest book is the edited volume *The Humane Metropolis: People and Nature in the 21st Century*.

Victor Rubin, director of research at PolicyLink, leads knowledge-building, evaluation, and qualitative and quantitative analysis activities to build a strong research base for equitable development strategy, community capacity building, and policy advocacy. Rubin previously directed the U.S. Department of Housing and Urban Development Office of University Partnerships, where he administered grants to institutions of higher education for community engagement. He also served for 13 years as director of research and community programs at the University-Oakland Metropolitan Forum, a partnership based at the University of California, Berkeley, where he was concurrently an adjunct associate professor of city and regional planning.

Patricia L. Smith is director of special initiatives at The Reinvestment Fund (TRF), where she is responsible for coordinating targeted initiatives involving two or more lines of business. She previously directed the city of Philadelphia's Neighborhood Transformation Initiative (NTI), a $295-million redevelopment bond program she designed to address decades of urban blight and stimulate new investment in Philadelphia neighborhoods. Her career spans the foundation, government, and nonprofit sectors and includes public policy advocacy, program development, strategic planning, and housing bond financing. She was featured in the Philadelphia segment of the PBS series *Edens Lost & Found.*

Robin Thompson is visiting professor of planning at the University College of London Bartlett School of Architecture and is the former planning director for the County of Kent in England's southeast region. He is currently an adviser on city planning to London's Mayor Ken Livingston. He led many aspects of the Thames Gateway Project and is now responsible for integrating sustainable development into London's development plans.

Domenic Vitiello, an urban planner and historian, teaches in the urban studies program at the University of Pennsylvania. He has been involved in several capacities in the "LANDvisions" international design competition for the reuse of vacant land in the city (also known as "Urban Voids"), organized by the City Parks Association of Philadelphia, Pennsylvania Horticultural Society, Pennsylvania Environmental Council, and The Reinvestment Fund. His current research and planning focus on community development in immigrant communities, urban arts and cultural planning, and the impacts of peak oil and changing energy use in cities and regions.

Susan M. Wachter is codirector of the Penn Institute for Urban Research, Richard B. Worley Professor of Financial Management, and professor of real estate and finance at the Wharton School of the University of Pennsylvania. She served as chair of the Wharton School's real estate department from 1997 to 1999. She is also a professor of city and regional planning at the university's School of Design. She studies real estate economics, urban economics, and housing finance. She served as assistant secretary for policy development and research at the U.S. Department of Housing and Urban Development from 1998 to 2001. A founding director of the Wharton GIS Lab, Wachter is a national expert in housing analysis and the first woman to head the American Real Estate Urban Economics Association. She has recently completed a study on the economic impacts of greening on neighborhoods in transition, "The Determinants of Neighborhood Transformation in Philadelphia: Identification and Analysis."

Rachel Weinberger teaches city and regional planning at the University of Pennsylvania. Her areas of specialization include urban transport, land use, and transportation planning and sustainable transportation. While on leave from the University of Pennsylvania, Weinberger served as senior adviser on transportation policy for New York Mayor Michael

Bloomberg's 2030 sustainability plan, PlaNYC. In that capacity she was the primary author of the New York Mobility Needs Assessment, from which the current article is drawn. Other recent publications include "The High Cost of Free Highways" in *Idaho Law Review* and "Men, Women, Job Sprawl and Journey to Work" in *Public Works Management and Policy*.

Harry Wiland, co-president/CEO of the Media & Policy Center Foundation and co-executive producer/director of the *Edens Lost & Found* project, is a versatile producer with an Emmy Award-winning career as a television producer/director and cross-disciplinary media innovator. He has produced and directed numerous specials on network, public, and cable television, including the Emmy-winning productions *Showdown at the Palace*, an internationally syndicated special, and *Bridge over Troubled Waters*. Wiland is the cofounder and former CEO of Leonardo Internet, which developed educational multimedia software. With his partner, Dale Bell, he was executive producer/director/writer of the award-winning *And Thou Shalt Honor. . .* , a two-hour special PBS broadcast on family caregiving, hosted by Joe Mantegna. For their innovative approach to public policy and use of the mass media for social advocacy, in the spring of 2006 Wiland and Bell were elected as Ashoka Fellows, joining a global organization of social entrepreneurs committed to addressing social issues and encouraging social change.

Stockton Williams is responsible for external affairs, public policy, fund-raising, and communications functions at Enterprise Community Partners, Inc. He came to Enterprise in 2000 as director of public policy and in 2004 was promoted to vice president for external affairs and later to senior vice president. He leads Enterprise's Green Communities initiative, a $550-million effort to create more than 8,500 environmentally healthy homes for low-income families. Before joining Enterprise, he was a senior legislative and policy associate at the National Council of State Housing Agencies. He also worked for nonprofit community development organizations in New York City, Baltimore, and Charleston, South Carolina. He is a trustee of the National Housing Conference, and a member of the board of directors of the Affordable Housing Tax Credit Coalition, the steering committee of the New Markets Tax Credit Coalition, and the Trust for Public Land's Real Estate Council.

Kathleen L. Wolf is a research social scientist at the Center for Urban Horticulture and College of Forest Resources at the University of Washington, Seattle. Based on theory and methods of environmental psychology, she investigates people's perceptions and behaviors with regard to urban landscapes. Based on professional experiences early in her career—as an urban horticulturist in south Florida and a landscape architect in the Midwest—she became interested in how natural environments influence people's attitudes, values and actions. Her research of the human dimensions of open space, urban forestry, and natural systems include public preferences and perceptions regarding urban public landscapes; costs, benefits, and perceptions of urban forestry in retail and commercial districts; integration of urban nature and transportation systems; developmental benefits associated with youth participation in urban greening work; and effective integration of science and policy through technology transfer.

Robert D. Yaro is president of the Regional Plan Association (RPA). Founded in 1922, RPA, headquartered in New York City, is America's oldest and most respected independent metropolitan research and advocacy group. He is also practice professor in city and regional planning at the University of Pennsylvania. He chairs the Civic Alliance to Rebuild Downtown New York, a broad-based coalition of civic groups formed to guide redevelopment in lower Manhattan in the aftermath of September 11. He is coauthor of *A Region at Risk* and *Dealing with Change in the Connecticut River Valley.*

Acknowledgments

Inspired by the PBS's *Edens Lost & Found,* a series that highlighted grass-roots initiatives in Philadelphia, Chicago, Seattle, and Los Angeles to transform cities and neighborhoods into more beautiful and sustainable urban landscapes, the Penn Institute for Urban Research (Penn IUR), the Pennsylvania Horticultural Society (stars of the Philadelphia episode, *Edens Lost & Found: The Holy Experiment*), and Harry Wiland and Dale Bell, producers of *Edens Lost & Found,* organized a two-day conference, Growing Greener Cities: A Symposium on Urban Environmental Issues in the 21st Century, which took place October 16–17, 2006, at the University of Pennsylvania.

In addition to exploring cutting-edge research methods and innovative best practices in urban greening, the conference featured a keynote address by Nobel-prize winner Wangari Maathai, founder of Kenya's Green Belt Movement. The more than 300 conference participants—scholars, design and environmental science practitioners, neighborhood leaders, policymakers, and students—made enormous contributions through their presentations, questions, and discussions to a national dialogue on transforming urban places to green, sustainable cities, creating a sense of vision, energy, and commitment that we hope this volume captures. We are especially thankful to the Pennsylvania Horticultural Society and the *Edens Lost & Found* producers for their help in convening so many of the individuals whose work appears here.

We are grateful for the generous support from foundations and institutions dedicated to urban sustainability for hosting the conference, including CDM, the Citizens Bank Foundation, the William Penn Foundation, SCA Americas, the University of Pennsylvania's Office of the Provost, School of Arts and Sciences, and Institute for Environmental Studies, the White Dog Café, and the Philadelphia Water Department.

In addition, we are most appreciative of the thoughtful guidance and advice of the Penn Institute for Urban Research Advisory Board, Executive Committee, and our Faculty Associates, many of whom have contributed in several ways to this volume.

We are indebted to the leadership and editorial staff at Penn Press who made this book, which is part of Penn Press's The City in the

Twenty-First Century series, possible. In particular, we would like to thank Peter Agree, editor-in-chief, who has provided invaluable oversight from start to finish, and William Finan, developmental editor, who has offered meticulous reviews and editing. Above all, Penn IUR's publication manager, Amy Montgomery, has kept this project on course with her gentle nudges and attention to the many details of such a volume.

We are tremendously grateful for the contributions from all the authors. The work they produced in such short order is a testament to their expertise and dedication to making urban places more equitable, more enduring and greener.